New Perspectives on the Irish in Scotland

New Perspectives
on the Irish in Scotland

Edited by
Martin J. Mitchell

First published in Great Britain in 2008 by

John Donald, an imprint of Birlinn Ltd
West Newington House
10 Newington Road
Edinburgh
EH9 1QS

www.birlinn.co.uk

ISBN 10: 1 904607 83 7
ISBN 13: 978 1 904607 83 0

British Library Cataloguing-in-Publication Data
A catalogue record for this book is available on request from the British Library

Typeset by Carnegie Book Production, Lancaster
Printed and bound in Britain by Bell & Bain Ltd., Glasgow

Contents

Preface

Irish emigration to Scotland is one of the most important events in the modern history of the nation. Other immigrant groups have arrived over the past two hundred years, and have made major contributions to Scottish society. But arguably none has had the same impact as the Irish on the social, economic, political, religious and cultural life of the country. Irish immigrants were vital to the success of the Scottish economy during the industrial revolution of the nineteenth century, and they played an important role in the creation of the trade union and labour movement.

The impact of Irish immigration is still apparent in twenty-first-century Scotland. Today there are over a million Scots who are descendants of those who crossed the North Channel from the 1790s onwards. Between two-thirds and three-quarters of the new arrivals were Roman Catholic, and their presence led to the re-emergence on a large scale of sectarianism and religious bigotry. These problems continued into the twentieth century, and indeed to the present day, although there is some considerable debate as to the current extent of anti-Catholicism in Scottish society.

Some of Scotland's major institutions would either not exist or would be insignificant if there had been little or no Irish immigration. The Roman Catholic Church in Scotland is a prime example. In the 1780s, prior to the arrival of the Irish, there were only around 30,000 Catholics in Scotland out of a total population of around 1.5 million, or 2 per cent of the total. Today there are over 800,000 Catholics in the country – the bulk of whom are of Irish descent – who make up around 16 per cent of Scots. In the 1780s most Catholics in Scotland lived either in the western highlands and islands or in the north-east. In the western lowland counties Catholicism was all but extinct. Irish immigration changed this geographical pattern. By the 1830s the west of Scotland had become the centre of Catholicism and the Catholic Church, and remains so to this day: around 70 per cent of Scotland's Roman Catholic population live in the region.

Other contemporary institutions are the creations of Irish immigration. Between one-quarter and one-third of the Irish in nineteenth-century Scotland were Protestant, and these immigrants brought over their own culture and heritage, part of which for some was Orangeism. Orange lodges were established in areas of Protestant Irish settlement, and throughout the nineteenth century their membership was drawn overwhelmingly from that community. Today the order and Orangeism are important features of the lives of tens of thousands of Scots. Finally, one of Europe's most famous sporting institutions, Glasgow Celtic Football Club, was founded in 1887 by and for members of the city's Catholic Irish community.

Despite the Irish having made a vital contribution to the creation of modern Scotland, the immigrants were for a long time neglected by academic historians. In the 1940s James Handley published two histories of the Irish in Scotland; but it was 40 years before another monograph appeared on the subject, namely Tom Gallagher's study of the Irish in Glasgow. In the intervening period the subject was kept alive through articles and essays by historians such as John McCaffrey, Bernard Aspinwall, William Walker and Ian Wood.

The past two decades have seen a resurgence of scholarly interest in the Irish in Scotland. Monographs, theses, articles, essays, conferences and symposia on the subject have all contributed to a better understanding of the immigrant experience. This volume brings together most of the leading scholars of the Irish in Scotland. New perspectives are offered on some of the major themes of Irish immigration, such as communal relations and sectarianism, the relationship between the Catholic Irish and their clergy, Catholic devotional life, the Famine Irish, immigrant political activities, the impact which the Protestant Irish had on the Scottish Episcopal Church, Orangeism, Catholic Irish involvement in the First World War, and the experience of the Catholic community in Scotland since the end of the Second World War.

More research is needed on the Irish in Scotland. The approaches and methodologies adopted by the contributors demonstrate the ways in which the subject can be advanced. Some areas need more research than others. For example, little is known of the experience of Irish women, or of the Irish middle class in Scotland. The study of Irish involvement in local politics is in its infancy. Detailed local studies of Irish communities are essential for a fuller understanding of immigrant life, as comparisons can then be made to determine if the Irish experience was uniform throughout Scotland, or differed according to the social and economic context of individual towns and villages. Finally, comparisons need to be made with Irish immigrant communities throughout the world, in order to place the Irish in Scotland firmly in the context of the study of the Irish Diaspora.

Most of the essays in this volume were first given at a symposium held in the AHRC Centre for Irish and Scottish Studies, University of Aberdeen, as part of its major research programme on the Scottish and Irish diasporas. I am grateful to the late Janet Hendry, the then administrator of the centre, and to the founding director, Professor Tom Devine, for their support. I also wish to thank Jean Fraser who helped to prepare the text for publication with her usual efficiency and enthusiasm.

Martin Mitchell,
University of Strathclyde

Contributors

Bernard Aspinwall, Honorary Research Fellow, Department of Adult and Continuing Education, University of Glasgow.

Thomas M. Devine, Sir William Fraser Chair of Scottish History and Palaeography, University of Edinburgh.

John Foster, Emeritus Professor, Social Sciences, University of the West of Scotland.

Muir Houston, Research Fellow, Institute of Education and Centre for Lifelong Learning, University of Stirling.

Eric Kaufmann, Reader in Politics and Sociology, Birkbeck College, University of London.

Elaine W. McFarland, Professor of History, Glasgow Caledonian University.

Chris Madigan, Former Senior Lecturer in Sociology, University of the West of Scotland.

Ian Meredith, Team Rector of the Scottish Episcopal Churches at Ayr, Maybole and Girvan.

Martin J. Mitchell, Lecturer in History, University of Strathclyde.

Máirtín Ó Catháin, Lecturer in Modern History, University of Central Lancashire.

Michael Rosie, Lecturer in Sociology, University of Edinburgh.

Geraldine Vaughan, Lecturer, Department of English, University of Rouen.

1 Irish Catholics in the West of Scotland in the Nineteenth Century: Despised by Scottish workers and controlled by the Church?

Martin J. Mitchell

The prevailing view among historians about the Irish in nineteenth-century Scotland is that the Protestant Irish immigrants were, in the main, welcomed and accepted – because they shared the same religious beliefs and culture as most of the Scots; whereas the Catholic Irish were despised by the bulk of the native population on account of their race and religion, and because they were employed mainly as strike-breakers or as low-wage labour. As a result of this hostility the Catholic Irish, it has been argued, were unwilling or unable to participate in strikes, trade unions and political movements with Scottish workers; instead, they formed isolated and self-contained communities, centred on their Church, in the towns in which they settled in significant numbers, and politically were interested almost exclusively in issues affecting Ireland, Catholics and the Catholic Church.[1] For example, Tom Gallagher, in his major study of the Catholic Irish in Glasgow, argued that prejudice towards them was 'endemic throughout society'[2] and as a result they constituted a separate and isolated community.[3] He added: 'Finding religious intolerance and sectarian hate in many areas of nineteenth Century Scottish life, the immigrants preferred to remain expatriate Irish rather than strive to make common cause with the Scots in their midst.'[4] Michael Fry claimed that in the late nineteenth century:

> There was hatred in all classes for Irish immigrants. Scots workers were infuriated when they allowed themselves to be used as strike-breakers, keeping down wages and crippling trade unions. The higher orders deplored the squalid social habits to which they saw them irretrievably given up. The Irish, in the face of such bitter hostility were unassimilated, maintaining their own identity and institutions.[5]

A contributor to a popular academic history of modern Scotland argued that:

> Irish Catholics ... found themselves strangers in a strange land. Forced to take whatever jobs they could get, they remained firmly on the bottom rung of the Scottish social ladder. Herded into ghettos, and facing

hostility from the local community, their identity focused on their church. Catholicism and Irishness mutually reinforced one another.[6]

Callum Brown maintained that 'partly through the use of immigrants as strike-breakers and partly through sectarianism, Catholics were generally isolated from the trade unions and Labour movements before 1890'.[7] Moreover, he concluded: 'In the context of a hostile Presbyterian reception, the incoming Irish turned to the chapel and its activities for cultural and ethnic identity.'[8]

Other historians have argued or suggested that within the Catholic community the Church and its clergy exercised a considerable degree of power and authority over the Irish. In an influential article published over 30 years ago, William Walker detailed 'the creation of an exclusive and intense Irish community life ...', in which the priest was the dominant figure, exercising almost total control. According to Walker: 'Within their substitute society the immigrants were exhorted to the virtues of docility and resignation while, institutionally, the structure of parochial organizations compelled precisely this quiescence.'[9] Tom Gallagher has described the creation of a 'self-enclosed world' by the Catholic Irish, which was presided over by 'the parish priest, an undoubted figure of authority ...'.[10] Chris Harvie and Graham Walker argued that the Catholic Irish population in urban Scotland 'was disciplined by its priests as well as the hostility of the native Scots into retaining an Irish identity which, until a very late date, resisted industrial and class pressures to assimilate'.[11] Graham Walker later claimed that: 'There is little doubt that the Catholic Church functioned as the fulcrum of this immigrant community and exerted great influence in the social, educational, and political spheres of life ...'[12]

Indeed, some have claimed that the Church was so powerful and influential that it was able to control and direct the political activities of the Catholic Irish. William Walker contended that in the late nineteenth century the Church was able to prevent the Irish from joining the ranks of the emerging labour movement.[13] He suggested that one way in which the Church was able to do this was through the clergy's deliberate – and perhaps 'devious' – promotion of Irish nationalism and Home Rule among the immigrant community, which co-existed alongside their continual attacks on Socialism and the cause of labour: 'It is distinctly possible that priests fostered the politics of nationalism as a distraction from the politics of class.'[14] In his recent history of the Scottish working class, Bill Knox is more forthright in his interpretation of the role of the clergy. He maintains that hostility and prejudice throughout society 'saw the Irish Catholics retreat from the embrace of the Scottish labour movement and into the arms of a reactionary priesthood, which channelled Irish political energies into the struggle for Home Rule'.[15]

This chapter will critically assess these views of the Catholic Irish in the nineteenth century. The first section will determine whether the immigrant community was as isolated and despised as some have claimed. It will not deal with the attitudes of the Protestant churches and the middle classes, as these have been well documented.[16] Instead, it will focus on the Catholic Irish and their relationship with those beside whom they lived and laboured – the Scottish working class. The second section will establish whether the Catholic Church and its clergy were able totally to dominate and control the lives of the Irish. The chapter will deal exclusively with the west of Scotland, as this is the region in which the majority of the immigrants settled.[17] Moreover, the bulk of the research on the Irish in nineteenth-century Scotland relates to the west of the country.

I

It is undeniable that Irish workers – Catholic and Protestant – were used to break strikes, and, as a result, incurred the wrath of Scottish workers. However, most of the evidence of this relates to the coal and iron industries of Lanarkshire and Ayrshire from the mid-1820s to the mid-1850s.[18] The vast majority of Irish workers in the nineteenth century were not employed in the mining industry and were not used as blackleg labour.[19] Furthermore, even in the mining districts of the west of Scotland the Irish experience was more complex than some historians have suggested. In many instances Irishmen who were used as strike-breakers were not new to the industry but were already employed in and around the pits as labourers, and had apparently lived and worked alongside the Scottish colliers without incident.[20] Alan Campbell has argued that, once part of the mining workforce, most Irish workers during the middle decades of the nineteenth century were unwilling to join their district unions, for social, economic and cultural reasons.[21] Yet there is, as he acknowledged, evidence that some Irish workers participated in strikes to protect or improve their wages and conditions during the 1840s and 1850s.[22] Campbell and others have also shown that from the 1870s onwards Irish miners – Catholic and Protestant – were prominent both in the rank-and-file and in the leadership of miners' trade unions in Lanarkshire. For example, it has been estimated that by 1900 the Irish made up almost three-quarters of the total membership of the Lanarkshire Miners' Union. At this time at least one-third of the executive of the Airdrie branch of the county union were of Irish Catholic extraction, including its secretary, P. J. Agnew. By 1911 the Catholic Irish constituted the majority of the membership of the Lanarkshire branch of the National Iron and Steelworkers Union.[23] Catholic Irish miners also participated fully in industrial disputes during this period, including the major stoppages of 1874 and 1912.[24]

Irish workers in other occupations also played a prominent role in strikes, in trade unions, and in the labour movement in the west of Scotland throughout the nineteenth century.[25] For example, Irish handloom weavers were involved in industrial action from the 1800s to the 1840s. In 1834 a Glasgow Cotton Manufacturer stated that:

> With regard to combination among the weavers, the Irish are rather urged on by the more acute and thinking among the Scotch; but when the emergency comes the Irish are the more daring spirits; and as they are in

themselves less reflective, and worse educated they are more prone to use violence, without regard to consequences.[26]

By the late 1830s around 40 per cent of the membership of Glasgow's weavers' associations were born in Ireland. If weavers born in Scotland of Irish parents are taken into account, it is probable that the majority of the membership were Irish.[27]

The majority of cotton spinners in Glasgow and Paisley during the first four decades of the nineteenth century were Irish or of Irish descent. These workers were the driving-force behind the Glasgow Cotton Spinners Association, which in the 1820s and 1830s was the most powerful and active workers' organisation in Scotland.[28] Indeed, in the aftermath of the disastrous spinners' general strike of 1837 a member of the association informed the authorities that '… almost all the jobs done in the union … were done or originated by Catholics and Irishmen'.[29] Two Irish Catholics, Patrick McGowan and Peter Hacket, were particularly active in the affairs of the union at this time. The association, which throughout its existence had a large Irish membership – Catholic and Protestant – was also an integral part of the labour movement in the west of Scotland in these years. It was represented on Glasgow's Trades' Committees during the 1820s and 1830s and was prominent in the various working-class agitations of those decades. The association was the driving force behind the campaign in the west of Scotland for a reform of working conditions for all workers in all factories, and appears to have been the principal backer of the *Liberator*, the newspaper for the Glasgow working class.[30]

There is not much evidence, apart from that which relates to the Lanarkshire coalfields, of significant Irish involvement in trade unions and strike action in the west of Scotland from the mid-1840s to the late 1880s. As most of the successful unions in non-mining areas in this period were organisations of skilled workers, and most Irish men and women in these localities were unskilled or semi-skilled, this is not surprising. However, in Glasgow in the 1850s Irish labourers managed to form their own association, which was affiliated to the city's Trades Council. This organisation, known as the United Labourers, did not survive the depression of the late 1870s. It was re-established in 1890 as the National Labourers Union, and by 1892 was the largest subscriber to the Glasgow Trades Council.[31]

Irish workers were heavily involved in the New Unionism of the late nineteenth century. In 1889 the National Union of Dock Labourers was established in Glasgow by two Irishmen, Richard McGhee and Edward McHugh. According to Kenefick, the dockers in the city were 'overwhelmingly Catholic Irish in composition', and formed the backbone of the organisation. Moreover, the union played a full part in the labour movement of the time; for example, during the 1890s it was a leading subscriber to the Glasgow Trades Council.[32] Elsewhere in the city, Irish workers were prominent or dominant in the Corporation Workers Union, the Municipal Employees Association, and in the Gas Workers and General Labourers Union. Catholic Irish workers were likewise involved in the Glasgow Trades Council in this period. For example, in 1888 Owen Kiernan was the tailors' representative and in 1892 Hugh Murphy was the delegate of the Cabinet Makers Union.[33] In Airdrie and Coatbridge the Catholic Irish were present in significant numbers by the 1890s in the Gas Workers and General Labourers Union, the National Society of Smiths and Hammermen and in the Amalgamated Society of Railway Servants.[34]

Throughout the nineteenth century the Catholic Irish in the west of Scotland were deeply concerned about issues affecting Ireland. In the 1840s they were heavily involved in the campaign for repeal of the British-Irish Act of Union of 1800, and from the early 1870s onwards they were enthusiastic supporters of the movement for Irish Home Rule.[35] However, the Catholic Irish in the region were not interested solely in Irish political affairs: during the nineteenth century there was also a significant Catholic Irish presence in most of the working-class agitations for political reform. Members of the immigrant community were neither isolated from the social and economic pressures of urban Scotland, nor indifferent to the demand for the franchise and the benefits which political reform was expected to bring to the working class, of which they, of course, formed a significant part. Concern for Irish or Catholic issues and support for political change in Great Britain were not mutually exclusive. For example, in the autumn of 1819 Andrew Scott, who was the sole Catholic priest in Glasgow, informed the Home Secretary that the secret revolutionary organisation in the city was attempting to recruit into its ranks members of his congregation. He later revealed that, despite his efforts to dissuade them, a number of Irish Catholics had joined the insurrectionary movement. There is also evidence which suggests that the bulk of the Catholic Irish supported the aims of the revolutionaries, and participated in the general strike which took place during the 'Radical War' of April 1820.[36]

Members of the Catholic Irish community participated in the great processions and demonstrations in Glasgow in 1831 and 1832 for the Reform Bills, and in similar events held to honour the visits to the city of the Earl of Durham and Daniel O'Connell – both noted advocates of political reform – in 1834 and 1835 respectively. Moreover, Catholic Irish involvement in these and in other reform activities during this period was not insignificant, but was on such a scale as to be noted and welcomed by Scottish participants.[37]

A number of Irish Catholics were prominent in the Chartist movement in the west of Scotland, and there was also a Catholic Irish presence in its rank-and-file in Glasgow between 1838 and 1842; for example, Irish workers participated in processions and demonstrations for the Charter. However, the bulk of the Catholic Irish community in the city, and probably elsewhere in the region, did not participate in the agitation during this period. The majority of the Glasgow Catholic Irish community remained loyal to Daniel O'Connell, the political leader of Catholic Ireland and the idol of the immigrant community, who urged his followers to eschew involvement in a movement dominated by his bitter rival Feargus O'Connor. Instead, the Catholic Irish in the city supported the Complete Suffrage movement, a branch of which was established in the city in 1842. This organisation also advocated the Six Points of the Charter, but sought to unite middle-class and moderate working-class reformers, and most important of all as far as Irish Catholics were concerned, received the blessing of O'Connell. Leading figures in the Catholic Irish community in Glasgow became prominent members of the city's Complete Suffrage Association. However, like Chartism, Complete Suffragism went into rapid decline after 1842.[38]

There is not much evidence of Scottish and Catholic Irish workers participating in joint political activities in the mid-Victorian period. Furthermore, from the early 1870s onwards the Catholic Irish in Scotland were involved in the campaign for Irish Home Rule, a subject not high on the list of priorities of Scottish working-class reformers and radicals. The Catholic Irish, however, were not interested solely in the movement for an Irish legislature; they were also concerned about the same issues as their fellow Scottish workers, and were active in agitations and organisations alongside them, particularly from the mid-1880s onwards, and mainly at the level of local politics, as historians such as Ian Wood and James Smyth have demonstrated. For example, in the 1893 Glasgow municipal election three of the candidates endorsed by the city's Trades Council were Irish Home Rulers, two of whom were Roman Catholic. In 1896, the Workers Municipal Elections Committee was established in Glasgow to run candidates at the local election. Four groups were involved in this body – the trade unions, the co-operative societies, the Independent Labour Party and the Irish National League, the organisation for Glasgow's Irish Home Rulers. Six of the eleven candidates put forward by the committee at the 1896 municipal election were Irish. By the late 1890s, the Glasgow Trades Council and the city's Irish National League branches were co-operating to get jointly-approved candidates elected to parish councils in the city. Similar developments occurred in Paisley during this period.[39] Some historians have argued that the Catholic Irish did not move over to the labour movement until after the First World War. The work of the aforementioned scholars demonstrates that, at the local level at least, the shift had occurred as early as the 1890s.

Another example of considerable co-operation between Irish Catholics and Scottish Protestants in nineteenth-century Scotland can be found in the temperance 'craze' of the 1830s and 1840s. The temperance movement expanded rapidly in these decades and many members of the Catholic Irish community became enthusiastic advocates of total abstinence. Although they established their own temperance societies, the Catholic Irish teetotallers worked closely with their Scottish counterparts. For example, in July 1841 between 5,000 and 7,000 Catholic and Protestant Total Abstainers marched through Glasgow before holding an open-air meeting. In August 1842 members of the Catholic and Protestant temperance societies in and around Glasgow walked in procession and held a demonstration to honour the visit to the city of the renowned Irish temperance advocate, Father Theobald Matthew. The procession was led by Father Matthew and James Enraght, an Irish priest serving in Glasgow. On their return to Glasgow Green the marchers were welcomed by a crowd which numbered around 50,000. During his three days in the city Matthew administered the teetotal pledge to upwards of 40,000 people.[40]

At the beginning of this chapter it was shown that the prevailing view about the Catholic Irish in nineteenth-century Scotland is that they were despised by the bulk of the native population, and as a result formed separate and isolated communities in the towns in which they settled in significant numbers. Yet, the evidence surveyed thus far has demonstrated that during the nineteenth century members of the Catholic Irish communities were involved – often in significant numbers – in strikes, trade unions, trade union campaigns, political agitations and in the temperance movement alongside Scottish workers. Moreover, this involvement was both welcomed and sought by native participants. However, not all Scottish workers were strikers, trade unionists, political reformers or total abstainers. Perhaps those who participated with the Catholic Irish in collective action were more enlightened and less bigoted than those who did not. What now needs to be examined is the relationship which existed between the Catholic Irish and the Protestant working class in general.

Some historians have highlighted sectarian riots and disturbances in Scotland in the nineteenth century as proof that there was considerable Protestant working-class hostility towards the Catholic Irish community. Many such incidents indeed occurred: Alan Campbell has compiled a list of over 50 of them involving Irishmen in Lanarkshire alone, during the period from the early 1830s to the mid-1880s.[41] Callum Brown looked at the evidence of sectarian violence as set out by Campbell and others and concluded that: 'the frequency of recorded confrontations ... suggests that the unrecorded cases represented an artery of hate operating throughout Scottish urban society'.[42]

However, if these events are looked at more closely, it is apparent that the situation is not as straightforward as some have suggested. For example, most of the incidents which Campbell notes or discusses did not involve Scottish workers, but instead were 'Orange and Green' disturbances involving Protestant Irish and Catholic Irish immigrants. The available evidence either states or suggests that most Scottish workers were not participants – they remained aloof and let the two immigrant groups continue their old battles.

Of course Scottish workers were, as Campbell and others have shown, involved in some rioting against Irish workers, but this was confined almost exclusively to certain industrial disputes in the coal and iron industries of Lanarkshire and Ayrshire from the mid-1820s to the mid-1850s. These incidents were not of the sectarian character as those already discussed: they were disturbances against the Irish – Catholic and Protestant – as strikebreakers, and were not primarily attacks on the Catholic Irish on account of their religious persuasion or ethnic background.[43]

Indeed, if the attacks on Irish strikebreakers are put to one side, what is noticeable – given what has been written about Scottish working-class attitudes towards the Catholic Irish – is that there was comparatively little open popular hostility towards the immigrant presence. There were in fact only a few anti-Catholic riots in the whole of the west of Scotland throughout the nineteenth century: in Airdrie (1835), Greenock and Gourock (1851) and in Greenock (1855).[44] There is, however, evidence of small scale anti-Catholic activity, such as the breaking of the windows of Roman Catholic churches, and the shouting of abuse at priests,[45] and there were also a number of drunken brawls between Catholics and Protestants.[46] It is not clear, however, how representative such actions were of the Scottish Protestant workforce as a whole. Yet overall, as John McCaffrey pointed out over 20 years ago, the extent of 'communal friction' in Scotland was far less than in the north of England and Wales in the second half of the nineteenth century.[47]

Of course the absence of widespread native rioting against the Catholic Irish does not necessarily mean that the bulk of the Scottish workforce was not hostile to the presence of the immigrant community. Scottish workers could have expressed their displeasure in other ways. Yet there is little evidence that they did. For example, they did not give significant support to organisations or activities which were anti-Catholic, or anti-Catholic Irish. Membership of the Orange Order in Scotland in the nineteenth century was drawn overwhelmingly from the Protestant Irish community.[48] There was little or no support at local or national level for Scottish politicians (or others) who played the sectarian card, unlike in the 1930s when the anti-Catholic demagogue Andrew Ratcliffe achieved success in Glasgow municipal elections.[49]

In the 1850s there was an upsurge in 'No Popery' sentiment in Scotland, caused mainly by the restoration of the Catholic hierarchy in England. Numerous anti-Catholic meetings were held and pamphlets published. Yet apart from the riots in Greenock and Gourock in 1851, there were no major outbreaks of violence against the Catholic Irish community, nor was there much popular support for those who sought to exploit the situation for their own ends.[50] By the mid-1850s the furore was over, and when, in 1878, the Catholic hierarchy in Scotland was restored, there was no return to the 'No Popery' of the 1850s, nor was there any sectarian uproar or backlash against the Catholic Irish community.

The absence of significant open popular hostility towards the Catholic Irish, and the lack of support for anti-Catholic organisations and activities, does not necessarily mean that the bulk of the native workforce were happy with the Catholic Irish in their midst. For example, Helen Crawfurd (1877–1954), a suffragette and member of the Independent Labour Party, recalled that during her upbringing in Glasgow she looked 'upon the Fenian and Catholic Irish as sub-human'.[51] In the 1930s a Glaswegian recalled that in the Calton district in the late nineteenth century:

> The Irish were looked upon as an inferior race, hewers of wood and drawers of water, who should be treated with consideration but kept in their place. The less we had to do with them the better. Their religion was not our religion, which was the best; and their customs were different from

ours, as was their speech. Doubtless there were good folk among them, but the unruly and turbulent ones showed us what we might become if we did not keep to our own people.[52]

Rather than engage in public acts of hostility, Scottish workers who shared such views of the Catholic Irish may simply have chosen to ignore members of the immigrant community; for example, the skilled working class – the 'aristocracy of labour' – may have distanced themselves socially, culturally and physically, in the same manner in which they removed themselves from the unskilled and semi-skilled native workforce.[53]

However, there is evidence which suggests that members of the Catholic Irish community enjoyed good relations with some Scottish workers and in fact associated with them to a considerable extent.[54] For example, one reason why sections of the Scottish middle class were hostile towards the Catholic Irish was that they recognised that the immigrants were mixing with Scottish workers, and believed that this was a cause – for some the principal cause – of the perceived decline in the moral condition of the native population.[55] Evidence submitted to the 1834 inquiry into the Irish Poor in Great Britain clearly demonstrates this. For example, one Glasgow businessman maintained that the Irish were

more addicted to drink, to lying, and to swearing, than the natives; by mixing so much with them, they have lowered the tone of morals among the Scotch, whilst they, the Irish, have been in a greater proportion improved.[56]

Moses Steven Buchanan, the senior surgeon of the Glasgow Royal Infirmary and an elder and deacon of St John's Parish, stated that there were no streets or districts in the city exclusively inhabited by the immigrants, who appeared to him 'to be quite amalgamated and mixed up with the poor population ...'. He added:

In consequence of the large numbers of Irish who come here, and their great ignorance, both intellectual and religious, their morality is inferior, and this has a tendency to lower the Scotch. You may educate and raise the native population as you will, still there is a constant influx of ignorant and uneducated Irish, who, by their example and association, deteriorate the condition of the natives.[57]

James Wright, a cotton manufacturer, argued that the Irish were

extremely ignorant, those who come here being generally the lowest of the population, and their mixing with the natives produces a bad moral effect on them, from their want of religious education. Generally I think that the Irish have contributed considerably to demoralize the working classes of

Glasgow by their example, arising from the want of religious and moral training, and by evil communication.[58]

In the late nineteenth century such views were still widespread. For example, the author of the introduction to the Census of Scotland for 1871 described the Catholic Irish community in the following terms:

> The immigration of such a body of labourers of the lowest class, with scarcely any education, cannot but have most prejudicial effects on the population. As yet the great body of these Irish do not seem to have been improved by their residence among us; and it is quite certain that the native Scot who has associated with them has most certainly deteriorated. It is painful to contemplate what may be the ultimate effect of this Irish immigration on the morals and habits of the people, and on the future prospects of the country.[59]

Not only did many Irish Catholics mix and associate with Scottish Protestants – a considerable number also married them. For example, in 1850 an Irish priest was upset to find during his visit to Glasgow that too many spouses of Catholics were Protestant. In Saltcoats in 1858 one in six marriages was mixed.[60] In 1871 the priest at Ayr informed Archbishop Eyre of Glasgow that the moral condition of his congregation was 'truly frightful', and that he had many mixed couples in his Mission.[61] In 1878 the priest at Helensburgh lamented that almost one-half of his marriages were mixed;[62] that same year the priest at Airdrie informed Eyre that the chief abuse prevailing in his charge was '… company keeping with protestants ending in marriages often at the Kirk'. He added that they were 'the curse of the place'.[63] In the early 1880s the Bishop of Galloway told Rome that mixed marriages were common in his diocese, which included most of Ayrshire.[64] Bernard Aspinwall's analysis of baptismal registers of the Catholic Church at Kinning Park, Glasgow, between 1875 and 1896 shows that 18 per cent of baptisms were of children of mixed religious parentage.[65] Moreover, Aspinwall's figure relates only to mixed marriages sanctioned by the Catholic Church; there may have been other mixed marriages which occurred outwith the Church, such as those complained of in 1878 by the mission priest at Airdrie. It has been suggested that intermarriage between Protestants and Catholics decreased markedly as the nineteenth century progressed, as the Catholic Church developed institutions and organisations which locked its adherents into an isolated, self-contained 'cradle-to-the-grave' community.[66] It is now apparent that by the late nineteenth century the issue of mixed marriages was one which still greatly vexed the Catholic Church.

II

The Catholic Church, its clergy and its institutions played a vital role in the lives of Catholic Irish immigrants in the nineteenth century.[67] The local priest in particular 'was the pivotal point in parish life. He assumed the leadership in the mission, and encouraged the various spiritual and parochial activities of his congregation.'[68] However, although the clergy were important and influential figures within their missions and parishes, it does not necessarily follow that they were able to exercise their authority to the extent that some have argued. In fact, one of the major themes in the history of the Catholic community for much of the first seven decades of the nineteenth century is the conflict between the Scottish clergy who ran the Church and sections of the Irish laity: conflict over politics, and over the governance and identity of the Church in the region.

In October 1823 a number of Irishmen in Glasgow established a Catholic Association, which soon became involved in Daniel O'Connell's campaign for Catholic emancipation.[69] A year later, Andrew Scott, priest in charge of the Glasgow Mission, resolved to crush the organisation. He believed that its mere existence not only damaged the image of Catholicism in the city, but also posed a serious threat to the security and well-being of the Church. Several leading Protestants had complained to Scott about the association; there was a concern that it was a radical organisation similar to those which had engaged in insurrectionary activities from 1816 to 1820, and no doubt there was hostility among some against the very aim of emancipation – to allow Catholics to enter Parliament and to hold public office.[70] Monetary considerations were vital to Scott's decision. Leading members of the Glasgow Catholic Schools Committee had suggested to him that many Protestants would withdraw their financial support from the schools if the association continued, particularly since the leading figures in it – the brothers William and James McGowan – were teachers in the Catholic schools. Also, the Catholic Rent – funds raised in the city and sent to Dublin to assist O'Connell's campaign – deprived the impoverished Glasgow Mission of vital funds. When the Glasgow Catholic Association refused Scott's orders to disband the issue of control became prominent. In February 1825 Scott wrote to his superior, Bishop Cameron:

> I am fully convinced from experience that if such rebellions be not quelled in the bud, it will very soon become impossible to manage such congregations as we have here. This is the most numerous and consequently the most difficult to manage ...[71]

The association could not be allowed to defy the orders of the clergy. Its members were denied the sacraments, and in late 1825 Scott engineered the dismissal of the McGowan brothers from their teaching posts. Yet despite such measures, the Glasgow Catholic Association continued to campaign publicly for emancipation, and disbanded only when the measure was achieved in 1829.[72]

Events in the subsequent two decades further demonstrate that the Catholic clergy in the west of Scotland were not able to impose their will on large sections of the immigrant community, and dictate to them on political matters. In December 1832, during the first general election campaign under the terms of the Reform Act, Andrew Scott – now bishop in charge of the Church in the west of Scotland – tried to persuade a meeting of Catholic electors in Glasgow to vote for the Tory candidate. Only 12 out of a Catholic electorate of around 300 took Scott's advice, and this attempt by the bishop to get the Irish to vote against the reform candidates aroused much comment and controversy in the Glasgow press.[73]

Catholic Irish involvement in the campaign for the Reform Bills, and in subsequent movements in the 1830s for an extension of the franchise, greatly alarmed Bishop Scott, who, as has been shown, was a social and political conservative. He not only opposed such agitations, but also believed that the Catholic Irish should keep their heads down and not become involved in any political activities – such as campaigns to give some or all of the adult male working class the vote – which were opposed by the bulk of the Protestant middle class. Such participation would draw attention to the Catholic Irish community and its Church, and Scott feared that – as with the involvement of some in the movement for Catholic emancipation – this could result in increased Protestant hostility. However, despite Scott's opposition to reform, there was little he could do about it. Catholic Irish support for political change was simply so great that Scott, and his coadjutor Bishop John Murdoch, did not even attempt to prevent the involvement of their flock.[74]

The same is true of the movement for the Repeal of the British-Irish Act of Union, which gained tremendous support from the Catholic Irish in the west of Scotland during the 1840s. Both Scott and Murdoch were opposed to the measure but such was the popularity of repeal among the Irish that – as with the situation with reform – the bishops decided not to interfere.[75] Furthermore, despite the bishops' ban on clerical involvement in the agitation, some of the Irish clergy – who first arrived in the region in the late 1830s as a result of the shortage of Scottish priests – privately promoted the cause, much to Scott's chagrin.[76]

Until the late nineteenth century there was a significant section of the Catholic Irish community which was opposed to the dominance of the Scottish clergy within the Catholic Church in the west of Scotland. These Irish Catholics maintained that since the bulk of the Catholic population in the region, and indeed in Scotland as a whole, were Irish or of Irish descent, they should be served by Irish priests and be governed by Irish bishops. These demands were first raised in the late 1820s;[77] however, it was not until the 1860s that matters came to a head with the assault of the *Glasgow Free Press*, the newspaper of the Catholic Irish community, against the Scottish bishops and clergy. It also supported the campaign by a section of the Irish-born clergy against the way in which the Church was run and dominated by their Scottish colleagues. This bitter civil war ended only when Rome intervened and, in late 1868, appointed an Englishman, Charles Eyre, to take charge of the Church in the west of Scotland.[78]

In comparison with the era of the Scottish bishops, Eyre's period in charge of the Catholic Church in the west of Scotland (1869–1902) did not witness any major conflicts between him and the Catholic Irish over politics, the running of the Church or over what identity it should have.[79] Furthermore, Eyre's reign saw the Church expand rapidly, with a marked increase in the number of priests, chapels and schools, as well as the creation of a number of welfare, charitable, social, devotional and recreational organisations.[80] Some have suggested that one consequence of this was that the Church was able to tighten its grip over the Catholic Irish.[81] However, in the late nineteenth century, as with the previous period, the Church's control and influence was not as great as some have argued. This can be demonstrated with reference to four major themes: politics, secret societies, temperance and mixed marriages.

As shown in the introduction, William Walker suggested that the Catholic Church in Scotland promoted Home Rule and Irish nationalism as a means of directing Catholic Irish political activities away from the labour movement and socialism. This may well have been the case in Dundee, the focus of Walker's study, but it was not so in the west of Scotland during the episcopate of Charles Eyre. Eyre did not advocate Home Rule, and indeed did not get involved in national politics in general, except, of course, when the interests of Catholicism or the Church were at stake.[82] The Church in the west of Scotland concentrated almost exclusively on local politics in order to protect or promote Catholic interests. Indeed, in order to avoid conflict or confusion, an understanding was reached between the Church and the Irish nationalist organisations (such as the Irish National League and later the United Irish League) whereby the former would contest school board and parochial board elections, while the latter would organise the Irish vote in municipal and national elections.[83]

Despite the Church's willingness to co-exist peacefully with the Home Rule movement, and indeed to co-operate at times with nationalist bodies over issues concerning religion, Eyre occasionally distanced his Church and clergy from the politics of Irish nationalism. For example, in February 1886 he expressed concern that Irish National League meetings were still being held in the school at Carfin, and 16 years later he refused a branch of the United Irish League at Motherwell the use of the Catholic schools in the town.[84] In December 1885 a priest at Airdrie, following Eyre's 'advice', severed all links with the Irish National League.[85] Six years earlier, Henry Murphy, the parish priest at Irvine in Ayrshire (in the neighbouring diocese of Galloway) spoke at a major Home Rule meeting in Glasgow, and at other nationalist gatherings in the city. This infuriated Eyre, presumably because he feared it could encourage some of his own clergy to participate in such events. Eyre insisted to Bishop McLachlan of Galloway that Murphy should be prevented from attending nationalist meetings, and, under episcopal pressure, Murphy quickly apologised for his actions. The following year, after a lengthy and bitter dispute over money with his bishop, Murphy was dismissed from his diocese.[86]

Other Irish priests, however, were heavily involved in Irish nationalist politics, seemingly without being censured or disciplined by Eyre.[87] Indeed, Michael Condon and James Danaher, two senior clergymen in the archdiocese of Glasgow, were prominent advocates of Home Rule.[88] It is not known why some priests were allowed to participate in Irish nationalist politics, while others were not. Yet the role of Irish clergymen in the Home Rule movement should not be exaggerated. As Ian Wood pointed out in the 1970s, 'clerical influence was not tantamount to clerical control'.[89] During the 1885 general election, Charles Stewart Parnell, the leader of the Home Rule movement, instructed Irish voters in Great Britain to vote for Tory candidates. The Wishaw branch of the Irish National League expelled a member who had refused to obey this directive; as a result, the local priest attacked the branch for its decision, and withdrew the use of his school rooms for its meetings. The Wishaw INL upheld the expulsion, stating that 'they would be pleased to sit under Father McCoy in religion, but in politics we will be guided by the leaders of the Irish people.'[90] Those priests who actively supported the cause of Home Rule were not, as the Wishaw case illustrates, the dominant figures in the local branches. Leadership in the west of Scotland came mainly from the Catholic Irish laity; moreover, the towering figure in the Home Rule movement in the region was in fact an Ulster Protestant, John Ferguson.[91]

There is other evidence which shows sections of the Catholic Irish community rejecting the 'advice', or more accurately the orders, of some of the clergy on political matters. In August 1875 the Irish in the west of Scotland planned to celebrate the centenary of the birth of Daniel O'Connell by holding a large demonstration in Glasgow. However, some Irish nationalists wanted to turn the celebration into a political event and pass resolutions in favour of Irish Home Rule and amnesty for Irish political prisoners. Some of the senior Catholic clergy in Glasgow, such as Alexander Munro, a Scot, and Bernard Tracey, an Irishman, opposed this, and called on the Irish to support a non-political celebration, which would be led and controlled by them. Two rival demonstrations were then held on the same day; according to Handley twice as many attended the clergy event.[92] Nevertheless, the fact that thousands attended the political gathering, whose speakers included Michael Condon, demonstrates that 'clerics were not always able to control their parishioners' political movements as easily as popular opinion imagined they were.'[93]

Eight years later clerical advice over another demonstration was likewise ignored. In August 1883, the priest at Motherwell, the Irishman James Glancy, was opposed to a planned Home Rule meeting. He even went as far as issuing posters which read:

> Dr. Glancy wishes it to be distinctly understood that the so-called Irish demonstration announced to take place here on Saturday has been organized against his express order by a secret society formerly condemned by the Holy See, and that it is in no sense an Irish Catholic demonstration. He wishes the public of the burgh to consider all those taking any part whatever therein as acting in direct opposition to ecclesiastical authority, and he hopes that the peaceful Catholic population of the town will not be held responsible for the disreputable conduct of a few self-willed adherents of secret societies.[94]

Despite such public hostility from Glancy, around 400 Home Rulers from in and around the town assembled and then left to attend a demonstration in Coatbridge. On their return to Motherwell they were attacked by Orangemen and fighting continued over the next two days.[95]

Some Irish Catholics were even willing to defy the Church during local elections in which Catholic interests were at stake. For example, in March 1882 Henry Murphy, who since his dismissal from the diocese of Galloway had been publicly campaigning for the Irish nationalist cause, stood in the Glasgow School Board election as a Home Rule candidate. Despite incurring the wrath of the hierarchy and the senior clergy, and indeed being a sacked priest, he was elected ahead of the three Catholic Church candidates, one of whom was the Rev. Alexander Munro. Murphy's success also meant that one of the three Church candidates was not elected.[96]

Another area in which many Irish Catholics refused to obey the clergy's instructions was involvement in organisations which were proscribed by the Church. Catholics were forbidden to join societies such as the Ribbonmen and the Fenian Brotherhood. The Church in Scotland, as in Ireland where Ribbonism and Fenianism originated, opposed these secret oath-bound bodies on account of their violent activities and their revolutionary political aims and ideals, and because they were considered to be anti-clerical. Known members of these societies were denied the sacraments of the Church.[97] Yet despite this, some Irish Catholics seem to have been active in Ribbonism and Fenianism, and throughout Eyre's period in charge of the Catholic Church in the west of Scotland he received letters from his clergy seeking advice on how to deal with those who were involved in these activities.[98] Indeed, such was the concern that in 1882 Eyre established a 'Commission on the Subject of Secret Societies'. It concluded that societies such as the Ribbonmen did exist and were 'pernicious'. In order to disguise their activities and escape ecclesiastical sanction, the societies sometimes took the form of benefit societies. The commission recommended that all the organisations it named should be banned,[99] and as a result Eyre issued a circular on the St Patrick's Hibernian Society and the St Patrick's Fraternal Society. The clergy of the archdiocese were directed to prevent members of their flock from joining these proscribed organisations, and to do everything they could to persuade those who were members to leave.[100] In 1889, the Ancient Order of Hibernians, which according to Handley 'had a strong representation among the immigrants', was banned by the Catholic hierarchy in Scotland. The order insisted that it was simply a friendly society but the Church was convinced that it was mainly a front for Ribbonism.[101]

Despite the ecclesiastical ban and the exhortations of the clergy, members of the proscribed societies carried on regardless. The priest at Shieldmuir in Motherwell informed the archdiocese in 1897 that there seemed 'to be a very strong branch of the "Fenians" in this district', and gave an account of its activities.[102] The following year, Eyre was informed that 'the "Ribbonmen", or as they call themselves "St Patrick's Fraternal Society"', were holding meetings in Greenock.[103] The Ancient Order of Hibernians continued to operate openly, and eventually in 1909, 'in view of recent statements, and in view of the reformation of the rules', the ban on it in Scotland was lifted.[104] Indeed such was the concern in the archdiocese about the continuing activities of the secret societies, that Eyre's circular of 1882 was reprinted in 1888 and 1889, and was reissued in 1899 with the addition that 'all other similar societies (the "Ancient Order of Hibernians" being included)' were to be condemned.[105]

It was not only in the political or radical sphere that Irish Catholics rejected the wishes or instructions of their Church and clergy in the late nineteenth century. Temperance is a case in point. By the 1880s, if not before, drunkenness was regarded as a major problem within the Catholic community.[106] In October 1888, after a wide consultation with his clergy, Charles Eyre decided to establish a branch of the temperance organisation The League of the Cross in every parish in Glasgow and its suburbs.[107] The following May, encouraged by the success of the new venture, Eyre decided that the society was to have branches in all the parishes throughout his archdiocese.[108] This was soon achieved; indeed, at a great League of the Cross meeting in Glasgow City Hall on St Andrew's Day 1890, Eyre proudly informed his audience that the archdiocese of Glasgow was the first diocese in all of the United Kingdom to have a branch of the organisation in every parish. The secretary of the league reported that there were 68 branches in total, with a 'practical' membership of between 16,000 and 17,000.[109] Within a year and a half the society had expanded further. In March 1892 Eyre informed the laity that the number of branches had now risen to 128 – 64 for men, 40 for women and 24 for children – and announced that over 30,000 Catholics had taken the total abstinence pledge.[110] Moreover, the Church usually provided the organisation with the use of its halls and premises, and the parish priest was normally the leading figure in the local branch.[111]

Eyre's establishment of the League of the Cross throughout his archdiocese is seen by some historians as one of the main achievements of his episcopate.[112] However, a closer examination of the organisation reveals that in some parts of the west of Scotland in the 1890s it struggled either to attract or to keep members. For example, in March 1890 the priest at Larkhall informed the archdiocese that, in spite of all his efforts, there was no branch of the League of the Cross in his parish for men.[113] In October 1891 the priest in charge of St Mary's Hamilton, Peter Donnelly, told a parish meeting that the local League of the Cross 'did not come up to his expectations. It had not gathered into the ranks all those who were drinking to such an extent that they were unworthy of the name Christian. It was true that the League had accomplished a great deal, but it still had a large field before it.'[114] The following March the president of the branch stated in his annual report that although progress had been steady, 'the falling off at times was distressing ...'[115] In 1899 the parish priest at Longriggend stated that, 'The evil of drunkenness is ruining the large majority of the people and I find it very hard to keep up the league of the cross.'[116] Indeed, it would appear that the League of the Cross was not the success that some have suggested, and that the bulk of the Catholic Irish in the west of Scotland in fact rejected Eyre and the Church's entreaties to embrace the cause of total abstinence. The League of the Cross Annual Report of 1901 revealed that there were 65 branches in the archdiocese, with a total membership of 33,327 (23,943 men, 7,500 women and 1,884 children); the number of Catholics under Eyre's charge at this time was around 330,000. Mary McHugh's analysis of the report concludes that 'barely ten percent of the estimated Catholic community had even a nominally active involvement, and even within this group, very few followed the League programme with unswerving devotion'. According to McHugh, the League of the Cross went into decline thereafter and quickly 'lost ... any importance it may have possessed'.[117]

Finally, as was revealed earlier, even as late as the 1880s the issue of mixed marriages was still of great concern to the clergy. Throughout the nineteenth century the aim of the Catholic Church in the west of Scotland was to create and maintain a self-contained Catholic community in which the Irish remained true to the Catholic faith, and married within that community. From the 1860s onwards in particular, the Church established a wide range of social and recreational groups and activities, in part to negate the need of its adherents to look outwith the parish for them. The great fear was that if the Catholic Irish mixed socially with wider Scottish society, intermarriage would result: this could lead to Catholics being lost to the Church, and the children of such unions being raised as Protestants.[118] That many Irish Catholics did in fact choose to marry outwith their faith demonstrates once again that the grip of the Church was not as firm as some have claimed.

III

In the introduction to this chapter it was shown that the dominant view among historians about the Catholic Irish in nineteenth-century Scotland is that they were despised by the native population, and as a result constituted a separate and isolated community which was controlled by the clergy. Such a view, however, is not compatible with much of the evidence surveyed in this chapter. Many members of the Catholic Irish community in the west of Scotland participated in strikes and trade unions, and in political and other movements with Scottish workers. While most Scots might have disliked Catholicism as a religion and the Catholic Church as an institution, it is clear that many did not let their personal religious beliefs prevent them from participating in joint activities or associating with – or even marrying – members of the Catholic Irish community in the region.

It is evident, therefore, that the extent of popular opposition to the Catholic Irish in the west of Scotland in the nineteenth century has been greatly exaggerated. Some historians appear to have noted the hostility towards Irish strike-breakers in some of the mining districts in Lanarkshire and Ayrshire from the 1820s to the 1850s, and assumed that Scottish workers elsewhere in the region were equally opposed to the Catholic Irish presence, and for the same reasons. Yet outwith these mining areas there was in fact little economic rivalry between the Catholic Irish and the Scots. The nineteenth century saw rapid and massive industrial expansion in the west of Scotland, demand for labour was high and as a result Irish immigrants were absorbed into the growing economy with relative ease.[119] Indeed, as James Handley demonstrated, most Irish workers – Catholic and Protestant – in the major towns in the west of Scotland did not deprive the Scots of employment, simply because they took the jobs that no-one else wanted:

> For much of the labour that they undertook the Irish had no competitors among the native population. As builders' labourers, as stevedores, at the canals and reservoirs, on the railways, in road-making and mending, in pipe-laying, in brick kilns and potteries, at gas works, in quarries, in sugar refineries, in cotton factories, the Irish had no rivals to dispute their presence, for the native avoided such employment either on the ground that it was too strenuous for him or because it fell below his aspirations.[120]

It must be emphasised that the most intense and sustained period of popular hostility to the Catholic Irish community in Scotland over the past 200 years occurred not in the nineteenth century when the economy was booming and jobs were plentiful, but in the twenty years after the First World War, when the country suffered a severe economic depression and a crisis in national identity.[121]

This is not to suggest that there was little opposition to the Catholic Irish in the west of Scotland in the nineteenth century. The hostility of the Protestant Churches and sections of the middle class, particularly during the famine years[122] and the No-Popery agitation of the 1850s, was fierce, and reinforced Irish Catholics' sense of communal identity, as did the presence of Orangeism in the region. Irish strike-breakers in mining areas incurred the wrath of the native workforce, and bitterness towards the immigrants in such districts continued long after the industrial disputes were over. Elsewhere in the region, there were Scottish workers who disliked the Catholic Irish in their midst. However, it is currently impossible to gauge the extent of such hostility, as it did not usually manifest itself in ways which are easily measured; for example, there were few anti-Irish riots, and little support for anti-Catholic organisations and activities. An examination of nineteenth-century working-class newspapers and literature may reveal more about popular attitudes to the Catholic Irish. While further research will undoubtedly produce evidence of working class hostility to the Catholic Irish presence, it is likely that it will also show immigrants associating and integrating with, and even marrying, the native population.

With regard to the relationship between the Catholic Irish and their clergy, it is strange that a number of historians have chosen to portray the immigrant community as docile, deferential and easily controlled and manipulated by the priests and bishops. After all, over 60 years ago James Handley discussed in some detail a number of the disputes between priests and people over politics, and over the running – and indeed the identity – of the Church.[123] The Catholic Irish bowed to the will of the Church in the spiritual and religious sphere, and had great respect and admiration for their priests for the role that they played in community life. However, in matters concerning how the Church in the region should be governed, and in political and social affairs, many members of the Catholic Irish community showed a strong independence of mind, and rejected the views, advice and even the orders of their priests and bishops.

More local studies of the Catholic Irish are needed. By examining individual Catholic communities in depth, the relationship which the immigrants had with both the native population and the clergy can be placed firmly in the social, economic, religious and cultural context of the locality. Comparisons can then be made over time and across the region, and indeed with Catholic Irish immigrant communities throughout the world. Only then will the Catholic Irish experience in the west of Scotland in the nineteenth century be fully understood.

2 The Great Irish Famine and Scottish History

T. M. Devine

The Great Irish Famine of the 1840s was not only the greatest human disaster in nineteenth-century Europe but, proportionally, more lethal than the majority of famines of modern times. The calamity killed one-eighth of the entire population or just over a million people, most of whom succumbed to famine-related disease. The repeated failure of the potato crop, the primary source of subsistence for the small farmers, labourers and their families, was not simply a terrible ecological tragedy because the crisis also had profound consequences for the future demographic, economic, political and cultural history of the island of Ireland.[1]

However, the results of this epic catastrophe were not simply confined to the Irish nation. Emigration from Ireland had been taking place on a substantial scale from the early eighteenth century and the Great Famine massively accelerated the scale of that exodus. An estimated 2.1 million men, women and children left for overseas destinations in the decade between 1845 and 1855, with 1.5 million sailing for the USA, another 340,000 for British North America (later the Dominion of Canada) and between 200,000 and 300,000 settling in Great Britain. One scholar has suggested that more emigrants left Ireland during these years than the entire two and a half centuries which had gone before.[2] It was inevitable, then, that each of these receiving countries, plus Australia, which absorbed an additional several thousand, would be affected to a greater or lesser extent by this vast incoming tide of humanity.

In absolute terms the movement of the famine refugees to Scotland was less significant numerically than elsewhere because fewer than 100,000 came to Scotland during the crisis years.[3] In relative terms, however, this was an enormous and unique burden for a small country which contained only around 2.8 million inhabitants in 1845 and which also suffered an acute industrial depression in 1847–48, a cholera epidemic in 1848 and a subsistence crisis in the Highlands between 1846 and the early 1850s, where the failure of the potatoes also threatened an Irish-type calamity. Yet, despite its significance, the impact of the famine immigrations has been little studied by historians of Scotland. While several scholars touched on aspects of the event, only James E. Handley, in a book now nearly 60 years old, treated the topic at any length.[4] More recently, Frank Neal considered the experience of Glasgow during one famine year, 1847, as part of a wider volume on Britain and the Famine Irish.[5] Then, in one of his last publications, the late John

F. McCaffrey produced a valuable account of Scottish reaction to the Irish Famine which, nevertheless, stressed that there was much still to be said on a subject which was of such major consequence to contemporaries.[6]

This present essay does not pretend to be the final word on Scotland and the Great Famine. Its aims are the more modest ones of outlining some relevant themes: the nature and scale of the migration; the response of civic authorities, charities and churches to the huge army of the poor, diseased and hungry who landed on Scottish soil; and the longer-term significance of the Great Famine for Scottish history.

As the exodus from the stricken areas of Ireland to Scotland gathered pace in the summer of 1847, contemporaries started to react in a state of semi-panic. Under the heading, 'The Irish Invasion', the *Glasgow Herald* depicted a city over-run by a starving multitude: 'The streets are at present literally swarming with vagrants from the sister country and the misery which many of these poor creatures endure can scarcely be less than what they have fled or been driven from at home. Many of them are absolutely without the means of procuring lodging of even the meanest description and are obliged consequently to make their bed frequently with a stone for a pillow.'[7] In similar vein, *Blackwood's Edinburgh Magazine*, one of the most influential journals in nineteenth-century Scotland, described the human deluge which was now visited on the country. The 'influx of Irish hordes' had resulted in 'the inundation of Glasgow' which was taking place at the rate of more than 1,000 famine refugees a week fleeing to the city from across the Irish Sea.[8] The impact of this vast immigration would, thought the *Glasgow Chronicle* in 1847, be disastrous as: 'it will ultimately corrode the vitals of society and render property almost valueless in all the hives of industry.'[9] But perhaps most revealing and eloquent of all was the correspondence of the Catholic bishop, John Murdoch, and his priests of the western district who had to minister to the poor. In April 1847, Murdoch was in melancholy mood as he contemplated the developing tragedy: 'The starving Irish are flocking into Glasgow, by every boat and are literally ruining us. This is going to be a terrible year in the west.'[10] By June of that year he was even gloomier: 'I think some malediction must have fallen upon the west.'[11] A human catastrophe of great magnitude was unfolding.

The apocalyptic reaction of those who lived through these crisis years is easily comprehensible. Partly, of course, it was simply a response to the many thousands of famished, ragged and often diseased men, women and children who descended on the west of Scotland after 1846. The language almost universally employed in the press to describe the Irish dehumanises them and also captures the sense of a host society overwhelmed by weight of numbers: the terms 'hordes', 'invasion', 'swarms', 'shoals' and 'inundation' were commonplace. The immigration at this time was on a quite new scale. In 1841, the first census to trace people by birthplace showed that there were already 126,321 Irish-born in Scotland. By 1851 this total had risen to 207,367. In 1841 the Irish-born represented 4.8 per cent of the Scottish population; by

1851 the figure was 7.2 per cent. This relatively low figure does not, however, fully convey the demographic background to the widespread contemporary alarm. The immigrants did not spread across the country but instead concentrated in particular areas. It was this pattern which helped to form the graphic impressions of a society under siege. In 1851 nearly a fifth of the populations of the cities of Glasgow and Dundee had been born in Ireland with very high numbers also recorded in Lanarkshire (16.8 per cent), Wigtownshire (16.2 per cent), Dumbartonshire (11.9 per cent) and West Lothian (9.4 per cent). In all cases there had been substantial increases since the last census of 1841 before the Great Famine. As John McCaffrey concludes: '... some 120,000 Irish must have arrived over the 1840s; and, since the bulk obviously came after 1845, the conclusion must be that 40,000 came in the first half, giving a rate of 8000 per annum, and 80,000 in the second half, giving a rate of 16,000 per annum, over double the rate experienced in the later 1830s ... It represented the addition of a sizeable new industrial town each year in the later 1840s and early 1850s.'[12]

However, the crisis was not simply a matter of a massive increase in numbers. There are also good reasons to believe that the famine migrations were even more skewed to the very poor than had been the case in the decades before the 1840s. Some scholars suggest, for instance, that those with some means left for America. The poorer opted for the British mainland because of quicker access and cheaper fares. It was reported, for instance, from Sligo in March 1847 that there was 'much emigration going on and in contemplation'. Those with money were heading across the Atlantic while the paupers were taking ship for Glasgow and Liverpool.[13] It was a view confirmed by the Roman Catholic Bishop of Glasgow. Not only were the most destitute arriving in the Clyde in large numbers but, once any meagre savings had been made, the more fortunate also sailed for America. As the Rev. John Murdoch reported in October 1848, '... still times are bad and the best of our people continue to cross the Atlantic so that by and by we will be left with a congregation of beggars'.[14]

The regional pattern of famine in Ireland also influenced the social and religious composition of the migrations to Scotland in the 1840s. Louis Cullen once memorably remarked that the Great Famine was a regional not a national calamity because of the dramatic differences in the incidence of potato failure, and in local economies; and because of the diversity in social structures which led to considerable variation in both death and emigration rates.[15] Traditionally, most Irish migrants to Scotland had come from the historic province of Ulster. The embarkation ports for the Clyde were Belfast, Londonderry and Larne. But the worst hit counties in Ireland were broadly outside this region. Clare, Cork, Galway, Kerry, Mayo and Roscommon in the southern and central districts had especially high mortality rates. On the other hand, the eastern Ulster counties of Antrim, Armagh and Down, were among the most resilient with the lowest levels of destitution throughout the island during the famine years.[16] Indeed, across the entire province of Ulster destitution was negligible with less than 5 per cent of the population on the poor rates for at least one year between 1846 and 1850.[17] Antrim and Down were overwhelmingly Protestant counties where the Scots had settled in the seventeenth century. Linen manufacture was still important in some parts of the region, especially in the Lagan valley, the area to the south of Lough Neagh and the middle Bann valley, where more than half of men employed were engaged in linen production. This, together with a more varied crop regime, afforded a security which was absent from the regions of near potato monoculture elsewhere in Ireland.[18]

The evidence therefore suggests that crisis emigration was very limited from the eastern counties of Ulster and, as a result, the Protestant element in the movement to Scotland was also diminished. The famine migrations therefore seem to have been mainly Catholic with south Ulster, parts of Donegal, Cavan, Monaghan and Sligo well-represented.[19] This pattern was a clear break with the past when substantial numbers of Ulster Protestants had come to Scotland in the first four decades of the nineteenth century. For example, an analysis of the birthplaces of (mainly aged) Irish paupers on the poor rolls in Wigtownshire in 1845 (who had arrived in Scotland in the previous four decades) suggests that around 75 per cent were born in 'Protestant' counties, with nearly 45 per cent originating from County Down alone.[20] The overtly Catholic identity of the famine refugees exaggerated the widespread fears of a Scottish Protestant nation under siege from a vast, alien invasion emanating from across the Irish Sea.

Several other factors helped to feed these apprehensions as the failure of the potatoes which triggered the catastrophe seemed unending. Rather than a one-off crisis in 1845 and 1846 there was another massive shortage in 1848 and then repeated shortfalls until 1852. As a result the hungry Irish also brought with them epidemic disease. The scourge of 'famine fever' (typhus), dysentery and diarrhoea accompanied those fleeing from Ireland and aggravated the epidemic which was building up in urban areas as a result of the trade depression of 1847–48.[21] Death rates in the west of Scotland rose spectacularly as the contagions spread. In 1845 there were 8,259 burials in the city of Glasgow and its environs. By 1847 this figure had more than doubled to 18,886.[22] One of the most poignant indicators of the health crisis was the deaths among Catholic priests who were ministering to the sick poor. During 1847, Frs John Bremner, Richard Sinnot, Daniel Kenny and William Walsh all succumbed to typhus. Other towns in addition to Glasgow were seriously affected. Kenny died in Houston, Renfrewshire and Sinnot in Greenock. A number of other priests fell victim to the disease but eventually recovered.[23] The pressure on those who were still healthy was enormous. Bishop Murdoch wrote in despair in April 1847:

I am in a mess here just know. Four of the priests of this House are now lying: Kelch has passed the crisis: Gallagher is in the balance: whether life or death will be the result is very doubtful. Hanly and Gordon have both taken to bed to day with all the symptoms of fever on them. The sick calls at all the chapels are very very numerous, sometimes not less than 80 or 100 a day. One of the St. Mary's priests is also drooping and scarce fit for work. All the others have stood out yet: but how long I cant tell. We are fatigued and fagged almost every day. I hope the present visitation will soon pass or we'll be all Kilt [sic].[24]

Despite these horrors, however, Glasgow and the west of Scotland did not top the league table in Britain of famine-induced immigration. That dubious pre-eminence belonged to Liverpool which, during 1847 and 1848, handled more than twice the tonnage of Glasgow and five times the traffic of London from Irish ports.[25] But, unlike the pattern in England, western Lowland Scotland was also confronted with the challenging reality of two subsistence crises in close geographical proximity. John Strang, City Chamberlain of Glasgow, described how, in 1848, the city had to contend with 'wretched and starving immigrants' not only from Ireland but also the Scottish Highlands:

During the last twelve months no city almost in Her Majesty's dominions has been more burdened with so many wretched and starving immigrants ... hundreds of families were found hurrying daily from Ireland and the Highlands to Glasgow as a city of refuge, those families bearing with them the last rags of poverty, and exhibiting, but too frequently, the last symptoms of famine fever. Thousands, in fact, while they fled from their starving homes to live, arrived here only to die and have thus not only tended to swell the figures of our city mortality but to increase to a fearful extent the amount of our parochial rate ...[26]

In several ways the Highland famine mirrored the greater disaster in Ireland.[27] The lethal blight of *phytophora infestans*, which brought the Irish to starvation, also decimated the potato crop in 1846 in the crofting region and for several years thereafter. Early estimates in the autumn of 1846 suggested that the main source of subsistence had failed in over three-quarters of the crofting parishes. Press reports described how the stench of rotting potatoes pervaded many townships along the west coast and throughout the Hebrides. The Free Church newspaper, *The Witness*, concluded gloomily: 'The hand of the Lord has indeed touched us' and proclaimed the calamity to be 'unprecedented in the memory of this generation and of many generations gone by, even in any periods of our country's history'.[28] One major consequence was a marked increase in movement to the cities of the south for work throughout late 1846 and 1847. By this time seasonal migration had become a well-established feature of Highland society. But the numbers involved now, because of the potato failure, were many times greater than before. In Kintail, for example, the people 'were going off to the south in every steam-boat ... few of the young men and women remain'. Similarly, in neighbouring

Glenelg, 'as many as can had left to seek employment in Glasgow'. From the estates of Maclean of Ardgour and Cameron of Lochiel 'multitudes had gone ... with every steamer about a score depart'.[29] So extensive was the exodus from Skye that observers feared a repeat of the crisis the following year because only a few were now available to prepare the croft lands for planting and harvest peat for fuel.[30] Recent work on these migrations has shown that they were much more extensive than before, especially in the Outer Hebrides, because they now included areas with previously weak migrant traditions. The social composition of the migrants also changed. No longer was the movement confined to young, single men and women from cottar families. Older men and heads of households from the tenant class were now travelling in considerable numbers to seek work in the Lowlands.[31] For town and city authorities already harassed by the 'hordes' of Irish pouring into the country, this additional exodus from the north of Scotland added to the sense of being swamped by successive waves of destitute poor. When a serious industrial recession started to develop in the autumn of 1847 and then intensified in 1848, it seemed to contemporaries little could now save the west of Scotland from a human tragedy of historic proportions. As the *Glasgow Herald* memorably reported in March 1847: 'the enormous number of Irish vagrants poured in upon us by steamer that arrives in the Clyde, threatens *to eat us up.*'[32]

Moreover, the famine immigration helped to fuel the typhus epidemic of 1847. Death rates rose dramatically for a time and the refugees from Ireland also endured much suffering and privation. Yet, against all the odds and in spite of the worst fears of people at the time, the crisis was contained. In Glasgow, which was at the sharp end, burials started to level off after 1847, even though the city was also assailed by an outbreak of cholera in 1848. The peak of burials was reached in 1847 at 18,886. Thereafter, the number fell to 13,179 in 1848, 12,731 in 1849 and 10,589 in 1850.[33] The relative stabilisation of mortality levels was accompanied by a dramatic fall in the number of Irish claiming relief from the city's poor rates. For instance, in the Irish migrant heartland of Barony parish, the number of Irish-born claimants fell from 13,952 in 1847 to 2,709 the following year. Spending on poor relief declined even more dramatically from £9,092 in 1847 to £1,107 in 1848, though some of this was a result of a major fall in per capita payments.[34] In addition, after 1848, comments in the press about the immigration of the famished Irish became much rarer and, by the early 1850s, virtually disappeared. Between January and 30 November 1847, an estimated 49,993 'destitute' Irish had landed at the Broomielaw, a figure which did not include those other unfortunates who disembarked at other Clyde ports or elsewhere along the west coast. By the early 1850s this great multitude had declined to a trickle.[35] The city and its environs had apparently been spared the full long-term horror which some observers had dreaded.

This deliverance came about in part because circumstances became much more favourable for the western Lowlands after 1848. For one thing, the feared massive permanent movement to the south of destitute Highlanders did not happen. There was, indeed, a substantial exodus from the north-west and islands but this mainly took the form of emigration across the Atlantic and to Australia. Furthermore, the extensive relief effort organised by some landowners, the Free Church of Scotland and Lowland charities was broadly successful and so prevented a major mortality crisis.[36] Charles Withers' work confirms that the traditional patterns of permanent migration to the cities of the south were not significantly altered by the potato famine. While levels of temporary movement did rise, the southern and eastern Highlands, which were much less affected by crop failure, remained the main source of new Highland migrants to the urban areas.[37] The *Reports of the Glasgow Night Asylum for the Homeless* confirm the relatively limited rate of the migration of the destitute from Gaeldom. Thus, from July to October 1849, only 75 (or 2.4 per cent of admissions) were from Highland counties, which is to be compared to 935 from Ireland.[38] Similarly, in 1851, Highlanders accounted for 145 admissions (or 3.8 per cent of the total) while the number of Irish registered was 762.[39]

In addition, as good luck had it, the serious economic recession of 1847–48 started to wane by 1849. Market reports for seasonal harvesters suggested a recovery by 1850 and by 1851 and 1852 demand for workers in most Lowland areas started to exceed supply. The urban labour market also showed more buoyancy as did railway construction activity.[40] This propitious upturn in the economic cycle more than any other single factor made for better prospects for poor Irish immigrants who, long before 1846, had become well-established in general and casual labouring jobs in Scotland in construction, agriculture and industry.

Town authorities also mounted a substantial relief operation. Frank Neal has conducted an extensive analysis of these measures for Britain as a whole with special reference to the year 1847. His broad evaluation is positive: 'Overall a tentative conclusion regarding the response of local British poor law authorities during the 1847 famine crisis is that they fulfilled their responsibilities regarding the welfare of the Irish Famine refugees. They were not generous but they were not generous to the British poor.'[41] In Glasgow the response was one of a mix of punitive and benevolent strategies. In early 1847 hundreds of vagrants were arrested on the streets of the city for begging, most of whom were Irish.[42] Even in 1849, when conditions had marginally improved, the parochial authorities were sending paupers back to Ireland at the rate of 1,000 a month. In total, between 1845 and 1854, 47,000 Irish paupers were repatriated though doubtless unknown numbers successfully returned.[43] But this policy was paralleled by support for the destitute and the sick. A soup kitchen established in St Enoch's Square was serving 4,000–5,000 Irish a week in the winter of 1847, many of whom were 'emaciated by disease and want'. No discrimination on religious grounds was practised.[44] The authorities also acted swiftly to commandeer empty buildings as temporary fever hospitals.[45] Some officials and doctors performed heroic service: four surgeons, six poor

law officers and three nurses caught typhus and died.[46] Temporary poor relief
was given to the Irish from the parochial board at a cost of £21,306 in 1847.
The individual level of relief was very low, only enough to support a minimal
level of existence. But this was an accepted axiom of the time, a policy based
on the fear of encouraging dependency among the poor. At least there seems
to have been a broad equality of treatment with Irish refugees being treated
little differently from Scottish paupers.[47]

In some ways this response was surprising given the negative press which
the Irish attracted as immigration gathered pace after 1846. They were
blamed for importing typhus fever, corrupting the lower orders of Scotland
by setting the most pernicious example of dependency on parochial aid, and
accused of spreading criminality. In addition, examples appeared regularly in
the newspapers highlighting instances of poor, ragged Irishmen being caught
with money on them despite claiming destitution and pleading for relief. The
Glasgow Herald summed up the mood of hostility:

> We have applied to the Legislature, in vain, for a remedy against the annual
> inundation of pauper Irish with which we are afflicted. They are landed
> by thousands, we may say, since the Irish famine by tens of thousands ...
> We have thus to bear the expense of supporting the lives of perhaps the
> most improvident, intemperate and unreasonable beings that exist on the
> face of the earth, who infest us in shoals and beg our charity because the
> land of their birth either cannot or will not support them. Our hospitals
> are filled with them, our police are overwrought by them, our people are
> robbed and murdered by them.[48]

Yet, in the first years of the famine migrations at least, two factors
encouraged a more positive treatment by the poor law and hospital
authorities. The first was pragmatic – if the immigrant Irish were indeed
seen as the vectors of fever then they perhaps above all deserved medical
intervention and support if the epidemic was not to spread uncontrollably.
Second, the reactions to this invasion of destitute strangers were complex.
In one sense there was an explicit conflict between the Victorian consensus
that people were poor because they were at fault and, on the other hand, the
need to respond to the desperate search of the Irish for support. The attitude
to the immigrants was also suffused with racism and sectarianism. The
Free Church organ, *The Witness*, was unambiguous: 'Popery is peculiarly a
religion of dependency and indigence and it is its direct tendency to militate
against the self-relying spirit.'[49] Yet the mid-Victorian middle classes were
also deeply religious and therefore also felt the duties and responsibilities
of benevolence and charity called for by Christian conscience. In the same
way as they contributed many thousands to the relief of destitution in the
Highlands, so they were also willing to be supportive, for a time at least, of
the hungry Irish.

This complexity was perfectly caught by Peter Mackenzie who was partly responsible for establishing a Sunday soup kitchen for the destitute in Glasgow in 1847. On the one hand he bitterly denounced the Irish landlords who 'to save their own pockets from pauper assessments, were shipping off whole cargoes of their population by steamers to Glasgow to live or die as beggars amongst us in Scotland'. The Irish race had also, in his view, managed to produce nothing but 'anarchy and squalid misery' and they were now exporting these maladies to other lands. Equally, however, Mackenzie was so affected by the physical reality of actually seeing Irish families in the streets of Glasgow, enduring terrible distress, 'a most dismal sight, sufficient to touch a heart of a stone', that he became an enthusiastic advocate of providing free soup for the immigrants.[50]

Public support from the poor law and civic authorities is also well-documented. Less familiar is the role of the Catholic Church and the resident Irish population who had settled in west-central Scotland before the Great Famine. At the census of 1841 there were 126,000 Irish-born already in Scotland with the majority settled in the western Lowlands. Also, the Catholic Irish had an institutional and cultural identity which was buttressed by loyalty to the Catholic Church. William Sloan estimates that Glasgow's Catholic population numbered over 40,000 in the late 1830s with just over a third of them attending mass on a regular basis.[51] The 'better off' of the working class were more likely to observe their religious duties. Even non-practising Catholics seem to have maintained a sense of Catholic community and identity which was manifested by religious pictures and ornaments in the home, membership of Catholic organisations, such as temperance clubs, and continuing loyalty to the Church by contributing to collections on a regular basis.[52] Most Irish workers were concentrated in jobs which offered low levels of pay and status. But, as recent research has shown, not all were employed in menial occupations. Apparently, 'a significant proportion' of Irish immigrants were building tradesmen, glass and pottery workers and were also to be found in the skilled textile sector as spinners, printers, warpers and tenters.[53]

It would have been strange indeed if such a community had not offered aid and support to the famine refugees, many of whom were not only their co-religionaries and fellow Irish but had come from broadly the same districts in Ireland which had sustained migration to Lowland Scotland since the later eighteenth century. Bishop Murdoch organised a soup kitchen in 1847 which served over 400 men, women and children every day. He also praised his congregation at St Andrew's Cathedral which was acting 'very generously' although he feared if the crisis continued much longer 'its means will ... soon be exhausted'. It was the case that 'crowds collected daily at chapel houses' to receive money while Catholic priests were required to give daily two to three shillings from their 'slender salaries' to help the destitute.[54] The Church also developed and managed a Catholic Orphan Institution which in 1848 was described as being of 'immense service during the recent pestilence'. The initiative had originally come from Protestant subscribers but 'Catholic money and zeal carried it through to completion'.[55]

However, despite all the relief efforts and the clear signs during the crisis of inter-denominational goodwill (which even extended in Glasgow to Catholic priests being invited to open the public soup kitchens for daily business with prayers for their people), the experience of the Irish Famine did leave an enduring scar on Scotland. True, there was little of the venomous sectarian violence which disfigured Liverpool, New York and Boston as a consequence of the huge Irish migrations into those cities.[56] But a Protestant backlash of sorts did take place in the early 1850s. The restoration of the English Roman Catholic hierarchy at the beginning of that decade, though of no direct relevance to Scotland, was dubbed 'papal aggression'. This, together with native hostility to the successive waves of Irish immigrants, sparked off a period of sectarian unrest. Anti-Catholic demagogues, such as John Sayers Orr, the self-proclaimed 'Angel Gabriel', and Alessandro Gavazzi, a former priest, attracted a good deal of attention.[57] Some rioting also occurred in several towns in the western Lowlands and anti-Catholic journals, like the *Bulwark* and the *Scottish Protestant*, were founded. The latter drew a direct causal link between the flood of famine immigrants and the menace of popery on the march: 'If the hopes of Popery to regain her dominion of darkness in this kingdom of the Bible light are beginning to revive, it is because she is colonising our soil from another land with the hordes of her barbarised and enslaved victims whom she proudly styles "her subjects".'[58]

But this phase of virulent and overt hostility lasted only a few years and was over by the end of the 1850s. More subtle and significant was the consolidation of a new racial analysis of the Irish and their descendants as feckless, inferior and undisciplined who had brought the catastrophe of famine upon themselves. Colin Kidd has demonstrated the importance of racist thought in Victorian Scotland – George Combe, Robert Knox and Thomas Carlyle were among the leaders of the movement and Combe's treatise, *The Constitution of Man* (1828), its most influential text, going through eight editions by 1847 and selling more than 80,000 copies.[59] His followers believed in the absolute superiority of the Saxon and Teutonic stock of Lowland Scotland and England over the benighted Celts of Ireland and the Scottish Highlands. The thinking of the Teutonists lent a spurious intellectual legitimacy to anti-Irish racism of the time which was also given a special impetus by the arrival of the famine refugees. Newspapers, such as the *Scottish Guardian* and the *North British Daily Mail*, demonised the arrivals and in his racist diatribe, *Scotland for the Scotch*, John Steill bitterly protested against the Irish 'invaders' as 'clouds of the vilest specimens of the human animal in the face of the earth' whose baleful influence contaminated the Scots through exposing them to 'Irish crime, Irish dirt, Irish disease and Irish degradation'.[60] Steill was one of the more extreme commentators, but that stereotype of the Catholic Irish as an inferior race was to endure and embitter relations between indigenous Scots, the immigrants and their descendants for generations to come.[61]

Acknowledgement

This essay is part of a wider study on the Catholic Irish in Scotland, 1845–1939, funded by the Leverhulme Trust and the Arts and Humanities Research Council (AHRC) and conducted under the auspices of the AHRC Centre for Irish and Scottish Studies at the University of Aberdeen. I am very grateful to both the trust and the AHRC for their support and also my colleague, Dr Martin Mitchell, who was a joint investigator on the project.

3 Catholic Devotion in Victorian Scotland

Bernard Aspinwall

'We Catholics need much solidarity. We are addicted to snobbishness and split up into cliques and coteries. Yet we ought to be taking the lead in healing breaches of society and in dissipating the flames of class.'[1] So wrote convert Jesuit Rev. Charles Dominic Plater in 1920. Almost 70 years earlier, St Margaret's Association had sought a similar objective: to unite aristocrats, converts, Highlanders and Irish in one harmonious body of faith.[2]

Unity was essential for a common identity, for political protection and self-defence, to raise funds for churches, schools and orphanages, to establish and maintain a connection with incomers, and to prevent leakage. The transformation of a vague rural Highland or Donegal folk religion into a dynamic controlling worldview of faith demanded an effective framework. That strategy required a cultural transition; a redistribution of resources; a managerial and organisational revolution within Catholicism. Rome, Romanticism and respectability combined. Unity was more than the Latin Mass.

That brings us to the extent and influence of 'Italian' devotions in Scotland. The traditional view of Emmet Larkin and his followers saw assertive Ultramontanism in the introduction of novel Italianate devotions as characteristically Irish responses to a cultural and pastoral crisis, an interpretation vigorously challenged by Mary Heimann and others who emphasise continuity and competitive parallels with Protestantism.[3]

Scottish experience somewhat differs. There was continuity *and* a devotional watershed. Outsiders, Irish, French, Italian, English and converts, transformed a rather staid Catholicism. Ethnic division fuelled Ultramontane zeal and precipitated the restoration of the hierarchy. Irish clergy saw it as an excellent means of controlling unaccountable Scottish bishops and clergy – and exalting 'pure' Irish Catholic culture against pagan Scottish industrialism.[4] Experience subsequently suggested the new hierarchy later saw it as a means of reaching and controlling the Irish.[5] The Catholic aristocracy saw it as a means of upgrading and 'civilising' their coreligionists in that old and convert families were united. The internecine clashes are well known, but shortage of resources, scattered locations, inaccessible workplaces and the demographic profile of the faithful demand we rethink nineteenth-century Scottish devotional life.

Money and its control were central.[6] Money – or its lack – dictated most apparent 'Ultramontane' responses. Bishop Carruthers scorned an Edinburgh college 'in some future time or century'.[7] Revivalist practices gave a greater spiritual return on investment of resources and manpower: less debt, more effective use of priests and maximum impact. Whatever caused the introduction of 'Italianate' practices in English-speaking countries, their growth here was a practical response to uniquely Scottish problems.[8]

Scots knew of Catholic revivalism as early as 1820.[9] It undoubtedly had an effect. In 1832 Protestants were astounded at the opening of Dumbarton chapel as some 3,000 attended *Missa cantata* and Benediction.[10] An Irish Gaelic-speaking Oblate was immensely successful in an 1851 Edinburgh mission.[11] Soon Bishop Murdoch rejoiced in mission successes.[12] In 1875, at Greenock, a Redemptorist mission produced 5,000 confessions and 700 confirmations.[13] The phenomenon repeatedly occurred throughout the central belt. By the 1880s parallel to several visits by Moody and Sankey, Archbishop Eyre was promoting multi-centre citywide missions in Glasgow. Missions invariably drew huge attendances.[14]

It was a transformation in the spiritual life of the community. *The Religious Census; Scotland 1851* (1854), although flawed, gives some indication of earlier Catholic spiritual life and practice. Allowing for thirteen known omissions and errors, several points emerge. Sunday Mass attendance was put at 48,771 or perhaps a third of the Catholic population, with 2,377 at afternoon and 15,439 at evening services. Information concerning Catholic devotional life in these returns is patchy. Eleven areas (Buchan, Caithness, Clackmannan, Haddington, Kincardine, Linlithgow, Nairn, Orkney, Shetland, Selkirk and Sutherland) were untainted by Catholic services. Even areas with Sunday Mass considerably varied.[15]

Several factors may explain these variations: the nature of the group; difficulties of travel; distance from a permanent chapel; the nature of local occupations, agricultural or industrial; or simply a shortage of priests – in many areas priests covered several chapels or celebrated Sunday Mass only once a fortnight or month. Perth, for example, served a fifty-mile radius.[16] Add numerous baptisms, Sunday schools, marriage preparations and other demands; a priest had little time left. Ill-prepared sermons were normal.[17] The cost and availability of heating, lighting, candles or oil lamps, were further disincentives until the introduction of gas or, more remarkably, electric lighting from 1880 in Cumnock. Laity at a distance, lacking transport and working long shifts may also have had limited commitment.

Rural areas had 31 Masses but only two afternoon and no evening services. In eleven shires (Aberdeen, Argyll, Bute, Elgin, Inverness, Peebles, Ross and Cromarty, Roxburgh, Stirling and Wigtonshire) 42 Masses were not followed by any afternoon or evening services. In Fife, two Masses were followed by only one afternoon service. Ayrshire had four Masses but only one evening service. At the other extreme Glasgow and Lanarkshire Catholics had the luxury of 13 Masses attended by almost 14,000 and some 45 per cent of these, 6,280, were at the six evening services.[18] Edinburgh had five Masses with 2,650 faithful and four evening services attended by almost 1,100, approaching 40 per cent of the morning attendance.

Observance was highest in Dumbarton and Paisley. Almost 3,000 Renfrewshire

Catholics attended seven Masses while four evening services brought out 1,683 faithful or three fifths the morning attendance. Kirkcudbright had three Masses but only one evening service, which attracted 40 per cent of those at the Masses. Differences between rural and urban congregations are clear. In short there were few opportunities for Catholic revivalist practices. Those few chapels with afternoon or evening services had Vespers but that was already changing.

These practical concerns reinforced the conservatism of Scottish Catholic clergy, elite converts and 'old' Catholic families. Emphasis upon immediate needs demonstrated the severe limitations of the few Catholics who had passed beyond basic survival level: visionaries would only emerge when they achieved basic levels of comfort. In their often rootless, short, brutal lives they sought 'their' space, spiritual support and reassurance of an after life. To priests, those fleeing famine in the Highlands and Ireland, who were often employed on short-lived projects, invariably victims of Victorian economic fluctuations and frequently moving on to the south or to America, posed immense pastoral problems. They made overwhelming demands on resources, spiritual and temporal. Roots were a prerequisite to spiritual nourishment: a self-consciously shared experience of basic literacy, catechism, portable medals, scapulars or hymns was the preliminary to abiding faith.

Those were brought to newcomers by priests from Banffshire, Ireland, England, Italy, the Low Countries, Germany, repressed Poland or Lithuania: after all there were as many Canadian and English-born Scottish bishops as Irish in the nineteenth century – one of each.[19] Irish, French and English nuns similarly inculcated their devotions in the classroom, sick room, boarding and Sunday school.[20] The Miraculous Medal, public recitation of the Rosary, or devotion to a particular saint infiltrated in this way: few religious objects were available before 1829. Jesuits sustained these approaches through missions, sodalities, sermons (particularly at the opening or rededication of chapels) and dominance of the confessional.[21]

The Great Famine generation, overwhelmingly in the childbearing age group, married, began families in Scotland or departed overseas. Faith had to be grafted onto folk religion. In 1888 the Rev. Michael Condon found his two parishes had 35 per cent under 14 years of age but by the eve of the First World War only about 17 per cent of Catholics were.[22] A more mature, settled pattern emerged as growth accelerated astonishingly in urban areas: the Glasgow archdiocese population grew 225 per cent and Edinburgh 181 per cent in the half century from 1881.

Numbers of priests increased from 100 in 1850, to197 in 1870, to 540 by 1910. A clericalised Church made huge demands on them: over-worked dispensers of the sacraments had little time for angst or reflection.[23] A quinquennial sampling from 1885 to 1920 shows baptisms increased from just fewer than 14,000 to more than 23,000, while marriages almost doubled to 5,894. Long hours in confessionals increased priestly influence and exhaustion.[24] Bishops were equally hard pressed. Confirmations grew from 6,467 to almost 17,000. Despite high infant mortality in Glasgow, the community was overwhelmingly young: it needed tradition, roots, routine, discipline and warmth of shared experiences. Parish missions regularly revitalised those needs. Catholic revivalism stressed the individual sense of guilt, repentance and reassurance within the group: colourful ceremonies, theatrical sermons and popular hymns recognised their anguish, hardship, grief and offered hope. They instilled an indelible, portable sense of Catholic spiritual identity.[25]

The prevailing ethos – the Famine and failed Irish revolts of 1798, 1848 and 1866 – dampened potential political firebrands and reassured Protestants. Traditional quiet Scottish Catholics avoided confrontation; aristocrats and elite converts sought to win Protestant respect and occasional financial support by example and to prevent raw, embittered incomers falling prey to atheistic demagogues, futile violence or utopian schemes. The Church was to inculcate behaviour suitable for the Victorian drawing room, the anteroom to eternity.

Such considerations dictated spiritual life: 'We please the Lord', wrote aristocratic convert Passionist, the Rev. Ignatius Spencer to fellow convert Agnes Traill, 'by our present devotion of heart and joyful obedience in present duties; by not wasting our thoughts in speculation about the future. Tomorrow will provide for itself.'[26] While not binding Catholicism to the existing order, that approach emphasised individual responsibility within an evolving organic social order: it rejected revolutionary confrontation, encouraged self-improvement and mutual support as a means of individual and communal advance. It walked purposefully rather than ran in several directions.

The year 1846 was decisive in Scottish Catholic history. The Great Famine began. In July the Rev. Charles Eyre of Newcastle, later Archbishop of Glasgow, attended the opening of Pugin's St Giles, Cheadle, when Bishop James Gillis' theatrical preaching horrified Newman, as ladies of quality moaned and swooned. In November, convert Sir William Drummond Stewart reopened his ancient chapel of St Anthony at Murthly Castle. Reconstructed by Gillespie Graham, it had a full choir and organ under Signor Paolo Della Torre. In the morning, the Rev. Stephen Keenan, Dundee pastor and Irish author of an influential catechism reprinted throughout the century, preached and in the evening, at Vespers, the Rev. J. S. McCorry, an inveterate pamphleteer. The congregation included Old Catholic families like the Earl of Traquair and wealthy converts like Robert Monteith. The following month, the judicious pamphleteer, the Rev. Paul McLachlan, claimed that over 1,000 poor Irish were scattered for miles around his Falkirk district.[27]

A few years earlier in 1837 the Constable Maxwells at Dumfries had the first altar consecrated since the Reformation.[28] The following year Scottish bishops and eventually nine elite laymen supported the defensive propaganda of the new Catholic Institute of Great Britain.[29] Subsequently the Edinburgh Holy Guild of St Joseph, a socially inclusive body, epitomised the Romantic character of the revival. Its members enjoyed sickness and death benefits and attended Requiem Masses of their humblest brothers in exquisite robes designed by Pugin.[30] A return to medieval harmony was preferable to radicalism: religion was essential to social order.[31] Aristocratic and convert social self-confidence as much as Ultramontanism helped to restore hierarchy. A new assertive character was forming.

Catholicism experienced remarkable growth. Even before the Famine, the Western District in 1845 reportedly contained 140,000 faithful.[32] To Scottish-born clergy Irish priests and people were a passing phase: they were alien transients who made few concessions to Scottish sensitivities. Their departure might be welcomed but the likely aftermath of heavy debts and renewed anti-Catholicism made undemonstrative Scots-born Catholics apprehensive. Even after the Famine generation, congregations were 'liable to be scattered by the exhaustion of minerals, the dullness or trade and other causes'.[33] Enterprising Highlanders and Irish emigrated to America, leaving behind ever more demanding poor and pauperised.[34] In 1855 a priest reported some 500 Catholics in two Glasgow poorhouses.[35] Typhus, cholera and frequent death in densely packed slum areas further exacerbated pressing pastoral and social problems.[36]

Startling growth then followed the shift in power from the Highlands and Islands to the new industrial centres of the central belt. By 1835 only 20 priests ministered to almost 70,000 faithful in the western district yet 25 priests still laboured for 14,000 in the sparsely populated northern district,[37] where local cohesive cultural Catholic communities existed, often with good relations with Protestant neighbours, if not their Protestant landlords. The central belt differed markedly, with social change, competition and xenophobia. If less remarkable in numerical terms than England and Wales, the impact in Scotland was still astonishing: 83 priests, 52 permanent chapels, a nunnery and an estimated 150,000 mainly Irish faithful in 1838 grew by 1855 to 131 clergy, four convents, about 100 chapels, and numerous Sunday and day schools for around 200,000 nominal faithful.[38]

Considerable efforts were made to meet their demands: in Glasgow schools went from one in 1834 to 17 in 1870, and numbers accelerated following the 1872 Education Act.[39] That was reflected in the frequent reprinting of Keenan's *Catechism* from 1846, with revisions especially after Vatican I, until the end of the century: rote learning was a straightforward response to manpower and literary shortages.[40] Hardship and survival left little time for angst. In 1850 St Mary's Edinburgh and a temporary Mass centre, Leith, struggled to provide basic education for over 1,000 children.[41] Women religious filled the breach with Sunday schools, which catered to over 7,000 children in Glasgow.[42] Later Confraternities of Christian Doctrine massively expanded as laity took responsibility. The Catholic Poor Schools Committee disproportionately aided Scottish education and teachers received full-time training in England. Only after 1894 was Notre Dame training college established in Glasgow.[43] Sheer numbers, more than Ultramontanism demanded discipline, rote learning and deference to authority. The Church mirrored the centralisation, consolidation and mass production of the late-nineteenth-century economic world.

Numbers of convents also grew markedly. The sole Edinburgh convent in 1838 became 17 nationwide by 1870: a decade later the previous handful of Sunday schools almost touched 200.[44] Dioceses varied: before 1914 less than 40 per cent of scattered Aberdeen churches had Sunday schools while three-quarters of sprawling Galloway diocese did. After 1872 evening schools declined markedly with enforced day school attendance. That pressure and the massive post-Famine generation birth rate bulge led to a rapid growth in schools. A more settled and disciplined body assumed responsibility.

In tandem with these developments regular instruction or sermons greatly increased.[45] They reflected more, less peripatetic clergy, more settled churches and congregations as much as any Roman influences. Congregational devotions greatly expanded. Rare, if not unknown, Benediction quickly became the most popular devotion: in 1798 the seminary at Aquhorties had a monstrance, but regular Benediction and the first Quarante 'Ore seem to have begun at St Margaret's Convent, Edinburgh in 1834 and 1842 respectively.[46] The eight Benedictions of 1855 climbed to 193 on the eve of the First World War.[47] The western district in 1860 offered one Benediction service, quadrupled a decade later and Glasgow archdiocese managed at least 70 weekly Benedictions by 1914.[48] Dioceses varied: in Dunkeld only four in ten but in Galloway three out of four chapels had Benediction. Vespers virtually disappeared during the country.

Parish Rosary assumed greater significance yet never had the appeal of Benediction. For the Rev. Thomas Keane, illiterates in Irvine poor-house responded more readily to tangible faith in a Rosary or medal where the more literate favoured a tract or booklet. Faith was literally their only possession; their Rosary alone was theirs, a last shred of dignity and identity.[49]

The most remarkable organisational transformation lay in a phenomenal expansion of voluntary associations. In 1838 there were none but they reached 51 by 1880. By 1914 1,010 parochial organisations operated including 463 in the Glasgow archdiocese.[50] Many undoubtedly had small memberships but a conservative estimate suggests thousands in all. Their primary loyalties rivalled political organisations; like building blocks they formed, cemented and expressed the community.

The Famine shocked the Church, and had unpredictable reverberations long afterwards as new industrial areas opened up or closed a generation or more later: Irvine doubled the number of faithful, baptisms and Easter communicants in less than six years while the Newton Stewart congregation virtually disappeared as local industry collapsed.[51] By the end of the Crimean War, in Glasgow alone a quarter of the total population, 100,000 were reputedly Catholics.[52] However reassuringly impressive that figure meant huge demands on very limited resources.[53] The structure could not cope.

Bishop John Murdoch among others had profound misgivings about the Irish, particularly the quality of their clergy in the west of Scotland.[54] Their arrival was not altogether welcome to their co-religionists; their poverty and among Irish clergy especially, their alleged abrasiveness, political sympathies and lack of education were embarrassing.[55] Bishop Smith, soon to be sent to

America on a begging trip, preferred quiet progress to Bishop Gillis' exuberant zeal with schemes for seminaries, a massive Pugin church in Edinburgh or one by Hansom in Leith.[56] To old Tory Bishop Andrew Scott of the western district, the Irish threatened authority in church and state.[57] More conciliatory, Murdoch still found them infuriatingly unreliable. Scottish clergy were generally suspicious, less welcoming and uneasy about their clerical brethren: one convert priest fierily denounced Irish clerical revolutionary zeal under pretended spiritual concern.[58] To Murdoch, 'Patriotism is the great idol before which all men fall down and worship.'[59] In the Glasgow *Free Press* controversies, Scottish clergy, hostile to a possible Irish bishop in either western or northern districts, demanded 'someone that would be faithful to the interests of Scotland' and opposed any Irish, English or 'any other foreigner' as a vicar-apostolic.[60]

Irish clergy and laity were equally antipathetic to their Scottish brethren. They bombarded Rome with protests and accusations; in 1868 Bishop James Lynch reminded Archbishop Cullen on several occasions that Scottish clergy were, with few exceptions, limited, lacking zeal and in many instances morally deficient.[61] Ethnic antipathy did not help Catholic cohesion. Ultramontanism would. And would also help the Irish.

Parochial gatherings were antidotes to division. At the simplest level, outings from the 1840s, with choirs, brass bands, sports and children's fun melded folk together in respectability on temperance trips to estates of Catholic lairds like Drummond Stewart, Monteith or Bute. Trips 'doon the watter' were similar parish occasions. Newspapers invariably noted the good order and decorum of large numbers of faithful.

A more overtly religious slant came later. In 1860 Charles Gordon, improving Catholic laird and later Jesuit missionary, led a band of 120 Glasgow Irish volunteers to fight for the Pope: English clerical suspicion of their revolutionary intentions meant they ended up cleaning papal privies.[62] Elite Catholics went on pilgrimage to Rome and to Paray-le-Monial in the 1870s. In 1897 Jesuits promoted the first official pilgrimage to Iona, with Presbyterian co-operation.[63] Two years later the first official Scottish pilgrimage to Lourdes followed; some 400 laity and numerous clergy entrained.

Newcomers raised considerable sums from their small means but immense problems remained. Catholics had drawn financial support from sympathetic Protestants on many occasions: in establishing the first Glasgow chapel, the first Glasgow Catholic schools with sermons by the Rev. Dr Thomas Chalmers, or for Barrhead chapel.[64] Protestants also supported Catholic poor relief in hard times.[65] Some priests learned the hard way: a Catholic or convert was not necessarily the most reliable workman.[66]

Catholicism remained heavily dependent on wealthy patrons or elite converts until the First World War. Sir William Drummond Stewart, already mentioned, gave oil paintings by American Alfred Jacob Miller to Dundee and assisted Crieff. But the outstanding convert, the Third Marquess of Bute, quietly aided chapels, schools, religious orders and charities from Oban to

Rothesay, Ayr, Irvine, Cumnock, Birnieknowe, Lockerbie and Whithorn.[67] Catholic Duchesses of Buccleuch, Hamilton and Leeds were benefactors. The Herries family, with six daughters nuns, generously aided New Abbey and Kinharvie while firmly defending Catholic interests.[68] The Lothians frequently supported good causes. Rev. Archibald Douglas, whose brother, the Marquess of Queensberry, owned most of Annan, preached at the opening of the new chapel there.[69] The owner of Auchen Castle underwrote Moffat until a permanent chapel was built.[70] James Hope-Scott established missions at Mingarry, Dunkeld and aided Oban; Douglas Dick, Montraive, Fife established missions at Cupar and Kirkcaldy; Mrs Stewart Menzies substantially aided Aberfeldy; Captain Hunter Blair bequeathed funds for a chapel at Kirkoswald.[71] Oswald Hunter Blair served as a Papal Zouave, became a Benedictine and exercised considerable conservative influence from Fort Augustus, a foundation lavishly aided by aristocracy.[72] Mr Cunninghame-Barre gave the chapel at Kirkcudbright. A close friend of Tennyson and numerous luminaries, Robert Monteith, heir to a Glasgow textile fortune, reputedly imported ten tons of religious statues into Lanarkshire, gave extravagant financial encouragement to the foundation of the Vincentian St Mary's church, hospital and library at Lanark, as well as Jesuits, Good Shepherd nuns and other religious orders.[73] The Cambridge and Oxford movements coincided with a general process of Anglicisation.

Old Catholic families like the Constable Maxwells, the Lovats, Gordons and Smith-Sligos of Inzievar were equally benevolent patrons.[74] They found a close affinity with the Ultramontane spearheads, the Jesuits who unlike the Irish secular clergy were drawn from a better class of (often convert) English Catholic background. Earlier John Menzies of Pitfodels had underwritten Blairs seminary, Aberdeenshire and St Margaret's convent, Edinburgh. In short, although the poor were proportionately generous, decisive financial backing came from the elite. They helped to create the conditions for the community to develop, expand and flourish within the faith. Not surprisingly men of cautious Banffshire or gentry stock like Archbishops Eyre, Glasgow or MacDonald, Edinburgh were reluctant to disturb that relationship – they shared a similar outlook: duty, obligation and noblesse oblige. This outlook enabled a united community to build a respectable base, enter the mainstream and yet maintain its integrity.

These sentiments were restatements of old feudal notions of service and obligation in an urban industrial world. As *The Times* stated in 1864: 'Land is the beast of burden on which everything is placed in this country. All local and social obligations, religion and charity, order, peace, all rest on the land ... The greater the income ... the loftier the position of a landowner, the more exigent and multifarious are the claims made on his money, his influence and his love.'[75] The Marquess of Bute maintained a choir school at Oban and a meticulous oversight of liturgy at Cumnock because he understood the evangelical possibilities of liturgical ceremonial.[76] Romantic medievalism, compassion and cohesion deflated class-consciousness.

The affluent alone could not build a structure of communal faith, but they effectively dictated its emphasis. In a harsh world they provided a much needed comforting, seemly drawing room for the poor, with music, stained glass and fulfilling shared experiences. They provided a formative devotional environment.

A sense of sin and duty inculcated through frequent parochial missions, services and spirituality bolstered clerical authority and may have diminished self-confidence or increased feelings of inadequacy among the laity. Missions coincided with a remarkable surge in advertised confessions: in 1860 the east advertised only two fixed Confession times, 12 in 1870 and over 60 by 1914 and the west only one in 1860 but 79 by 1910.[77] Stations of the Cross became more frequent: virtually invisible in 1850, they soon peaked to remain fairly static with a slight increase after mid-century to 22 in Edinburgh and Glasgow by the early twentieth century. That may reflect the absence of actual Stations in poor chapels as much as a shift in spiritual emphasis.

Frequent sermons and services with hymns stressing 'the tempest tossed church' or 'death's dark night' were shared experiences that helped construct an attitude of mind. In their holy poverty the faithful were powerless before God and man without the Church: out of the ark was no salvation. Emphasis upon communal support was a useful form of reassurance and containment.

Advances often depended on clerical leadership. The extraordinary Rev. Thomas Keane revolutionised his Irvine parish. In five years from 1867, he transformed his church, its décor, introduced numerous associations, parish reading rooms, opened a second church in Kilwinning and, aided by the Marquess of Bute opened a school. By visiting every home within miles, he reclaimed numerous souls, massively increased Easter communicants, established a strong sense of Catholic identity and won respect from all denominations. Not surprisingly the numbers of mixed marriages dramatically declined.[78]

Irregular marriages, common in the early days, receded as orthodoxy and respectability prevailed. Growth meant more potential partners: greater socialisation through parochial associations helped promote 'good' marriages. Antipathy to mixed marriages and concern for leakage, although both persisted on considerable scale, reinforced group and ethnic loyalties, which functioned as long as a large, low-wage, unskilled base persisted in a post-Vatican I Church.[79]

Mutual aid societies, savings banks and devotional bodies reinforced humility and communal solidarity under clerical leadership within 'their' space.[80] Conservative cohesion contained damage to individuals, families and aided ecclesiastical survival. Displaced through migration, unemployment or a rootless lifestyle, workers found stability attractive in reality and faith. Strikes put survival at risk. Death and disease in dangerous working conditions in mines, factories or appalling housing in a wildly fluctuating economy reinforced a deferential faith.

Catholic schools, as suggested, were established at an early stage. Numbers of potential pupils were overwhelming but many parents depended upon them for income: parents had first to be won to long-term objectives. Inadequate numbers of trained lay teachers was predictable in a poor community. Religious 'Romanising' orders were the obvious solution. The vicars-apostolic, however, were reluctant to go down that road: they were not so much Gallican as cautious over expenditure, future debt and potential Protestant backlash. Women religious, Ursulines, Franciscans, Sisters of Mercy, Sacred Heart, Good Shepherd and Passionists gradually arrived, often with sizeable lay support, from the 1830s.[81] Male orders were slower, partly through episcopal fear of a financial drain or violence, and partly through the inability of orders to supply priests until after 1856.[82]

The upwardly mobile phase began with the arrival of the Marists and Jesuits in Glasgow. Marists bolstered the surrounding primary schools and opened opportunities through their high school. Two convert Jesuit headmasters with glittering Oxford credentials, the Rev. Edward Bacon and the Rev. Eric Hanson, and convert John S. Phillimore, first Catholic professor at Glasgow University since the Reformation, spearheaded the drive for excellence and British respectability. Catholics began to enter university in increasing numbers, distinguishing themselves in bursary competitions and subsequent academic success.[83]

Traditional devotion as exemplified in the works of Bishop George Hay (1729–1811), or Bishop Challoner's *Garden of the Soul*, remained popular through the century and beyond. Bishop Murdoch and Bishop Strain both edited editions of his work in 1831 and 1872 respectively.[84] With Hay's support, Bishop John Geddes had published *A Collection of Spiritual Songs* (Edinburgh, 1823), although availability of organs or other musical accompaniment is unclear. Change coincided with the 'Ultramontane' upsurge of churches, extensions, installation of organs and more settled laity. But contemporary theories of man and music rather than Roman zeal may be the explanation. Scottish Cambridge and Oxford converts, Robert Monteith, Campbell of Skerrington and Edward Caswall wrote several popular congregational hymns to create a sense of belonging.[85]

Organisations were effective community building tools. Adult education in night schools, mainly for recent school leavers, helped the process; many early migrants neither spoke nor wrote English. The Rev. Eugene Small found his Irish flock were poor, ignorant, turbulent and badly instructed, while the younger generation were indifferent.[86] Drunkenness was rampant in good times and bad.[87] Seasonal Irish workers were further cause for concern. An Irish missioner claimed confraternities reduced sin twenty-fold and reported 'the Sodalities are so many Noah's Arks in which poor servants find a refuge from that deluge of corruptions and sins which inundates the world.'[88] Hope and roots were perquisites for conversion and social advance.

Bodies like the widespread Confraternity of Christian Doctrine, Catholic Young Men's Society or the fewer St Vincent de Paul Societies and parish libraries that mixed Catholic apologetics and Irish history helped. Temperance societies flourished from the 1830s, encouraged by Father Mathew's visit, by enthusiastic Irish clergy in the 1850s, and by Archbishop Eyre's demand every parish have a branch of the League of the Cross. Many juvenile branches were to save the next generation.

In Barrhead, Keane, like many priests in Scotland, supplemented his funds by begging tours in Glasgow and Liverpool. A more frequent preacher than others, he found his St Patrick's Society brought faithful together; 350 attended its annual Communion. After he began Benediction and evening devotions in 1858, processions, banners, medals and crosses further stimulated enthusiasm.[89] But his chapel's bare walls left much to be desired, with oil lamps fitted only belatedly and a harmonium only from 1860.[90] But a Rosminian mission in May 1860 and a Redemptorist one in May 1867 proved influential: soon candlesticks, sanctuary decorations and Stations followed. New vestments came in 1869 as Keane encouraged children's Mass attendance at another school he built in a distant part of his parish.

Leakage followed illiteracy and poverty. To proselytising tract societies, Catholics had few responses.[91] A community in print was unavailable. Numerous short-lived Catholic papers failed between 1818 and mid-century. In the 1850s Thomas Earnshaw Bradley campaigned with modest success to win readers for his *The Lamp*. Few parish libraries bought English, Irish and American Catholic papers: poverty was a severe handicap. Attempts to establish a popular Catholic paper after the collapse of *The Free Press* foundered.[92] Even then, local newsagents were reluctant to carry Catholic papers. Learned addresses were useless to Keane's flock.[93] Inadequate local laity, whether craftsmen or the St Vincent de Paul Society, made him more reliant on nuns and religious orders.[94] An aroused laity he hoped might question abuses of money and celibacy.

But the circumstances surrounding the restoration of the hierarchy made Eyre favour a centralising policy.[95] He influenced the subsequent nature of the Church as his massive archdiocese dwarfed the rest in numbers of clergy, churches and faithful. He recruited clergy from all over Europe, established his own seminary and rigorously disciplined his clergy. He was aided by the restoration, the introduction of canon law and railway travel: Trent had come to Scotland.

Eyre's mass-production of neo-Gothic Pugin churches visually reinforced uniformity and routine: Romanisation seemed dominant. But an examination of the dedication of chapels is revealing: of 124 archdiocesan churches built before 1914, 31 were dedicated to Scottish, Celtic or Anglo-Saxon saints, 24 to Our Lady, St Joseph and the Holy Family, 15 to Apostles and St John the Baptist, but only six to Ultramontanes, five to Jesuits, and one to St Alphonsus Liguori. Just three chapels were dedicated to post-Reformation saints (two to St Charles and one to St Vincent de Paul). Even if these are placed with chapels dedicated to Our Lady, only 24, less than a fifth, fall into an Ultramontane category.[96] Romanisation had severe limitations.

The implication is that ancient saints, the Holy Family and architecture redolent of the Middle Ages were highly valued. Even increasingly Roman-educated clergy did not promote Ultramontane figures. Mobilising ethnic folk culture, medieval romanticism and extolling the model of the Holy Family were more effective pastoral tools: bolstered by the glories of the past and the bulwark of the family in the present, the faithful were integrated into a British Ultramontane experience. In short they reinforced stability, roots, self-discipline, capital and values, which would guarantee individual and collective progress towards a better life here and in the hereafter. The family was the bastion of order, the forcing ground of dynamic faith, the visible sign of Christian love. Education was a vital component but required time to develop and improve: Glasgow would double its schools and quadruple its pupils inside thirty years.[97] In that process revivalism or so called Romanisation were important interim stages in building a community of faith and substance.

But even within his own family, Eyre showed the limits of Ultramontanism. In the 1880s he and his brother, a Jesuit at Stonyhurst, became embroiled in an unseemly legal battle over his father's will.[98] He ever after remained cool towards the society in Glasgow. The Archbishops of Edinburgh also clashed with Jesuits and their aristocratic patrons in the Borders: the society eventually left the area. As ever, seculars remained suspicious of Jesuit independence, influence, wealth and power.[99] After all it was the elite convert the Rev. Robert Belaney and convert laity who had brought Jesuits into Scotland.[100] Whatever their indirect influence through Jesuit devotions to the Sacred Heart or the flourishing Apostleship of Prayer in most parishes, it stopped episcopal doors.[101]

Scottish concern was with Scottish Catholic problems: poverty, education, leakage and pressing debts. Dreamy notions of Ultramontanism, like notions of Irish, or, in the Marquess of Bute's case, Scottish nationalism, or social concern were useful within certain bounds. If they kept the faithful loyal and supportive, well and good; if they became dangerously revolutionary or divisive they were challenged. Bishops demanded obedience to (their) lawful authority within a distinct Catholic space where devotion flourished. Bishops became 'mini Popes' enforcing submission of elites and masses alike: it was a devotional and cultural revolution. A diverse agenda had unforeseen if unifying 'Ultramontane' results.

After 1880 other voices were demanding a more socially aware Church but that required Catholic modest comfort, enfranchisement and leadership. Voluntary organisations as much as any political body were training grounds for that organising role. The influx of Lithuanians, Poles, Italians, Belgians, Gaels, even Basques and the continuing need for unity briefly masked that shift.[102] The power and wealth of the Catholic aristocracy like their influence within the Church was slowly eroding. Even then Eyre and Michael Davitt united as patrons of Celtic Football Club. Labour and increasingly enfranchised masses asserted themselves; as we saw at the start of this paper, the Rev. Dominic Plater, SJ and his retreat movement tried to contain atheistic class antagonism within the community.

After 1920, emigration, unemployment and the Second World War reshaped Scottish society. Sentimental togetherness lingered, as Heimann noted in Bruce Marshall's novels, but Vatican II, affluence and education destroyed worthy regimentation that served in the darkest days.[103] As in contemporary urban renewal, many Catholics moved out and moved on as they became more diversified. As Patrick Macgill's Moleskin Joe had forecast years before, a new world was 'acomin".[104]

Acknowledgments

I wish to acknowledge the kind hospitality and assistance in Rome from the late Thomas Cardinal Winning, Mgr John McIntyre, Rev. Michael Conroy, Rev. Atli Jonsson and the seminarians at the Scots College, Rome.

4 Irish Migrants in the Scottish Episcopal Church in the Nineteenth Century

Ian Meredith

The nineteenth century was a time of growth for the Scottish Episcopal Church, with the number of its churches increasing from 81 in 1840 to 355 in 1900 (see Table 4.1). This can partly be accounted for by the fashion among some within middle-class and aristocratic circles to convert to Episcopalianism. While these men provided leadership, finances and clergy for the burgeoning Church, their numbers were not that significant. The growth was mainly due to migration from England and Ireland, yet no detailed study has been done to ascertain the proportion from each country. The assumption has been that they came mainly from England: 'The Irish perhaps were less numerous ... For the English congregations were built by the Scottish Church which, as a result, was often called "English" because of this new membership.'[1] Moreover, Episcopalians have been seen as a 'rural based, crypto-Catholic, Anglocentric elite'.[2] Brown's conclusion that 'The Scottish Episcopal Church has never lost its identification with rural landowners and with a culture connected closely with that of the English upper classes,'[3] continues to be the popular perception.

Table 4.1 Scottish Episcopal Church: number of churches, 1840–1900

Diocese	1840	1884	1900
Moray, Ross & Caithness	12	31	30
Aberdeen & Orkney	20	48	57
Brechin	9	28	33
St. Andrews, Dunkeld, & Dunblane	14	37	61
Edinburgh	14	47	67
Glasgow & Galloway	8	62	73
Argyll & The Isles	4	29	34
Total	81	282	355

Source: *SEC Journal* May 1851; *Scottish Church & University Almanac*; *SEC Year Book* 1900

This chapter challenges these assumptions by bringing to light a largely forgotten and lost people – the Irish Episcopalians. Ireland gave to the Scottish Church one bishop (John Dowden of Edinburgh, 1886–1910), dozens of parochial clergy, tens of thousands of members, and the impetus for starting most churches in the diocese of Glasgow and Galloway during the nineteenth century. Indeed, the Irish constituted by far the greatest number of Episcopalians in the west of Scotland for most of the nineteenth century, as an article in one of the Church's papers, the *Scottish Guardian*, made clear in 1872: 'Our Church people are to a large extent Irish, and not native Churchmen.'[4]

Yet despite their predominance, little is known of the Irish Episcopalians. They have not only been marginalised, they have become subliminal. The cause of this collective amnesia may have been that, as the clergy in the west realised, the Irish came with their own particular memories, interpretation of history and worship preferences, which would lead in many instances to conflict between them and innovating clergy. It is said that history is written by the victors, and the contemporary Episcopalian historian Rowan Strong admits that: 'By [the 1920s and 1930s] Episcopalian history was being almost exclusively written by clergy who were themselves products of Anglo-Catholic theological colleges.'[5] Episcopalian historians have tended to ignore elements in the Church of whom they had either little or bad experience, or with whom they had little sympathy.[6]

The Irish presence in the Scottish Church has also been ignored by Irish Church historians, like Alan Acheson who has written appreciatively of the Irish contribution in the foundation of Anglican churches in America and Australia,[7] but has said nothing of Scotland. More recently, however, historians from outside the Church, such as Irene Maver, have noticed 'an intriguing Irish connection with the Church in urban communities ... In yet another of Scottish Episcopalianism's many contradictions'.[8] Elaine McFarland has also commented that 'there was an influx of thousands of migrant workers from Ulster ... into the Scottish Episcopal Church',[9] and Callum Brown has been aware of their numerical presence, yet marginalisation from the Church.[10]

This chapter will also consider how the Church responded to the Irish in terms of opening churches, evangelism and schools. It was to meet the spiritual needs of mainly Irish Episcopalians that most of the earliest work in the home missions of the diocese of Glasgow and Galloway[11] was directed. The mission to the Irish was not to a target group like 'The Mission to Seamen' or Highland Gaelic congregations. The first criterion was that as former members of the Church of Ireland they were Episcopalians and thus, at least, nominally under the spiritual care of the Scottish Episcopal Church in their adopted land. Their Irishness was in a sense coincidental, yet it was the cultural baggage of their ethnicity which was to create difficulties, which were not there to the same extent in, for example, the English or the Welsh.

Swift and Gilley in their *Irish in the Victorian City*, admit that what is missing in their book is any study on the Protestant Irish, and challenge its neglect and assert that we need to know more on this topic. Likewise, T. M. Devine expresses his concern that the weakness in the traditional historiography of the Irish in Scotland has been its almost exclusive concern with the Catholic Irish.[12] James E. Handley's pioneering work *The Irish in Scotland*[13] comes into this category. William Sloan has also excluded Protestant Irish participation in congregational life 'mainly due to lack of evidence'.[14]

Evidence of such participation in congregational life is offered in this chapter, and given the large number of Protestant Irish with strong religious views who migrated to Scotland in the nineteenth century, such evidence was not difficult to uncover. Akenson claims that 'from 1815 onwards the migration out of Ireland attracted Protestants and Catholics in equal numbers.'[15] This does not mean that they migrated to Scotland in similar proportions. The smallest estimate, given by Gallagher, is that Protestants constituted 20 per cent of all the Irish.[16] Walker favours 25 per cent[17] while McFarland suggests that the proportion was at least 30 per cent.[18] However, in the 1830s several Catholic priests claimed that Protestant Irish outnumbered Catholic Irish in their localities,[19] and this was often the case certainly until the Great Famine in 1846. Thereafter in several towns they continued to dominate, such as in Larkhall, Armadale, Irvine and parts of Glasgow. Elaine McFarland and Graham Walker have recently sought to fill the gap in Protestant Irish studies, but have concentrated mainly on the social, economic and political aspects of the diaspora. This present study concentrates almost wholly on the religious aspects of Ulster Protestantism.

I

If one common stereotype has been to equate Irish with Catholic, another has been to equate Protestant with Presbyterian. This is based firstly on the fact that the Presbyterians in Ireland have for the most part been more numerical than the Episcopalians, and therefore it is assumed that these proportions would be reflected in migration patterns. Secondly, it is supposed that Presbyterianism was more anti-Catholic than Anglicanism, and therefore that Presbyterians would be more interested in joining the Orange Order. Walker thinks so: 'It should ... be noted that there were some ... Anglican Protestants among the emigrants, although they were nowhere as numerous as the Presbyterians.'[20] Later in his article, however, he seems to have second thoughts about this: 'those Protestant migrants who had been adherents of the Church of Ireland – and there may have been a higher proportion than is often thought ...'[21] His high percentage of Presbyterians is based on the religious demography of the Ulster counties from where most of the migrants came. However he admits, 'had figures been available, for example, for County Armagh where the Presbyterian presence was not as dominant among the Protestant denominations, the numbers may well have been more balanced.'[22]

It is my contention that Episcopalians formed the majority, or were at least half, of the Protestant Irish in Scotland. Until the 1820s and from the 1880s to the present, Presbyterians did in fact outnumber Episcopalians in Ireland.

During the eighteenth century there was massive Presbyterian emigration to America, continuing in the 1820s with dissatisfaction with the Tithe laws which compelled them to support the Established Church. Thus by 1834 the balance had tipped, and there were now 853,160 Episcopalians compared with 643,058 Presbyterians.[23] The religious census of 1861 showed that the Church of Ireland figures had dropped to 693,357, while the Presbyterians were showing an increase. Several historians have stated that the famine and emigration did not affect greatly Presbyterian numbers: 'The physical help given by organisations like the Belfast Relief Association was substantial, partly because few Presbyterians suffered to any extent during the famine years.'[24] That Ulster Protestant emigrants were more likely to be Anglican than Presbyterian was also noted by Houston and Smyth in their study of Irish emigration to Canada, principally between 1816 and 1855. They found that 'approximately 55 per cent of Irish settlers in Canada were Protestant, and predominantly Anglican rather than Presbyterian.'[25] These figures for Canada correspond with those for Australia. By 1911 the Australian census data on religion stated that 14 per cent of the Irish-born professed Anglicanism, 9 per cent Presbyterianism, and 3 per cent Methodism.[26]

On the basis that most of the Irish migrants to Scotland were poorer than those who could afford to go further, the Protestant poor were more likely to be Episcopalians. The Church of Ireland did contain most of the aristocracy, gentry and landowners. However, as the established Church in that land, it was also, at least in theory, responsible for the spiritual state of every soul in its parishes. While the Presbyterians undoubtedly had working and labouring classes among them, 'The social background of the Presbyterian ministry reflected the interests of the predominantly middle-class rural community.'[27] The Presbyterians admitted that few aristocrats belonged to their community, 'But neither did the poor.'[28] It was noted that in Belfast, Londonderry and Monaghan workhouses in 1853, a quarter were Roman Catholics, a quarter were Presbyterians, but half were Episcopalians.[29] This is also reflected in statistics for Scottish poor-houses. In a sample of Irish admissions to the Dundee Poor House in 1861 it was noted that 5 per cent put down as their denomination 'Established Church' (in Scotland, the Church of Scotland), whereas 8 per cent had put down 'Episcopalian'.[30] This is even more striking considering that in Scotland the Episcopalian figures were a fraction of those of the Presbyterians.

Another misapprehension is that most Orangemen in the nineteenth century were Presbyterians rather than Episcopalians; for example, James E. Handley dismissed 'The Twelfth of July' as the brainstorm of Presbyterianism.[31] This would be truer of the twentieth century, especially the present day, as Joseph Bradley stated in 1995 that 73 per cent of members of the Orange Order claimed adherence to the Church of Scotland.[32] Episcopalians, however, would have been more dominant in the Irish Order, certainly until later in the nineteenth century, and this would have been reflected in the Scottish membership, which was, in the first generation, mainly from Ireland. Bowen, writing of Orangeism in Ireland in the 1820s, says that most Orangemen were members of the Church of Ireland.[33] The Presbyterian historian A. C. Anderson agrees: 'It was from their ranks (The Church of Ireland) and not from the Presbyterians that the Orange Order drew the great majority of its members between 1795 and 1830.'[34]

Allied to this, there had always been a radical and republican strand in Irish Presbyterianism. Disadvantaged by various Penal Laws in the eighteenth century, many Presbyterians had emigrated to America. Among those who remained, resentment against the Anglican Church and the Protestant Ascendancy led them to join Roman Catholics in the formation of the United Irishmen in 1791. Disillusioned by what they saw as sectarian violence, especially in the south, most Presbyterians soon left the movement.[35] Several emigrated to Scotland, where in the 1790s they helped to foster radical views among the weaving community.[36] Presbyterian involvement in the Orange Order did not begin in earnest until the 1870s, after the disestablishment of the Church of Ireland.[37] But by then Irish migration to Scotland was in decline.

There is a great deal of evidence to suggest that Orangemen were involved in the formation of many of the Episcopal churches in the diocese of Glasgow and Galloway in the nineteenth century. Mr. R. J. Speir, a prominent Episcopalian layman and convenor of the Church's Home Missions Committee, reported to Bishop Wilson of Glasgow that: 'There were Orangemen in the congregation, which I am quite aware must be the case in every poor congregation in the west of Scotland in your diocese.'[38] In some congregations they predominated, as at Springburn in Glasgow where the Rev. W. E. Bradshaw wrote: 'The majority of those attending the Mission have always belonged to that narrow and bigoted Order.'[39] By 1882 the predominance of Orangemen within the Episcopal Church in Glasgow was noted by the *Scottish Guardian*: 'It is a well known fact that an immense number of the professed members of the Church in this city are from the Sister isle, and belong to the Orange ... Society.'[40]

The assimilation of Irish Episcopalians into their sister Church in Scotland was not without its problems. Unlike the Church of Ireland, which had maintained a 'low church' (lack of ceremony, as advocated by the more stark and Calvinistic forms of Protestantism) form of worship, and where innovations and ritualism in a 'high church' direction were indicative of a capitulation to Romanism, the Scottish Episcopal Church had embraced many of the ritual practices associated with the Oxford movement. The Anglican Archbishop of Armagh, John Beresford had read John Henry Newman's *Tract 90* in 1840, 'With deep concern, and I must say with considerable indignation'.[41] In this tract, Newman claimed that the Thirty Nine Articles, regarded as the de facto creed of Anglicanism, suggested that Anglicanism was compatible with the Church of Rome. Newman's later defection to Rome in 1845 confirmed the view of many that the Oxford movement and its associated rituals were simply precursors to bringing the whole Anglican Church back into the Roman fold. When the Irish Episcopalians arrived in Scotland they were certainly aware of the implications of the theological issues causing a storm in the Anglican world. A letter describing the formation of St John's Episcopal Mission in Irvine in 1887 states: 'The Protestant Irish predominated the Mission and would stand nothing in the nature of "high church" which sometimes we had to suffer on the fourth Sunday, and then down went the attendance. It took a lot of coaxing to bring them back. They were well versed in Dr. Pusey, etc.'[42] In 1881 the Grand Orange Lodge of Scotland, aware that Orangemen were attending 'ritualistic churches', introduced the following rule: 'Every brother who is presently attending any Ritualistic Church, because he is aiding and abetting the re-introduction of Popery ... be suspended for two years until he give proof of true repentance.'[43]

Of the seven dioceses that made up the Scottish Episcopal Church, the remainder of this chapter will focus on Glasgow and Galloway, which covered the west of Scotland, the area of greatest Irish concentration. Of all the dioceses, Glasgow and Galloway suffered most from the triumph of Presbyterianism over Episcopalianism in 1689: 'Elsewhere ... a few remnants of the Church survived the catastrophe of the Revolution ... But in Glasgow and Galloway we were violently and absolutely annihilated root and branch.'[44] Bishop Harrison contrasted the growth during the nineteenth century with its near extinction in the eighteenth, and admitted that the growth had come from outside the area: 'The Episcopal Church in the west of Scotland seems to have been entirely wiped out. I can never find a West of Scotland man who is a hereditary Episcopalian. The Church seems to have been wiped away just as a man wipes a dish and turns it upside down.'[45] The nineteenth century opened with just four Episcopal churches in the west of Scotland, and with probably around 400 Episcopalians living in the area.[46] By 1923 there were almost 110,000 Episcopalians in the diocese, which by then was the largest in Scotland, containing one third of the Church's membership.

II

This section will look at the Glasgow diocese through case studies of five local churches. These churches have been selected firstly because they represent a geographical diversity, showing that issues which affected the Irish in Glasgow churches were also being reflected in Ayrshire and Renfrewshire. The second reason is that they have yielded significant amounts of primary source material in terms of church registers (particularly baptisms), a lively series of correspondence held in the diocesan archives, and a fair amount of public reporting both in the local and in the Church press.

Glasgow: St Andrew's by the Green

It was in the 1830s that the presence of many thousands of Irish Episcopalians was first noticed in Glasgow. The City Chamberlain, James Cleland, calculated that in 1831 there were 8,551 of them in Glasgow and its suburbs.[47] St Andrew's, opened in 1750, was the first Episcopal church to be built in Glasgow since the revolution of 1688. It was part of that group of churches known as 'qualified chapels', in that they qualified for toleration under the law, having seceded from the Scottish Episcopal Church, and 'qualified' to minister under various Acts of Parliament between 1712 and 1748 which laid down conditions for lawful Episcopalian worship, especially after the Jacobite risings of 1715 and 1745. Their clergy swore the oath of allegiance, and prayed for the Hanoverian royal family by name. During the incumbency of the Rev. William Routledge, from 1805 to 1843, it underwent a transformation. Firstly, it united with the Scottish Episcopal Church in 1805, and secondly, its neighbourhood, once fashionable, became known for its overcrowded slums. The parish included the Irish areas of the Briggate, Saltmarket, Tradeston and Hutchesontown, Routledge reporting in 1815 that 'the congregating included the poorer sort, who are chiefly tradesmen and labourers from England and Ireland.'[48] An analysis of the baptism register of 1842 shows 33 fathers listed whose place of birth was England, but most of these were connected with the army stationed at the nearby barracks and thus not permanent. Forty-one of the fathers listed were from Ireland and belonged to more local occupations such as weavers and labourers.[49]

In 1844 Dr James Gordon began an incumbency at St Andrew's which was to last for almost 50 years. His liturgical style would not have appealed to the Irish. Described as an 'advanced high-churchman', in 1857 he was the first Episcopalian priest to wear eucharistic vestments while conducting the communion service. Gordon, for his part, held the Irish in contempt, bemoaning the fact that his missionary forays into the Irish areas south of the River Clyde had produced very little fruit. In 1858 he told the Diocesan Synod that the Irish, ' were often in receipt of high wages, and though they spend them in tobacco and whisky and extravagant weddings, yet any offering for the offices of the Church is like pulling a tooth out of their heads. In Glasgow the evil is much worse, and much worse to amend. Manufacturing towns are generally the reservoirs into which the idle and dissolute of both sexes pour; and it is quite notorious that it is only the worst of the Irish who come over here, who were bad "at home" and become tenfold worse when they get up to town tricks.'[50] By the time Gordon retired in 1891, the congregation numbered just a handful. This may have been due to his somewhat paternalistic attitude towards his Irish congregation, his confrontational style with dissidents and his growing personal eccentricities. Anthony Mitchell took over St Andrew's in 1895, and later recalled: 'The church was deep in debt. The congregation, never large, had lost what cohesion it once possessed, and the district was a slum. The church was, for more reason than one, a byword in the neighbourhood.'[51] The Scottish Chronicle stated that Mitchell's ministry there was 'to awaken the whole Church to the crying needs of East Glasgow, where multitudes of poor people, from Ireland particularly, were waiting to be gathered into the Church to which they had been brought up'.[52]

Glasgow (Mile End): Christ Church

As the population of Glasgow increased, a large number of Irish migrants found accommodation in the eastern parts and suburbs. There were about seven Orange Lodges meeting in the Calton and Mile End area in 1830, a part of the city renowned for weaving and its high number of Irish Protestants. In 1831, of the 6,890 Irish in this area, only 2,688 were Catholics.[53] Episcopal services were started in hired halls in 1834. A year later, the Rev. David Aitchison formed them into a congregation called Christ Church. In his evidence to the Royal Commission on Religious Instruction in Scotland in 1837, Aitchison stated that the congregation was comprised of 1,300 persons, who were 'overwhelmingly poor and working class, mostly handloom weavers and a few tradesmen. Most were Irish ...'[54] As well as his own congregation, he reckoned there were another 7,000 Irish Episcopalians in Glasgow not connected with any church.

The congregation had been gathered by Aitchison through pastoral visiting in the area. Weaving had become depressed, and pauperism left many families in Calton with few resources. He worked tirelessly for the Irish poor in his parish, and in 1838 helped found the Bridgeton Board of Health which organised visitation and care for those in the area suffering from diseases such as typhus and cholera. The following year he lamented that having 'endured the famine' in Ireland, it was a shame that they now had to face disease and poverty in Glasgow.[55] Aitchison's printed sermons, however, suggest a growing frustration with his parishioners. Many, he felt, had no interest in the church, preferring to spend what little money they had on drink.[56] His approach was somewhat high-handed and paternalistic, but he certainly laid the foundation for one of the east of Glasgow's strongest churches.

Glasgow (Springburn): St James the Less

Glasgow's foremost home mission church was St Mary's in Renfield Street. This congregation had its antecedents among the city's Jacobite Episcopalians, and had not qualified for toleration during the eighteenth century. However by 1807 the Scottish Episcopal Church had, by abjuring its former Jacobite allegiance and declaring its loyalty to the Hanoverian monarchy, re-emerged into 'respectable' Scottish religious life. By the 1860s the more affluent of the congregation had moved to the city's western suburbs, leading to St Mary's leaving Renfield Street and relocating to a new Gothic edifice on the Great Western Road. In order 'to accommodate his poor Episcopalians' who were inconvenienced by the move, St Mary's incumbent, the Rev. Richard Oldham, began a Mission at Townhead in 1865.[57] It attracted a large congregation, not only from its immediate surroundings, but also from Springburn and Garngad. In order to accommodate Episcopalians from these two districts, another mission, later to be called St James the Less, was formed at Springburn in 1875.

The mission got off to a shaky start, but an offer from a lay reader, Mr W. M. Biggar, revived the work of caring 'for at least 2,000 members of the Anglican Communion in Springburn and the immediate neighbourhood'.[58] The baptismal register of 1875 shows that 75 per cent of the families had either one or both parents born in Ireland. There seems to have been concern at the Diocesan Home Mission Council about a grant being given to what they perceived was becoming purely an 'Orange church'. A letter to the bishop in 1878 from the Rev. W. E. Bradshaw, the clergyman in charge of the Springburn mission, assured him however, that 'attendance at the Mission has never to my knowledge, been made a party question'.[59] He did say that there were tensions with the local Orangemen, who very much wanted their own way in church matters. Bradshaw admitted that most members of the mission were Orangemen, and that they had tried to put pressure on him, but he had firmly resisted them. Mr Speir, convenor of the Home Mission Board, remained unconvinced: 'With the power they possessed, the Orange Lodges would use their influence there. Any priest working in that place might find his usefulness and services hindered and thwarted unless he was willing to dilute his teaching down to the level of what is considered among Orangemen as orthodox Protestantism.'[60] Indeed, a former clergyman of the Episcopal Church, who had worked briefly at Springburn as a curate, the Rev. Joseph Rice, established a breakaway church under the auspices of the English Episcopal Church. Rice, an Irishman and an Orangeman, had seized on the vulnerability of the mission, believing it was not making sufficient inroads into the Irish community.[61]

An English-born curate at St Paul's, Charing Cross, the Rev. Charles Hyde Brooke, was put in charge of the struggling Springburn mission. Brooke had been a missionary in Melanesia and for the past three years had been in charge of the mission at Jordanhill, to the west of Glasgow. He regarded Orangemen with some ambivalence: 'I found the Orangemen at Jordanhill gradually adopted some of my views ... Once gained, this Orange element is a tower of strength. As has been well said – they will either kill you or die for you.'[62] Brooke succeeded in building a church, St James the Less, which opened in 1881. Whether by congregational clamour or diocesan strategy, in 1883 the Episcopal Church appointed an Irish minister to succeed him. The Rev. Patrick Phelan had been a converted Roman Catholic priest. But on another front, he would have been an able defender of the main Episcopal Church against their English Episcopal rivals, having been himself a clergyman in that schismatic group when he was curate of St Silas', Glasgow, from 1878 to 1883. Phelan's ministry lasted from 1883 to 1886 during which time the congregation increased considerably, from 150 to 500 adherents. Irish migrants dominated: the baptismal register for the same period shows that they accounted for 86 per cent of the families.

After Phelan's departure to pastor another of the Irish missions, St Stephen's, Cartsdyke, Greenock, the church suffered another split. In 1886 a breakaway church was formed under the auspices of the Reformed Episcopal Church, which later amalgamated with the Free Church of England to create a new congregation known as 'Holy Trinity Protestant Church of England' which met in Keppochhill Road. By 1910 this schism was still an issue, as the *Scottish Guardian* alerted its readers that 'Although such congregations are weak in numbers and influence, their very existence is harmful to the Church in many ways. The title "Church of England" is misleading … Its services being of a very bald type, many Irish people are led to believe that it is an Irish Church specially adapted for them, and in full communion with their own Church at home. If, as it usually happens, the minister is an Orangeman, they need no further proof of its genuineness.'[63] It is not clear if the Rev. R. J. Campbell, Trinity's first rector, was an Orangeman, but his rhetoric showed the constituency he was aiming at: 'They had an object in holding their meeting near "Derry Day" [18 December]. Their motto was that of the men who lay behind the walls of Derry – "No Surrender." They had not surrendered and they did not mean to surrender.'[64]

Ayrshire (Girvan): St John

The Ayrshire village of Girvan had a sizeable Irish community early in the nineteenth century. The number of Irish in the 1830s was stated to be three-quarters of the population. The chief trade of the town was weaving and it was estimated that four-fifths of the weavers were Irish, with the local Presbyterian minister, the Rev. Peter McMaster, noting that 'more than half of them were Protestants'.[65] Making no secret of his dislike for the Irish (both sorts) he wrote: 'In no part of the kingdom are people more respectable than the native inhabitants of this parish … So much, however, cannot be said of that portion which is Irish.'[66] The first Irish Protestants to arrive in the village were Presbyterians with the radical views of the United Irishmen. They congregated at the northern end of the town, near the parish church, in what became known as 'little Ireland'. Along with Irish Catholics and local Presbyterians, they took part in a series of reform demonstrations which clashed with Orangemen, and led to the 'Girvan Riots' of 1831. A larger and more sustained stream of weavers came next, and this group, who were supporters of Orangeism, would have been Episcopalians. They settled in the southern end of the town in weavers' cottages in an area called Newton. It had a street called Sandy Row, a part called the Orange Arch, and by 1830 two Orange Lodges met in William Young's Inn.[67] In July 1831 'the reform party, joined by the Irish Catholics, attempted to stop a 12 July parade of orange Lodges from in and around the town.'[68] A series of reprisals ensured that the town was in some ferment for several months, resulting in a policeman being shot by an Orangeman. Between these incidents and the anti-Irish prejudice of the parish minister, it is unlikely that the Orangemen and their families from Newton would have found much solace in the parish church.

In 1837 McMaster stated that 'there is no Episcopalian chapel in the parish.'[69] The Episcopalians would have attended William Wilson's church at Ayr, some 20 miles away. In March 1846 Bishop Russell received a petition in

Wilson's handwriting asking for an Episcopal Church to be commenced in the town:

> That the number of Protestant Episcopalians (of all ages) in Girvan is considerable above 400. Most of whom are either natives of Ireland or the children of Irish parents, of the established church in that country. The nearest Episcopalian church being in Ayr, 21 miles away. That as most of them are poor persons of the operative and labouring classes, it is not in their power to provide the means of supporting a clergyman, or defraying the other expenses necessarily attending on the maintenance of public worship, but they are willing to contribute to the utmost of their ability and they trust that they will be aided by their wealthier brethren in obtaining for themselves and their children, the benefit of that spiritual instruction and superintendence of which they have long been destitute and which their limited means prevent them procuring by their own unaided exertions ... They ask the Bishop to endeavour to bring them more effectively within the pale of the Church, many of her children who have long been as 'sheep without a shepherd.'[70]

In 1859 St John's Church was built on Piedmont Road, in the southern end of the town where the Orange and Episcopalian community was concentrated. In 1870 the services there were described as 'simple, but hearty. The congregation consists for the most part of people engaged in that poorest of all trades, handloom weavers. Most of them are either of Irish birth or descent and on a clear day can still behold the hills of the Green Isle in the home of their adoption.'[71]

However, Girvan was about to change, and this would be reflected in the congregation. The population had peaked through immigration to 8,588 in 1851, but by 1901 it had dropped by almost half to 4,872. The decrease was due to the gradual disappearance of the weaving industry and to the decline of the port, as ships became too big for the small harbour.[72] The church, being almost entirely composed of weaving families, went into decline as its members moved to the central belt of Scotland in search of new work.

Paisley: Holy Trinity

Trinity Episcopal Church was founded in 1817 and as such was the first to be built in the west of Scotland after the repeal of the Penal Laws. The initial congregation may not have been Irish, as the Rev. William Wade, its first minister, recalled: 'Our little society did then comprehend not a few wealthy persons; still the expense of providing a chapel would have fallen heavily upon them.'[73] However, within just a few years of the church opening, the make-up of the congregation had changed: 'deaths, removals and other circumstances have considerably diminished in number the original and more opulent seat holders. So that, although the congregation is much increased, and fast increasing ... it consists very principally of persons engaged in different kinds of manual labour, a class whose earnings of late years lessened in amount.'[74] Certainly by the 1830s the Irish had become prominent in the congregation. In 1833 Wade maintained that the number of Episcopalians in Paisley was growing almost daily 'owing chiefly to the resort of Irish families hither, in quest of employment'.[75] That year the new Trinity Chapel was opened in St James Place, in the area known as 'The Sneddon'. According to a historian of Paisley, this was a district in which large numbers of the migrants settled; indeed 'there were closes or tenements wholly inhabited by the Irish and known as "Wee Ireland".'[76] Some decades later an Irish clergyman recalled that it was 'beyond all question that Trinity Church was built to accommodate Protestants from the north of Ireland', and that the building fund received contributions not only from Scotland, but also from England and Ulster.[77]

The connection between Trinity Church and the town's Orange Lodges appeared to have been quite convivial. One of Wade's successors, the Rev. James Stewart addressed the Orangemen at their annual 5 November Soiree in 1856 and spoke of the 'mutual benefits Scotland and Ireland have received from each other from the very earliest of time ... in the field of religious controversy, as well as in that of actual warfare, the two nations are brethren, and, shoulder to shoulder, they will stand or fall.' He went on to defend Orangeism against its attackers:

> If I had entertained any doubt as to the propriety of my being present at this meeting tonight, it would be completely removed on seeing the highly respectable and orderly company now before me. It is a fact too notorious to be called in question, that a very strong prejudice exists in the minds of many in this country ... against the Orange Society ... on account of the numerous scenes of riot which they have been led to believe it has been the cause. This I well know to be the slander of the enemy ... You have the truth on your side, and, therefore you need not fear the result; contend for your principles as Christian men may be expected to do, firmly and honestly, giving soft words, but hard arguments.[78]

It was no surprise therefore, that one of the earliest Orange Lodge church parades in Scotland was to Trinity Church in 1868.[79] Stewart also supported the Conservative Party and in the 1868 general election campaigned for Colonel Archibald Campbell.[80] Campbell, a leading Orangeman, successfully contested West Renfrewshire for the Conservatives in 1873 and was later raised to the peerage as Lord Blythswood.

In 1871 the Rev. William F. Mills became incumbent. Prior to his institution, The *Church News* hinted at the challenges at Paisley which lay before him: 'The good folk of Trinity Church, we have been told, have been in the habit of keeping nothing but "The Sabbath" ... and we trust will be taught by their new Incumbent that Orangeism in itself is not Churchmanship; that there are holy days to be observed.'[81] Soon after his arrival, he was the speaker at the annual Orange Soiree where his enthusiasm for Orangeism was fulsome:

> I am glad to see that the Orange tree is in good condition, carrying many blossoms and giving promise of much fruit. No doubt it is making progress in the land ... and if you only continue to increase as you have been doing so during the period I have known you, you need not care for, or fear Popery. The Orange principle is good – it is scriptural; and we are not here tonight for the purpose of expressing our hatred of our Roman Catholic fellowmen. We are here for higher and holier purposes – to give thanks to God for past mercies, and to honour and revere those who, with the help of the King of Kings crushed Popish ascendancy – may it be forever.[82]

Mills was moving closer to Orangeism and in 1882 joined the lodge. The Minute Book of King William L.O.L. 102 recorded on 26 June, 'Bro. Mills passed in the Purple degree. Bro. Elliott congratulated the Lodge on being fortunate in having Bro. Mills as a member of the Lodge. Bro. Mills expressed his gratification at being amongst us.'[83] Furthermore, he rose to prominence in the order, becoming Grand Chaplain in 1883.

The marriage between Mills and some of his Orange friends, however, soon came into difficulties, as it was obvious that other influences had also been at work in his life. Mills, it was claimed by later historians, 'came under the influence of the Oxford Movement.'[84] This may not have been in any extreme sense and extended mainly to a re-ordering of the interior of the chapel, along with some modest changes in the ritual of the services. The 1885 Annual General Meeting of the church proved stormy. A considerable section of the congregation greeted the proposal to build a chancel with violent opposition. This and other innovations lead to a breakdown between Mills and a large section of the congregation who claimed Mills had allegedly described them as a lot of 'dirty Irish'.[85] A series of letters from 1885 to 1888 between the parties involved reveals in some detail the grievances and the various attempts at reconciliation. Eventually there was secession, and the 'Irish element' left to form a congregation, styling themselves as 'Christ Church Reformed Church of England'.[86] However, not all the Irish or even Orange left Trinity Church. The breakaway group lasted barely ten years and there are indications of a sizeable Irish congregation at Trinity at least until the 1920s.

III

Table 4.2 lists the churches founded in the diocese over the past 200 years, and shows that from 1817 until 1902 most of those opened were in areas of Irish concentration. However, after 1905 new churches, with few exceptions, were located in areas not associated with Irish migration. This reflects both a growing English-born element, such as at Gretna and Eastriggs, and Scottish working-class congregations such as those at Kilmacolm, Troon, Prestwick and Clarkston. By contrast, the churches closed at this period were all in Irish areas such as Partick, Gorbals, Harthill, Kingston, Balgray and Larkhall.

A census of the membership of the diocese in 1912, ascertaining their country of birth, resulted in: Scottish 36 per cent, English 36 per cent, and Irish 28 per cent.[87] This shows the Irish by then to be the smallest of the ethnic groups represented. However, it must also be considered that the survey was of the committed members, rather than the wider constituency, and that among the Scots-born would be many children and grandchildren of the Irish. An interesting comparison is that by 1891 the majority of Roman Catholics in Glasgow and the west of Scotland were also Scots-born, but it is conceded that these would be second and third generation Irish.[88] The membership of the diocese became more English as the twentieth century progressed, in keeping with the general population trend. In Glasgow, the English increased in population from 2.45 per cent in 1851 to 3.62 per cent in 1901. During the same period the Irish decreased from 18.17 per cent to 8.88 per cent. By 1911 the percentage of English-born had overtaken the percentage of Irish-born in Scotland, their numbers being similar. This trend continued for the remainder of the twentieth century.

In February 1909 the *Scottish Chronicle* brought the following to the attention of the Church:

> A noticeable feature of the increased population in the West of Scotland during recent years has been the continuous flow of Irish immigrants. The Church in these parts has been alive to her responsibilities in welcoming and shepherding members from the sister Church in Ireland, yet it is generally conceded that in spite of all efforts made to weld together Church people from the two countries, there has been a vast leakage in our ranks, which is somewhat depressing.[89]

There were several reasons why many Irish left the Scottish Episcopal Church. In terms of the Church's own response in the Glasgow diocese, there was a lack of any central strategy to deal with the thousands of Irish migrants. Initiatives for mission came from parochial clergy in response to local needs. In most cases, however, they reported that they were simply overwhelmed with the numbers calling on their ministrations. The lack of clergy was a crucial element in the impotence of the Church to shepherd effectively their adherents. Several of the missions survived only through lay leadership. The Church put far more emphasis on acquiring or improving buildings than on providing more clergy. This was in contrast to the Roman Catholic Church whose strategy was to put emphasis on the provision of many priests, being content for the buildings to come later.[90]

On the other hand, and ironically, the opening of fine and spacious new churches was often the point where the Irish poor left the church. This was not because they felt uncomfortable or were unappreciative of beauty, but because the buildings, the accompanying liturgical development, and the oratory of the preachers were attracting more middle-class congregations. With increased expenses, the clergy depended more on the moneyed middle classes to keep up these buildings, as well as their stipends. At Springburn, Anderston and Govan, extra early morning or afternoon services were held for 'the poorest of the poor', but these in most cases were short-lived experiments.

The *Scottish Churchman* in 1926, looking back over the past few decades, noted that many new people had come from England, but admitted that 'A still larger number have come from the Emerald Isle – men and women who have been baptised and trained in the Church of Ireland.'[91] That not all in the Church had been understanding of the Irish and even critical of them was also hinted at: 'There are some who belittle the Church of Ireland and who almost sneer at her efforts to make her services attractive to and appreciated by her people. We emphatically disclaim such an unchristian view, for we have seen many good God-fearing families brought up in the plain simple Church of Ireland form, men and women who were most catholic in things fundamental.'[92] In the 1860s, Dr Gordon of St Andrew's by the Green had made no secret of his dislike of the Irish, and the fact that efforts to evangelise them had been met with indifference. Other clergy and laymen had written to bishops to complain that the Orange Irish were resisting all efforts to lead the churches in a more Catholic direction. Several churches had seen their congregations divided through Irish opposition to perceived Rome-ward trends, and this must have left some bitterness. One priest in particular who expressed his frustration with the Irish was the Rev. William Jenkins who had worked with them, both as Curate of St Luke's, Grafton Street and then as priest-in-charge of St Columba's, Clydebank. He wrote a series of letters to the *Scottish Chronicle* which began in 1910 and continued to 1919. Jenkins' own church had seen such a schism, which perhaps led to his outbursts. Some of his complaints seemed valid: part of his problem was that the clergy of the Church of Ireland were mainly to blame for the attitude of their people in Scotland. He wrote of 'the persistent failure on the part of the Irish clergy to send letters of commendation to our Scottish clergy. There are thousands of Irish Episcopalians in Clydebank, and I regret to say that since I was licensed two and a half years ago, only one member of the Irish Church has been commended to me by any clergyman.'[93] In 1912 Jenkins referred again to the schism which had divided his congregation as having been indirectly caused by the Church of Ireland clergy themselves. Previously he had hinted that they had not taught their people any Church principles, or the importance of remaining faithful to their Anglican heritage, or the necessity of being in full communion with recognised sister Churches. He then revealed that 'Some of the Irish who left my church actually told me that their Irish clergy had encouraged them to go to the schismatic group [Reformed Episcopal Church] rather than go to the Scottish Episcopal Church.' Jenkins further claimed that many of the Irish clergy regarded the Scottish Episcopal Church as being papistical and looking similar to the Church of Rome: 'I found that a large proportion of these Irish immigrants separated from the Church when they came to Scotland. They would not listen to the meaning of schism; as long as they attached themselves to any religious body that was anti-Roman Catholic, they did not mind what it was … their Bishops have perpetually praised the "no-popery" cry against the Scottish Church. For instance, I have heard the late Bishop Wilkinson condemned by an Irish Bishop as a papist.'[94]

'Ulsterman', writing to *The Scottish Chronicle* in March 1909, said that many of the Irish who came to Scotland had attended church regularly back home, particularly in country areas, but since coming over here had succumbed to the stress and temptations of city life. He continued: 'There are too many who never were Church-goers at home, perhaps once a year on the Sunday before "The Twelfth". The fact is that the Irish problem is only a part of a much greater problem. There are plenty of Scots and English who do not want to go to church, but "Ritualism" is the Irishman's excuse.'[95]

Ritualism, or changes in the ceremonial of worship in a more Catholic direction, slowly evolved within the Scottish Episcopal Church. Its earliest exponent in the Glasgow diocese was the Rev. Alexander D'Orsey who introduced changes at St John's, Anderston in 1850, drawing the ire of his bishop who wrote: 'I need not remind you that there are no members of the Church so sensitive as to anything that looks to them like Romanism, as the Poor Irish; nor with any whose very natural prejudices on that subject it is more a duty to deal tenderly. To build a Church for The Poor, and then introduce a mode of conducting the services, which was almost sure to be a stumbling-block to them, does seem to me to be sadly marring your own good work.'[96]

Strong notes that 'One of the most useful interpretations of Anglo-Catholicism in the last decade has been that by John Reed who has proposed that in its later ritualistic development, Anglo-Catholicism was deliberately provocative and challenging to prevailing religious respectability.'[97] Reed added that the degree of ritualism, the strength by which it was enforced, and the sensitivities which it disregarded amounted to 'a bemusing lack of common sense'.[98] Differences between Protestantism and Roman Catholicism mattered in the period under examination. For example, Mr John Davies, an Ulsterman who had worshipped for many years in the Scottish Episcopal Church and personally had no problem with ritualism, wrote to *The Scottish Chronicle* in 1912: 'I can see in my mind's eye a parishioner from most of our Belfast churches carrying letters of commendation, to, say, the rector of Christ Church, or St. John's, Anderston or St. Peter's, Cowcaddens. I am certain that he would not continue his attendance at any of these churches, and the probability would be that he would find his way to the Established Presbyterian Church.'[99] The Church of Scotland in the early 1920s was going through its most anti-Catholic phase. Its Kirk and Nation Committee's report, *The Menace of the Irish Race to our Scottish Nationality*, with its insistence that the 'Orange Irish' were not under the same condemnation, as they were 'loyal and the same religion as ourselves',[100] would have proved a welcoming overture to Episcopalians disillusioned with their Church.

The Methodist Church would have been another alternative. Although Scotland had proved hard ground for their cause, Methodists succeeded in founding several churches in the industrial west of Scotland, particularly in places like Girvan with its weaving tradition, and Partick with its strong migrant community. The Rev. Frank Binns, the last rector of St Margaret's, Bellshill wrote to his bishop in 1940 just as the church was closing, after struggling on with a few members for many years: 'The Methodist Minister here has informed me that there were a few on his roll who used to worship at St. Margaret's, but who, because of the changes and nature of the services introduced here, left the Church. We have lost them, when we could have kept them.'[101] A further option for disillusioned Irish Episcopalians could have been the various independent mission halls which sprang up in Glasgow following the evangelistic mission of the American evangelists D. L. Moody and Ira Sankey to the city in 1874. These included the Tent Hall in the heart of the Irish Saltmarket area. These halls attached a great importance to hearty singing, simple preaching, and lack of formality and hierarchy, which gave them an edge over the established churches, as far as some of the working classes were concerned.[102]

The greater part of Irish Episcopalians in Scotland would have ended up being attached to no church. Many of them had been nominal in their allegiance in Ireland, had been indifferent towards the claims of the Episcopal Church in Scotland, and their religious denominational affiliation on admission to hospital or when being buried would have been very tentative. Their descendants today would probably be part of that secular sectarianism, whose Protestantism would amount to no more than the fact that they were not Roman Catholics.

The Irish were not the only group lost to the Episcopal Church by the early part of the twentieth century: the Highlands were also largely lost. When one concerned church member suggested to the Bishop of Argyll and the Isles strategies for bringing them back into the fold, he was told, 'They were far better away, and had better be left alone.'[103] It is possible that others felt similarly about the Irish.

Table 4.2 Table of churches and missions opened and closed in the diocese of Glasgow and Galloway, 1817–1973

Churches opened			Churches closed		
Year	*Town/Area*	*Dedication*	*Year*	*Town/Area*	*Dedication*
Diocese of Edinburgh 1817–37					
1817	Paisley †	Holy Trinity			
1824	Greenock †	St John			
1834	Glasgow (East) †	Christ Church			
Bishop Michael Russell 1837–48					
1837	Blythswood †	St Jude			

Churches opened			Churches closed		
Year	Town/Area	Dedication	Year	Town/Area	Dedication
1841	Helensburgh	St Michael			
1841	Annan	St John			
1842	Hamilton	St Mary			
1843	Coatbridge †	St John			
1846	Anderston †	St John			
1846	Airdrie *	-			
1847	Dumbarton †	St Patrick			
1847	Girvan †	St John			
1847	Maybole †	St Oswald			
Bishop Walter Trower 1848–1859					
1849	Largs	St Columba	1856	Glasgow/Calton	†Green St Mission
1850	Baillieston †	St John			
1851	Kilmarnock *	Holy Trinity			
1853	Lanark †	Christ Church			
1854	Port Glasgow †	St Mary			
1855	Castle Douglas *	St Ninian			
1853	Jordanhill †	All Saints			
1855	Glasgow/Calton	†Green St Mission			
1856	Gourock	St Bartholomew			
1858	Lamington	Holy Trinity			
1855	Moffat	St John			
Bishop William Wilson 1859–88					
1863	Glasgow	St Silas	1874	Pollokshaws †	Mission
1865	Partick †	St Silas Mission	1874	Partick †	St John Mission
1865	Townhead †	St Luke			
1866	Southside †	St Ninian			
1867	Cowcaddens †	SPeter			
1870	Pollokshaws †	Mission			
1870	Partick †	St John Mission			
1870	Maryhill †	St George			
1870	Lenzie	St Cyprian			
1871	Greenock/ Cartsdyke †	St Stephens			
1871	Charing Cross †	St Paul			
1873	Johnstone †	St John			
1873	Dalbeattie	Christ Church			
1875	Springburn †	St James			

Table 4.2 continued

Churches opened			Churches closed		
Year	Town/Area	Dedication	Year	Town/Area	Dedication
1875	Govan †	St Michael			
1875	Newton †	St Columba			
1878	Harthill †	Mission			
1877	Alexandria †	St Mungo			
1878	Kirkcudbright	Greyfriars			
1879	Garngad †	Mission			
1879	Renfrew *	St Margaret			
1880	Stranraer †	St John			
1882	Gorbals †	St Margaret			
1882	Motherwell †	Holy Trinity			
1882	New Galloway	St Margaret			
1885	Polmadie †	St Martin			
1886	Dalry †	St Peter			
1887	Langholm	All Saints			
1888	Kinning Park †	St Mark			
1888	Clydebank †	St Columba			
1888	Uddingston	St Andrew			

Bishop William Harrison 1888–1903

Churches opened			Churches closed		
1889	Irvine †	St John Mission	1888	Charring Cross †	St Paul
1890	Wishaw	St Andrew	1891	Blythswood †	St Jude
1890	Paisley (West) †	St Barnabas	1902	Blythswood †	St Barnabas
1890	Port Patrick *	St Ninian			
1891	Kelvinside	St Bride			
1891	Govan †	St Gabriel			
1891	Maxwelton	St Ninian Mission			
1891	Port Dundas †	St Saviour			
1892	Lockerbie	All Saints			
1893	Ayr (Wallacetown) †	St John Baptist			
1893	Blythswood †	St Barnabas			
1894	Bridgeton †	St Columba			
1894	Gorbals †	St Mungo			
1895	Possilpark †	St Matthew			
1895	Gartcosh †	St Andrew			
1896	Milngavie	St Andrew			

Churches opened			Churches closed		
Year	Town/Area	Dedication	Year	Town/Area	Dedication
1897	Bearsden	All Saints			
1898	Partick †	St Patrick Mission			
1898	Kirkintilloch	Mission			
1898	Kingston †	St Paul Mission			
1898	Newlands	St Margaret			
1899	Mossend (Bellshill) *	St Margaret			
1899	Balgray †	St Christopher			
1899	Cambuslang	St Cuthbert			
1899	Shettleston *	St Serf			
1900	Greenock (East) †	St Ninian			
1902	Dennistoun *	St Barnabas			
1902	Gallowgate †	St Cuthbert			

Bishop Archibald Campbell 1904–21

Churches opened			Churches closed		
1905	Kilmalcolm	St Fillan	1906	Gorbals †	St Margaret
1906	Parkhead *	St Paul	1907	Gorbals †	St Mungo
1906	Rutherglen †	St Stephen	1910	Partick †	St Faith
1907	Bridge of Weir	St Mary	1911	Partick †	St Patrick
1908	Neilston	Holy Trinity	1918	Stevenston †	Mission
1909	Gatehouse	St Mary	1920	Harthill †	Mission
1911	Troon	St Ninian			
1912	Scotstoun	St David			
1914	Shotts *	St Catherine			
1914	Stevenston †	Mission			
1915	Larkhall †	All Saints			
1915	Prestwick	St Ninian			
1916	Gretna	All Saints			
1916	Eastriggs	St John			

Bishop Edward Reid 1921–31

Churches opened			Churches closed		
1924	Blantyre	All Saints	1925	Kingston †	St Paul
1924	Clarkston	St Aidan	1927	Balgray †	St Christopher
1924	Mosspark	The Ascension	1930	Larkhall †	All Saints
1926	Knightswood	Holy Cross			
1927	Cumbernauld Rd	Holy Trinity			
1931	Kings Park	St Oswald			

Churches opened			Churches closed		
Year	Town/Area	Dedication	Year	Town/Area	Dedication
Bishop John Derbyshire 1931–38					
1932	Inchinnan	All Hallows	1931	Neilston	Holy Trinity
1934	Barrhead	Holy Spirit	1934	Garngad †	Mission
1938	Hillington	Good Shepherd			
Bishop John How 1938–52					
1944	Hillington	St Phillip	1940	Inchinnan	All Hallows
			1949	Blantyre	Mission
			1951	Gallowgate †	St Cuthbert
			1951	Greenock (East)	†St Ninian
Bishop Francis Moncrieff 1952–73					
1953	East Kilbride	St Mark	1952	Mossend (Bellshill) *	St Margaret
1955	Drumchapel	Mission	1952	Townhead †	St Luke
1958	Cumbernauld	Holy Name	1953	Kinning Park †	St Mark
			1953	Parkhead *	St Paul
			1954	Port Dundas †	St Saviour
			1954	Ayr (Wallacetown) †	St John Baptist
			1955	Kirkintilloch	Mission
			1957	Hillington	St Phillip
			1959	Anderston †	St John
			1961	Newton †	St Columba
			1961	Pollokshaws †	Mission
			1963	Govan †	St Michael
			1963	Cowcaddens †	St Peter
			1965	Barrhead	Holy Spirit
			1967	Bridgeton *	St Columba
			1968	Rutherglen †	St Stephen
			1970	Scotstoun	St David
			1971	Greenock/ Cartsdyke†	St Stephen
			1973	Gorbals †	SS. Magt & Mungo

Key: Significant Irish presence at foundation (proved) †
   Significant Irish presence (assumed) *

Source: Bertie, Scottish Episcopal Clergy, 'Diocese of Glasgow & Galloway', pp. 585–612.

5 Sectarianism, Segregation and Politics on Clydeside in the Later Nineteenth Century

John Foster, Muir Houston and Chris Madigan

Report by Liberal Party canvassers, 1889 By-election, Govan
The first thing that caught their eyes when they had gone in was a portrait of the Pope on one side of the mantelpiece and a portrait of William of Orange on the other. The good woman noted their looks and said: 'I am afraid my man will not vote for Mr Wilson [the Liberal candidate] for he is an Orangeman and I am a Catholic. He is one of the best men in Govan but goes mad once a year on 12th July and then he takes down the portrait of His Holiness, throws it on the floor and dances on it. As soon as he goes out I take down King Billy and put him in the pawn. After he comes out of his madness, he takes Billy out of the pawn and buys me a new Pope, and then I have the best man in Govan for another twelve months.[1]

Some years ago Steven Fielding stressed the need to research the potentially transforming relationships between nineteenth-century Irish immigrants to Britain and the host population.[2] There was, he argued, an unhistorical tendency to treat Irish immigrants as socially isolated and, often in consequence, to assume them to be demographically homogeneous and culturally unchanging. By contrast, studies of contemporary immigration show the process to involve highly diverse patterns of interaction with host populations. Sometimes such contact will entrench existing internalised identities among immigrant populations; sometimes they will transform them and sometimes erode them altogether in a process of rapid assimilation. Methodologically, however, contemporary studies have one key advantage: the possibility of precise, locally-focused observation of the process of change. For the historian any identification of change over time is highly problematic. Attributing cause is even more so. For this reason this study approaches the issue on a strictly limited basis. It looks at just one aspect of behaviour: residential segregation. It confines this to the Irish immigrant population in terms of segregation between Catholics and Protestants. And it focuses on just two Clydeside townships: the shipbuilding burgh of Govan and the adjacent dockside and railway burgh of Kinning Park. It does so in an attempt to relate the changing intensity of this segregation to what was happening socially and politically in these specific industrial localities over a fairly long time period: the four decades between 1861 and 1901.

In summary, the evidence from census household schedules shows that in Govan and Kinning Park Catholic and Protestant immigrants from Ireland did tend to live in different streets and that this trend was established in the 1860s, consolidated in the 1870s and then levelled off in the 1880s – with some indications of a slight decline in the 1890s. Most of these immigrants came from the north of Ireland where religious segregation was already strongly marked in the 1870s.[3] Unlike Clydeside, however, the scale of segregation in Belfast and other urban centres continued to increase thereafter – doing so particularly sharply in the 1880s and 1890s and by then assuming a level of intensity quite unlike that in Govan and Kinning Park.[4] The question is therefore why patterns of behaviour diverge at this point. Clydeside had the highest concentration of Irish immigrants in Britain and was relatively unusual in the degree to which Irish immigration remained at a high level right up until the beginning of the twentieth century.[5] Why then did immigrants coming from a background of intense sectarian conflict in the 1880s and 1890s not reproduce these relations to the same extent on Clydeside? What factors within the host communities might have impacted on this behaviour?

This study represents the second stage of a project on Clydeside's Catholic and Protestant immigrants. We start with a brief summary of the previous findings based on the 1891 census and of the methodology used to attribute religious affiliation.[6] This sets the context for the new data on spatial separation in Govan and Kinning Park and the question of why such segregation, though present, was so different from that in the north of Ireland – focusing particularly on the higher level of trade union organisation and class activity on the Clyde.

Catholics and Protestants: Identification and Findings

Census schedules in Britain provided no information on religious affiliation. Those in Ireland did and the methodology for attributing religion is based on a large sample of first names drawn from the 1901 Belfast census. This permitted the identification of those male first names where there was a high association with being either Protestant or Catholic. Names such as Adam, Albert, Andrew, David and Samuel were exclusively Protestant in more than 95 per cent of cases. Names such as Bernard, Patrick and Michael were equally exclusively Catholic. These associations were then checked against a similarly sized sample of Irish-born prisoners in Glasgow's Barlinnie jail for years on either side of the 1891 census. The levels of association were found to be similar. Combining the two data sets makes it possible to select cohorts of Irish immigrants from census schedules that can be assumed to be principally of one religion or the other – depending on the exclusivity of the names chosen. For the current research nineteen of the twenty chosen 'Protestant' first names had an association in the 80–100 per cent range. The twentieth, Isaac, had a 75 per cent association. A similar level of exclusivity was used for 'Catholic' names.

In practice, considerably more Protestants than Catholics took names that were religiously specific at the 80 per cent level and so the 'Protestant' cohort is considerably bigger proportionately than it would have been in real life. For the Govan and Kinning Park in 1881 the identified 'Protestants' make up 45 per cent of selected 'Catholic' and 'Protestant' households combined. The actual proportion of Protestant immigrants is likely to have been nearer a quarter. Moreover, an outright majority of Irish males had names which fell outside the required level of exclusivity. In 1881 the combined number of selected 'Protestant' and 'Catholic' households constitute only 30 per cent of the total.[7] Consequently, the selection of households based on this methodology is not intended to reproduce a representative sample of the Irish population as a whole but to produce cohorts that are likely to have been very largely Catholic or very largely Protestant. What is important is the confidence with we can compare the profiles of the two cohorts and know that a large majority in each will have been either Catholic or Protestant.

The previous stage of this research was based on a structured random sample of over 1,500 schedules drawn from all households recorded in the 1891 census for six Clydeside shipbuilding communities: Greenock, Dumbarton, Clydebank, Linthouse, Govan and Partick. Cohorts of putative Catholics and Protestant Irish immigrants were selected from the wider sample of Irish households and analysed to discover their different occupational and demographic profiles. Surprisingly, the two cohorts were found to be identical. This was so in terms of age, family size, skill level, size of house occupied and types of occupation entered. Compared to the general population both Catholic and Protestant male heads of household were also found to be equally disadvantaged. The great majority were in unskilled jobs. Moreover, this disadvantage was in contrast to the other major immigrant community on Clydeside, the Highlanders. These mainly non-industrial and non-urban migrants generally secured jobs in the semi-skilled range.

While these findings were initially unexpected, challenging some long-held stereotypes about the relative characteristics of Catholic and Protestant immigrants, they do in fact match what is known about labour markets in Belfast and on Clydeside.[8] Wages for skilled workers, particularly in engineering and shipbuilding, were slightly higher in Belfast throughout the later nineteenth century and there would therefore be little reason for any skilled Protestant to emigrate to Scotland – although skilled Catholics might wish to do so to escape workplace harassment. On other hand, the wages of unskilled workers were over a third lower in almost all Belfast trades and there was a chronic over-supply of labourers, both Protestant and Catholic. There was therefore every reason for *unskilled* Protestants to emigrate on the same scale as Catholics. What is perhaps less predictable is the evidence that Catholics and Protestants appear to have fared equally badly once they got to Clydeside. There is no evidence, in terms of occupation and skill levels, of more discrimination against Catholics than Protestants. In fact Catholic immigrants appear to have been slightly better represented than Protestants in shipyard labouring. The only evidence of statistically significant difference between Protestants and Catholics was in settlement patterns: Catholics preferred Dumbarton and Clydebank and Protestants Partick.

On this basis it was suggested that occupational disadvantage or discrimination was experienced on Clydeside in a quite different way from that in Belfast. In Belfast it mainly operated through closely controlled exclusion from entire industrial sectors. Catholics were excluded entirely from all jobs, skilled and unskilled, in most shipbuilding and engineering works and certain docks. Usually, this exclusion was reinforced by exclusion from the relevant neighbourhoods as well. On Clydeside all Irish immigrants in general were relegated to the less skilled jobs – but had access to the full range of industrial and service occupations. There is even some evidence that the adult sons of some Irish families, both Catholic and Protestant, were by 1891 securing apprenticeships and beginning to move into skilled trades.

Our conclusion was therefore that occupational discrimination on Clydeside did not primarily operate on a sectarian or religious basis and, in so far as discrimination did exist, it tended to operate to the detriment of *all* Irish immigrants equally. Occupational discrimination was also, compared to Belfast, weak. At least an element of the disadvantage appeared to derive from generational positioning – with Highlanders having opened up networks of industrial involvement in shipbuilding somewhat earlier. It was suggested that this particular positioning of the Irish immigrant had to be understood within the culture and politics of the host community at the time, the rapid expansion of the industrial labour force and particularly the relative tightness of demand for unskilled labour. This made possible active processes of class formation and union organisation among semi- and unskilled workers that did not occur in Belfast.

If there were exceptions, they appear to have been generated by Irish immigrants themselves. There is some evidence that, once on Clydeside, attempts were made to replicate Belfast-type patterns of exclusion by monopolising certain unskilled workplaces and surrounding locales. Lobban found evidence of this in Greenock.[9] There Protestant immigrants sought to control access to labouring work in the cotton mills and sugar refineries and settled in adjacent streets, while the Catholics did the same in the docks. Our own research identified attempts, in one case at least supported by dock employers, to create similar Protestant and Catholic-controlled enclaves in particular docks and quays on the upper Clyde. However, these attempts were ultimately unsuccessful and foundered amid the general trend toward unskilled unionisation from the late 1880s.

The research reported here is designed to investigate these issues of spacial segregation between Catholic and Protestant immigrants in greater depth and, in particular, over a time period that could reflect longer-term trends. It takes advantage of the machine-readable transcription of the 1881 census to abstract *all* households with Irish born heads for the two burghs. On this basis it is possible to secure very large cohorts of presumed Catholic and Protestant households at an over 80 per confidence level: 405 'Catholic' households and 336 'Protestant'. This, in turn, makes it feasible to plot concentrations of settlement street by street and secure the basis for comparison with settlement patterns for the same streets in preceding and subsequent censuses. The large cohorts also make it possible to test somewhat more conclusively the findings reached for 1891: that Catholic and Protestant immigrants to Clydeside were demographically and occupationally very similar.

Govan and Kinning Park: Profiles of Development

Govan was by 1881 a major industrial town on the south side of the Clyde some five miles west of Glasgow. It had been a centre for linen and cotton weaving from the eighteenth century but had remained very small with a population of fewer than 5,000 into the 1850s. Pictures from the 1830s show it as a small village with thatched cottages, green fields and a ferry across the river to Partick. This rural idyll changed very quickly over the following two decades. Shipbuilding and engineering works began to move downstream from Glasgow to gain additional space and deeper water. Napiers, the pioneers of fast, efficient marine steam engines and iron ships, moved from Glasgow to the yard just east of Govan Cross in 1842. Elders opened an even bigger yard just to the west in 1860. Stephens, a shipbuilding firm originally from Aberdeen, took the next available section of the river bank at Linthouse in 1868 after having occupied a site at Kelvinhaugh since 1848. Each of these yards employed well in excess of 1,000 workers. Smaller yards and specialist engineering and iron works followed.

By 1849 38 per cent of all iron ship tonnage built in Scotland had been produced in Govan, the great bulk at the Napier yard. Substantial Admiralty orders followed in the 1850s as Govan became acknowledged leader in the new iron and steam technology.[10] The world's first all iron warship was completed at Napier's yard in 1856. Forges in the Lanarkshire coal and iron fields east and south of Glasgow supplied the cast iron – as they had previously provided the iron rails for Britain's new rail network.

Govan's population increased rapidly from less than 4,000 in 1851 and 8,000 in 1861 to 18,000 in 1871 and 49,000 in 1881. As the transition from wood to iron proceeded, so the composition of the shipbuilding labour force was transformed.[11] Previously the trade had a relatively skilled profile: dominated by shipwrights who worked with apprentices and one or two labourers. With the move to iron, boilermakers and platers became the key skilled occupations. Iron drillers were needed to drill the plates and riveters to rivet them. The riveters worked in gangs with unskilled 'holders on' and rivet boys to heat the rivets. Large numbers of less skilled and labouring jobs were also created – from caulkers to stokers. Almost all these workers were recruited from immigrants to the immediate area. Just less than half came from Lowland Scotland and over a quarter each from the Highlands and from Ireland. Most of the shipyard workers lived in streets on either side of the Govan Road, which ran parallel to the river frontage from Glasgow to Renfrew (Map 5.1). Labouring and semi-skilled families occupied one-roomed tenement houses in conditions of serious overcrowding, and a substantial proportion of these were immigrants from Ireland. By the early 1860s an Irish population of several hundred households existed – many concentrated in the streets directly opposite the gates of the Napier yard, the so-called 'Irish 'Channel'. A red brick Catholic chapel with accommodation for 300, St Anthony's in Govan Road, was opened in 1864.[12]

The 1860s was the decade in which Govan was definitively transformed into an industrial community. The population trebled as Elders and Stephens joined Napiers along the riverfront and major industrial struggles unfolded as these giant employers sought to impose a new division of labour based on iron technology and to destroy the power previously exerted by the shipwrights. In the 1850s and 1860s wages were some 25 per cent lower than in the established English shipbuilding centres on the Thames and Mersey.[13] There is, however, evidence of a strong union presence. Union resistance in 1856 compelled employers lower down the Clyde to abandon an attempt to impose a no-union rule on workers.[14] Although, as trade worsened in 1864, employers enforced a 10 per cent wage cut and broke the resulting strike across the whole river, there were further strikes in Govan in 1865 to resist wage cuts.[15] In 1866 the iron trades took the offensive to demand a 57-hour week without loss of pay across the Clyde. The employers responded by forming the Clyde Shipbuilding and Engineering Employers Association to lock out 18,000 workers across the Clyde and attempted to enforce a no-union rule.[16] The strength of trade union organisation was again sufficient to secure a negotiated settlement with a reduction in hours to 57 – though without pay for the three hours' reduction. A Clydeside employer explained the philosophy of the new employers' association to the 1869 Select Committee: 'our main objection both to arbitration and conciliation as palliatives of Unionism is that they sanction, nay necessitate, the continuance of a system of combination as opposed to that of individual competition.'[17] At this stage the main organised trades were the shipwrights, the boilermakers (based on Tyneside but organising on the Clyde from the 1850s), the blacksmiths (based on the Clyde from 1858 but organising in England from the 1860s) and the engineers.

It was during these years that Govan secured its status as a police burgh in 1864, with power to raise its own police force.[18] It appears that some attempt was made to use this local power in a way which sought to accentuate divisions on ethnic lines. In 1867, well after the main Fenian emergency had passed, the Council persuaded the Home Office to supply fire-arms to its police force. There was in Govan it was argued, 'a large labouring population, mixed in nationality, a considerable proportion of whom would be doubtless susceptible to Fenian influence'. A massive additional force of 900 special constables was enrolled. At its first parade this force was told by the chief magistrate: 'we may give all Fenians a touch of the Auld Scottish thistle and remind them that none may assail it with impunity.' Early in 1868 this force, armed with batons, was

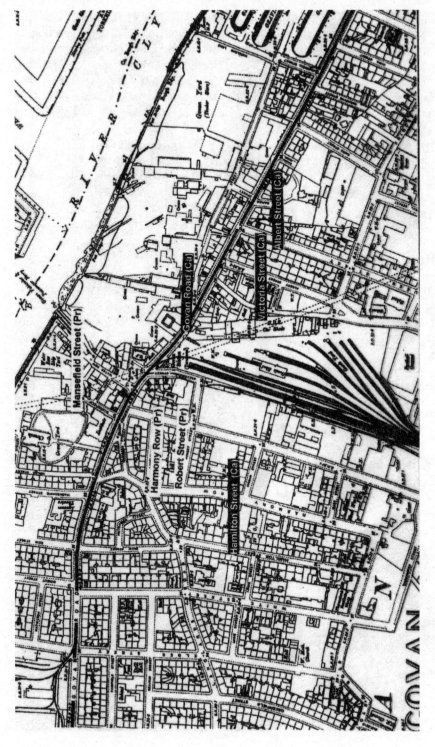

Map 5.1 Govan 1881: Streets indicated where Protestants or Catholics exceed expected by 10 per cent

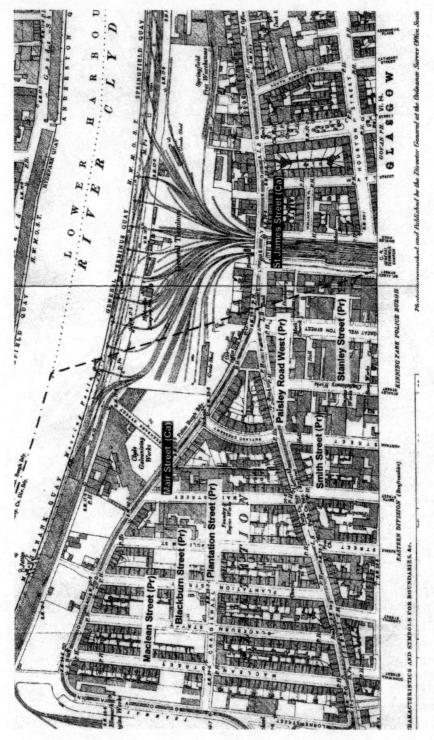

Map 5.2 Kinning Park 1881: Streets indicated where Protestants or Catholics exceed expected by 10 per cent

marched through the streets with a heavy Irish population directly opposite the Napier yard.[19]

Kinning Park was up until 1871 administratively part of Govan Police Burgh and occupied the area to the east directly on the border with Glasgow. It emerged as a dockside and railway centre in the 1840s and 1850s. The first streets were on either side of the Paisley Road, which ran west from Glasgow, and immediately adjacent to the new railway opened in 1841. This ran west to Paisley and then divided to go south to the Ayrshire coalfields and west to Port Glasgow and Greenock. Railway yards and small iron foundries provided employment together with the docks that were spreading down the river from the Gorbals. The first was Windmillcroft Quay which was linked by tramways to Dixon's coal works two miles south. The most important development was the creation of a rail spur to the river in 1849 and the construction of the General Terminus Quay. This, together with Springfield Quay, opened in 1850, became the major hub for exports of coal and imports of iron ore and manganese. The docks and associated railways and carting firms provided employment for hundreds of dock and transport workers. Streets now developed on either side of the spur along with further iron foundries and galvanisers. In 1858 Mavisbank Quay was opened which specialised in grain and other food imports across the Atlantic – leading to the opening of flour mills, bakeries, starch works and sugar refineries. Plantation Quay, furthest down the river towards Govan, was opened in 1872. This catered principally for the Allan line and the Canada trade. Further tenements sprang up opposite these docks (Map 5.2).[20]

Kinning Park's creation as a separate police burgh appears to have been closely linked to the perception of Govan Burgh as one dominated by local employers. In a period of rising union militancy during 1870 and 1871 Glasgow Trades Council ran a campaign for the amalgamation of Kinning Park to Glasgow. This was resisted by local property owners and employers fearful of higher rates. A competing proposal, eventually successful, was made for the creation of a separate police burgh. In the elections for the new Council 'working-class' candidates linked to Glasgow Trades Council, including its chair Andrew Boa, won five of the twelve seats.[21] The burgh was always significantly smaller than Govan and in 1881 its population was just over 11,000. A relatively large Irish population existed from the late 1840s mainly living in the streets immediately adjacent to the new rail link and General Terminus Quay. The first make-shift Catholic school was established in St James Street in the 1860s. A stone built school and chapel were opened in Stanley Street in 1874. Four years later an Orange lodge was established which was eventually to occupy a hall 300 yards away in Lorne Street. By 1881 the burgh formed part of continuous urban development along the south side of the Clyde from the Glasgow border to the western edge of Govan Burgh.

In 1881, therefore, both Govan and Kinning Park were established industrial communities and both overwhelmingly working class in composition. Of Govan's occupied males 82 per cent were classified as industrial. Of the 15,000 in work 3,300 were shipbuilders, 2,700 machine and implement makers, 1,500 in conveyance and 1,400 in housing trades. Of Kinning Park's 3,500 occupied adult males 2,600 were classified as industrial and 700 as commercial. Kinning Park had far fewer shipbuilders (only 158) but 564 of its adult males were in conveyance (most of the commercial category), 353 in machine and implement making, 369 in food production and 409 in housing.[22] Both Govan and Kinning Park had established Irish populations with origins going back over three decades. Of Kinning Park's adult males aged 20 and over 643 were Irish-born, 719 Highlanders and 1,312 Lowland Scots. Govan had 3,382 Irish born against 3,632 Highlanders and 5,497 Lowland Scots.[23]

Irish Immigrants in Govan and Kinning Park in 1881

How far, then, did the 'Catholic' and 'Protestant' cohorts of those recorded as 'Irish-born' in the 1881 census differ occupationally and demographically? Table 5.1 gives the results for a range of demographic variables.[24] Given the very large sample, even minimal differences should be expected to show up. But none does. The two populations are headed by men who are of similar age, marry women of similar age, have a similar number of children and start their families at the same age. Demographically, they are identical. The only difference to emerge as statistically significant is the very slightly greater number of lodgers taken by Catholic households. The average for Protestants is 0.44 per household as against 0.61 for Catholics, a difference of 0.17.[25]

Table 5.1 Govan and Kinning Park 1881. Putative Catholic and Protestant households: demographic characteristics

	Average Catholics	Average Protestants	T	df	Sig. (2-tailed)
Number present in household	5.45	5.18	−1.7	739.0	0.10
Number of children present	3.15	3.22	−0.2	739.0	0.88
Number of lodgers	0.61	0.44	−2.4	738.5	0.02
Age of head	38.68	37.58	−1.3	736.0	0.19
Age of spouse	35.27	35.25	0.1	694.0	0.94
Age of first child	19.8	18.8	−1.8	216.0	0.08
Children modified for unmarried			−0.3	739.0	0.77

Column T gives the raw figure for the significance test tau; df the degrees of freedom that qualify that figure; and Sig. the resulting probability of a particular test being significant, i.e. that there was a true difference between the Catholics and Protestants for this variable. Conventionally, anything less than 0.05 is considered significant, i.e. that it has a more than 95 per cent probability of being a true difference.

Source: 1881 census enumerators' schedules for Govan and Kinning Park Burghs: households with Irish-born heads only

Another potentially revealing variable is the birthplace of spouses. Wives of Irish-born heads were not necessarily born in Ireland and their birthplaces enable us to compare whether either Catholics or Protestants were more prone to marry into local communities in Scotland. Again, however, we can find no important difference. Protestants show a very slight, but not significant, tendency to marry Highlanders and those from Lowland Scotland. Catholics were more likely to marry those born in Glasgow. But the great bulk of men from both religions were married to women born in Ireland – whether before or after emigration we do not know.

Table 5.2 Govan and Kinning Park 1881: birthplace of spouse

		Glasgow	Clydeside	Other Lowland	Highland	Ireland	Total
Protestant	Count	26.0	25.0	18.0	15.0	217	301
	Expected	31.9	23.4	13.5	11.7	220	301
Catholic	Count	45.0	27.0	12.0	11.0	273	368
	Expected	39.1	28.6	16.5	14.3	270	368
	Total	71	52	30	26	490	669

Source: 1881 census enumerators' schedules for Govan and Kinning Park Burghs: households with Irish-born heads only

Table 5.3 shows results of significance tests on birthplace of spouse and also of the three first-born children – a useful way of testing for differences in the experience of migration and in particular for different time periods. Again there is no significant difference.

Table 5.3 Birthplaces of spouse and older children (same range of birthplaces as Table 5.2)

	Tests of significance between Catholic and Protestant Irish			
	Chi squared	*df*	*p*	*Cramers V*
Birthplace of spouse	6.7	4	0.15	0.1
Birthplace of child 1	5.3	3	0.15	0.09
Birthplace of child 2	1.9	3	0.59	0.06
Birthplace of child 3	0.8	3	0.86	0.05

Chi squared is used to test for the independence of two criteria in the classification of qualitative data. The raw figure is qualified by the degrees of freedom (df) to give the probability of association (p) where anything less than 0.05 is considered significant at more than 95 per cent probability. Cramer's V is an appropriate test of significance where at least one variable is nominal. 1.0 would indicate full significance,
Source: 1881 census enumerators' schedules for Govan and Kinning Park Burghs: households with Irish-born heads only

This lack of difference is so striking that it might lead to scepticism as to the effectiveness of the first name selectors for 1881. However, when we turn to the first names of spouses we do find a large and statistically significant difference. Catholic men, collectively, are revealed as choosing spouses with a quite different range of first names compared to their Protestant counterparts.

Table 5.4 presents this in terms of the probability of a particularly named female being chosen by a Protestant male. The choice of Bridget as a spouse solely for Catholics is not surprising, though Rose, Susan and Catherine are perhaps more so. The more Protestant names of Martha, Eliza, Agnes, Elizabeth and Sarah have a biblical resonance – as do a number of the favourite first names for Protestant men (Samuel, Benjamin, Isaac). The cross-tabulation was statistically significant with a probability of 0.000.

Table 5.4 Spouse's first name

	Total	Religion Protestant	Protestant as %
Bridget	29	0	0.0
Rose	18	1	5.6
Susan	12	3	25.0
Catherine	48	14	29.2
Mary	140	49	35.0
Ann(e)	67	24	35.8
Helen	13	5	38.5
Ellen	15	6	40.0
Total	607	265	43.7
Isabella	16	8	50.0
Margaret	76	43	56.6
Jane	51	30	58.8
Sarah	34	22	64.7
Elizabeth	49	32	65.3
Agnes	15	10	66.7
Eliza	12	9	75.0
Martha	12	9	75.0

chi squared = 83.5, 15df, p = 0.000, Cramers V = 0.37
Source: 1881 census enumerators' schedules for Govan and Kinning Park Burghs: households with Irish-born heads only

When we turn to occupation we find variations but no major differences. The census descriptions of occupations are fairly full and have enabled us to categorise as in Table 5.5. The largest single group is the 262 non-shipyard labourers (over 25 per cent of the total sample). The next biggest category is those working in the shipyards: 206. In terms of expected numbers (as against incidence in the overall population) there are slightly more Catholics than Protestants among the non-shipyard labourers, but, as in 1891, just as many Catholics as Protestants worked in the shipyards. There are somewhat more Protestants than Catholics in the skilled shipyard trades but more Catholics than Protestants in the semi-skilled jobs (riveters, caulkers and drillers) and the unskilled ones. At a finer level of detail there were more Catholic riveters (16 as against 13 expected) and fewer Protestants (7 as against 10 expected).

There are also surprisingly more Protestants and fewer Catholics among the drillers – a trade considered significantly less skilled than riveting and barred from membership of the Boilermakers Society.[26] Outside the shipyards there were more Protestants than Catholics in skilled building trades but more Catholics than Protestants in other skilled trades. There were more Catholics than Protestants in general non-shipyard labouring but more Protestants than Catholics in other areas of labouring (carting, transport and iron foundries) and equal numbers as quay labourers. Overall these variations show up in Table 5.5 as statistically significant – though not at a particularly high level given the size of the sample. It is slight compared with the very strong association found between the religion of household head and spouse's first name. If the shipyard occupations in Table 5.5 were taken separately the difference would be just significant for the shipyards (chi squared = 8.11, 2df, p = 0.017) and even less so for the non-shipyard occupations (chi squared = 13.36, 6df, p = 0.038).

Table 5.5 Occupations of heads of household

		Skilled shipyard	Shipyard semi-skilled	Shipyard labourers
Protestant	Count	48	14	28
	Expected	38.3	18.0	34.3
Catholic	Count	39	27	50
	Expected	48.7	12.9	43.7
Total		87	23.0	78

		Skilled non-shipyard	Skilled building	Non-shipyard labourers	Quay labourers
Protestant	Count	23	21	101	18
	Expected	23.7	15.4	115.2	18.5
Catholic	Count	31	14	161	24
	Expected	30.3	19.6	146.8	23.5
Total		54	35	262	42

		Carters	Transport labourers	Iron foundry labourers	Total
Protestant	Count	6	14	26	299
	Expected	4.8	9.2	21.5	
Catholic	Count	5	7	23	381
	Expected	6.2	11.8	27.5	
Total		11	21	49	680

chi squared = 21.5, 9df, p = 0.011, Cramers V = 0.18
Source: 1881 census enumerators' schedules for Govan and Kinning Park Burghs: households with Irish-born heads only

Table 5.6 Shipyard and non-shipyard occupations

		Shipyard	Other	Total
Protestant	Count	90	209	299
	Expected	90.6	208.4	
Catholic	Count	116	265	381
	Expected	115.4	265.6	
Total		206	474	680

chi squared = 0.009, 1df, p = 0.92, Cramers V = 0.004
Source: 1881 census enumerators' schedules for Govan and Kinning Park Burghs: households with Irish-born heads only

Again we find, as we did in 1891, a tendency for sons to be moving into more skilled occupations – particularly in the shipyards. Table 5.7 shows that in the shipyards there is very little difference between the skill levels achieved by Catholic and Protestant sons. Outside the yards there is a very slight advantage to Protestants. There is again an interesting concentration of Protestants in certain areas of specialist labouring: iron foundries, carting and transport. None of the differences, however, is at a statistically significant level.

Table 5.7 Occupations of eldest sons

		Skilled shipyard	Riveters	Shipyard labourers	Skilled non–shipyard
Protestant	Count	4	5	7	9
	Expected	4.4	3.9	7.9	6.6
Catholic	Count	6	4	11	6
	Expected	5.6	5.1	10.1	8.4
Total		10	9	18	15

		Non-shipyard labourers	Foundry labourers	Total
Protestant	Count	39	3	67
	Expected	39.4	4.8	
Catholic	Count	51	8	86
	Expected	50.6	6.2	
Total		90	11	153

chi squared = 3.57, 5df, p = 0.61, Cramers V = 0.15
Source: 1881 census enumerators' schedules for Govan and Kinning Park Burghs: households with Irish-born heads only

In conclusion, therefore, we can reaffirm – even more so for 1881 than 1891 – that the occupational and demographic characteristics of Catholic and Protestant immigrants on Clydeside were more or less identical. Occupationally, Protestants and Catholics were disproportionately represented in labouring jobs. Demographically, they lived in households that were the same size and they arrived on Clydeside over the same time period. The main reasons for this similarity would be, as in 1891, economic. Most Catholics and Protestants immigrants came from the same labouring background in the north of Ireland and sought similar jobs but at higher wages on the Clyde. For Catholics, however, escape from occupational harassment was probably an increasingly important additional factor as sectarian conflict gathered pace from the 1860s.[27]

Residential separation of Catholic and Protestant Immigrants in Govan and Kinning Park in 1881

The experience of sectarian conflict forms a significant backdrop to the immigration to Clydeside. Much of central Belfast saw violent street expulsions in 1857. Sectarian conflict in 1864 had a clear occupational focus with Catholics expelled from linen mills and battles between Protestant ship carpenters from the yards and Catholic navvies from the docks. Further expulsions occurred from the shipyards in 1872 and particularly violent street confrontations took place in 1880 and 1886.[28] After that date violence was mainly focused on frontier areas between religion-specific territories. Parallel processes – although usually with a lower level of intensity – occurred in Derry, Coleraine, Lisburn, Lurgan and Portadown.

This process directly poses the question as to how far the cultural background of Irish immigrants – and in some cases immediate memories of expulsion prior to emigration – affected spatial patterns of settlement in Scotland. The data from the 1881 census enables us to investigate this in some detail. The figures in Table 5.8 for individual streets in Govan and Kinning Park relate solely to those Catholics and Protestants immigrants identified as such by their first names. This excludes the majority of Irish-born households which could not be identified in this way. It also excludes all non-Irish-born – in most cases the majority of households in any street. Consequently the figures relate to only a fraction of those actually living in any one street. Nonetheless, the figures do represent a reliable proxy for the degree to which Catholic and Protestant immigrants favoured one street as against another.

As can be seen, street by street differentiation was widespread and this differentiation is not immediately explicable in economic or demographic terms. Protestants were no more able to afford better quality housing than Catholics, the range of family sizes was identical and the period of settlement similar. Yet clearly Protestants tended to choose different streets from Catholics. In the case of Harmony Row (Protestant) the street ran directly parallel, north to south, some 50 yards from Hamilton Street (strongly Catholic) – both ending opposite the Elder family's giant Fairfield shipyard in Govan (Map 5.1). In Kinning Park the Catholic St James Street was next door to the rail line which ran down to Terminus Quay (mainly for coal and iron ore) while the strongly Protestant Plantation Street, 300 yards to the west, ran north to Mavisbank Quay which catered for the Atlantic trade (Map 5.2).

Table 5.8 Govan and Kinning Park streets in 1881: percentage of Protestant as against Catholic Irish-born

	Combined number of households	Protestants	% Protestant	Ward
Victoria St	67	10	15	2
Albert St	47	11	23	2
Hamilton St	69	20	29	1
Govan Rd	15	5	33	9
Mair St	14	5	36	4
St James St	14	5	36	5
Anderson St	33	12	36	5
Eaglesham Rd	10	4	40	4
Marlow St	15	6	40	5
Queen St	31	14	45	2
West Scotland St	11	5	45	5
Langsland Rd	17	8	47	1
Fairfield St	12	6	50	1
Linthouse Buildings	10	5	50	9
Logie St	12	6	50	1
Blackburn St	30	16	53	4
Maclean St	26	15	58	4
Harmony Row	17	10	59	1
Mansfield St	20	12	60	1
Smith St	15	9	60	5
John St	11	7	64	1
Paisley Rd	11	7	64	9
Robert St	12	8	67	1
Plantation St	19	13	68	4
Stanley St	13	9	69	5
OVERALL	741	336	45	

Streets with fewer than 10 religiously specified Irish households have been excluded from this table – although not from the wider analysis.
Source: 1881 census enumerators' schedules for Govan and Kinning Park Burghs: households with Irish-born heads only

Even within streets this type of variation continues. Victoria Street was the heaviest area for concentrated Catholic settlement in Govan and lay opposite the gates of the Napier yard. Twenty-three of the 57 Catholic households are to be found within three closes: Nos 20, 22 and 24. There is one Protestant household in No. 18 and another five in No. 26 but most of the other eight live away from the densest area of Catholic settlement. In Queen Street running south from Victoria Street – where there are many more Protestants – the

Protestants tended to live at the end furthest from Victoria Street (ten out of 14 at numbers above 15) while 14 out of 17 Catholic households are at and below No. 15. Similarly in the strongly Protestant Plantation Street in Kinning Park, which led onto the Mavisbank Quay entrance, eight out of 13 Protestant households are below No. 100 – that is, closest to the quay – while five out of six Catholic households are above No. 100.

Taking ward level boundaries, we can test for the statistical strength of segregation across the whole area. Wards 1–4 are north to south strips across the Govan Burgh starting with Ward 1 at the western edge; the only oddity is that part of Ward 4 continues along the river to the north of Kinning Park. KP represents the western area of Kinning Park Burgh included in the sample:

Table 5.9 Irish immigrants: religion by ward, 1881

Religion		Ward					Total
		1	2	3	4	KP	
Protestant	Count	115	37	16	68	61	297
	Expected	109.8	67.6	8.4	56.5	54.7	297
Catholic	Count	132	115	3	59	62	371
	Expected	137.2	84.4	10.6	70.5	68.3	371
Total	Count	247	152	19	127	123	668
	Expected	247	152	19	127	123	668

chi squared = 43.1, 4df, p = 0.0000, Cramers V = 0.25
Source: 1881 census enumerators' schedules for Govan and Kinning Park Burghs: households with Irish-born heads only

This test gives a very significant indication of segregation. Protestants are under-represented in Ward 2 and over-represented in the other four areas. Ward 2 contains the strongly Catholic Victoria and Albert Streets. Even if the anomalous Ward 3, which was much smaller, is dropped, the analysis still leaves a significant relationship (chi squared = 10.7 with 3df, p = 0.014, Cramers V = 0.144) between religion and ward.[29]

Comparisons of Residential Segregation

Simply describing this spatial separation leaves the question of its relative magnitude unanswered. The figures may be statistically significant and appear to be considerable. But this does not answer the question as to whether it represents a high level of segregation compared, for instance, to the segregated communities of Ulster. Or locally in Govan whether it was high or low compared to what went before or came after. At both of these levels, the available comparative data is limited.

Because the pre-1901 Irish census schedules have not survived, any data on Catholic and Protestant residence patterns for nineteenth-century Ulster have to rely on the published census. Even for Belfast there is no detailed analysis of religion below constituency level. Worse still, the boundaries of these constituencies were in some measure gerrymandered to cut across areas of potential Catholic voting strength. The constituencies are also very big: just four for all Belfast. Effectively, therefore, any statistic based on this material only makes sense in comparison with itself over time. However, trends are revealed and segregation shown increasing at each census from 1871. The index of dissimilarity is that calculated by Doherty where zero would indicate a distribution in each constituency exactly proportionate to the distribution of sub-populations in the overall population and an index of 1 would indicate complete segregation. While the figures do not mean very much in themselves, they do show a sharp and continuing increase from 0.133 in 1871 to 0.182 in 1881 and 0.216 in 1891.[30]

A more meaningful comparison may be found by looking at Lurgan in 1911 – where streets have been analysed from surviving census schedules. Lurgan was a predominantly Catholic town where the proportion of Protestants was roughly similar to that in Govan and Kinning Park. The research by Hepburn reveals that the bulk of the population lived in streets where there was either a very high proportion of Catholics or of Protestants. This permits a fairly direct comparison with Govan and Kinning Park in 1881 using the data from Table 5.10 below. The pattern is strikingly different. Lurgan effectively reveals two populations concentrated on either side of the graph. Govan displays what is near enough a normal distribution curve – albeit with a slight dip in the middle. Only 10 per cent of Govan households lived in streets where there was less than 20 per cent of the other religion and 80 per cent lived in streets that were more mixed than 20 per cent. In Lurgan over three-quarters of the population lived in streets with less than 20 per cent of the other religion. Hepburn's figures

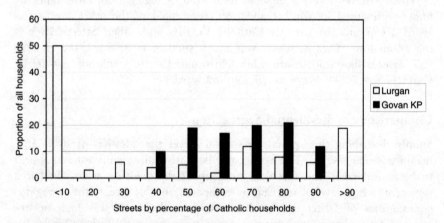

Figure 5.1 Percentage of households in total sample population living in streets with specified percentage of Catholic households: Govan 1881 and Lurgan 1911 (Source: 1881 Census enumerator's schedules for Govan and Kinning Park Burghs, households with Irish heads only; A. Hepburn, *A Past Apart*, p. 55 for Lurgan)

for the neighbouring and predominantly Protestant town of Portadown reveal
a similar though somewhat less marked pattern of exclusivity.

Hepburn has also undertaken sample-based analysis of streets in Belfast
using the 1901 census schedules.[31] This uses the criteria for 'mixed' streets
and 'Catholic' and 'Protestant' developed by Boal, Murray and Poole for the
mid-twentieth century. Catholic and Protestant streets were defined as those
with a minimum 90 per cent exclusivity for either religion. 'Mixed' covered the
streets in between.[32] It will be immediately apparent that all Govan streets were
mixed, in terms of Irish immigrants, in 1881. The one exception is Victoria
Street with 85 per cent Catholics. If we make allowance for the over-represen-
tation of Protestants in terms of name identification, it would just qualify as
Catholic. There would be no other Catholic street and no Protestant streets.
All other streets would qualify as mixed. By contrast, Hepburn found 60 per
cent of the population of Belfast living in religiously exclusive streets in 1901.
By 1972 it would be 77 per cent.

The other way of assessing the 1881 Govan figures is by comparing them
across time within Govan. In order to do this, streets with a high Catholic or
Protestant density in 1881 are examined – in terms of proportions of identifiable Catholics and Protestants – for the censuses before and after. As part
of this exercise some smaller streets have also been used (that is, streets not
shown in Table 5.8) and the streets grouped in terms of their location within
Govan and Kinning Park. The percentage of Protestants in each street (in
bold) is given alongside the numbers of Protestants and Catholics – with the
expected random figure being 45 per cent. See Table 5.10.

The picture that emerges is that of the pattern of differentiation being
established between 1871 and 1881 – with both Protestant and Catholic streets
in general becoming more rather than less exclusive over the decade. After
1881 this trend continues, though not dramatically so – with some evidence of
Catholics and Protestants switching locally into 'their' streets. This seems to
be the pattern in both East and West Govan and in Kinning Park. There were
certainly exceptions and some sharp switches – the most obvious being Stanley
Street in Kinning Park where the building of the Catholic Chapel appears
to have been followed by an exodus of Protestants. There is no evidence of
a decline in differentiation between 1881 and 1891. By 1901, however, there
does seem to be some evidence of convergence towards the 45 per cent mean
in East and West Govan and South Kinning Park – while North Kinning Park
remains more or less the same.

There are a couple of questions which stem from this finding. The first
is how far we are simply dealing with a process of settlement accretion
– whereby once an immigrant household is settled in one street it will tend to
attract relatives and friends. This is a process we can to some extent test for
by checking how far our identified immigrant households of 1881 were still
living in the same street ten years later in 1891. The answer appears to be that
there was only limited continuity at the level of individual streets. Taking 11
streets, covering just about a third of our sample households in 1881, we find

Table 5.10 Streets in Govan and Kinning Park: Protestant/Catholic numbers and
           percentage of Protestants (in bold)

Table 5.10a: Ward 1 streets: West Govan (Fairfield Shipyard)

Street	1861	1871	1881	1891	1901
Hamilton	*	3/5 37	20/49 29	17/52 25	13/34 31
Harmony	*	0/3	17/10 63	11/5 68	9/4 69
Mansfield and Water Row	0/3	3/3 50	5/12 41	5/13 38	0/0+

Table 5.10b: Streets in Ward 2: East Govan (Napier shipyard and Govan railway
           terminus)

Street	1861	1871	1881	1891	1901
Albert	10/17 37	14/21 40	11/36 23	8/32 20	10/34 23
Queen	*	1/2	14/17 45	17/14 55	9/28 32
Victoria	7/13 35	2/1	10/57 15	3/54 5	8/54 13

Table 5.10c: Streets in South Kinning Park (railways and engineering works)

Street	1861	1871	1881	1891	1901
Anderson	–	3/2	12/21 37	6/7 46	9/11 45
Marlow and Vermont	*	4/6 40	11/8 58	12/9 43	3/11 21
McLellan	*	–	8/1 89	11/2 85	12/5 70

Table 5.10d: Streets in North Kinning Park (docks and quays, railway)

Street	1861	1871	1881	1891	1901
Blackburn	*	–	16/14 53	12/13 48	16/17 48
Maclean	*	–	15/11 58	13/7 65	15/7 68
Plantation	*	*	13/6 68	11/4 73	13/5 72
Eaglesham and Rutland	–	2/0	8/9 47	7/10 41	1/3+ 25
St James	–	3/1 75	5/9 36	2/5 29	9/17 35
Stanley	*	1/2	9/5 64	1/6 14	1/6 14

* no housing – no Irish identifiable by religion
+ housing clearance and redevelopment
Source: Census enumerators' schedules for 1861, 1871, 1891 and 1901

that of 97 Protestants living in these streets in 1891 only 14 had been living
there ten years earlier and only 26 of the 155 Catholics. In percentage terms
this is 14.4 per cent of the Protestants and 16.7 per cent of the Catholics
– again showing the similarity between the two sub-populations. Nor does
there seem to be particular tendency for movement away from strong Catholic
or Protestant streets. One of the five 1891 Catholics in the Protestant Harmony

Row had been present in 1881 – but none of the 11 Protestants. Four of the 17 Protestants in the Catholic Hamilton Street in 1891 had been present in 1881 compared with 12 of the 51 Catholics. Two of the eight Protestants in the Catholic Albert Street in 1891 had been present in 1881 as against three of the 32 Catholics. We have therefore to conclude that the Catholic or Protestant character of particular streets, which on the basis of our census analysis appears to be relatively stable, was in fact continuously re-created in the course of a decade.

Another possible explanation for what therefore appears to be a continuously recreated separation is the relation between residence and employment. In Belfast employment location was probably the key factor in residential segregation. Catholic or, much more frequently, Protestant populations would seek to exclude those of the other religion from territorial access to particular workplaces. We have already noted that Lobban's ground-breaking analysis of Clydeside Irish settlement produced evidence of a similar process in Greenock's sugar refineries and docks.[33] In our earlier article we suggested that something of the same kind may have been happening in the vicinity of Mavisbank Quay and account for the very strongly Protestant character of Plantation Street in 1891. Table 5.11 gives a breakdown of occupations and skill levels for a range of streets in 1891. It covers all Irish-born heads of household and not just those identified as either Protestant or Catholic.

Table 5.11 Occupations of all Irish-born 1891 by selected streets: percentages

	Harmony	Hamilton	Albert	Queen	Blackburn	Maclean	Anderson/ St James
Retail/ Service	12	8	1	9	4	12	8
Shipbuilding skilled	45	18	18	27	13	3	5
Other skilled	10	3	8	9	25	17	19
Shipbuilding labourer	27	53	58	27	5	2	0
Dock labourer	0	0	3	1	28	29	8
Other labourer	7	18	12	26	25	37	69
Total	101	100	100	99	100	100	99
Numbers of Irish households	40	180	112	87	79	75	62

Chi squared = 414.7, 30 df, p > 0.001 (or over 99 per cent probability of significance)
Source: Census enumerators' schedules for 1891

The most striking finding is the very strong localisation of employment by place of residence. People lived very close to where they worked. Harmony Row and Hamilton Street, close to Elders' Fairfield yard in West Govan, are overwhelmingly shipbuilding in character: the first 73 per cent and the second 71 per cent. The second pair, Albert Street and Queen Street situated in East Govan opposite the Napier yard, was also very strongly shipbuilding: 76 per cent in the case of Albert Street; 54 per cent for Queen Street. None of the streets in either East or West Govan had any significant number of dock workers. By contrast, Blackburn Street and Maclean Street in Kinning Park housed large numbers of dock labourers but few workers in shipbuilding. Finally Anderson Street and St James Street, also in Kinning Park and just 300 yards away from the docks, had very few dock labourers and a great many general labourers.

How far, then, is there evidence that street differentiation is in some way related to processes of workplace monopolisation? The evidence from Kinning Park might point in that direction. Maclean and Blackburn Streets, like Plantation Street, faced onto the Mavisbank Quay docks which handled Atlantic trade, much of it food, where the largest employer was the anti-union Allan Line. Both were fairly strongly Protestant. None of the identified Catholics in Maclean Street worked in the docks – five did in Blackburn Street (although we do not know which docks and whether it was at the less favoured iron and coal terminus further upstream). There is a possibility that either the streets immediately ringing Mavisbank Quay were seen as hostile to Catholics wanting to work there, or, maybe more likely, that the employment practices inside were preferential to Protestants. There might also be some indication of similar processes regarding labouring work in the Napier shipyard – in favour of Catholics. It is notable that the proportion of shipyard labourers in Albert Street, directly facing the yard, was twice that of the almost equally labouring but more Protestant Queen Street – with the labourers there working more in non-shipbuilding workplaces. Again, however, it should be noted that six of the identified Protestants in Albert Street were shipyard labourers and four in Queen Street. Finally there is the very illuminating contrast of Harmony Row and Hamilton Street in West Govan. 'Protestant' Harmony Row is revealed as a street of largely skilled shipyard workers – while the more Catholic Hamilton Street is dominated by shipyard labourers. It was earlier noted that overall it was difficult to explain spatial differentiation in terms of different wage levels – because skill levels were identical for the total population. But once we get to local level it is clear that this is not necessarily the case and wages might well be a factor. In this part of West Govan, around the Fairfield yard, there do seem to be a somewhat greater number of Protestant skilled shipyard workers (and we are dealing with fairly small numbers) able to afford the rents of somewhat better quality housing in Harmony Row. Balancing this across the other side of our area is the congregation of unskilled Protestant labourers around the docks.

So, to sum up: what is it that explains the pattern of spatial differentiation between Protestant and Catholic immigrants? We have examined the possibility of settlement accretion and found it could have had some effect – but at a demonstrably low level. Over the course of a decade the occupation of most houses in any one street will have changed. What we have to explain is the continuing re-creation of the spatial differentiation over time – and here the identification of constant factors impacting on the spatial environment is particularly important. The street level analysis of occupations has shown the significance of the localisation of employment and the possible impact of some form of preferential access to particular workplaces. Again it is difficult to tell whether this occupational differentiation is the result of street-level exclusion, workplace discrimination or the gradual build up of contacts and networks inside particular occupations. There is also clearly a wage element operating at the micro level of particular employment locales.

Overall, however, what is striking is the degree to which, compared to the north of Ireland, Catholics and Protestants did live in the same streets. As we have seen, by Hepburn's criteria almost all streets in Govan and Kinning Park are 'mixed', most deviating by only 20 per cent from the norm. And, in stark contrast to Belfast, segregation does not increase after the entry of Home Rule to domestic politics. On the contrary, spatial segregation if anything declines – despite the continuing stream of new arrivals from an increasingly conflict-torn Ulster.

Labour Organisation and Sectarianism

This brings us to the final stage of our assessment: how to explain this degree of residential mixing among Irish immigrants to Govan and Kinning Park in terms of wider cultural and political developments on Clydeside.

In his essay comparing Belfast and Glasgow politics in the late nineteenth century Anthony Hepburn makes very similar points to Steven Fielding on the need to understand the dynamic relationships between immigrants and the host population. Examining how far Belfast's residential and industrial segregation and its very particular breed of nationalist politics were transferred to Clydeside, Hepburn finds elements of both cultural continuity and quite striking transformation. In particular he notes the climacteric divide of 1920. In Belfast Labour was 'forced steadily back into its ethnic compartments'. In Glasgow ethnic conflict was contained. It was, he suggests, the removal of the Irish question from the centre of the British political stage that cleared the way for the 'translation of the Glasgow Irish community into support for the Labour Party'. He identifies the previous two decades, and particularly perhaps the work of John Wheatley, as important in preparing the ground for this transformation.[34]

It is this issue of labour identity that we will examine next. In our study of the 1891 Clydeside census we examined industrial relations in the most concentrated area of Irish employment on the Clyde: the docks.[35] We found clear evidence of employers seeking to use sectarian conflict to halt the growth of unskilled unionisation – to the extent of recruiting a 'Protestant only' force of scabs in Belfast in 1888. We also found that this particular attempt failed. In addition, there was some evidence that the conflict between the Glasgow Harbour Labour Union and the National Union of Dock Labour (NUDL) in the 1890s had sectarian overtones – with the pro-employer Harbour Union being based very much round the docks of the Allan Line in Protestant Kinning Park. We also noted the significance of the joint Catholic and Protestant leadership of the NUDL, Edward McHugh and Richard McGhee, and its ability to outgrow and ultimately absorb and take over the Harbour Union in 1899. This would appear to show that the process of unionisation, even in the depressed late 1890s, was sufficiently robust to overcome sectarian attempts to impose workplace exclusivity.

While docks had the highest level of Irish concentration, shipbuilding was the biggest single employer of Irish labour and the character of its industrial relations was relatively unique. It was strongly unionised, prone to large-scale confrontations and generated high levels of inter-workplace and community solidarity.

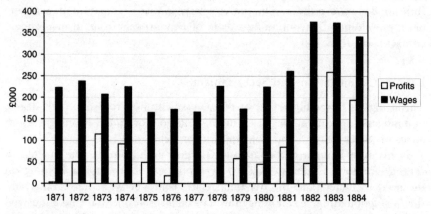

Figure 5.2 Profits and wages: Fairfield Yard. Source: Glasgow City Archives UCS 2/7/5

Figure 5.2, which gives wage and profit figures for Govan's biggest yard, illustrates one of the causes: the highly cyclical character of the industry. To take the cycle in the early 1880s: between 1879 and 1882 something like 3,000 additional workers would have been taken on in the Fairfield yard alone. Given the concentration of three major yards in Govan, plus a number of smaller ones, up to 8,000 additional workers would have been required over these years. Conversely, employment fell even more dramatically between 1883 and 1885. It was the strength of these demand swings, amplified across the Clyde, which drew so many immigrants over from Ireland. They also meant that periodically the labour market, even for unskilled workers, would be extremely tight. It was during these relatively brief periods of labour shortage that the unions had to maximise their positions in the knowledge that later in the cycle the employers would seek to seize back these gains. In 1854–55 Clyde shipyard workers secured a 57-hour week but had to concede 60 hours again by the early 1860s. In 1866 a 57-hour week was restored and in 1871 this was converted to a 54-hour week on the same wages as 57. By the end of 1872 a 51-hour week had been secured across the Clyde. This gain was reversed to 54 hours in 1877 and 57 hours in 1879 as the slump continued. Fifty-four hours was then regained in the early 1880s.[36]

Compared to England, trade union activity also faced considerable obstacles. The laws of contract and conspiracy were more frequently invoked, and both legally and in terms of recognition by employers, trade unions did not possess anything like the same status. Yet, despite this, despite the massive swings in employment and a very mobile workforce, there were very significant levels of unionisation in Clydeside shipbuilding. Indeed, a number of trades appear to have maintained a virtual closed shop from the 1850s. Greenock's biggest shipbuilding employer reported that 90 per cent of his workers were trade union members in 1866.[37] Riveters are recorded as striking to enforce a closed shop and exclude non-union members in 1866 and again in 1871.[38] Very significantly for our understanding of the environment facing immigrant Irish labour, unionisation appears to have extended to relatively unskilled groups. Rivet heaters are recorded as being on strike in 1866; rivet boys, helpers, holders on and hammermen in 1868; and caulkers in 1871 and in 1872.[39] Foremen, key figures for labour recruitment, were also often union members, generally of the shipwrights union.[40]

Strike action had another notable feature in Clydeside shipbuilding. This was the high level of solidarity action between workplaces and between trades. This involved both the raising of financial support from other workplaces and the provision of alternative employment for strikers. Massive sums were paid out in strike pay – sustained by levies on workplaces not on strike.[41] In 1876 the joiners union made payments totalling £3,300 at a time when a week's wage was approximately £1.40.[42] The immediate employment for strikers elsewhere on the Clyde could be equally effective.[43] For some trades, joiners and painters particularly, employment could also be found outside shipbuilding in domestic house building. In these circumstances a badly handled strike could face employers with a disastrous long-term loss of critical skills – as happened to Denny's shipyard in Dumbarton in 1855.[44]

The employers' response was to take collective action across the Clyde. In 1865, relatively very early in the development of iron shipbuilding on the Clyde, the big employers organised the Clyde Shipbuilders Association to provide collective resistance to workers and specifically to prevent solidarity action between workplaces. Their main tactic of response to strike action was the lockout. This could involve dismissing all workers in a single workplace when one trade went on strike or locking out all workers in one trade across the river. It could also, as in 1866 and 1877, mean locking out every single worker in all twenty-seven main shipbuilding yards in order to cut off all sources of financial support.[45]

In shipbuilding communities, with the population densely clustered around the shipyards, this type of confrontation seems to have generated more general attitudes of community solidarity. Strikes themselves would be highly visible. They involved the display of wall posters announcing strike action which were distributed across all the shipbuilding communities to deter anyone seeking work in a strike-stopped workplace – re-enforced by vigilants or pickets in the vicinity of the workplace.[46] The employers used police to deter pickets and increasingly plain-clothes detectives, sometimes disguised as scabs, to secure convictions. The organised importation of strike-breakers, sometimes from as far afield as Germany, created major set piece confrontations.[47]

Already by the 1860s this relatively newly created workforce was demonstrating high levels of solidarity. The employers' association secretary, John Smith Paterson, described how his association tried to halt a joiners' strike in Greenock by announcing that no firm anywhere on the river would employ union joiners. 'The result was that not only those belonging to a union but also the great proportion of the non-unionists went out. We did not turn them out. They made common cause.'[48] There was also significant organisation between trades. In preparing for strike action to enforce a 57-hour week in 1866 an interim committee was formed representing engineers, smiths, boilermakers, tin smiths, joiners, brass founders and shipwrights. The mass meeting which launched the demand was attended by representatives from 74 different shipyards and engineering works – as well as delegates from Tyne and Teesside.[49] When the Interim Committee initiated action by pulling out workers in selected workplaces, the employers retaliated with a total lockout. This involved all workers, whether union members or not, and included labourers. In Govan the workers met in mass meetings irrespective of trade – with calls being made for unions to create subsidiary sections for labourers.[50] This ethos of solidarity extended to support for other regional shipbuilding centres. At the meeting launching the 57-hour demand in 1866, the secretary William Latta announced that it was 'in solidarity with workers in England whose demand for 57 hours was met by the claim that employers could not compete with the Clyde'.[51] In 1876 collections were taken in support of Belfast workers striking against an attempt to re-impose a 60-hour week.[52]

What is notable in the very full reportage of union activity is the lack of any mention of sectarian conflict or exclusion on the grounds of religion – despite the ethnically very mixed character of the shipbuilding labour force.[53] Semi-skilled trades, such as riveter and caulker, contained significant numbers of both Catholic and Protestant Irish. Yet they were repeatedly to the fore in strike action. Shipyard labourers, many of whom were Irish, worked in squads with riveters, joiners and smiths and in general were not unionised till later in the century. But again there is no mention of labourers being used as strike-breakers. There seems to have been a well-founded expectation that in periods of good trade labourers could readily secure employment outside the industry. A relative freedom of movement appears to have existed between rural and urban markets for unskilled labour as well as a surprising degree of organisation. In 1858 labourers were among the trades listed as represented at the founding meeting of Glasgow Trades Council whose first secretary, Andrew Cumming, was organiser for the Carters and Storemen's Friendly Society.[54] In March 1866 mason's labourers in Edinburgh and Leith, whose Labourer's Society was chaired by a Michael Dolan, went on strike, and the stoppage continued into April during which time many labourers moved through to Glasgow. This strike was reportedly assisted by the shortage of rural labourers and a campaign by farm labourers on wages and hours that spread from the Lothians to west and central Scotland during the year.[55] At the end of March 1866 platelayers on the North British Railway struck for a 10 per cent increase and in May all grades of workers on the Caledonian Railway in south Glasgow are reported as meeting to demand an increase.[56] In January 1870 the Railway Carters of Glasgow were meeting to demand an increase from the two main rail companies operating south of the Clyde. Two months later the horse-keepers for one of the main South Glasgow transport companies were on strike and in September workers on the Caledonian railway operating between General Terminus Quay and Motherwell.[57]

This level of organisation among labourers, even if intermittent, is important for understanding the environment in which Irish immigrants found themselves when they arrived on Clydeside. Unskilled Irish workers finding employment either in the yards or in the carting companies or railways of Glasgow's southside encountered a density of union activity and assumptions that was in stark contrast to the religion-based exclusion that was increasingly characteristic of Ulster workplaces.

We have therefore two quite separate, though related, phenomena that distinguish Clydeside from the urban environment in the north of Ireland. One is the mixing of Catholic and Protestant immigrants in the same workplaces and surrounding locales – a phenomenon which would seem to result from the way labour was recruited and the periodically very high level of demand for semi-skilled and unskilled labour. The other is the experience of unionisation and labour solidarity and the demands this placed on these workers. Analytically, it seems difficult to find a way of distinguishing their relative impact on attitudes and behaviour. Joint work in the same workplace, and familiarity bred by proximity in the surrounding streets, might itself result in tolerance. On the other hand, most studies of ethnic conflict do not see proximity itself as an active factor in overcoming what would be entrenched and historically rooted hostilities. It might be posited, therefore, that labour solidarity was the key causal factor and that the relatively intense confrontations between capital and labour which punctuated the 1860s, 1870s and 1880s were important in challenging attitudes and imposing a different ethos.

It is possible to test, at least partially, for the attitudinal effects of such labour activity by examining the impact of Home Rule on politics in Govan. The demand for Home Rule, and particularly its endorsement by Gladstone in 1886, has been seen as a major catalyst for intensified conflict in the north of

Ireland. In the ensuing riots at least a dozen people were killed and hundreds injured. In Govan the 1885 election (the first after Govan became a parliamentary constituency) and the subsequent 1886 election have a particular interest because of the way they were contested by the owner of the Fairfield yard, William Pearce.

Pearce, a Conservative, bought the yard from the Elders, politically Liberal, in 1878 after previously being their yard manager and then partner. Once in charge, Pearce, originally an Admiralty naval architect at Chatham, took a far more aggressive stance on wages. As chair of the Clyde Shipbuilders Association from the early 1880s, Pearce was the driving force behind the united employer front that faced down demands for wage increases during the boom, using scab labour from England, and in 1885 enforced a 7.5 per cent wage reduction on all iron workers.[58] Pearce's yard increasingly specialised in warship orders, which were generally much more lucrative than merchant shipping. It was probably for this reason that Pearce wanted to reinforce his existing Admiralty links at a higher political level. In 1880 he sought to get elected as a Conservative candidate for Glasgow but was heavily defeated. In 1885 he fought the newly created Govan constituency and won it. He won it again in 1886.

It was his manner of winning in both 1885 and 1886 that is particularly revealing for our purposes.[59] In 1885 the Conservatives were temporarily allied with Parnell. Pearce, whose inclinations would almost certainly have been otherwise, was not able to use the Orange card and the Liberals, after period of intense internal conflict, had selected a radical with socialistic leanings. In what was likely to be an extremely close contest, Pearce decided not to stand as a Conservative. Instead he sought to reinvent himself politically as a 'working man' standing in the interests of Labour. Originally he attempted to get himself nominated as a 'trades' candidate through the good offices of a leading figure in the boilermakers union.[60] When this attempt was spiked by a revolt among the members, he continued to present himself as fighting for the interests of Labour (always capitalised) in what he described as a 'working class' constituency.[61] In face of fierce challenge as to his credentials, he made a series of public statements about his philosophy and policies. His speech to his final public meeting gives an idea of his defensive posture on class issues. 'The address I issued has been very much criticised, and an attempt has been made to show that I am incapable of representing the interests of labour ... the reason put forward is that I am a capitalist.' He then went on to redefine his position. 'If I were a capitalist in the sense that we know a capitalist, if I lent or invested my money in stocks and shares ... and went away from the district in which my money was invested, then what they said might hold good. But I have invested my money in a special industry ... and I am entirely dependent on the labour around me to reap the advantage. Without labour I would be compelled to realise my property.' In face of hostile questioning Pearce then went on to make some remarkable concessions. He announced his support for a trade union amendment to the Employers Liability Act to stop employers opting out – an act to which he had previously been implacably opposed. He backed state intervention to enforce safety on the railways and in shipping and an extension of the Factory Acts. He stopped short of supporting the nationalisation of land but said he would not oppose the nationalisation of railways out of hand.[62] Pearce won by 3,677 to 3,522. His majority of 155 depended on the 300 votes delivered by the local organisers of Parnell's Irish League.

In 1886, by which time Parnell had endorsed Gladstone and the Home Rule section of the Liberal Party, Pearce took a quite different position, and stood as an Anti-Home Rule Unionist. The Liberals put up a Home Rule Irish Protestant, previously Liberal MP for Tyrone. Pearce dropped any pretence of being a labour representative and plastered the constituency with giant red, white and blue Union flag posters. He went out of his way to fan sectarian fears: 'there were two types of Irish vote. One was the loyal Protestant vote. The other was the Irish League Roman Catholic vote.' He explicitly linked a strong empire policy to his ability to secure warship orders and bring employment to the constituency. Pearce's vote went down to 3,574. His Liberal opponent's dropped further to 3,212, giving Pearce victory by a margin of just 362.[63]

The significance of Pearce's candidature is twofold. One is to demonstrate the degree to which Pearce had to acknowledge the mass influence of the trade union movement and to engage with it using a relatively sophisticated level of class discourse. He was not the kind of person who would do this unless he saw it as essential. The second is the relative lack of success of his use of the Orange card in 1886. Pearce got elected but his actual vote went down. The use of anti-Catholic rhetoric scarcely seems to have compensated for the loss of the Irish caucus. According to the *Govan Press*, Pearce's resort to sectarianism was treated with disdain by the majority of working-class voters and, as in 1885, his main electoral appeal derived from his promise to use his parliamentary position to secure more jobs at a time of serious depression. By contrast, Belfast saw its worst rioting of the century in 1886.

No riots occurred in Govan in 1886 and only one in the 1870s. This happened in 1874 when Orangemen returning from the 12 July demonstration in central Glasgow were involved in a fracas with Home Rulers. Three Orangemen and three Home Rulers were arrested. There were no serious injuries and the riot was limited to Govan Road and the area outside the Orange rooms in Portland Street.[64] Across the river in Partick, where there was probably the biggest concentration of Irish Protestants on Clydeside, a serious sectarian riot did occur in 1875. A Home Rule demonstration in honour of O'Connell, held in central Glasgow, was used as the pretext. A Catholic chapel was attacked, there were a number of serious injuries and the Riot Act was read. In Govan, on the other hand, no disturbances occurred in 1875. The magistrates of the Police Burgh took steps after the first day of Partick rioting to swear in 200 special constables. These are described as being secured from the 'the principal shipbuilding yards and consisted of picked men of good character and physique and who were totally unconnected with any religious society or organisation'. The presiding Sheriff stated 'before swearing in, he must ask if any of you were in any way connected with any society on either side – he meant of the Orangemen and the Home Rulers'. One of the local magistrates urged them 'to do their duty irrespective of country or creed'. Another ruled that they should not parade in full formation ('which would be a rather formidable thing') but in detachments of 50.[65] These comments indicate that, while magistrates were aware of potential dangers, they saw them as localised within the Irish immigrant community and sought publicly to distance themselves from any association with loyalism. If sectarianism was being stigmatised it was as a phenomenon associated with the Irish community as a whole and not simply Catholics. In doing so, the magistrates reflected the generally Liberal political alignment of local shipbuilding employers – who were also well aware of their continuing dependence on the supply of Irish unskilled labour. This conduct is in clear contrast to the more provocative stance of the Govan magistrates in 1867–68 when the council was still largely controlled by local small property owners.

Overall, therefore, sectarian hostility does not seem to have had dominating impact on political or social life in Govan and Kinning Park and by the 1880s there appears to have been a fairly conscious rejection by organised labour of any attempt to exploit sectarian attitudes. Earlier the question was posed about causation: of how far it was the level of mass involvement in trade union conflict with employers that changed attitudes. The evidence we have reviewed seems to confirm this was the case. In contrast to Belfast, particular workforces were religiously mixed. In the shipyards union-led activity involved, formally or informally, all grades of workers, whether skilled, semi-skilled or unskilled. It is also clear from the conduct of the two elections in 1885 and 1886 that the language of working-class solidarity was by this stage dominating political discourse on a mass scale. For those coming into the area, especially those with experience of the bitter Ulster conflicts of the 1880s, local employment and residence brought them into contact with an entirely different social universe

Conclusion

This essay on the spatial separation of Protestant and Catholic immigrants in Govan and Kinning Park has shown two things. First, there was a tendency for Protestants and Catholics to live in different streets. Second, the strength of this tendency was quite different from that found in Belfast and other urban centres in the north of Ireland. The patterns established in the 1870s seem to have remained generally constant up to the beginning of the twentieth century and appear to have been closely linked to workplace differentiation. Some at least, at micro-neighbourhood level, seem to have been determined as much by occupational and income factors as religious and ethnic allegiance. These findings are in very strong contrast to the sharply increasing segregation in

Ulster through the 1880s and 1890s. On Clydeside we find a characteristic mixing of Catholics and Protestants *within* unskilled workplaces, especially in the shipyards, and, no less important, in the streets outside. This was definitely not the case in Belfast.

At the outset we asked why this should have been the case. The supposition of this article has been that the main factor was the active process of class formation then taking place on Clydeside. Evidence has been presented on the growing scale of unionisation, the incidence of strike action and the degree to which class-based assumptions had become central to political debate by the mid-1880s.

If this explanation is rejected, it is difficult to find effective alternatives. Some might point to the existence of some wider Scottish 'national' culture that was actively inclusive. But, as a major cause of attitudinal change, this has little to recommend it. Irish immigrants were not automatically 'included' and all suffered discrimination at the hands of the host population on national if not religious grounds. And, in terms of establishment cultures, Scots were distinctly non-inclusive even to each other. Religion split them three ways. The rhetoric of the two main Presbyterian denominations, the Church of Scotland and the Free Church, was both mutually antagonistic and somewhat anti-Catholic. The Episcopal Church, traditionally a haven for Highland immigrants, also took on an increasingly anti-Catholic aspect as it became the main recipient of Church of Ireland Protestants from Ulster.

Employer attitudes and the management of industrial relations could have been an important factor. But again it is difficult to point to any consistent pattern. The position of local shipyard employers in the 1875 was to minimise open sectarian conflict. But this does not seem to have been so much the case in the 1880s. There is Pearce's use of the Orange card in the 1886 election and the evidence of employer attempts to manipulate religious divisions in the docks in 1887 and after.

The only way employer attitudes could be claimed as significant would be in a more indirect manner: patterns of labour recruitment. This was, as we have noted, very important. It meant that Catholics and Protestants worked together in the same yards, and to a large extent in the same labouring and semi-skilled occupations, and consequently, because of the close, work-bound character of residence, lived nearby in the surrounding streets. Compared to the situation in Belfast, the importance of this cannot be overestimated. But, as argued earlier, this itself was probably not enough to overcome deep-rooted hostilities. The active ingredient would appear to have been the prevalent culture of class solidarity – something that the shipyard employers definitely did not encourage.

It might be noted in conclusion that this growing culture of class solidarity was also – within 15 years – reflected in terms of political allegiance. In general, electoral support for the Labour Party in Scotland was lower than in England. But Govan was one of the exceptions. In 1905 the Labour candidate – a pro-Home Rule leader of the boilermakers' union – secured 4, 200 votes, almost a third of the total against Conservative and Liberal opponents. By 1913 Labour candidates in the largely shipbuilding Central Govan and Fairfield wards (by then incorporated into Glasgow) were achieving an amazing 62 per cent of the vote. In the same election Labour also gained a majority in the Kinning Park ward and only failed to win the Plantation ward by 39 votes.[66] The scale of these votes must mean that many Irish Catholics and at least some Irish Protestants were voting Labour. So, in answer to Anthony Hepburn's question as to how far the basis for the post-1920 transformation was laid before 1914, we would be inclined to say that this was very much the case for parts of South Clydeside and particularly perhaps for Govan and Kinning Park – and that, important though Wheatley's intervention was, there were more basic processes of class mobilisation at work as well.

6 Shaping the Scottish Past: Irish migrants and local politics in the Monklands in the second half of the nineteenth century

Geraldine Vaughan

> A missionary canvasses the working classes for their souls just in the same manner as a town councillor canvasses them for their votes.
>
> Patrick McGill[1]

When Daniel Carlin, a native of County Donegal who had emigrated to Airdrie in the late 1840s and had sat as a member of the local parochial boards during half a century, died in 1907, the local paper stated that his death 'removed another of the few remaining links with the Airdrie of nearly half a century ago'.[2] Thus an Irishman, who had fled to Scotland during the Famine years and started off in life as a miner in the Monklands, was being depicted as a link, a connection between two eras of Scottish local history. This suggests that the part played by Irish migrants in towns of central Scotland, especially on the local political scene, has to be reassessed – as it might tell us something more about their part in the making of Scotland's history.

Whereas Irish Catholic participation in national politics, for instance the development of the Home Rule movement in the 1870s, has been thoroughly analysed, less attention has been given to Irish involvement in local politics. In nineteenth-century Scotland, the key to power lay in local institutions, as T. M. Devine puts it: 'Scottish control was still paramount where it mattered most to people in the Victorian period, that is at the level of the city, the burgh, the locality.'[3] Locality is precisely the field where the Irish developed a certain sense of belonging – not only to a place, but perhaps also to the history of this peculiar 'nation without a state'.

The Monklands was a destination favoured by Irish transients: the region lying 20 miles east of Glasgow, with its two main coal-mining and ironworks towns, Airdrie and Coatbridge, was described in the 1850s as 'the nearest thing possible to two Irish colonies'.[4] In the mid-Victorian era, the sons of Erin and their descendants represented up to a third of the total urban population.[5] At that time local politics included a wide range of bodies: from parochial and parish boards to town councils[6] and the school boards established by the 1872 Education (Scotland) Act.[7] What was the participation of Irish immigrants in such bodies? This chapter will focus on Irish Catholics, as little evidence is available for Irish Protestants in local issues, although there seems to be a strong connection between the latter and the temperance movement.

If, in national politics (such as parliamentary elections), the Irish Catholic community was prepared to follow the nationalist guidelines, what happened in local political contests was a very different matter. Hence a close study of Irish involvement in local issues reveals a most interesting aspect of the immigrant community: the perspective is turned upside down – the new question being rather how far were the Irish prepared to forget national unity and give up Irish issues when it came to municipal elections? As regards decision-making within the Catholic Irish community, a re-examination of W. M. Walker's thesis on priestly political domination is required.[8]

In order to tackle these issues, first an overall account of Irish participation in local politics in the Monklands, with reasons for this, the main local Irish leaders involved and the organisation of voting, will be given. Second, the religious issues at stake, with clerical participation in local politics and the religious topics discussed on the various boards, will be examined. The third area to be covered will be the divisions which arose in the Irish community over local matters; and finally the Scottish perception of Irish political involvement.

The primary element to consider in this examination of Irish contribution in local matters is the motive for such an involvement. The first incentive was certainly of a financial nature: Catholic ratepayers' interests were paramount, the aim being to keep the rates as low as possible, or to prevent them from increasing too much.[9] This was especially true in educational matters – where the Catholics were not getting anything back from their rates.[10] This almost became a stereotype; the Catholics were viewed as obsessive misers, as is shown in a letter written to the local newspaper, *The Airdrie Advertiser*, in 1900: 'Here we have four Roman Catholics elected whose prime object ... is to keep down taxation.'[11] Yet this money-saving attitude was regarded as a great quality by Catholics; as the *Glasgow Observer* boasted in 1888, there were none 'more careful and economising than the Catholic members'.[12] The prime reason, therefore, for Irish Catholics entering politics was often an unconstructive or negative one – to oppose increases in the rates – which is the opposite of what they actually achieved by their action on the local boards. Economic interests could also mean the protection of trade – above all the wine and spirit trade;[13] during the 1855–1905 period, out of the ten most prominent Irish Catholic gentlemen, eight were spirit merchants.[14] Indeed, the Irishmen who engaged in the spirit commerce were often very active in local matters, as a means for them to keep an eye on the granting of licences,[15] and to oppose any attempts at passing too severe temperance bye-laws.

Next to keeping the ratepayers' burden lighter, came the religious interest – that of the protection of Roman Catholics who were under the jurisdiction of local councils and boards. This was true of parochial boards, which then became the parish councils (1894). These dealt with the administration of the poor: the churching of Roman Catholic inmates, the boarding out of Catholic children into Protestant families, the paying of school rates for Catholic children attending Catholic schools, the internment of Catholic paupers – such were the most familiar issues the Catholic members on these boards were keen to deal with. The religious question was also the focus in the elected school boards – created by the 1872 Education (Scotland) Act – where the delegates of the voluntary schools were eager to protect their interests.

Although these motives for entering local politics were to be a regular feature during the second half of the nineteenth century, others appeared later on in the period. Municipal socialism and the labour question became important factors in Irish involvement in Monklands politics in the 1890s. For instance, at an Airdrie town council monthly meeting in 1894, the Roman Catholic councillor Alexander McKillop moved that in contracts for the burgh, the working men should be paid the standard wages as agreed by trade unions, because 'the rights of labour should be looked after'.[16] In time, the Irish Catholics promoted their own labour representatives, such as James Donaldson, a miners' agent, elected in the 1894 elections for the Old Monkland School Board,[17] or John Cooper, a Coatbridge craneman, defeated in 1900.[18] At the beginning of the twentieth century, Patrick Agnew, an Irishman active in trade unionism, once the chairman of the first ward electors in Airdrie, was to be found regularly questioning candidates on their views on labour issues.[19] The need to municipalise gas and water companies found strong advocates amongst the Irish Catholic municipal leaders by the late 1890s.[20]

What kind of Irishmen became very involved in local politics? In this 50-year period, around a dozen Catholic laymen natives of Erin (or of Irish origin) became prominent local figures in both Coatbridge and Airdrie.[21] From the biographical details that are available, a few common characteristics emerge: the great majority were born in Ireland and were Ulstermen, they almost all belonged to the merchant class (a majority of them were spirit dealers), they were practising Catholics and very active in the Church, and once they had secured any municipal position they usually remained in place for an extensive period of time.

The first example of a prominent Irishman's journey to local honours was the exceptional career that James McAuley pursued in Airdrie. Born in 1813 in County Donegal, he trained as a teacher and then left for Scotland in September 1836. From 1836, he was a teacher (and then head teacher) at St Margaret's school, Airdrie. He retired in 1860 and then entered the spirit trade, as this left him more time to attend to his local duties. In the late 1850s he had become a member of the New Monkland parochial board, and at the first school board elections in 1873 he was returned for Old Monkland and Airdrie. Even the local newspaper acknowledged his great talent for politics: 'The Almighty had endowed him with the material necessary to constitute a leader. He was well educated, a fluent and ready speaker, a man of sound common sense.'[22] In Coatbridge were found equally brilliant Irishmen, such as Hugh O'Hear, Arthur Malone or Charles O'Neill – who left Glenravel, County Antrim, when he was 15 years old, and arrived in the 'Iron Burgh' in

1865. Originally a spirit dealer, which he remained throughout his life, O'Neill took a degree in medicine and botany at Glasgow University in 1892 (he retired from medical practice in 1898, but remained Assistant Professor of Botany in St Mungo's College). He was a well-travelled man: his undimmed fervour for the national cause – he was a member of the Fenian Brotherhood when a young man in Glasgow – led him to visit America twice, and numerous capitals of Europe.[23] Five years after arriving in the Monklands he was elected member of the Board of Guardians (1870), and in 1887 became a member of the Old Monkland School Board. He acceded to municipal honours in 1893 by being returned as a town councillor, and was appointed bailie in 1898.[24]

The Catholic Irishmen who managed to secure seats on local boards did so mainly through the support of Catholic voters. The problem the historian faces here is of finding a way of evaluating the numerical force of the Catholic vote. The lists of parliamentary and municipal electors give no indication as to the nationality or the religion of the voters. The first distinction however to be made, however, is of the gap between myth and reality, or the Catholic claims of voting power and the numbers actually on the electoral roll. As in national elections, the Irish Catholics boasted about their electoral might. As the *Glasgow Examiner* was proud to announce in a 1903 leader: 'The power and influence of the Irish vote is most eagerly sought in Municipal as well as Parliamentary elections.'[25] Earlier evidence shows the confidence Irish Catholics had as an electoral force to be reckoned with, and that led them to declare in 1862: 'We [Irish Catholics] by our united action have often put in our friends and expelled our enemies ... and [this] enables us to get at the different Civic Boards of the town [Airdrie] and parish every manner of justice and fair play.'[26] In Coatbridge in 1882, Father Thomas O'Reilly complained to the Old Monkland School Board about other members' behaviour, and declared that 'if he had known he was going to receive such treatment on the board, he would have caused his party to have nominated three Roman Catholics – and they would have carried them all.'[27] In 1889, Hugh O'Hear, a prominent local Irishman, declared to the Old Monkland School Board, while discussing the Bill against cumulative voting, that the Catholic body in Coatbridge had never abused its voting powers: – 'we could have returned three members,' he stated, but they voluntarily secured only one seat.[28] These assertions of might could be occasionally turned into a threat. For example, in an 1872 New Monkland Parochial Board nomination, on the refusal of Mr Robertson to withdraw a list of 16 nominees where there was no Roman Catholic, Daniel Carlin, a member of the board, replied that they, as Roman Catholics, had always had four of their number on the parochial board, and added that if Mr Robertson persisted in his refusal, 'we will give you some trouble.'[29]

What was the reality of such proclaimed electoral power? The first point is that, in fact, Irish Catholics managed to secure at least one member on every (parochial and school) board and council throughout the period in question. Was this a satisfactory result compared to their numerical strength? Catholics didn't always seem to think so: the nationalist paper *The Glasgow Star and*

Examiner complained in 1903 of the poor representation on the Coatbridge town council – only two Irish Roman Catholic councillors (John Lavell and Dr O'Neill) amongst the 15 members, when the Roman Catholic population represented one-third of the burgh population.[30] The sources only give scattered evidence of the number of Catholic voters: in 1868, the local paper mentioned 300 Catholic electors from a total of 1,670 (17.9 per cent, not far from a fifth of the total electorate) for Airdrie;[31] in 1895, the *Coatbridge Express* stated that in Airdrie's third ward 100 of the 741 electors were Catholics. As the list of voters for Airdrie in 1894–95 has survived, it gives us an opportunity to put the Irish-sounding name method to the test.[32] Only 59 Irish-sounding Catholic surnames (combined with first names) were counted, which is 40 per cent under the real total.[33] This proportion of fewer than one in five for Airdrie was small compared to the Coatbridge figures, where in 1897, in the fourth ward, 322 Catholic electors were to be found amongst a total of 996 (32 per cent of the electorate). The cumulative vote system for school boards did advantage 'minorities' as every elector was allowed to accumulate an allocation of votes on one candidate if they wished: this introduced some degree of proportional representation, fairer to minorities, and the voting franchise (£4 per annum) ensured a large number of the Irish flock, consisting mainly of labourers, could go to the poll. Thus Catholic candidates were often returned with very decent scores (James McAuley was returned third in the poll in the first Old Monkland School Board elections in 1873, as was Hugh O'Neill in 1891). This was a frequent subject of dispute on school boards, as a 'one candidate, one vote' correspondent put it in a 1900 letter: 'Minorities [Catholics] should scramble on to School Boards by ordinary means same as they do on other boards.'[34] On the whole, whether the Catholic vote represented 20 per cent or 30 per cent of the electorate at best in both towns, it meant that, as Charles O'Neill very frankly put it in a letter written to Archbishop Eyre in 1897, 'in no ward in the Burgh can a Catholic candidate hope to be returned either to the Town Council or the Parish Council, without a very large amount of support from the Protestant electorate.'[35]

Yet if the Catholics had a potentially great electoral force, the first need for local Irish politicians was to ensure that they registered as voters. Thus, Hugh O'Hear's unsuccessful re-election bid to the Old Monkland Parochial Board in 1888 was partly attributed to the fact that 'a lot of his supporters weren't on the rolls'.[36] Canvassing and electoral meetings played a central part in local elections, and Catholic papers insisted on this fundamental necessity: 'Pay your rates. Get your qualification. Look to your votes and those of your neighbours. Be dynamic.'[37] This call for enthusiasm was met in the numerous electoral meetings held throughout the period in both towns. On the Catholic side, political meetings were often held in the church hall and therefore frequently supervised by the local priest.[38] But there were also 'lay' meetings, and as early as 1859 a correspondent to the local paper mentioned that several meetings of Catholic electors had taken place during October in view of the coming Airdrie elections.[39] In November of that same year, a public meeting of electors and non-electors called by hand-bill was presided over by James McAuley and addressed by John Devlin in the Airdrie Assembly Rooms.[40] The practical aspects of elections such as canvassing and campaigning were often met by the local nationalist organisations: even if they were more preoccupied with national and purely Irish matters, getting the Irish Catholic on the voters' rolls for municipal elections (as well as parliamentary) and for the defence of Catholic interests at school boards was one of their essential aims (see, for example, the role of nationalists acting as defenders of Irish Catholics in the Voters' Registration Court).[41] Once the Irish voter was on the roll, the electoral committees wanted to make sure that Catholic electors would go to the polling stations on voting day. Some committees were so efficient that, for example, during the 1891 Old Monkland School Board election, one of its members, to avoid the loss of a voter 'took his place at one in the iron furnaces while the voter went off to the polling station, which was quite far away'.[42] This energy spent in canvassing was acknowledged by Protestant citizens,[43] as is shown in a newspaper commenting in 1900 on the high scores of the Catholic candidates in the Old Monkland School Board election: 'the spoils of the election are to those who canvass hardest.'[44]

Mixing political and religious matters was a characteristic of the Irish Catholic community, as W. M. Walker stated: 'Irish Catholic parochial life was a way of life, and one in which religious, political, economic, educational and recreational elements were so fused as to form a culture from which total withdrawal was unlikely and partial withdrawal appeared as inconsistency.'[45] In that perspective (although Walker's use of the word 'inconsistency' is undoubtedly excessive) priests were to play a key role in every form of politics – whether local or national. One particular institution which received the Catholic clergy's full attention from 1872 onwards was the school boards, on which many local clergymen were very active.[46] The *Glasgow Observer* explained in an 1888 leader: 'We can return our representatives to the Boards where they will act usefully in many ways. In most cases the Catholic representative is the Reverend manager of the schools in the district.'[47] In fact, the Monklands might have figured as an exception to this rule, at least in the first (1873) school board elections. Interestingly, the question of clerical participation on school boards – Protestant or Catholic – was a matter of debate in the region. In 1873 the main local newspaper's leader stated it would be best not to have any clergymen appointed on the boards because of the numerous different religious denominations; in that way, sectarianism would be avoided.[48] To this, the local priests reacted differently: in Airdrie, Father James McIntosh, the senior priest of St Margaret's Church, agreed to stand down in favour of a Catholic layman for election (to the discontent of some of his parishioners),[49] whereas in Coatbridge Father Michael O'Keeffe of St Patrick's Church[50] stood in the election with two other Catholic laymen, only to be defeated.[51] After the death of James McAuley, in 1881, Father Michael O'Keeffe sent the Old Monkland School Board a letter stating that a meeting of the Catholic parishioners had agreed on the nomination of Father Thomas

Reilly to replace the late member: the board unanimously agreed to it.[52] In the 1873–1903 period (during which 11 triennial elections were held), while the Airdrie School Board remained the Catholic laymen's realm, on the Old and New Monkland School Boards local priests sat at regular intervals.[53] This clerical involvement in local school board management implied active participation in electoral meetings, canvassing and so on. As already mentioned, the church hall and schoolroom provided a convenient meeting place for Catholic electors in the Monklands. For example, in 1891, Father Michael O'Keeffe, in view of the forthcoming school board elections, gave use of his schoolroom to the electoral committee preparing for the election and nightly attended the meetings during the month of April.[54] But how far were the local priests actually engaged in local politics?

The influence exercised by Catholic clergymen, in all aspects of Irish Catholic life (in spiritual as well as political matters), has been described by W. M. Walker as being of a dictatorial nature.[55] He mostly relied on the example of Dundee to prove his thesis: but in the area we are considering, the Monklands, Catholic clergymen do not fit this profile. On the whole, Catholic priests in Airdrie and Coatbridge cannot be accused of dictating to their parishioners.[56] There were, however, exceptions amongst them, and the involvement of one priest in local politics will be detailed at length in view of the turmoil it caused in the Irish Catholic community. Father John Hughes, born in County Kilkenny in 1850, was familiar with the Monklands: from 1877 to 1883 he served as an assistant priest in St Margaret's, Airdrie, and in 1892 he was appointed to St Augustine's Church, Langloan (Burgh of Coatbridge). This Irish clergyman was very charismatic. He was described as a 'priest of the most prepossessing character. Handsome, witty, and full of zeal ... His fame as a lecturer began too, at this early period ...'[57] He had a natural gift for politics. He was very active in local matters, and 'at School, Parochial and Parliamentary elections he was a force to be reckoned with'.[58] However, his intense participation was not appreciated by all the Irish Catholics in the district, and a series of incidents took place from 1892 onwards. Father Hughes' lead in the temperance movement led to him being labelled a 'modern Father Mathew', and his fight against the evils of drink was so determined that he resolved not to support Irish Catholic spirit dealers in local elections because he considered them first as publicans, and their religious creed made little difference. His crusade against spirit merchants and his strong involvement in local politics led to division within the Irish Catholic community. In the 1892 Coatbridge Town Council elections, Father Hughes and the 'Temperance Party' gave their support to two Protestant candidates in the third and fifth wards of Coatbridge, namely Mr Dick and Mr Fleming, opposing two prominent Irish Catholic men (spirit dealers), Dr Charles O'Neill and John Lavell. This led to the defeat of Dr O'Neill in the third ward by only 39 votes, to the candidate's great surprise: ' I had so far succeeded in establishing my position with the Protestant electors in the ward that I had every title to anticipate success had it not been for the grossly unfair and totally unexplainable conduct of Fr Hughes in connection with the election.'[59] What seemed even more unjust to the unfortunate Irish candidate was that Mr Dick was not a professed teetotaller, and was supported by the priest only to oppose the spirit dealer. John Lavell, the other Irish candidate, managed to secure his seat, but he was reported to have called Father Hughes' attitude 'clerical dictation'. The latter supported his own Roman Catholic candidate in this election, Charles Quinn, an Irish Catholic teetotaller, who lost against Mr Smellie, the Protestant candidate.

Not only did Father Hughes anger lay Catholics – he also entered into conflict with fellow priests. At the Old Monkland parish elections of 1895, he encouraged John Cooper, an engineman, to contest the fourth ward, where Father Curran (of St Mary's, Whifflet) was already a candidate.[60] In Charles O'Neill's opinion, the running of two Roman Catholic candidates for this ward divided the votes and resulted in no Catholic being elected at all.[61] Father Hughes' attitude in local elections caused his neighbouring fellow priests to be very upset: in 1897, Canon McCay, of St Patrick's, Coatbridge, who nearly resigned because of Father Hughes' behaviour, wrote to the archbishop: '... my opinion of Father Hughes' conduct at recent municipal elections, and former ones. I am of the same opinion still – and nothing I am sorry to say has occurred since the election to lead me to alter it or to withdraw the charge I had made against him at the chapter meeting, viz. that to him was due on that occasion the defeat of the Catholic candidate by a Protestant.'[62] Canon McCay was referring here to the 1897 school board elections in Coatbridge, where Father Hughes brought forward, against the wishes of the other local priests and the vicar general, Dr Maguire, a miners' agent, John Donaldson, whose catholicity was contested. In November that year, at the town council elections, Father Hughes chose not to support Bailie Benson, the Irish Catholic spirit merchant seeking re-election (a 'universally popular' figure amongst Protestants and Catholics)[63] in the fourth ward (Benson stood against Mr Arnott, a Scottish spirit merchant). Father Hughes proclaimed that he was going to abstain from voting for either of the two, and he 'made a house to house visitation of the Catholic electors in his division of the ward ... [stating] he had decided to keep his vote in his pocket and give it to neither of the candidates, and he would expect his parishioners to be guided by his example'.[64] An interesting insight into Father Hughes' canvassing methods was given on a former occasion (1894) when he remained all day at the entrance of the polling station, throwing 'abusive and insulting epithets to all he suspected to be voting for Benson [the Catholic spirit merchant candidate]'.[65] Thus this 'Modern Father Mathew' managed to anger his fellow ministers (in 1894, Canon McCay wrote that Father Hughes' attitude brought 'scandal – division amongst Catholics and the humiliation of the Catholic candidates')[66] and parishioners (even the very temperate and faithful Catholic Charles O'Neill described him as 'tyrannical and overbearing', and a 'Demon of discord'). This very exceptional case was linked to the strong personality and charisma of the priest: overall, if parish priests did have an influence in local elections in the Monklands, their role could not be generally described as dictatorial. The very fact that Father Hughes' attitude caused such chaos in the Irish Catholic community is proof that not all priests behaved in this authoritative way. As Charles O'Neill concluded in his long letter to the archbishop in 1897: 'no people under Heaven, but the Irish Catholics would stand the severe test to which they have been put, and this severe strain to which their faith has been put by his [Father Hughes'] general conduct'.[67] Thus, as John McCaffrey put it, on the subject of priests and politics: 'The stereotype of the Irish parish priest with his overpowering influence in moulding the attitudes of his flock through the schoolroom and the pulpit has to be seen, too, with the context of time. The influence of the clergy on their parishioners ... could have its local variations.'[68]

Other than clerical participation, the second aspect to consider here is the religious issues that arose in local politics, and the Irish Catholic response to them. The Catholics were anxious to secure seats on parochial, and later on parish boards: it was essential that the interests of the Irish Catholic poor should be looked after. Father McIntosh, in a letter addressed to the archbishop, wrote: 'The absence of Catholic members for the operations of the Parochial Board would be a serious evil. In Airdrie it would be simply disastrous.'[69] The Catholics' first concern was probably for children boarded in the poor-house or boarded out in Protestant families: it was feared what might become of them if they were brought up in a 'Protestant atmosphere'.[70] Various concerns could arise from the Catholic inmates (children and adults) boarded at poor-houses.[71] The Irish Catholic members were careful to ensure that the inmates could go to Mass freely and be taught the Catholic catechism. For example, at a meeting of the Poor-house Committee of the New Monkland Parochial Board in April 1865, James McAuley, the Irish Roman Catholic member, mentioned the case of Thomas Barrett, who had been sent to the poor-house as a test case by the inspector, and suggested that he might now be allowed to go out to the Catholic chapel on Sundays.[72] However the commission decided he be kept in for another three months, as he had already fled for a period of three days on a previous occasion. In 1892, Hugh O'Hear, the Irish Catholic member of the Old Monkland Parochial Board, fought against the rule that Catholic inmates should be debarred from attending Mass before a trial period of three months in the poor-house. The poor-house governor answered that the three-month period was necessary to assess their behaviour and morality before granting them this permission.[73] Nevertheless, after a lively discussion, O'Hear's motion that the inmates should be allowed to attend Mass at Whifflet under supervision was passed.[74] A variety of religious matters was discussed, ranging from the providing of Roman Catholic prayer books,[75] to the burial of Catholic paupers in the Catholic cemetery.[76] Concerning education, the parochial board, on examining parents' applications, could pay school fees: in 1878, for example, Father James McIntosh replied to the New Monkland Parochial Board which had requested a reduction in the fees of the Catholic school for children taken in charge by the board, that the fees could not be reduced, and that there were only 13 pauper children attending the school.[77]

On school boards, a wide range of material problems connected with religion arose. At first, the presence of Roman Catholic members on certain committees was not easily accepted: for example, in 1882 members on the Old Monkland School Board objected to the presence of a Catholic minister on the committee of a Protestant school.[78] Catholic members sought to protect Catholic children frequenting board schools: in 1873 McAuley opined that if the Shorter (Presbyterian) Catechism were to be taught in board schools, Roman Catholic children should be able to leave the class while this religious instruction was taking place.[79] The interest of fee-paying and rate-paying Catholics was defended by Catholic board members. For instance, the issue of double fees paid by Irish Catholic working men was tackled by the boards: in March 1878 James McAuley presented the parochial board with a list of 62 children whose parents had to pay double fees (the employers of the Summerlee Colliery, for instance, deducted one penny a week from wages to maintain a works Protestant school which Catholic children did not attend).[80] The school board members resolved unanimously to 'intimate all the public works that this practise ought to be discontinued henceforth'.[81] Keeping the rates low was an electoral motto for Catholics; thus, Irish Catholic members often supported motions against the increase of teachers and headmasters' salaries,[82] or the erection of a new school that did not seem desperately needed. The welfare of Catholic teachers was promoted by Catholic representatives: although the motion was not carried forward, Hugh O'Hear and Charles O'Neill in 1903 voted that the retirement allowances of Catholic teachers be paid by the school boards.[83] Often Catholic clergymen were appointed to the committee of management of a specific school, because of their experience as school managers. For instance, in April 1882, Father Thomas O'Reilly was appointed to the committee of Faskine school, one of the public schools managed by the board. Another member, Mr Allan, commented that he 'also thought that Mr O'Reilly would make an efficient member of school committee, as the Catholic schools were conducted on a much cheaper scale ... [this would] give the members of the Old Monkland School Board a lesson.'[84] Four Catholic members were appointed to committees at the Old Monkland School Board in April 1906: they were present on the 'Technical and Continuation Schools'; the 'Coatbridge and Gartsherrie Academy Schools' (as well as all the other schools committees); the 'Finance and Law'; and the 'School Attendance and Drill' committees.[85]

As 1903 began, the *Glasgow Examiner* boasted about the new comfortable social position acquired by Irish immigrants in the west of Scotland: 'Socially, also our people have progressed by leaps and bounds ... in the Town Boards we have representatives; a large number of gentlemen have been placed on the Justices of the Peace roll.'[86] In this statement, the new local political posts acquired by Irish migrants were cited as a sign of respectability, a notion dear to Victorian mentalities. It must be stressed here that the decorum that went along with municipal positions contributed to this newly acquired uprightness. The Irish Catholic municipal leaders became respectable and important figures of local life: regular sketches of their career were reported in the local Protestant press, in a laudatory tone. For example, Alexander McKillop, the first Roman Catholic councillor to be elected in Airdrie (1887), elected bailie in 1891, and who became JP in 1898, was thus described in the *Advertiser*: 'Mr McKillop was for some years the Irish leader (Co. Mayo) in the Parliamentary Debating Association and possesses a fluent speech and florid oratory; he has frequently lectured with marked appreciation ... Mr McKillop is a keen politician ... He is president of the local branch of the *National League*, vice-president of the *Airdrie Liberal Association*, and is now president of the *Airdrie Burns Club*.'[87] The Burns Club gave annual suppers, where local Irish leaders such as Alexander McKillop or Charles O'Neill took a prominent part, along with the most respected Scottish personalities of the town. The Irish members who took part in club gatherings or town council dinners did not object to toasting the Royal Family repeatedly,[88] whilst on various boards their reluctance to celebrate the British Crown was shown on different occasions.[89] Obituaries[90] offer a good source to demonstrate the respectability Irish gentlemen had acquired: when James McAuley died in 1881, the chairman of the Old Monkland School Board recalled his 'gentlemanly and courteous bearing toward his colleagues';[91] and when Daniel Carlin died in 1907, he was deemed as 'one of Airdrie's oldest and most respected townsmen';[92] while the late ex-bailie Bannen was described as a man 'possessing high ideals of citizenship' and was 'held in the highest esteem by all classes and creeds in the community'.[93] However, if some prominent Irish men achieved respectability, this was not the case for all the Irish community. Did this create tensions between the newly respectable middle-class Irishmen and the ordinary Irish working-class men? W. M. Walker, in the article quoted earlier, portrays the Dundee Irishmen's rejection of middle-class values, viewed as Presbyterian (for example, temperance and thrift). In a book written by a Dundee priest, *Boyhood of a Priest*, a quest for local and worldly fame by some Irishmen was perceived as treason by the Irish working classes: the example given was the famous case of 'Lord Provost O'Donnell', a notorious 'turncoat', who '... pitched his religion overboard and joined up with the genteel Freemasons and the Town Councillors. When a man appeared in a public house with a new collar and tie, he would be warned that he would be walking in the footsteps of Lord Provost O'Donnell.'[94] There is no evidence of this type of relation within the Irish Monkland communities. But if such social tension did not seem to be central in the Irish community, there was scope for political division in local matters.

Although Irish Catholics tended to vote according to nationalist instructions, the local elections were a different matter altogether. Voting orders in local elections were seldom given by the nationalist organisations, probably owing to the diversity of situations to be found in each particular town. A general guideline was handed out by the organiser of the Irish National League, D. J. Sheehan, in 1891, on municipal elections: when these were 'contested on political principles', the branches should 'support those candidates only who are supporters of Mr Gladstone's Irish policy'.[95] Thus, the main nationalist recommendation throughout the period examined was to favour, as in national politics, the Liberal Party. However, as D. J. Sheehan put it, this was true when local elections were disputed on political principles, which was not always the case. Hence, political division amongst Irish Catholic voters in local elections can be identified as early as 1859: a controversy in the *Airdrie and Coatbridge Advertiser* revealed that some 'renegade' Catholics had supported Tory candidates in the late municipal elections.[96] In 1860, an electoral meeting called by an Irishman, John Devlin, and chaired by James McAuley, was organised in support of two Conservative candidates, Mr Brown and Mr Fleming.[97] Surviving Airdrie municipal poll books (1861–67) give us an interesting insight into the political behaviour of different local Irishmen. Throughout this six-year period, the choices of at least five local prominent Irishmen (out of the claimed 25 voters)[98] who could be identified were examined.[99] The Scottish candidate in competition for municipal honours did not always claim a political allegiance, but an examination of the local Liberal paper the *Airdrie and Coatbridge Advertiser* is useful in deciphering the political preferences of the contestants. Besides, the key to Irish voting was given in an 1862 leader, in which an Airdrie Catholic was quoted: 'our mode of action in Airdrie ... we, some fifteen years ago, adopted the two following resolutions', that were firstly, always to hold a Catholic meeting where each candidate would be examined and 'the best men selected', and secondly, to be unanimous on three candidates 'leaving each other the power of voting for whom we please for the fourth'.[100] The analysis of the poll books reveals that such a pattern was usually followed: as a rule, the Irish went together to the polling station, at the same time of the day, and their choices, if different, varied over one or two men at the most. The Irishmen voted both for Conservative and Liberal candidates,[101] but their choices within that might differ: two Irishmen generally represented opposite tendencies, namely James McAuley (Liberal) and John Lavell of Airdrie (Conservative). Nevertheless voting patterns changed from one election to another: for example, in 1861, all Irishmen but John Lavell voted for three Liberal candidates and another who was 'the publicans' candidate' (Mr Black)[102] whereas John Lavell voted for two Conservative and one Liberal nominee.[103] Another controversy divided the Irish Catholic electors in 1862: at the Catholic meeting preceding the municipal elections, 15 members had promised to vote for Matthew Thom, a Liberal slater. In fact, on the way to the polling station, the Tory committee managed to convince four of them to vote for Conservative candidate.[104] This affair led to a heated correspondence published by the *Glasgow Free Press* (from this example one can see that the Irishmen identified in the poll books were predominantly Liberal). Each party accused the other of corruption, and some argued that they had not voted for Thom as he 'had opposed the admission of Roman Catholics on the Parochial Board'.[105] This led Thom to answer these charges in the same newspaper: 'I always believed and still adhere to that belief that Catholics are entitled, as a matter of right, to a fair representation at the Parochial Board.'[106] A few years later, in 1865, all Irishmen selected two Tory and two Liberal contestants.[107] From the results shown in Figure 6.1, it can be seen that the Conservatives got a fare share of the Irish Catholic polling; but this simply seems to confirm that in local elections, personal friendship and business relations played a greater role than political beliefs.

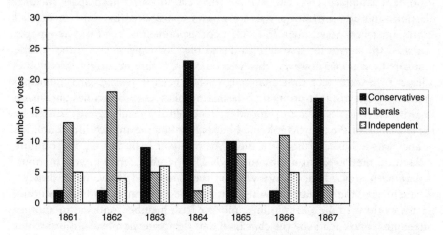

Figure 6.1 The Irish Catholic vote (number of recorded votes) in Airdrie municipal elections, 1861–67. Source: Airdrie Municipal Poll Books (1861–67)

The Irish Catholic community also split on matters other than purely political ones: as mentioned earlier, the temperance question could be a serious source of division. We reviewed Father John Hughes' involvement on that subject, with his promotion of temperance reformers as opponents to Irish Catholic candidates. The involvement of most prominent local Irishmen in the spirit trade was a steadfast feature of that period, as Dr O'Neill, himself a spirit merchant, explained in 1897: 'Some of us have been in the district for over a quarter of a century, and all the time have identified ourselves with the spirit trade [the] only business which we [the Irish Catholics] can practise with any hope of earning a livelihood.'[108] In that sense, temperance advocates were bound to oppose Irish publicans, who formed the majority of Irish Catholic candidates. In 1893, an Airdrie Catholic temperance writer and worker, Mary Grass, addressed a letter to the third ward Catholic electors asking them not to vote for Bailie McKillop, who although not a spirit dealer had acquaintances in the trade, but to support Peter Horn, a Scottish temperance worker.[109] The Irish spirit trade was sometimes accused of having links with the Tory Party: in a letter sent to the *Glasgow Observer* in 1895, a correspondent accused Irish publicans of having favoured a Tory candidate (John Benson, an Irish publican) in the 1894 Coatbridge municipal elections and also of having abused the Liberal one.[110] Furthermore, division within the community could be reflected by division of Irish Catholic members on local boards: for example, a much disputed issue in the Coatbridge Town Council in 1899, the reappointment of the town clerk, was approached in different ways by Irishmen, as Dr O'Neill voted against his reappointment, and Councillors Lavell and Bannen, along with the provost, voted in favour of the clerk.[111]

How were the Catholic Irish in local political life perceived by their Scottish Protestant counterparts? The will of Irish Catholics to participate in local elections and administration was not always appreciated by some prejudiced Protestant fellow townsmen. In 1868, a correspondent of the local newspaper criticised the Tories for having introduced the 'No Popery' cry in the Airdrie municipal elections; however, this seemed to be a rare occurrence, as it was alleged to be 'the first time that religion has been imported into municipal matters'.[112] Discrimination against Irish Catholics was sometimes shown on boards. Thus, in 1860, a correspondent reported the insulting words used by the chairman of the New Monkland board regarding the application of an Irish pauper whose husband had just died: 'Ay, my; you Irish as soon as you have a claim on the Parish, you die', to which Mr McAuley replied, with humour: 'I have been upwards of twenty years in the Parish and I have never died yet – (laughter) – and the last thing that either a Scotchman or an Irishman does in this world is to die'; Mr Collins, another Irish member, retorted to another offending remark made by the chairman that the expression 'was insulting, not only to the Irish applying for relief, but to the Irish members of the Board'.[113] In 1870, at a New Monkland Parochial Board meeting, James McAuley accused the chairman, J. C. Waddel, of excluding Roman Catholics from the House Committee.[114] The presence of Orangemen on school boards did not help soften sectarianism: in 1901, John Carter, master of a Coatbridge Loyal Orange Lodge and member of the Old Monkland School Board, complained about the presence of Roman Catholics on the board, by denouncing the 'impudence of Romanist meddling' with Protestant affairs.[115] When the Church of Scotland pastor Joseph Primmer,[116] well-known for his anti-Catholic views, addressed a Coatbridge audience in July 1901, he thundered: 'It is a disgrace … that in Coatbridge there should be 4 Papists looking after the education of their Protestant children,' and added 'while Protestants vote for them!'[117] Primmer was certainly always very extreme in his perception of Catholics, but nonetheless it can be said that many Protestant citizens tended to think that Catholics were not fit nor able to work on school boards, and that their numbers on boards were certainly too great. What were the accusations levelled by Protestant citizens at the Catholics on school boards? One essential reproach was that, in Protestant eyes, Catholics, in general, were less concerned with education. In 1875, a letter addressed to the local newspaper, signed 'Pat' and written in a simulated Irish brogue, entitled 'Paddy's opinion of schoolmasters and school boards', summed up the opinion Protestants had of Irish Catholic interest in education. In his letter, 'Paddy' pleaded against those 'skool boords', wondering why children had to be sent to school, when they should be at work, bringing back some money to allow their parents to 'have a drop of the crathur' – or, in other terms, to indulge in some drink.[118] This low opinion of Catholic educational prospects was linked to general prejudice against Roman Catholicism, commonly associated with ignorance, superstition, anti-Bible reading and so on. Moreover, why would Catholics be concerned in the least about the education of Protestant children? For Catholics were supposedly on school boards only to 'keep the rates low' and why should they care when they did not send their children to board schools?[119] As a correspondent to the local newspaper wrote in 1900: 'four Roman Catholics elected, whose prime object ... is keeping down taxation, and when it comes to touching the local purse, not to further education but to prevent it'.[120] Of course these were extreme, though not infrequent, views. A good majority of citizens simply thought that the Catholics were over-represented: as a correspondent of the local paper put it in 1900: 'I do not wish to say a word against our local Catholics, or to imply that we should not have some of them on Board, as under a system of single voting, I would have supported one or two of them, but, under such a system it is certain we should not have had so many as four.'[121]

Yet, on the whole, these incidents were quite rare, and the Scottish response to Irish participation in the town's affairs was one of acceptance and furthermore, in some cases, of gratitude.[122] The keen interest and active partici- pation of Catholic Irish councillors on local boards was recognised by their Scottish counterparts: for instance, James McAuley's devotion to parochial affairs was described at his death in 1881 by his colleagues as follows: 'For nearly half a century Mr McAuley had laboured earnestly in the interest of the Board and proved himself an able Counsellor in all matters of difficulty and of great assistance in managing its affairs. He had served on all its committees [New Monkland Parochial Board], and was intimately acquainted with its business in all its details so that his loss will now be keenly felt.'[123] On the work accomplished by Catholic members on school boards, a Protestant correspondent of the *Advertiser* stressed the 'important work [that] is done by R.C. members shows their fitness and willingness to take a full share of this responsibility in the educational interests of the Parish'.[124] On ex-Bailie Bannen's death in 1907, his long-term services to the town of Coatbridge were saluted: 'He fulfilled the duties of his position [as bailie] during his term of office with uniform dignity and with great acceptance to the community ... his colleagues – with whom he was always on terms of friendly intimacy ...'.[125] This friendliness referred to had its proof in electoral campaigns, where the Protestant vote was necessary to all Irishmen wanting to be returned. In 1868, when James McAuley was candidate for the Airdrie municipal elections, an 'election ballad' published in the Liberal *Advertiser* celebrated the formidable Irishman:

Ho! for the gallant Irishman,
M'Auley, tried and true !
Stand by him, Scottish Liberals,
As oft' he stood by you.

For where the fight was hottest
He aye was in the van
And staunch of heart and strong of arm
Was that real Irishman.[126]

Thus, electoral committees were found to be 'mixed': in 1895 there were ten Protestants and three Irish Catholics on the electoral committee of Mr McGeehan, who was standing as a candidate in the New Monkland Parish Council elections.[127]

On the whole, overall acceptance of Irish Catholic involvement in local matters was certainly a sign of a change that was gradually taking place (although this slow change did not follow a linear progression in time, as the Irish Catholics were to encounter great obstacles to integration in the inter-war period),[128] and the best example of what status could be achieved by local participation is that some prominent Irishmen ended up being considered almost as Scottish. On the occasion of ex-Bailie Bannen's death, the local newspaper wrote of him: 'his parents migrated when he was but a child, so that he may be said to have been a native of the burgh'.[129] John Lavelle, quoted earlier, a second-generation Irishman (his father emigrated from County Armagh to Airdrie in 1845), born in 1857 in Airdrie, who started his public career as a member of the Airdrie School Board and later became a member of Coatbridge Town Council before rising to the provostship was a striking example of local ascent. As James Knox, Lord Lieutenant of Lanarkshire, wrote in a foreword to John Lavelle's memoirs, *Looking Back* (a memorial volume) published in 1934: 'To quote his own words, "I have always felt a strong affection for the town in which I was born". He revelled in its history and traditions of which he was proud ... In short, the spirit of *local patriotism* was born in him.'[130] In this Scottish man's own words, a patriotism that overcame national differences existed, and the 'striking figure as he rose from the Irish benches to address the "House"' (Lavelle was a member of the local Parliamentary Debating Association) symbolised this merging of national characters into local pride.

Looking at Irish attitudes within the world of local politics helps us take a different view of involvement and divisions within the community. National elections offer a more, if not united, at least compact vision of Irish political mindsets, whereas in the world of municipal fights, individual priorities emerged. Some Irish would vote first as professionals (publicans defending their trade, for instance), while others had in mind social issues (emergence of labour politics in the late 1890s) – on the whole, various groups had their own agenda: the clergy's, the liberals' and so on. A subject certainly needing further investigation is the relationship between local Irish Catholic politicians and the nationalist movement:[131] in the Monklands, some of the prominent local Irishmen were also great figures in the Irish Nationalist Party in Scotland. Could the local political experience acquired on councils and boards be wisely used in national politics? Dr Charles O'Neill's political talents were acknowledged in the local press in 1909: 'Even those who most profoundly disagree with his politics will admit that Dr O'Neill's ability and wide experience as a public man, his life-long consistency, and his unfaltering devotion to the Nationalist cause ...' [132] The doctor was competing, for the second time, as a candidate in the South Armagh by-election, which he won.

With local governance, what made Scotland Scotland was fast reappearing;[133] and the Irish were certainly part of this movement. By participating intensively in specifically Scottish institutions, such as education (as McCaffrey put it: 'the educational system retained many of its traditional features and continued to mark out Scottish life in significant ways in its adaptation to British norms') [134] and by challenging the two other pillars of Scottish identity (namely the Presbyterian religion, along with law and order), Irish migrants were decisive in shaping modern western Scotland. This was a key to integration, as McCaffrey argued: 'Political activity necessarily entailed some involvement with issues and personalities outwith this parochial framework and therefore aided, albeit haltingly and with painful adjustments, integration into Scottish society.' [135] Whether the Monklands Scots approved of or condemned this phenomenon, they had no choice but to witness the slow rise of the sons of Erin in their local institutions.

7 A Winnowing Spirit: Sinn Féin in Scotland, 1905–38

Máirtín Ó Catháin

Writing in the early 1950s, the Glasgow Irish writer Colm Brogan declared: 'There is no reason why an Irishman of the third or fourth generation should fear to speak of "Ninety-Eight", but it would be a relief if he spoke of something else.'[1] Such a statement may well reflect Brogan's personal background rather than the broader socio-cultural observation it claims to make. His father, Denis, had forsaken the rural poverty of Killult, Falcarragh in County Donegal for the bustle and prosperity of Glasgow where he set up business in the 1880s. He became prominent in the Irish language movement through Conradh na Gaeilge[2] (or the Gaelic League), established in the city in 1895, but was also a member of the Irish Republican Brotherhood (IRB), or in colloquial parlance, he was a Fenian.[3] He was the first and last of that famous Glasgow dynasty, however, to tread the path of the archetypal Irish rebel, and his son's exasperation with the concerns of the 'old country', besides their apparent personal nature, were not at all unique. Sinn Féin, vibrant and well-established in Brogan's Scotland of the 1950s, was nonetheless an aberration – a cry from the margins of the Irish immigrant community as well as in the wider context of Scottish society. Such had been the case for a considerable length of time and the study of Sinn Féin's discordant voice across the space of four decades from 1905 to 1938 throws up some interesting aspects of the modalities of political change in the Irish community in Scotland (i.e. those born and descended from Irish immigrants), and their wider cultural significance.

I

The typology of physical force Irish republicanism, with which Sinn Féin became inexorably linked, had a long history in Scotland prior to that party's emergence. Indeed, one may well cite its antecedents in the aforementioned conflagration of 1798 with the exodus of numerous United Irishmen to Scotland after the collapse of that insurrectionary effort. However, more sustained attempts at forming an active organisational caucus among Irish republicans in Scotland did not take place until the later 1840s, when divergence from the much larger and more influential Repeal-Chartist axis, enabled the physical force men to chart a course towards Ireland that terminated abruptly with the dismal failure of the 1848 Young Ireland rebellion and its continued splutterings into 1849.[4] Of course, by this time,

Irish immigration had taken on immense proportions as a result of the potato famine. These people formed a generation whose memories, when added to their experiences in exile, were to inform the character and content of Irish nationalism in Scotland for the remainder of the century. After the quiescence of the 1850s, Irish republicanism not only made a comeback in the 1860s, but re-invigorated into the movement known as Fenianism or the IRB, which became established from a base in Glasgow soon after its foundation in Dublin on St Patrick's Day, 1858. With moderate constitutional nationalism largely sterile throughout the 1860s, the Fenians were able to carry the weight of Irish immigrant support in their pursuance of the Irish Republic, which would call home its 'wild geese' after freedom had been enthroned. How it proposed to create the economic turnaround in the British trade-dependent and impoverished island of their birth and extraction in order to facilitate the exiles' return was never coherently explained and was secondary anyway to the severing of the colonial link. The return motif should not be overemphasised – many, if not most immigrants simply longed to strike a retaliatory blow against the memory of the potato famine and the ongoing condition of exile, with its isolation, alienation, sectarian strife and socio-economic exploitation. It was a proxy movement which assimilated a variety of grievances and directed them against British rule in Ireland. This is not at odds with a genuinely held belief in the tenets of Irish republicanism, and such sentiment was imbued through a process of song and story in the warrens of the Briggait and the Cowcaddens as well as in the hills of Breffny or St. Columb's Wells in Derry. From here, Fenianism spread widely in Scotland aided by a succession of organisers as well as a spirit of self-organisation; and estimations of some 8,000 members by 1865 are not unreasonable. The collapse of the 1867 rising, though, and further set-backs in Scotland including the execution of the Glasgow IRB man, Michael Barrett in 1868, followed by the slow rise of the Home Rule movement scythed down membership to around a core of about 400 men by the later 1870s. This number rose during the 1880s but had settled down to a figure of 1,700 or so by 1898.[5] Obviously, the Irish community in Scotland had itself undergone substantial change during the second half of the nineteenth century. Firstly, Irish Protestant immigration, especially from Ulster, had increased in the 1870s in tandem with a wider campaign for Catholic education to be state-supported alongside the macro campaign for Irish Home Rule. The restoration of the Scottish Catholic hierarchy in 1878 and the establishment of the Land League in Scotland in different ways brought increasing numbers of the Irish into domestic political concerns, and the Liberal Party's support for Home Rule in the 1880s increased this trend.[6] There was thus a more heterogeneous Irish community in Scotland by the close of the nineteenth century – a mix of generations, religious denominations, political beliefs and priorities, which cut across class, culture and even individual families. Despite this, there remained a lively and collective sense of Irishness in a sub- or internal contextual form within the overarching or external context of Scottish society.

II

Sinn Féin made its appearance in Scotland at a time when the element had almost completely burned out of Fenianism. For more than a generation, if not from its very inception, the IRB had utilised the literary society as a front for its activities and as a means to initiating prospective recruits into the coda and culture of physical force Irish republicanism. In the 1860s it was the National Brotherhood of St Patrick; in the 1870s, the John Mitchel Irish National Association, '82 clubs and '98 clubs; and in the 1880s and 1890s, the most well-known, the Young Ireland Societies. However, a disastrous and abortive re-ignition of the dynamite wing of Fenianism in 1896 which largely terminated in Glasgow, and the death of the IRB's leader in Scotland for almost three decades, John Torley of Duntocher, near Clydebank in 1897, led Fenians in Scotland into something approaching terminal decline. In Greenock, a Young Ireland Society lasted on into 1899 and in Glasgow the Irish National Club, consisting of about 200 members, was founded the same year to replace the defunct Glasgow Young Ireland Society. It represented an ageing generation of Fenians, though, who were, on the whole, neither able nor willing to do much more than maintain a tradition in exile of anti-British sentiment and sentimental Irish revolutionary conspiracy, and but for some fortuitous developments between 1897 and 1905 that tradition would have been eclipsed entirely by a revitalising Home Rule movement.[7]

In 1900, when the Irish National Club became a more regular organisation and was operating a schedule of weekly meetings, despite the deaths of a number of key activists, a new movement only nominally Fenian in much of its inspiration was being established in Dublin. Cumann na nGaedheal, founded on 29 September, was at first a confederation of the various National and '98 Clubs along with the burgeoning Gaelic and Celtic literary society movement, but it soon became the epicentre of what Hutchinson has termed a 'politico-cultural revival' spearheaded by Arthur Griffith and D. P. Moran.[8] There was almost a mindset rather than a political conviction to this new brand of cultural nationalism and it could be quite unforgiving of previous revolutionary efforts in Ireland. In this sense it was a usurpation of traditional Fenianism and it is clear that although he was an enrolled member of the IRB, Arthur Griffith was unsatisfied with the republican mantra of Fenian separatism almost as much as he was opposed to constitutional nationalism.[9] It is important to consider this division of thought because the Glasgow IRB were very late and not entirely zealous converts to this brand of nationalism. Their priority was the preservation and presentation of an intact message which stressed not a social or a cultural revolution, though they conceived of and accepted the necessity of such, but rather a solid political revolution which would end British government in Ireland. Cumann na nGaedheal represented something not entirely in keeping with this traditional republicanism and the Fenians in Scotland kept to their little club even when a branch was finally established in their midst. They even sent apologies for being unable to send delegates to the annual conventions of Cumann na nGaedheal, but a winnowing membership, few resources and a creeping apathy definitely contributed to this.[10]

The natural constituency in Glasgow and elsewhere for this new cultural nationalist movement was among the members of Conradh na Gaeilge (or the Gaelic League). From its humble beginnings in Glasgow's Gorbals district in April 1895, Conradh had become an enthusiastic, influential and growing organisation in Scotland. By 1903, it had *craobhacha* or branches in Partick, Whiteinch, Coatbridge, Dundee, Port Glasgow, Greenock, Ayr, Rutherglen, Hamilton, Carfin, Motherwell and Maryhill in addition to those (eight or so) in Glasgow itself. On 8 June 1902 it brought a young barrister named Patrick Henry Pearse to Glasgow once more (he had visited in 1899), to give a well-attended lecture on the Irish language in Scotland, which he attached firmly to the national regeneration of Ireland and spoke of 'a battle to the death ... between the Irish mind and the English mind in Ireland'.[11] Symptomatic perhaps of the Fenian reception for this kind of Gaelicist gospel, there was only one IRB man, the prosperous city tailor and Conradh pioneer, the aforementioned Denis Brogan, listed as present at the Pearse lecture. It was therefore solely representatives of cultural nationalism in Glasgow who initiated the first branch of Cumann na nGaedheal in Scotland (named the Lord Edward Fitzgerald), on 16 November 1902, and set about the task of promoting Gaelic nationalism among the Irish exiles in Scotland from a base in Cumberland Street in the Gorbals. This does not tally with the founding of Cumann na nGaedheal in Belfast, Derry, Liverpool, Manchester or London, where Fenians completely dominated from the outset. After a couple of weeks a few individual IRB men such as the young Meath exile, William P. Hyland, M. O'Hora and Patrick McAllen of Killarney, an organiser in the Brotherhood, joined the Lord Edward branch, but these were younger and keener figures than the general Glasgow Fenian profile.[12] What exactly, however, the Irish National Club was doing as 1903 dawned is extremely difficult to ascertain. From about the middle of the previous year the club had lapsed into a state of listlessness once more and it was only to appear briefly for a final curtain call in April when it welcomed the IRB Supreme Council member, P. T. Daly to the city for a lecture on Wolfe Tone.[13] As was common, though, on these occasions, Daly had a tour of inspection of the IRB in Scotland and issued instructions from the leaders in Dublin. It is likely that two of these instructions or orders related to the infiltration of Cumann na nGaedheal in Scotland and the placement of men in the Ancient Order of Hibernians (AOH) with the aim of attracting new recruits. Both plans were duly carried through, although the instigation of a new branch of Cumann na nGaedheal rather than the infiltration of the existing branch was chosen by the Glasgow IRB, probably in order successfully to carry it off, but also to avoid the sometimes difficult impositions of Gaelic nationalism, which P. S. O'Hegarty described as being 'puritanical'.[14]

A new branch of Cumann na nGaedheal named 'Young Ireland', and later 'Éire Óg', was set up soon after P. T. Daly's visit to Glasgow and was clearly dominated by the same IRB figures as the Glasgow Irish National Club.

Although they met in the very central location of the Albion Halls in College Street, only two members from the defunct Lord Edward Fitzgerald branch (Michael McDonnell and W. P. Hyland), joined the Young Ireland branch.[15] This time the Cumann Lúthchleas Gael (CLG), or Gaelic Athletic Association, official John Brolly agreed to serve on the committee alongside such veterans as Dan Meagher, the Wicklow-born former Irish National Brotherhood (INB) man; James Ward, the Anderston IRB leader; and Derryman Bernard Havilan, a labourite and trade unionist. Their programme was of the traditional lecture and concert variety, but they were evidently totally incapable of countering either the Emmet or Manchester Martyrs events 'stolen' by the Home Rulers. Not only this, but they failed to attend Cumann na nGaedheal's annual conventions in 1903 and 1904, though by this second year they had probably disintegrated completely because a third and final launch of Cumann na nGaedheal in Scotland was made in January 1905. This time the same name, 'Branch Young Ireland', was re-adopted and under the supervision of Patrick Scullion, James Ward and Terence Fitzpatrick things began with a more determined air. A core of activists, most of whom were ardent Sinn Féiners, would remain in the IRB right up until and after the 1916 insurrection.[16]

With the help of a timely split in the AOH over personalities, politics and funds in 1906 and the creation of the so-called Registered AOH, based in Scotland and composed of supporters of the Sinn Féin policy outlined in Arthur Griffith's influential work, *The Resurrection of Hungary* (1904), Cumann na nGaedheal made a promising start. This was maintained despite quite acrimonious conflict with Home Rulers both in public and within Conradh na Gaeilge, and was buoyed up by the support of popular figures who visited Glasgow at this time, such as the Fenian veteran Jeremiah O'Donovan Rossa and the Donegal author and *seanachie* or storyteller, Séumas MacManus.[17]

The acquisition of various types and sizes of organisational buttresses, which strengthened and raised the Sinn Féin policy, while giving the IRB a wider base of operational influence throughout Scotland, did not impede the Fenian desire to evangelise. Members never appeared likely to give way to complacency, and the years 1907–8 saw a hive of activity. Not only did Sinn Féin run its own very successful *céilidh* concerts, outdoor trips and lectures, it also (at least in Glasgow) organised a branch dramatic club and industrial committee and published its own monthly magazine. It demanded that Irish history and Irish Gaelic be taught in Scottish schools, virulently attacked the establishment of a Catholic Boys Brigade in Glasgow's famous St Mungo's parish as reeking of British militarism, and took an increasing interest in the formation of independent Irish immigrant co-operative societies.[18] Lecture topics were wide-ranging and could include subjects such as 'Popular Control of the Education System in Ireland', 'Political Economy', 'Sinn Féin and Nationalism' or less specific ones such as 'What Can Poor Ireland Do?', 'Are We Degenerating?' and 'A Restatement of National Principles'.[19] Occasionally, topics for debate could be downright bizarre, as in August 1908 when the public display of a 'captured Mullingar leprechaun' in a Glasgow city centre emporium was discussed at a Craobh Éire Óg meeting, it being decided in the end to cause enquiries to be made by members with a view to stopping the exhibition.[20] The range of activities and self-confidence displayed by Sinn Féiners in Scotland, in almost total disregard to their size, became more evident. Their contributor to the *Peasant* newspaper looked eagerly towards a Sinn Féin–Home Rule parliamentary contest in North Leitrim promised by the resignation of the sitting MP, C. J. Dolan who had defected to Sinn Féin: 'Nationalists in Glasgow and the West of Scotland are prepared to aid him [Dolan] to the full extent of their purses, no matter how exalted the position of those from whom the opposition may come. This is a fight for national freedom, and all who are not with us are against us, and we mean to win.'[21] This bullish confidence was expressed organisationally as well when, in November 1907, a Coiste Ceanntair Albain (or Scottish Executive), was founded in Glasgow to co-ordinate Sinn Féin branch activities across Scotland through monthly delegate conventions. Its president was Craobh Éire Óg stalwart, Thomas McDonnell; its vice-president, Thomas Jennings of Motherwell; the treasurer James McLaughlin, the Renfrew IRB centre; and Port Glasgow's Patrick McCauley was chosen secretary.[22] It is also about this time that a number of women previously in the background of Sinn Féin suddenly achieve positions as office-bearers in Craobh Éire Óg, with one elected assistant secretary and another four taking up places on the executive committee. A few of these women, the O'Neill sisters, Sorcha and Máire, and Annie Gillespie were very possibly the daughters of two men long connected with Fenianism in Glasgow: James O'Neill and Francis Gillespie.[23] It is possible that Inghinidhe na hÉireann, Maud Gonne's Irish republican women's organisation did establish a branch in Glasgow sometime in 1908, but if this is so, it did not cancel out the growing participation of women within Sinn Féin in Scotland. In October 1908 Craobh Éire Óg increased its female representation by choosing Sarah O'Kane (who was actually the first woman in Scotland to join Sinn Féin), as treasurer and placing no fewer than nine women on the executive committee (containing 23 in all). The same cannot be said about Sinn Féin elsewhere, however, and the involvement of women was regularly restricted to their ability to provide displays of Irish dancing and singing. This no doubt prompted some women attached to the John O'Leary *craobh* in Shieldmuir in 1910 to propose forming their own *craobh*, though within a month some 20 of these women agreed simply to join the existing one, suggesting that they had been promised a more active role.[24]

III

With the debacle of the Irish Council Bill of 1907 and the Sinn Féin challenge in North Leitrim behind them, the Irish Parliamentary Party and United Irish League could afford at last to be more ambivalent about the arguments of the separatists. Sinn Féin's fortunes at this point mirrored those of its enigmatic leader Arthur Griffith whom the poet Pádraic Colum witnessed, 'had a difficult role to uphold, the role of a man who, while not a failure, has failed in certain spectacular attempts'.[25] To lift themselves and fight on with the same vigour was difficult, but in Scotland a resurgence in anti-Catholicism alongside continuing intolerable urban working and living conditions made their attempts to focus minds and mould passions around specifically Irish instead of Scottish issues increasingly arduous.[26] Both Seán MacDiarmada (the 1916 signatory and insurrectionary later executed for his part in the Easter Rising) and P. T. Daly made return visits to various Sinn Féin *craobhacha* in 1909, but the failure to initiate as promised three new *craobhacha* in August that year and the winding down of the Coiste Ceanntair Albain executive body which seems to founder around about the same time, indicates some degree of degeneration. Not that the United Irish League of Great Britain (UILGB) itself had a sound grip either in Scotland at this time. They did institute a very successful gentlemen's club in Glasgow city centre (the Irish National Club, Glasgow Limited), and exacted a form of revenge for the O'Donovan Rossa visit of 1906 by bringing Fenian turned parliamentarian supporter Captain Edward O'Meagher Condon and UIL of America organiser John O'Callaghan to the city in September, but the UIL was being far outstripped in both branches and membership by the AOH (Board of Erin).[27] Ironically though, Sinn Féin was also marginalised by the rise of an AOH wing as sympathetic towards, if rarely active within the party, as its Board of Erin rival was towards but similarly not entirely within the UIL and IPP. The so-called AOH (American Alliance) was a short-lived dalliance with Gaelic republicanism which raised the profile of that politico-cultural creed briefly and probably lingered on in some areas until 1916 at least before going the way of its Registered AOH predecessor, which had broken away at an earlier stage.

Sinn Féin in Scotland had slowed to almost a dead halt in 1910. It remained active, met weekly, held concerts, lectures and invited speakers but had, perhaps, gone as far as it was able. Difficulties had been increasingly apparent since 1909. In that year the IRB in Scotland selected a new commander and Sinn Féin gave notice of a new militant youth association, Na Fianna Éireann. Lloyd George's budget promised a clash with the House of Lords, which in time would lead to the removal of their veto on parliamentary legislation; and this was followed in 1910 by a general election which gave to the IPP the all-important balance of power at Westminster. With the passing of the Third Home Rule Bill in 1912, the UILGB was firmly in the ascendant, with 102 branches from Alloa to Dalmellington and 2,600 members in Glasgow alone, whereas physical force Irish republicanism, not for the first or last time in its history, was looking more like an irrelevance than an anomaly in the Scottish and British body politic.[28]

Difficult as the ignominy of 1912 proved to be for Scotland's militant Irish republicans, the following year was no better. No senior speaker from Ireland addressed the members of Craobh Éire Óg at the Emmet or St Patrick's Day anniversaries; and another attempt at organising internal Irish classes for Sinn Féin members drew only 18 applications out of what would have been at least a pool of 100 or so individuals.[29] The only positive note (of sorts) for Sinn Féin in the course of 1913 was probably their move from the hall in 26 High Street to 146 London Street, Glasgow at the beginning of May. While Craobh Éire Óg were in the process of this retreat from the central and comfortable premises of High Street into the ill-lit wynds of the Calton in the city's east end, the cheerleaders of Redmond to the number of 5,000 when he spoke in St Andrew's Hall in Glasgow in June, and a considerably larger 50,000 who listened to his Ulster and Scottish conductor Joe Devlin in August in Kilmarnock, Ayrshire, remained in the ascendant.[30]

IV

Since the foundation in Ireland of several paramilitary forces towards the end of 1913, Irish immigrants in Scotland appear to have been locked in debate over the merits and demerits of establishing branches of these forces in Scotland. Within a few days of New Year 1914, Cumann Lúthchleas Gael (CLG) or the Gaelic Athletic Association in Glasgow called a meeting of the city's Irish associations for 11 January to consider the formation of an Irish Volunteers corps for the west of Scotland area. This accordingly took place under the chairmanship of a high-ranking Sinn Féiner, IRB veteran and Irish National Forester's official from Renfrew called James McLaughlin. At length, a vote resulted in 43 for setting up a corps and 13 against, and thus the Sarsfield or the First Glasgow and West of Scotland Regiment of Óglaigh na hÉireann (the Irish Volunteers) was formed.[31] A provisional committee of 15, all delegates from various Irish groups such as the UILGB, Irish National Foresters, Catholic Benefit Society, Conradh na Gaeilge, CLG hurling and Gaelic football clubs and Sinn Féin, was set up contemporaneously to oversee the expansion of the Volunteers. It should be made clear, though, that the Home Rulers of the UILGB who participated did so more as individuals than representatives of their organisation, while for the first few months, the board of Erin AOH held aloof completely from the new body. It is a complex and unsatisfactory process trying to discover the actual number of Irish Volunteers in Scotland both before and after the organisation was divided as a result of Redmond's appeal for them to aid the British war effort. Numbers quoted when individual companies were started, taken together with conservative estimates, indicate a figure of around about 2,500, but Patterson's suggestion this narrowed in Glasgow to 70 anti-Redmondite Volunteers after the split is almost certainly too drastic.[32] Considering that there were sustained attempts by the IRB to place its men in Volunteer companies (or at least the ones it had not initiated), often concentrating on key posts due to their small activist base, and that Scottish membership at this juncture amounted to 250, in addition to post-split numbers given in the newspapers, the anti-Redmondite Volunteers in Scotland would have stood about 200 strong.[33]

Sinn Féin was all but drowned out by the guns of 1916, and even before the Irish Volunteers had been formed in Glasgow, the party had been replaced by the actionist emphasis and activities of the Fianna and Cumann na mBan, the women's republican arm which was established in Scotland in 1915. Nonetheless, in that year a little known Sinn Féiner from Templemary, near Buttevant, County Cork made his way to Glasgow and began a connection with Irish republicanism in Scotland that would last until his death in 1949. Seán O'Shea, blind at the age of 30, a musician, singer, composer, linguist and ardent Gaelicist, along with the similarly named Seán O'Sheehan, sent as a Sinn Féin organiser to Glasgow in 1918, were completely to rebuild Sinn Féin into a dynamic, nationwide organisation hardly recognisable from the almost folksy and marginal pre-Rising Sinn Féin. Beginning with the creation in 1916 of the James Connolly Cumann and amalgamating into it the remnants of Craobh Éire Óg, by 1919, a network of some 75 Sinn Féin clubs were involved in a range of activities, though with a primary emphasis on fund-raising and propaganda work.[34] The demise of parliamentary Irish nationalism and the subsequent rise and popularity in the cause of Sinn Féin that took place across Ireland, was replicated in Scotland and evidenced by the massive growth in Sinn Féin clubs, by the sympathetic response of the Scottish Catholic press under its post-war baron, Charles Diamond, and by the active and passive aid given to the Irish Republican Army (IRA).[35] The high point, as far as republicans themselves were concerned, came in 1920 with the visit to Scotland (he was banned from entry to Ireland, and from speaking in Manchester or Liverpool), of Sinn Féin advocate Archbishop Daniel Mannix. The archbishop spoke to large crowds of enthusiastic supporters in Edinburgh, Greenock, Dalmuir, Kilmarnock, Dumbarton (where the Sinn Féin cumann had 600 members), Cowdenbeath and Dundee. The Glasgow demonstration was blocked, and Mannix spoke to a defiant crowd of 50,000 to 60,000 supporters at Whifflet instead.[36] Events thereafter, such as the famous 'smashing of the van' prison escape attempt and the shooting of police officers in Lanarkshire during an arms raid, led the authorities in Scotland increasingly to consider Sinn Féin and the IRA as one and the same thing; a belief that did not end with the signing of the Anglo-Irish Treaty and the military defeat of the republicans.[37] Sinn Féin played a negligible role in the subsequent split in Scotland over the treaty, and Free State agents in Glasgow were effective in completely closing down any major republican activity by 1924, even if they had to deport people to Irish prisons in order to do so. They thus enjoyed little support in Scotland, and failed even to gather enough sympathisers for a Glasgow branch of the new Cumann na nGaedheal soon after.[38]

V

The majoritarian embrace of physical force Irish republicanism by the Irish in Scotland, historically brief though it was, turned the community outside in. In no way was this more apparent than in support for a political party that had no intention, nor ever had, of standing in Scotland. The importance of this fact cannot be overstated and it illustrates the depth of rootedness to Ireland rather than the traditional sense of rootlessness in Scotland amongst a largely anglicising minority immigrant population up until this point in history. Even the alliances made by Sinn Féiners with domestic politics in Scotland underlined their socio-political distance from that country. Links of fraternity and active co-operation in many parts of Scotland with both militant Scottish nationalists and equally militant communists did little to endear the Irish to a Scottish mainstream opinion that had already bracketed the immigrant community as a dangerous menace.[39] However, the 1919–23 period was more than the blip on the road to assimilation and/or integration suggested by some historians, for it embedded in the psyche of the immigrant community the notion of that remembrance – that they were immigrants, formed in another country and a different tradition whose unsettled and incomplete state was a perpetual reminder of their origin and exile. This was to remain with them as a sentimentalist but serious anchor long after they had ostensibly ceased to think of themselves as immigrants and drifted into a Scottish and/or Catholic identity.[40]

It is often assumed that, like Óisín of old, Sinn Féin in Scotland and Irish republicanism generally disappeared into some void-like Tír na nÓg after the civil war. The buying power of the 1918 Education Act for the Labour Party and the increase in the franchise, added to the dismay of the treaty split, partition and the military capitulation of republicans, are all given as the contributing factors towards the Irish abandoning nationality, tradition and culture for a more or less impromptu re-assignation as Scottish Catholic Labour Party supporters. Some observers have noted the dangers, even given the Irish links to Labour since its inception, that are inherent in this view: the stronger links to the Liberals historically, and the fact that most working-class UILGB supporters actually transferred loyalties to Labour rather than Sinn Féin, and that many of the Irish (definitely a majority of republicans) transferred their support post-civil war to groups such as the Independent Labour Party, Communist Party and the Scottish nationalists rather than mainstream Labour.[41] Most importantly, however, was the fact that a large number of Irish republicans remained (many took the option of emigration to the US), and continued to be active in the IRA and Sinn Féin, both of which survived with reduced numbers into the 1930s and beyond.

There has been great disagreement about IRA numbers in Scotland in the years 1920–22. The most recent estimation by Hart gives a figure of 600 for 1920, quoting Captain John Carney of 'C' company, based in Govan and writing in 1922, and rejecting as 'alarmist' Scottish police records which estimate 30,000 'Sinn Féin volunteers' (a figure which seems to include IRA, Cumann na mBan and Sinn Féin members). Prior to Hart, Aspinwall suggested 20,000, which was mainly based on Finlay and Handley, the latter of whom in turn based his figures on a *Daily Record* report, which also claimed 4,000 members in Glasgow. This 4,000 figure was used by O'Farrell, who gives a figure of 7,000 IRA members for Scotland as a whole. Patterson mainly relied on Scottish Brigade commander Éamonn Mooney's figure of 2,000–2,500 for 1921.[42] No matter which of these is most accurate, it seems certain that the drop in IRA members by 1926 to 100 volunteers (a figure that itself had halved since 1924) indicates a severe disenchantment with Irish republican politics on behalf of the Irish in Scotland. Naturally, Sinn Féin faced a similar demise, but as there was always more of an outlet for the propaganda and fund-raising activities of that party than for the arms raids, drilling and gun-running of the IRA, it was likely to prove a more robust organisation. From the autumn of 1925, and in spite of an internal feud in the IRA which may have hampered fund-raising, Sinn Féin's Comhairle Ceantair Albain was put on a more firm footing and held regular gatherings attended by James Connolly, Tom Clarke, Terence McSwiney, Liam Mellows, Patrick Pearse (all Glasgow), Michael Mallin (Govan), Roger Casement (Greenock), Major John McBride (Port Glasgow), Kevin Barry (Dundee), Rory O'Connor (Edinburgh), Pádraig MacPiarais (Hamilton), Coatbridge and Clydebank *cumainn*. Even before the March 1926 Ard-Fheis in Dublin which split the party and led to the founding of Fianna Fáil, Sinn Féin in Scotland made clear their opposition to the moves in the de Valera camp by submitting a resolution arguing against entering the Free State parliament, even if the oath of allegiance was removed. Their loyalty also held firm after Fianna Fáil had established a Comhairle Ceantair Albain containing seven *cumainn* in Glasgow (the only *cumainn* outside of the Irish Free State many of which lasted into later decades), which undoubtedly took a bite out of Sinn Féin in the city. Dev himself visited in December 1926 and elicited the support of the sister of Charles Carrigan (besides James Connolly, Scotland's only other 1916 martyr and a Sinn Féin pioneer in Scotland), and the son and namesake of the leader of the Fenians in nineteenth-century Scotland, John Torley (1852–97).[43] In spite of this challenge, Sinn Féin tried to carry on regardless, though they lost numerous members and even their central and commodious hall in Renfield Street in Glasgow city centre, and relocated to Séamus Connolly Hall at 51 Millar's Place in the Saltmarket. They established close links with a re-invigorating Fianna Éireann, which had the 1914–20 veteran Séamus Reader co-opted onto their ruling body in Dublin after an *ard-fheis* in October 1927. This, though, was the only event of note in 1927 and the year effectively saw a hiatus in Sinn Féin activities. The party re-emerged in 1928 with a modest enough Easter commemoration in St Mungo's Halls (indicating they had at least some clerical support), addressed by leading Belfast republican Peadar Murney, which was later repeated at Hamilton Town Hall for the Lanarkshire republicans. That summer, in an attempt, perhaps, to offset Fianna Fáil claims to the Fenian mantle and extend their calendar of events, republicans gathered in St Kentigern's cemetery at the grave of old Fenian, Sinn Féin and IRA member, Denis Canning (c. 1850–1917), for what was to be an annual occasion timed to coincide with the Wolfe Tone commem-oration at Bodenstown in County Kildare. It was organised by the Comhairle Ceantair Albain and continued into the 1960s, subscriptions being taken for a memorial which was unveiled in 1929. Sinn Féin's other main commemorative event was that for the Manchester Martyrs of 1867 during which tickets would be sold and a speaker and concert arranged (in 1928 they enjoyed the company of Professor Stockley, Sinn Féin Ard-Comhairle and Second Dáil member). Outside of these big events, Sinn Féin's activities followed a pattern set down in the first few years of its existence in Scotland – attendance at and support for *feiseanna*, regular debates, paper sales, outdoor trips and the running of Irish history and Irish Gaelic classes.[44] Seán O'Shea continued as president of Sinn Féin Scotland aided by a number of influential ex-IRB men like himself, such as Séamus O'Keeffe (who strangely was also blind),[45] Liam O'Donnell in Hamilton, Patrick McCauley, who divided his time between Derry and Port Glasgow and John Mulholland, former head of the IRB in Ireland and Scotland. Women continued to have a role in Sinn Féin and Cumann na mBan, maintaining possibly two branches in Scotland, though the Comhairle Ceantair Albain executive does not show as many women members as in previous years. Links with Scottish nationalists remained in place, after all a number of them – Willie Gillies, Amlaibh MacAindreas or Oliver Anderson, and Iain Mackenzie Kennedy had taken an active part in the Irish republican movement in Ireland alongside the quixotic founder of the small Scottish republican groupings Fianna na h-Alba and the Scottish Defence Force, Séamus Reader. Links to communists, however, did not persist and this may have been redirected through the Glasgow unit of the Irish Citizen Army, which claimed 25 members in Scotland in 1935.[46]

Down to seven active and affiliated *cumainn* going into the 1930s, Sinn Féin in Scotland was settling in for the long haul. The organisation in Ireland clearly had some time and esteem for those who remained faithful, but in the emigrant stakes Scotland's Irish republicans would always lag far behind the powerful and more wealthy Irish-Americans. Periodic immigration from Ireland added to Scotland's quota of physical force men, but this barely figured against generally declining figures; and while stalwarts like O'Shea in Glasgow, McCauley in Port Glasgow and O'Donnell in Hamilton kept going when Sinn Féin in Ireland was losing credibility, they could not disguise the lack of engagement that republicanism engendered in the wider Irish and Catholic community. Separating from that community increasingly since the treaty, but at the same time gaining some measure of unspoken sympathy and even admiration, Sinn Féin was still the representative of an inward-looking Gaelicist counter-culture running against the dominant, outward-looking, anglicised, labourist and Catholic culture of a majority of the Irish in Scotland. At ground level this dichotomy pitted the hurling and Gaelic football enthusiast against the erstwhile Glasgow 'Tim' whose life revolved around Celtic Football Club. However, between the two there was rarely a clash because there was rarely a meeting – the social circles between the first- and second-generation Irish and the third and fourth generations were increasingly drawing apart, hastened by loosening ties to Ireland from the latter and the ongoing socio-economic tussles with Scottish society from the former. Immigration was declining with lack of economic opportunity and increasing housing shortages, and Sinn Féin and the IRA continued to be overwhelmingly composed of first- and second-generation Irish.[47] Despite an avoidance of targeting Celtic countries in the 1939 bombing campaign, the 'S Plan', drawn up by past pupil of the select St Aloyisius' School in Glasgow, Séamus O'Donovan, represents the real spatial difference between the Irish republican mind in Scotland and the ordinary Catholic mind in Scotland. Much of the preparation work for the campaign was done by the Glasgow unit of the IRA, many if not all of whose members had come into the unit from Sinn Féin within a year or so of joining. Their anti-British focus on the eve of a war consolidation of British identity in the face of Nazi expansionism and aggression captures the psychological gulf separating generations of Irish immigrants with increasing starkness as the twentieth century progressed. However, while most Catholics in Scotland were not involved in Sinn Féin and the IRA, this does not necessarily mean that they were hostile to the aims of the republican movement.[48]

8 'Our Country's Heroes': Irish Catholics in Scotland and the Great War

Elaine W. McFarland

> I wandered where 'the Paradise',
> In all its silent grandeur lay,
> And fondly, prone to memorise,
> Recalled the charm of Celtic's play.
> Alas the war has brought us ills –
> Some Celtic lovers sleep in France,
> Some rest beneath the Turkish hills,
> Whilst others help 'The Great Advance'.
>
> J.C.[1]

Recent scholarship has done much to rescue the nationalist contribution to the Great War from the twilight territory it had previously inhabited in Irish popular memory.[2] The response of the Catholic Irish in Scotland to the war is worth equally detailed reassessment, offering a potentially vast canvas for this chapter. This is not least because a similar process of forgetting – or at best partial remembrance – gained ground almost as soon as the fighting had ended. Battalion histories, which emerged in great numbers in Scotland during the 1920s and 1930s, make no reference to the Irish presence, despite the fact that Scottish regiments like the Highland Light Infantry and the Cameronians accounted for the highest totals of Irish-born soldiers killed in non-Irish units.[3] However, if military commentators were anxious to stress the 'integrity' and 'continuity' of the Scottish military tradition, there were those among the Irish community who found the enthusiasm of their countrymen for the Empire's struggle almost as much of an ideological inconvenience. By the time of the first Peace Day in July 1919, the local Irish press refused to cheer military parades when peace was so clearly absent in Ireland.[4] Two years later, the young men of St Joseph's parish in Glasgow preferred to stage a 'Gaelic Carnival' for the benefit of 'victims of the present regime in Ireland, who are still called upon to make colossal sacrifices for upholding the ancient traditions of our glorious race'.[5]

'Sacrifice' had once carried an alternative meaning for this small parish. During the first two years of war, 700 of its congregation had left to join colours – already by January 1917, the death toll stood at 130.[6] Across Scotland, the rolls of honour of individual parishes and Catholic confraternities told a similar story. Indeed the picture nationally was a striking one. Statistics compiled by the United Irish League of Great Britain (UILGB) in November 1914 suggested that during the first three months of war the Irish Catholic population had contributed a total of 13,654 volunteers. This represented 16.4 per cent of total Scottish recruitment, though in some areas of heavy Irish concentration, such as Glasgow, the proportion was as high as 24.4 per cent.[7] Moreover, this was part of a much wider mobilisation among the Irish throughout Great Britain. Lord Macdonald of Swinford announced to the House of Lords in January 1915 that in round figures their total enlistments stood at 115,000: the north of England having provided 15,000; Yorkshire 20,000 and London 5000.[8]

The impact of the Great War was by no means restricted to demands for military manpower. The war years were a vital formative period for the whole Irish Catholic community in Scotland, which for decades had struggled doggedly for recognition and respect. The term 'community' is used advisedly in this instance, for the experience of war-time would strengthen its sense of collective identity, while beginning to shift the primary focus of that identity from 'Irishness' to Catholicism. In the short term, war was also to remove many of the old political certainties, while leaving few stable alternatives in their stead.

In examining the war experience of Irish Catholics in Scotland, the chapter will adopt a basic chronological approach, tracing the faltering path between exhilaration and disillusionment shared by most combatant populations across Europe.[9] The focus is on three main themes: the contours and motivations of participation in the war effort; the mechanisms by which the community absorbed the shocks of war; and the impact of war on their engagement with politics and society in Ireland and Scotland.

1914: 'Debt of Honour'

Irish Catholic volunteering demonstrated that the community was by no means immune to the collective pressures and extremes of emotion which coloured the opening months of the war.[10] Recent research, for example, suggests that the initial recruitment surge coincided with the short-term needs of many workers who were affected by the rapid contraction of Scottish industry on the outbreak of war. Scotland's eight main staple industries produced 60 per cent of its output, but by October 1914 her industrial sector had contracted by 11 per cent.[11] In these circumstances, the occupational profile of the Irish, over-represented in unskilled sectors of the labour market where casual work predominated, made them particularly receptive to the shelter of temporary enlistment.[12] In Glasgow, for example, 47.7 per cent of labourers in the building trade, which displayed particularly high enlistment rates up to July 1915, were Irish-born.[13]

Material imperatives may have been more significant for the Irish in Scotland than elsewhere, given the prevailing structure of local industry, but interpretations based solely on economic rationality should be treated with caution. As Fitzpatrick suggests for the case of recruitment in Ireland, subjective factors, drawing on workplace and parish networks and on kinship links, were also to shape Glasgow volunteering patterns. By the end of 1916, for example, a single local confraternity, Our Lady of Ganazzano, had 406 members in the forces.[14] Individual families also contributed heavily: one Leith widow received the king's personal congratulations on her seven serving sons, while another Govanhill family sent eight members to the colours.[15] Nor should an element of sheer impulsiveness be overlooked in triggering enlistment, as mobilisation brought an electric atmosphere in which war appeared as an individual 'test of fire'.

Pressures operating at a communal level were also decisive in encouraging recruitment. Indeed, it is impossible to understand how the Irish Catholic community was able to sustain itself in the face of the haemorrhaging of its youth, without grasping the great emotional investment that it placed in the war at its outset. Historians have traditionally viewed volunteer enlistment in Britain as the product of collective values, drawing on reserves of Victorian civic pride and Edwardian imperial patriotism.[16] In the case of the Catholic Irish in Scotland, specific issues of community identity combined with external developments in Irish nationalist politics to produce a distinctive articulation of ideals such as 'duty', 'honour' and 'service'.

The traditional bedrock of this identity was formed by loyalty to Redmondite nationalism, and above all to the Catholic Church. The strength of constitutionalism in Scotland was confirmed by ability of the local nationalist machine to channel the development of the anti-Carsonite Irish Volunteers in early 1914 – an initiative which in itself reveals the salience of romantic militarist sentiment on the eve of war.[17] Redmond's stress on a renegotiated imperial partnership had resonance in Scotland's export-orientated economy and similar 'aspirational imperialism' had gained ground among the Irish in the late nineteenth century. While condemning British imperialism, especially when it was directed against Ireland, many Irishmen saw their country's future firmly within the Empire, if only she could be elevated to her 'proper position' as a free nation.[18] For a community which had embraced Home Rule activity for decades, there was little novel in the rallying cries of 1914, which combined 'liberty', 'imperial loyalty' and the 'rights of small nations'.

In contrast to this expansive dimension in nationalist politics, the community's Catholicism had a more embattled quality. The Church retained a practical and an emotional pull among the Irish precisely because it had been vital to the maintenance of identity and cultural heritage. Despite a declining Irish-born population in the early twentieth century, there was an enduring sense of living in an enemy country, in which the battle lines were drawn by religion.[19] The outbreak of war at last presented the ideal opportunity to turn the concept of 'the enemy' outwards.

With the third Home Rule Bill blocked in the House of Lords and civil war threatening in Ireland, the local Irish Catholic response to the European crisis had originally been one of distracted support for Austria's legitimate grievances in dealing with 'a nation of assassins'.[20] Britain's declaration of war and the invasion of Belgium – 'Well done, gallant Catholic kingdom!' – shifted opinion dramatically. Charles Diamond, dynamic proprietor of the *Glasgow Observer*, took a lead in proclaiming that Catholics, 'knew their duty and would do it'.[21] The tone of the Scottish archbishops was initially more sombre and restrained. Trusting that the conflict was a scourge for the wickedness of the world, they implored their congregations to seek divine protection and succour.[22] However, the news of German atrocities in Belgium, where the Scottish clergy had close personal links, convinced them that a crusade was necessary to save European Catholic civilisation. Their support also reflected longstanding hopes that their Church might win an enhanced role in the Scottish national community. For the Bishop of Galloway, the sight of thousands of Catholics in 1914, standing shoulder to shoulder with the rest of the population for the defence of the realm, had already won them 'a war indemnity' in the form of 'equal justice in all matters regarding education'.[23] Calling on the 'Christian charity and patriotism' of their flock, both the Scottish hierarchy and individual parish priests gave unqualified encouragement for enlistment through the medium of sermons and pastoral letters. Some clerical enthusiasts preferred to lead by example: known as 'the parish recruiting sergeant', Father Stephen Thornton of Cadzow marched to the recruiting office at the head of his parishioners, before offering his own services as a chaplain.[24]

If the war engaged the Irish in Scotland as Catholics, they were also immediately drawn in by the response of their political leaders. In the first of a series of historic pronouncements, John Redmond on 3 August made a commitment of major strategic importance in which he pledged Irish support for the war, assuring Parliament that British troops could be withdrawn, as the coast of Ireland would be guarded by a united defence force composed of the nationalist and unionist volunteer corps.[25] Constitutional nationalists hailed his speech as a new dawn in Anglo-Irish relationships. Despite scepticism over the prospects of collective effort with the unionists, the *Observer* was positive that Ireland, admitted at last into the Commonwealth, 'now would become one of the sentinels of the Empire'.[26] This interpretation of the 'home defence' speech set the tone in Scotland as the various community organisations, such as the Ancient Order of Hibernians (AOH) and Irish National Foresters (INF) came to terms with the war. While the immediate impact was to boost Irish volunteer recruitment, Redmond's signal on Irish mobilisation may have exercised an indirectly encouraging effect on enlistment in the British army in the opening weeks of war, removing any stigma that might have remained after the recent use of the army to deal with recent civil unrest in Ireland.[27]

During the next six weeks, recruiting from the general male population in Scotland boomed, peaking in the first week of September when the country produced over 19,000 volunteers in a single week.[28] Crucially, just as this 'first rush' was beginning to fade, the specific Irish commitment was again dramatically boosted by external political stimuli. On 18 September, the Irish Home Rule Bill received royal assent. Two days previously, Redmond had already published a manifesto urging Irishmen to join the Volunteers or enlist in what he hoped would be an 'Irish brigade' in the British Expeditionary Force. The message was forcibly restated in an address on 20 September when he called on his audience to account for themselves as men, 'not only in Ireland, but wherever the firing line extends'.[29] While his actions appeared to seal a historic compact – Irish loyalty could be guaranteed now that Home Rule was on the statue book – as an experienced politician, he had left it deliberately vague whether the Volunteers or British army was actually the preferred formation.

In Scotland, any such ambiguity surrounding 'an Irishman's duty' was swept away in a powerful series of editorials in the Diamond press. The achievement of Home Rule, it was argued, marked a historical consummation:

> and from the hearts and lips of the sea-divided Gael may surely rise sentiments of gratitude and satisfaction that the shared struggle has ended at last, that the nationhood of Ireland is asserted and admitted and that the objective towards which so many generations of Irishmen have striven in blood and tears, by dungeon, gibbet and exile is at last attained. *Deo Gratias*.[30]

Not only Ireland was 'a nation once again' – as a true hallmark of her restored status, she had also become a nation in arms. For the Irish in Scotland, faithfulness to Redmond's 'compact' entailed personal as well as national obligations. 'Instant reciprocity' on the granting of Home Rule required hastening to the defence of the Empire: 'Ireland no longer need look on the Union Jack as the ensign of their country's enslaver. Ireland stands side by side with her sister countries as enemies of the German despot ... The real line of defence for Irish freedom is the line of allied armies holding back the Germans from Belgium and France.'[31] This interpretation of Redmond's 'debt of honour' policy won the endorsement of the network of mainstream Irish organisations in Scotland.[32] It did not, of course, go unopposed. The small Catholic Socialist Society found the spectacle of Irish nationalists draped in the Union Jack quite ludicrous, condemning the war as the product of a capitalist system that, 'has delivered us into hell'.[33] Meanwhile, advanced nationalists organised around Sinn Féin pointed out the insulting nature of the Home Rule settlement and, as an alternative to the Crown forces, championed enlistment in the Irish Volunteers, 'an army of her own sons for her own defence'[34] As in Ireland, however, the Volunteers now split, with the great majority supporting Redmond and reconstituting themselves as the 'National Volunteers'.[35] Heavily dominated by the Irish Republican Brotherhood (IRB), some of the minority rump at first drilled openly, while others went on to undertake covert operations, or, more mundanely, to pull down recruitment posters.[36] The trajectory of the Redmondite grouping was quite distinct; after seven months they were forced to discontinue operations, after experiencing a 'fully fifty per cent' loss in membership due to members joining the services.[37]

1915: 'A Common Fight for Freedom'?

As the fate of the National Volunteers suggests, Irish Catholic recruitment appears to have held up into the first half of 1915. By February, UILGB returns showed that some 25,747 Irishmen had joined the colours in Scotland. Indeed, with enlistment flagging generally, the Irish contribution – now 21 per cent of the total – loomed larger than in the first phase of the war.[38] The impact of recruiting on parish communities was still profound. During May, for example, 24 new recruits joined the 2nd Highland Brigade, Royal Field Artillery in Dundee; while St Joseph's, Woodside saw a further ten of its parishioners join up in a single week.[39]

Sustained voluntary enlistment was only part of a communal war effort, which may in itself have helped neutralise dissident voices. Civilian mobilisation among the Irish developed on an impressive scale. This drew initially on their instinctively defensive posture in Scottish society, with fears of proselytisation spurring the clergy into participation in relief committees for servicemen's families.[40] The arrival of the first Belgian refugees in Scotland in October 1914 as part of a government dispersal scheme had an even more galvanising effect. By the middle of 1915 their numbers had swelled to almost 11,000, bearing dramatic personal witness to the impact of the German onslaught.[41] While the refugees were officially the responsibility of the civic authorities, the Church quickly stepped in to distribute them to parishes throughout Scotland.[42] Secular organisations in the Irish community also gave enthusiastic support: the AOH, for example organised an 'Irish flag day' for Belgian relief during February 1915, involving 150 local collections in the west of Scotland, Dundee, Edinburgh and the east.[43] Indeed, the unfolding fortunes of war created new opportunities for patriotic and charitable impulses, such as the *Observer* and AOH collaboration, launched in May 1915, to provide tobacco and other comforts for Irish POWs.[44] Reducing in a similar fashion the conceptual distance between the fighting front and the home front was the loving and painstaking task of creating parish 'rolls of honour'. In St Peter's, Partick over 40 parishioners were drawn into this activity – originally listing the serving, but increasingly also the fallen.[45]

Commitment to the war effort on this scale was not intended to merge the Irish with Scottish society. Instead community leaders believed that they were making a contribution that was distinctive and worthy of recognition. The AOH flag day, for example, was hailed as a magnificent success, not only for its fundraising achievements, but because its sponsors believed it had, 'done a great deal to soften or dispose of racial prejudices and ... perpetuate neighbourly feeling between the Irish and Scotch in Scotland'.[46] As the war dragged on, such hopes were increasingly tempered by the realities of war.

Despite a major propaganda push throughout Britain in the first half of 1915, the early momentum of recruiting among the general male population proved impossible to recapture.[47] Meanwhile, casualties had begun their inexorable rise. In homes across Scotland, individual tragedies began to build a grim picture of national loss. Before the introduction of official casualty lists, news filtered back slowly though the obituary columns of the local press. The first soldiers to be killed in action from the Irish community had been from regular battalions engaged in the retreat from Mons and Battle of the Aisne during the opening weeks of war. Following the intensification of British offensive operations at Neuve Chapelle in March, it was the turn of the reservists. By May, the landings at Gallipoli had brought weekly casualty figures in the *Observer* to over 30, now also drawn from territorial battalions with a heavy Catholic representation, like the 5th Royal Scots.[48] In September came the Battle of Loos, with heavy losses in two Scottish volunteer divisions. Casualty totals now rose almost 60 in a single week. The local burden could be devastating: in St Anthony's parish, Govan, six men fell in this single engagement, including four brothers in the Conlon family who had contributed seven sons to the forces.[49]

With manpower demands pressing from both the armed forces and the war industries, the introduction of the National Registration Act in September signalled that the end of the voluntary system of enlistment was at hand. This scheme, which required every British subject on the mainland between the ages of 16 and 65 to make themselves known to the government, revealed that some 150,000 men in Scotland were still theoretically available for military service.[50]

Against this background, recriminations began to gain ground regarding the relative contribution being made by various social, ethnic and religious groups in Britain.[51] The denizens of 'villadom' were early targets in Scotland, but in the course of the year two sets of developments external to the community ensured the Catholic Irish would also struggle to escape censure. In the ranks, as Dooley suggests, new, corporate loyalties may have grown in battle conditions, but on the home from it soon became clear that war service had neither untangled historic sectarian rivalries nor acted as a solvent on smaller, 'routine' acts of bigotry.[52]

In the first place, the community was thrown onto the defensive by Pope Benedict XV's repeated public pronouncements on the neutrality of the Holy See. As head of a universal Church, he refused to accede to the rising clamour in the summer of 1915 to back the Allies. Theological controversy was subsequently waged with mid-Victorian fervour. Indeed, for some Scottish Protestant clergymen it was 'the Jesuits' who had actually caused the war in the first place.[53] In contrast to Ireland, where Cardinal Logue, acting in support of Vatican policy, refused to allow the Church to be used directly in recruiting, Catholic Church leaders in Scotland responded by redoubling their own recruiting efforts in conscious display of loyalty.[54] In the forefront was Archbishop McGuire of Glasgow, who in July launched a major appeal directed at both Irish and Scottish Catholics to avoid the disgrace of compulsion by enlisting immediately. He had his own answer to the pope's universalism, arguing that the war was 'a common fight for freedom', as the use of submarines and poison gas meant that Britain was 'not merely fighting a foreign foe, but an enemy of the human race'.[55] To the parents of young men eligible for service he offered the consolation:

> Even if you should lose your son dying honourably for his country, remember that you might lose him in some other way: he might die in some hideous accident of pit, or furnace, or factory; worse still he might yield to the temptations of life, and make you wish he had died when a child, or that you had let him go into battle.[56]

Challenges springing from the impact of the war in Ireland proved even more difficult to dispel. Despite the commitment of the local community to the war effort, the poor recruitment record of Ireland itself proved an irresistible target, especially for the Conservative press.[57] Between August 1914 and December 1915, 7.8 per cent of the country's male population between the ages of 15 and 49 enlisted, compared with 26.9 per cent in Scotland – nor was the National Registration scheme compulsory there.[58] Historians have recently suggested that the rate of decline in Irish enlistment was, in fact, almost proportionate to that in England, Scotland and Wales.[59] Nevertheless, the energy with which Irish parliamentary leaders refuted accusations of 'lagging' suggests the hold such perceptions rapidly gained in popular opinion. Moreover, despite their best efforts to argue that Irish figures were the product of demography or War Office incompetence, they were widely viewed as a reflection of the country's prevailing political distemper.

Tensions were particularly explicit in the case of Motherwell, which witnessed a surge of visceral anti-Irish sentiment during the anxious summer of 1915. The town was, of course, no stranger to inter-communal conflict, but this had been boosted by a faltering pre-war economy and given new populist voice by the militant Protestant orator, Hugh Ferguson who became councillor for the Forth Ward in 1904.[60] On the outbreak of war, recruiting in the town had initially been brisk, but once the first rush was over, as an area of heavy munitions production there was considerable local sensitivity to accusations that its inhabitants were 'hiding behind the button' – in other words sheltering from military service by claiming to be engaged on essential war work.[61] The result was a tendency to seek scapegoats, in contrast to the image of 'civic unity' and 'common sacrifice' carefully constructed after the war.[62]

While in November 1914 the local Liberal MP, J. Duncan Miller, had been careful to pay tribute to the patriotic response of Irish Catholic constituents, there was a persistent belief in the town from the outset of the war that the most enthusiastic recruiting grounds had been in its Orange enclaves.[63] At a series of recruiting rallies in May 1915, addressed by Mr George Clark of the Parliamentary Recruiting Committee, two strands of accusation were interwoven: not only were the 'unpatriotic Irish' in Ireland refusing to enlist, but they were coming to Motherwell to take the well-paid jobs of (by implication, Protestant) Scots who had left the factories for the armed forces.[64] These sentiments, one local commentator believed, rendered the war service of the local Catholic Irish population invisible, as, 'ever since the Irish are being insulted in public works, and told they are disloyal and that the Irish won't join the army'.[65] A further escalation of the anti-Irish campaign followed news of the town's heaviest military losses to date, with the engagement of the local territorial battalion at the Battle of Festubert in June.[66] It was now that Hugh Ferguson made a characteristic intervention, denouncing the Irish from an Orange platform for failing to answer the nation's appeal: 'What did the Irish expect to get from the war? They expected to get, and were getting, the good jobs of Scotchmen and Englishmen. The Party who thought they would get the Irish to enlist were up Queer Street.'[67] In these circumstances, sensitivities to 'Irish disloyalty' were already heightened by the time of the National Registration census in August. The town circulated with reports that the Irishmen who recently had entered booming local industries were now fleeing to avoid the requirements of the National Registration Act.[68]

Further local studies are necessary to establish how representative the Motherwell experience actually was. In Dundee, for example, with historically lower levels of sectarian tension, Irish Catholic participation in the war seems to have been more readily acknowledged.[69] However, it is interesting that local consternation in the steel town did gain a hearing in the national Scottish press during August 1915. As a result 'the flight of the Irish' threatened to create a broader moral panic in the west of Scotland, as returning harvesters and even Irish businessmen setting off for their regular holiday break across the North Channel were drawn into the net.[70] At Greenock, for example, the small numbers actually boarding the 'Derry and Dublin steamers did not stop a hostile crowd throwing potatoes at them from barrels on the quayside, shouting "Go and 'list!"'[71]

Such controversy increasingly politicised the recruitment of the Catholic Irish in Scotland. At one level, the response of community leaders was straightforward. The UILGB had figures to hand which showed that no fewer than 797 Catholic Irishmen had joined the colours from Dalziel parish alone, while Craigneuk and Motherwell had sent over 1,000.[72] Also evident was a more strident and combative reaction, contrasting 'Irish Catholic valour' on the battlefield with 'persecution and petty tyrannies' of the home front. This response illustrated too the mutually reinforcing nature of the sectarian dynamic. Almost instinctively, the *Observer* struck out at other groups it claimed were resisting the recruitment call: the real culprits in the Greenock incident were 'Orange' dockers who had come from Ulster attracted by high wages and who were 'pro-German to a man', while those fleeing were 'well-to-do Scots and even Jews availing themselves of the opportunity of non-registration by fleeing to Ireland'.[73] Meanwhile, the paper's correspondents displayed an intense fascination with the Germanic antecedents of the Scottish Reformation, at the same time discovering in Germany's Protestantism a new taunt for their Orange opponents.[74]

A defensive reinforcement of ethnic consciousness during 1915 may also be identified in growing concerns over the destination of Irish recruitment. During the opening months of the war, the great majority of Catholic Irish recruits had enlisted in Scottish regiments. Convenient local recruiting mechanisms assisted this process, but in any case General Laurence Parsons, Commanding Officer of the 16th (Irish) Division explicitly rejected mainland 'slumbirds' in favour of 'clean, fine, strong, temperate, hurley-playing country fellows'[75] From the few rolls of honour available where regiments are listed, it would appear that in 1914 around 75 per cent were in Scottish regiments, with only between 10 per cent and 15 per cent in Irish units[76] Indeed, some Glasgow units, such as 1st/7th Highland Light Infantry (the Bridgeton Battalion) acquired the reputation of being predominately Irish Catholic.[77] As national political leaders argued, these figures were not taken into account when 'Irish' recruitment was measured.[78] With the identity of Irish regiments threatened by casualties and falling enlistment, they became more determined that new recruits would be channelled appropriately.[79] This stance received enthusiastic local support from the *Observer*, whose columns offered practical advice and encouragement on how to join 'the Irish Brigade'. A vigorous advertising campaign followed Archbishop McGuire's July pastoral, with the 8th Inniskillens and the Tyneside Irish in competition for volunteers who wished to follow the episcopal call.[80]

These tactics may have had some success with those who did decide to enlist in advance of conscription, but the days of high-volume recruitment were over.[81] After more than a year of war, casualties and controversy battered the Irish Catholic community. Nevertheless, faith in Redmond and his 'compact' with the Empire had endured in Scotland. On the question of whether the Irish leader should join the new coalition cabinet in May 1915, the majority of local opinion was in favour. As Bailie McLaughlin of Dundee pronounced: 'the cause of the Empire today is the hope of Ireland. She has given freely of her sons ... let Redmond show the Empire the value of Irish statesmanship in the councils of the nation.'[82] Crucially, Redmond's refusal to accept such advice allowed the initiative on Home Rule to pass to uncompromising unionists in the new cabinet, such as Carson and Bonar Law. Without this prize, the landscape of Irish politics would alter more rapidly than traditional allegiances in Scotland could encompass.

1916: 'Breaking Eggs'

With every month that the war dragged on, the gap in experience widened between the Irish in Scotland and their countrymen at home. The high proportion of enlistments in the former case meant that the escalation of casualties had a particularly concentrated effect. Indeed, the death toll began to eat into the fabric of daily life during 1916, undermining parish communities and voluntary organisations alike. With 28 men already killed in St Joseph's parish, Kilmarnock, a crisis fund was necessary to meet financial stringency; the ranks of Irish Forestry and the Catholic Young Men's Society were also thinned, while St Patrick's Day, once a highlight of the local calendar, passed almost unmarked.[83] A new feature of the mass battles of this year was the rising number of officer casualties, usually in service battalions of Scottish regiments or in new formations like the Royal Flying Corps, indicative of the community's growing middle-class presence.[84]

As in Scottish society generally, the popular reaction to such losses was not revulsion about the war but a determination to 'see it through'. In this terse phrase was enshrined the belief that the collective sacrifice to date had to be made worthwhile. As the *Observer* commented in the wake of the Somme: 'This week's casualty lists ... are frightfully high. Of course you can't make an omelette without breaking eggs and when contrasted with the German's terrible losses at Verdun ... our casualties are only the minimum price for victory.'[85] Indeed, the newspaper, whose circulation had been handsomely boosted by the hunger for war news, was unwavering in its belief that this was no conventional conflict, but, 'our fight for the world's eventual peace'.[86] Its column 'Our Country's Heroes', which profiled fallen and decorated soldiers and sailors, underlined the sense of collective effort towards this goal. Meanwhile its actual war coverage had by no means abandoned the traditional conventions of gallant charges and death and glory stands, substituting Irish heroics for the Scottish iconography employed by the mainstream press, as it turned to drama, history and mythology to make the waging of modern war comprehensible to its audience.[87]

For those unable to find comfort in dispassionate rationalisation, the Catholic Church provided sustenance in various forms. The Scottish bishops and other senior churchmen remained vocal in encouraging recruitment. Catholics claiming the status of conscientious objectors on the grounds of the pope's neutrality were incredulously brushed aside.[88] For Dean McNairney of Partick, discouragement was 'the malady of cowards', while Archbishop McGuire was equally unblinking on the question of Catholic honour.[89] Despite feeling deeply for those left to mourn, 'he cannot regret that he called on them to do their duty, to fight as their forefathers had fought, for liberty and civilisation against the powers of despotism and barbarism'.[90]

Sensitive to the need to prove Catholic readiness to defend the Empire, the Church also busied itself with the work of quantifying its contribution. The archdiocese of Glasgow considered a roll of honour, which would list the 30,000 names, across 80 parishes, of those at the colours.[91] In Edinburgh and St Andrews a detailed census was undertaken in March 1916: this revealed that 12,684 were in the armed forces – 9.16 per cent of the total Catholic population – with 794 of these fatal casualties to date.[92]

The contribution of Catholicism in helping the community to bear its losses is perhaps best understood at a theological level. The Church possessed a clear set of rituals to deal with death, including sudden death, and did not require the notion of an 'immediate reward' for sacrifice on the battlefield. This had been poignantly demonstrated in November 1915 when the news of casualties from the Loos offensive had filtered through during the 'Month of the Holy Souls', the traditional period of intersession for the souls of the dead. As one priest explained: 'The Church is a great family, the living and the dead, we do not merely mourn our dead, we strive to help them by our prayers and good works that they may sooner have the joy of the Beatific Vision,'[93] Indeed, the war saw a wider popularity among Protestant churchmen for the practice of prayers for the dead and even for the doctrine of Purgatory.[94] Yet by no means did this signal the end of sectarian competition. For Diamond, such a development was merely evidence of Catholicism's superiority over 'heretical and unscriptural Calvinism', while the old suspicion persisted among many Protestants in Scotland that priests were actively profiting from masses for the dead.[95]

The changing nature of warfare also brought new challenges for the Catholic ideal of the 'good death'. Whereas in the opening months of the war, relatives could be consoled that their loved ones had been personally fortified at the point of death by the rites of the Church, this proved impossible amid the massive, mechanised slaughter of the Western Front. Instead, they were forced to rely on the blanket assurances of chaplains that Catholic soldiers had received the sacraments before battle, or to call upon reserves of traditional piety:

And when the strong hand clenches,
In death's last grip of pain,
Our Lady of the Trenches,
Be Thou there with the slain.
Nor let their heart's devotion,
To thee be all in vain.[96]

It is only against the background of the relentless grind of war that the community's reaction to external political developments, such as the Easter Rising, can be understood. To some degree, the 'moral deterioration' of constitutional nationalist politics, which Fitzpatrick identifies for Ireland, had begun before this episode.[97] The apparent resolution of the Home Rule question in 1914 had led to queries over the future utility of the local UILGB organisation as its continuation might threaten the 'isolation and segregation of the Irish people'.[98] John Redmond's reputation had apparently recovered from the coalition controversy, but the Irish parliamentary leadership again encountered fierce criticism in January 1916 when they refused to vote against the Conscription Bill on the grounds it was a 'purely British measure', and would not extend to Ireland. At least one correspondent felt betrayed:

What about the thousands of Irishmen in Scotland and England whom the bill will effect? Has the Irish Party no concern for them in this crisis? For years past, at election after election, the Irish Party had appealed to the Irish in Britain to vote for the parliamentary candidates recommended by the Party ... Is it too much to ask that the Party oppose this compulsory bill? The Irish Party will in all probability make further appeals ... to assist them to see that a parliament is again established in College Green. Would the Irish in Britain not be justified in refusing such support ...[99]

The Rising in April 1916, however, actually rallied the community around the Irish Party and its leader. Dismissed in the local Irish press as, 'unpatriotic folly: rash, blind, headlong, stupid and wrong', the harshest condemnation was reserved for the 'vile vermin who took German money to do German work'.[100] Meetings in support of Redmond were organised by Irish organisations throughout Scotland, and there seems little evidence to doubt the claim of the Home Government Branch that the bulk of local sentiment was firmly behind him.[101] The episode even put a new spurt of life into some UILGB branches in Paisley and Hamilton.[102]

The response to the rising in Scotland also drew on the Irish community's persistent sense of vulnerability. Its leaders were profoundly grateful for the recognition in the Scottish press that local loyalty was with Redmond rather than the extremists.[103] Unfortunately, popular opinion did not always make such distinctions. Again, Motherwell proved a flashpoint. Tensions over the wave of new Irish migrant workers in local industries had worsened from the previous autumn, with the shadow of conscription falling heavily on a town where the Derby scheme had very clearly failed.[104] As a vituperative article in the local press suggested, the charge was not only that the Irish were evading military service and filling the well-paid jobs of those who had enlisted; they had now become the 'Sinn-Feiner In Our Midst' – a threat to public peace: 'Paddy is to all intents and purposes an "undesirable alien". He comes here purely as a parasite on a decent patriotic community, and, as he cultivates the friendship of his own class only, he gradually becomes more of a parasite – he becomes an enemy to the country in which he is getting along so well.'[105] These sentiments later found a practical outlet in an anti-Irish 'jehad', as the *Observer* termed it, with police raids on the town's factories and lodging houses in August resulting in the round-up of over 50 men.[106]

Although hailed in retrospect as a turning point, the rising was only one episode in a complex and ambiguous process of political readjustment for the Irish in Scotland. Attitudes towards the rebels began to soften over the coming months as the British administration pursued its policy of executions, and as the first republican prisoners who arrived in Scotland turned out to be, 'excellent specimens of young Irish manhood'.[107] Sympathy with their plight was not extended to their political principles. The Redmondite establishment in Scotland during 1916 continued to benefit from a lack of alternative leadership in the community. Republican activity was limited to a minority of enthusiasts.

The advance of Sinn Féin had long been stoutly resisted in many areas by the AOH, and the IRB and remaining Volunteers were still poorly organised – despite the apprehensions of the Motherwell citizenry, for example, the two IRB 'circles' in the area were largely inactive and had first read of the rising in their morning newspapers.[108] Meanwhile, although the war had brought some rapprochement with Labour politics in the west of Scotland, this was still fragile and easily undermined by squabbles over municipal representation.[109] When the old politics finally crumbled in Ireland over the next two years, this would be in response to the creeping acquiescence of its leaders to partition and their failure to make Home Rule a reality. The process had a finality that caught some onlookers unawares.

1917: 'Dogged Effort and Heroic Sacrifice'

After the harshest winter on record, 1917 was to be one of the grimmest and most frustrating years of the war. Military stalemate on the Western Front continued, with now even Scottish priests who had joined as chaplains among the fallen.[110] Despite the new Irish Convention in July, disputes over a Home Rule solution dragged on without resolution. Similarly, on the surface little seemed to have changed for the Irish in Scotland. The pope's peace initiative in August raised the usual local backlash, but civilian mobilisation for the war effort carried on regardless, with its accustomed round of Irish Flag Days and concerts for the wounded.[111] The *Observer* continued to trumpet its support for Redmond's recruitment, trusting that 'the more the Irish assist recruiting now, the more Home Rule will be accelerated and the more it will be worth when it comes.'[112]

Yet the war ensured that subterranean shifts in community politics and identity were already at work. One indicator was in evolving attitudes towards new Irish labour migrants. The original controversy surrounding these workers had its roots in the lack of a co-ordinated manpower policy at the outset of the war.[113] Workers in key wartime industries had been permitted to volunteer in 1914, but labour shortages had soon required the government employment exchanges to bring over men and women from Ireland. Others were encouraged to migrate spontaneously by the high cost of living in rural districts. By 1916, as the Motherwell case indicated, the hunger of the local military authorities for men led to a new attempt to bring such migrants under the terms of the Military Service Act, exploiting ambiguities over the concept of 'ordinary residence' which were implicit in the legislation.[114] During the early stages of the crisis, those caught in the net had received support from a range of local political and religious leaders as essential war workers, suffering short-sighted victimisation from local bigots. However, ethnic solidarity had its limits. After a further debilitating year of warfare, it was difficult to maintain a reasoned stand when men of fighting age were apparently taking the places of Irish Catholics, as well as Scots, who had volunteered or been conscripted. In September 1917, the Glasgow

County Board of the AOH were active in their discouragement of further male and female migration. They warned of the moral and social dangers that lay ahead: 'the strange surroundings ... so many temptations and – in the case of the men especially – the resentment of the friends and dependents of those, who having been taken up for the forces, are having their vacated jobs filled – as they say – by imported Irishmen'.[115]

By the end of the year, it seemed that some of the more articulate voices in the community were also losing patience with Irish Party leadership, repudiating their supine response both to Lloyd George's machinations and to a new electoral onslaught from Sinn Féin. As late as August 1917, after the debacle of the East Clare by-election, Charles Diamond had contrasted the 'effervescence of Valeraism' with Redmond's record in, 'keeping a policy of commonsense before the country ... and acting a worthy and patriotic part'.[116] A personal tour of Ireland in the autumn, however, convinced him that the party's days were over as a serious political force. In a series of angry articles he condemned its 'narrow, conceited and intolerant view of its own virtues', while predicting that 'the new government of Ireland will be bigger, better, more virile, more competent and patriotic than could ever have evolved from Mr Redmond's leadership and following'.[117] This was too rapid a shift for the bulk of the community whose political horizons had long been framed by expressions of 'unswerving loyalty' to the Home Rule cause. Even Diamond did not feel able to transfer his allegiance to Sinn Féin, which was beginning to make a small foothold in Scotland during 1917.[118] In an attempt to rescue the impetus of constitutional politics, he called on the superior insight that local Irishmen had gained from their wartime experiences:

> the Irish in Great Britain (who have endured countless sacrifices for the Irish cause) also are entitled to be heard. They can judge establishing an Irish republic by force of arms from a more detached standpoint ... if only for the reason that they see more of the game. They are intimately connected in the prosecution of the war: they have all the evidence in front of them of the tremendous military strength of the Empire, and they know that further appeal to arms in Ireland will mean ruthless repression, the result of which will destroy all hope of an Irish settlement for a generation.[119]

Although agitation on the mainland could no longer hope to influence the direction of Irish politics, Diamond's tone was indicative of a new assertiveness among the Irish in Scotland. Crucially, this was also directed at the society around them. If the prospect of Irish Home Rule in return for war service seemed as far away as ever, there was a growing determination at least to win practical recognition in Scotland for their war-time contribution. This sense of a 'claim' or 'entitlement' was to intensify, when, after three years of 'dogged effort and heroic sacrifice', they considered that, 'the coming of peace is assured as tomorrow's sunrise'.[120]

1918: 'And you are safe'

John Redmond's recruitment strategy had been predicated on a short war. In the event, he did not live to see the end of the conflict, dying in March 1918 shortly before Germany's last desperate offensive on the Western Front. In Scotland, his obsequies were testament to how moribund the UILGB had become. In Glasgow, mourning was led by the burgeoning AOH, now a leading conduit of Irish ethnicity, while in smaller towns, like Kilbirnie, it was the local Catholic Church who stepped in to prove that 'national spirit' still survived.[121] Redmond's career was read as a tragedy, not because of his support for the war, but because he had not carried through conciliation fully, refusing to fight 'Ireland's cause' in the coalition cabinet, when thousands of young Irishmen were doing so in the firing line.[122]

The decision to extend conscription to Ireland a few weeks later seemed to offer precisely the sort of galvanising political issue that the expatriate Irish had once relished. At once, the *Observer* denounced the proposal as 'insane' – a deliberate ploy to kill Home Rule by discrediting Ireland, arguing that coercing Ireland would diminish Britain's moral force in the struggle against 'Prussianism'.[123] In reality, the conscription crisis is perhaps more significant for what did *not* happen in Scotland. There were no monster meetings, no mass petitions or floods of protest resolutions. Instead correspondents repeatedly bewailed the 'indifference' of the mainstream of the community to 'the annihilation of what remains of the finest Catholic manhood in Europe'.[124] Eventually, it fell to the Sinn Féin clubs to establish an Irish National Aid Committee to assist the anti-conscription struggle in Ireland, after the established bodies like the AOH and INF declined to participate.[125]

This circumspect response was not due merely to internecine rivalries between republicans and constitutionalists. It should firstly be placed in the larger context of the renewed hostility towards the Irish that the conscription crisis had stimulated throughout Great Britain, even amongst former Liberal supporters.[126] Wearily, the community in Scotland found itself rehearsing the old statistics on Irish Catholic enlistment and casualties. Indeed, the very extent of its own commitment to the war also made a dispassionate analysis of the plight of 'dear old Ireland' additionally difficult. The breach was by no means open, but one former soldier, writing to the *Observer*, may have spoken for many when he proposed a solution to the Irish conscription crisis: 'Although there is a Military Service Act in operation ... volunteers for the Army and Navy are willingly accepted, and I would suggest that the only honourable way of avoiding conscription in Ireland is for the Irish to enlist in numbers large enough to leave no necessity for compulsion.'[127] Indeed, even the Catholic Socialist grouping condemned the Sinn Féin stance as selfish rather than principled, neglecting the fact that conscription was already in operation among Irish 'exiles'.[128]

The community's apparent 'indifference' to Irish conscription in the spring of 1918 should also be set beside its greater eagerness to engage with burning local issues in Scotland. By the spring of 1918, attention was focused on the type of society that might follow the war, and on the possible gains secured by war service. Significantly, politics were becoming increasingly articulated in terms of the community's religious rather than national identity. Looming franchise reform, for example, made it necessary to consider tactics to maximise the Irish vote: in some constituencies it was the Catholic Union which emerged to undertake the work of canvassing and registration previously performed by the UILGB.[129] The impending Education Bill for Scotland raised even greater passions. As the Bishop of Galloway explained, the war had already imposed heavy financial burdens on Catholic education, raising interest rates, removing key benefactors and reducing the value of teachers' salaries.[130] Fearing submersion in a new state system, the *Observer* now called for 'Justice to our Schools, or War to the Knife'. Much more was expected after years of sacrifice: 'Are our sons, fathers and brothers to fight and die so that their children may be driven into secular or Presbyterian schools to be robbed of their faith?'[131]

Whatever its impact in Scotland, the conscription crisis had a decisive effect in Ireland, giving a major boost to Sinn Féin, whose principled abstentionism contrasted favourably with the impotence of the parliamentarians. World opinion was the audience that this new political force craved.[132] Rejecting the old strategy of working through existing British institutions and influencing British public opinion, Sinn Féin had little need for a dependable electoral adjunct among the Irish on the mainland. The situation for the Irish Party was very different. With its power waning, T. P. O'Connor launched a last desperate appeal for the Irish in Great Britain to organise themselves for battle against Sinn Féin.[133] It was, however, highly doubtful that his call would be answered on any credible scale. As Charles Diamond argued: 'We want for Ireland what Ireland wants for herself, and not what we think she should ask or take. Her affairs are those of her own citizens, from whom we may differ, but against whom we will never fight.'[134]

Community politics clearly were in state of flux during the last months of the war. In the past, discussion of political principles had been smothered as dangerous to 'unity', but the new mood was signalled by Diamond's own call in August 1918 for the Irish vote to move behind Labour. His unfolding position did not mean abandoning Ireland – on the contrary Labour, rather than discredited Liberalism, was her 'best hope of freedom' – but it was indicative of the beginning of a broader shift away from enclave politics. 'Inside Labour ranks', he argued, 'the Irish and Catholic electors will be powerful and effective. They can gain influence and weight. Outside they will be mere pariahs, flies on the wheel ...'[135] His prescription was also linked to a bigger, more confident vision of the British Commonwealth in which Irish Catholics, unstained by the sins of the past, would have a special duty, 'of healing, of charity, of brotherhood, of ministration'.[136] As the 1918 general election was to demonstrate, for others reared in the constitutional tradition, old loyalties proved harder to break. Indeed, contributors to the

AOH electoral fund in October were proud of Scotland's long record of support for the party, proclaiming that, 'the van is in the right of the Irish Brigade'.[137] Preparations for this election were well under way when the war suddenly ended.

On the first Sunday following the Armistice, Dean McNairney consoled his parish: 'They died to save you. And you are safe. From heaven above, where surely their fiery ordeal had already found them a glorious home, they look down on this glorious day ...'[138] It would be many more months before the human cost of the war became clear. Casualties continued to rise during 1919 and beyond through deaths from wounds and disease, and as the 'missing' failed to return.[139] By this point, however, Irish Catholic remembrance of war service was already beginning to sit uncomfortably with the British army's new 'policing' role in Ireland. 'Our Country's Heroes' became the stuff of *in memoriam* columns rather than of spirited editorials. The old political ideals which had sustained enlistment seemed bankrupt or unachievable. Unlike the Irishmen who had served in Australian or Canadian corps, there would be little opportunity to forge war-time experience into a new 'national mythology'.[140] Quietly, the community's grief was to be individualised, ritualised and depoliticised.

In conclusion, the Great War was not simply an external event to those who lived through it. Rather, it assumed a pervasive presence in their everyday lives. During the years 1914 to 1918, 'nations' across Europe were defined and redefined both to include and exclude those living within their physical boundaries. In the case of the Irish in Scotland, this process of transformation had two dimensions. Significant communal participation in the national war effort mediated their response to the unravelling of politics of their homeland. The European Armistice of November 1918 was only the beginning of revolutionary turmoil in Ireland. The new Ireland which emerged might have claimed their symbolic loyalty, but it had little practical need for the energies which for generations had been directed towards campaigning for 'Home Rule'. However, if the Redmondite project, with its subtly variegated patriotism, was at an end, accommodation with the society around them was unlikely to be a straightforward process, as the strains of war had not diminished sectarian tensions on the Scottish home front. This fact would also colour Irish attitudes to their record of war service and fuel their claims for full social and political participation in the post-war settlement.

9 Protestant Action and the Edinburgh Irish

Michael Rosie

Few recent examinations of Scotland's 'sectarian problem' (whether addressed in terms of Protestant-Catholic relations or of the Irish in Scotland) have failed to note two phenomena from the inter-war period: the Kirk's Disgrace, and municipal No Popery. Many accounts assume or imply that the second (the brief successes of the Scottish Protestant League (SPL) in Glasgow Corporation elections and the Protestant Action Society (PAS) in Edinburgh) more or less followed on from the first (an official and collaborative campaign by Scotland's Presbyterian churches against 'the menace' of Irish immigration, conducted c.1921–38).[1] In this chapter I hope to highlight an interesting disjuncture between these two phenomena, at least as far as Edinburgh's experience is concerned. In essence this disjuncture resides in the evolving rhetorical strategies of a Protestant Action campaign contrasting sharply with the strategies previously employed by the churchmen – whilst the clerics advocated a policy of 'No Irish', the militants were explicit in their cry of 'No Popery'.

Of course, it can be objected that this distinction is over fine, and that, after all, the terms 'Catholic' and 'Irish' have long been synonymous in lowland Scotland. In the 1940s James Handley complained that 'the Scottish equation: Irish and therefore Catholic = Catholic and therefore Irish' served to deny 'absorption into the stock to descendants of [Irish] immigrants ... so long as they remain Catholics'. In a similar and more recent vein, Joseph Bradley insists that: 'Irish and Catholic are clearly not the interchangeable terms they once were, though for those of an explicit anti-Catholic disposition, they remain so.'[2] Yet both Handley and Bradley themselves – amongst others – routinely and uncritically conflate 'Irish' and 'Catholic', marginalising both non-Catholic Irish and non-Irish Catholics. It seems important in the face of such habitual and banal conflation to problematise, rather than routinise, the connections between these terms. It is also worth noting that conflating the terms may, potentially, serve two distinct political projects. Conflation need not portray Catholicism as essentially alien and 'disloyal' to Scottish values; it can also serve to identify Scotland's Catholics as an unjustly beleaguered minority within a divided and 'sectarian' society. Bernard Aspinwall argues that: 'Irish equals Catholic is a useful tool for interested parties on both sides. Unfortunately it was not always true in Scotland. Reality is somewhat more complex.'[3]

There is a direct and pressing reason to question the 'Scottish equation' in the context of this chapter – the very deliberate care taken by many involved in the Kirk's Disgrace to disentangle the terms Irish and Catholic, to separate matters of religion from matters of nationality. The campaigners repeatedly insisted their motivation was 'race' rather than faith. In 1927 leading campaigner the Rev. John White reassured the Church of Scotland's 1927 General Assembly that: ' They dealt with this very difficult, delicate, and important question entirely from the racial point of view. The religious factor did not enter the question at all … Uncontrolled immigration was always a menace to a community, especially if it was to continue alongside the emigration of young and energetic native-born citizens.' The following year White again gave assurances that the anti-Irish initiative was not some narrow, bigoted sectarian one, 'He hoped the discussion … would be from the point of view of race and not of creed.'[4]

Few believed that the campaign was entirely free of self-interested religious bigotry, but the fact remains that this aggressive assault on a disadvantaged minority sought respectability and support through arguing a 'racial' rather than religious case. The campaigners consciously and deliberately moved away from the historic Protestant critique (that the errors of 'Rome' were contrary, or in direct opposition, to the teachings of Christ and the Gospels) and into an 'objective' discourse of race and nationality. Such discourses had a scientific respectability in the inter-war period difficult to grasp in the post-Auschwitz era. While the Presbyterian campaign failed in all its objectives, not least in that it further reduced (rather than reasserted) Presbyterian political influence, it ensured that attacks on Scotland's Catholics were – albeit indirectly – granted an almost unprecedented degree of legitimacy. Although there were almost no demonstrable links between the Kirk campaign and the militant Protestant fringe, the campaign inadvertently afforded 'respectability' to the militants. Ironically it was the success of the SPL and PAS in the mid-1930s that finally persuaded the leading campaigners (aggrieved that their 'noble purpose' had been hijacked and undermined by unsavoury radicals) to cease their activities.

There is insufficient room here to describe in detail the rise of militant Protestant parties in Edinburgh and Glasgow, their sudden successes in municipal politics during the 1930s, and their equally rapid evaporation. However, it is worth drawing the broadest contours of the phenomenon to frame the following discussion. In Edinburgh, following a Sinn Féin rally in 1920, Alexander Ratcliffe launched his Scottish Protestant League. The league was billed as a 'new aggressive Protestant movement', with the stated intention to oppose 'spiritualism, Christian Science, and various other systems of anti-Scriptural teaching [as well as] Roman Catholic Sinn Féin'.[5] Despite this broad remit the SPL focus was resolutely upon the activities of the Catholic Church. Although a handful of independent evangelical ministers were initially drawn to the SPL, their support rapidly melted away. In 1925 the SPL manufactured a localised controversy over Catholic schools, on the back of which Ratcliffe was elected to the Edinburgh Education Authority. The election was, however, a disappointment for the SPL: Ratcliffe was elected by the very narrowest of margins with his fellow candidates polling abysmally. Ratcliffe's tenure on the authority was an unhappy one, and he concluded that Edinburgh was poor soil for his No Popery politics. After polling well in Falkirk and Stirling Burghs during the 1929 general election Ratcliffe moved the SPL to Glasgow. They rapidly made progress, winning two seats in the 1931 municipal election in hitherto solidly Moderate and Labour wards. The SPL entered Glasgow politics at a time of great ideological flux, against a deeply discredited right and a deeply divided left. Taking another seat in 1932 the SPL peaked in 1933, taking four seats and 68,000 votes, 22 per cent of the total and only marginally behind the Moderates. Yet from here they disintegrated as Ratcliffe's autocratic style alienated supporters, and all seven SPL seats were lost at their first defence. This was the end of electoral Protestantism in Glasgow – a spectacular but ultimately brief phenomenon, whose unintended legacy was to reduce the ability of Moderatism to resist the rise of the left. The Labour Party took control of Glasgow in 1933, thanks in no small part to the SPL erosion of the Moderate vote, and has ruled it almost uninterrupted since. As Iain McLean wryly notes, 'It was an idiosyncratic way for a city to "go Red".'[6]

Whilst Ratcliffe's experience suggested that Edinburgh was barren ground for No Popery politicking, the achievements of Edinburgh's militant Protestants were to exceed those of the SPL in Glasgow. At its 1936 peak the loose alliance of militant Protestant factions captured almost one third (31 per cent) of the Edinburgh vote, constituting a bloc of nine councillors. Yet in the early 1930s militant Protestantism lay at the very outermost margins of the city's political life. Between 1932 and 1935 the tiny militant fringe was locked into a bitter rivalry between John Cormack, a former SPL member, and James Graham, a former Catholic. Cormack's faction, formalised from 1933 as the PAS, felt confident enough in 1934 to put forward two candidates in the municipal election, whilst Graham's organisation put forward another. To general surprise Cormack emerged victorious in North Leith, one of the poorest wards in the city, unseating a popular and influential Moderate. Accused of lacking genuine policies on the issues affecting local people, Cormack responded bullishly: 'We have only one "plank". It is a comprehensive one. Wherever in the political life of our country, municipal or national, the Papist beast shows its head we must crush it or, at least, keep it in subjection. Our party is composed of Protestants of every political party who want Protestantism to have its rightful place in our country's jurisdiction, in other words, to defend our Protestant faith'. Defence of that faith demanded removal of state support for Catholic schools; the expulsion of religious orders from Scotland; and the purging of 'Papists' from armed services and judicial bench.[7] In essence, PAS advocated the re-imposition of historic Catholic disabilities, utilising the very arguments from the point of 'creed' that the Presbyterian campaign studiously avoided. While the churchmen talked of 'race', PAS insisted 'the Reformation must be fought again.' PAS did make reference to Catholic Irish ('Free State') immigration, but it is clear that members genuinely viewed their enemy as a global system, and their struggle as merely one local skirmish between their Protestant faith and a political conspiracy aiming at human enslavement.

Although it is generally agreed that inter-war militant Protestantism marked a key point in Protestant-Catholic relations in Scotland (and indeed, a crucial moment in the Irish Catholic immigrant experience), it has in fact received scant scholarly attention. Most recent authors have seemed content to rely on the mid-1980s studies published by Steve Bruce and – in particular – Tom Gallagher.[8] These authors are to be commended for their pioneering work, but like all pioneers they could only sketch the outlines and contours of the phenomena they were exploring. And like all pioneers, they need to be followed by others filling in gaps, and redrawing the contours. Here I specifically want to revise Gallagher's view of PAS, as this has been the most influential. Gallagher effectively picks up the story from late 1934, the point at which PAS enters the council chamber, and says little about the movement's early development. Gallagher's work focuses mainly on the personality of John Cormack and the 'Long Hot Summer of 1935'. Indeed, Gallagher went so far as to claim that: 'The rise of Protestant Action owed more to the angry eloquence of its leader, John Cormack, than to the prevailing political situation or previous sectarian unrest. For a brief period he showed that, even in the absence of deep and readily understood divisions, a city or community can be almost torn apart by the sudden emergence of a charismatic individual who can move people to deeds which they would never normally contemplate.'[9]

Cormack's oratorical gifts and personal charisma undoubtedly played an important role in PAS' success. But success also relied on the contribution of several other key figures, both from within the organisation itself and from a broader web of gospel halls and evangelical missions. Cormack represented South Leith from 1938 to 1962 but was joined in the ward by two other Protestant councillors. Rev. James Trainer served South Leith as a councillor (from 1936 to 1945), as did George Horne, an evangelical preacher with strong PAS connections (from 1935 to 1958). Leith in general and the South Leith ward in particular became the heart of the Protestant movement. To some degree understanding why Leith emerged as the Protestant stronghold is the key to understanding the PAS phenomenon. Gallagher's focus, however, lies several miles south and west, to one rowdy demonstration in the leafy suburb of Morningside, with religious violence rather than electioneering.

Various protests against high profile Catholic events in 1930s Edinburgh have been described as 'riots'.[10] Yet high profile Catholic activities in the city encountered no protests throughout the 1920s and early 1930s. There were major public events celebrating the emancipation centenary and the consecration of Archbishop MacDonald in 1929, and regular lectures with leading Catholics in the city's more prestigious halls. Such public displays of Catholic faith drew no significant protest and Catholic life proceeded without notable harassment from militant Protestants. It was February 1934 before militants organised against Catholicism, James Graham leading a demonstration against an Usher Hall lecture. Later that spring Graham was prosecuted after a sectarian 'melee' between rival groups at the Mound.[11] These, though, were isolated events with Catholic functions in late 1934 and early 1935 passing off without incident. It was reaction to a planned council reception for the Catholic Young Men's Society (CYMS) which ignited the sectarian issue, and PAS capitalised enormously from Catholic plans for a eucharistic congress in the city.

From its electoral debut PAS had a reputation for roughness, Labour activists complaining 'they could make no progress against rowdyism, even at outdoor meetings.' Cormack retorted: 'Why squeal now when the same medicine is administered to themselves, which they loved to administer to their opponents?'[12] Certainly PAS' electoral tactics during 1934 and 1935 were no rougher than Labour's in the general election of 1935, and considerably less so than Labour's parliamentary campaign in Leith in 1929.[13] Yet PAS did utilise the aura (if not the actual delivery) of violent physical confrontation as a useful propaganda tool. Addressing supporters at the Usher Hall, Cormack warned that Edinburgh would learn 'what a real "smash up" was' if the CYMS reception went ahead. Supporters were urged to protest peacefully, but told 'they could leave the other part of the business to the young fellows'.[14] PAS demonstrations in 1935 were large and boisterous – 10,000 gathered for the CYMS protest, and 10,000 for the main anti-congress demonstration. An indeterminate number, in a city unused to large-scale public protest, were thrill-seekers and the curious rather than committed anti-Catholics. These events have been described as 'the most violent anti-Catholic riots seen in Scotland this century',[15] yet were characterised less by confrontation than by noisy confusion. The CYMS protest 'passed without any serious developments'.[16] As the eucharistic congress approached, PAS focused its campaign on its closing Mass in St Andrew's Priory, Morningside. On the opening day of the congress PAS rallied at the Usher Hall, its followers deliberately drawn away from confrontation. After minor scuffles, however, PAS announced an impromptu demonstration for the second day, picketing a rally of Catholic women. Gallagher is wrong to claim that 'A suitable opportunity for venting hate did not present itself until ... the second day of the Congress'[17] – rather it seems that PAS plans were overtaken by the enthusiasm of its followers. Cormack, perhaps nettled by his lack of control, did not attend the picket. Involving 1,500 demonstrators, this proved the most violent PAS event although heavy policing ensured 'the situation never got out of hand'. Eleven arrests were made and nine men subsequently convicted, the court deliberately imposing punitive sentences.[18] The following day 10,000 Catholics gathered in the priory grounds with 10,000 others outside to demonstrate (or to spectate). Alarmingly, several buses carrying Catholics were stoned – but these were isolated incidents on the fringes of a night tinged with confusion. Cormack spent the evening desperately trying (and failing) to assert some authority over 'his' crowd, and the image of a priory besieged by demonstrators is inaccurate. Some priests left the priory grounds unaware of the protests.[19] One priest recalls protestors 'cordoned off by a fairly strong contingent of police' and 'no major incidents of violence to mar the day'. He recalls, however, a palpable sense of tension: 'The atmosphere was not calmed by the presence of a group of [Catholic] men who set up camp in the grounds as self-appointed guardians that weekend, and armed themselves with a strange assortment of items to serve as clubs. Fortunately their martial arts were not called upon.'[20] The night yielded only four arrests, all involved in the stoning of a bus. The four were heavily fined and warned that a subsequent conviction would see them jailed.[21]

Small-scale confrontation continued throughout the summer with occasional clashes between PAS and a recently formed Catholic Vigilance Association (CVA), intended to defend church property from vandalism. In response to publicity surrounding CVA activities, PAS announced the formation of 'A Real Vigilance Association': Kormack's Kaledonian Klan. Much has been made of the 'Ks', but it amounted to little more than a grandiose and puerile title for the 'young fellows'. The name was both a conscious reference to the North American Klan (in the inter-war years characterised by urban anti-Catholicism rather than rural racism) as well as a sneering reference to an obscure and short-lived Ratcliffe 'bodyguard', the Knights of Kaledonia Klan.[22] A study of the local press – which reported 'sectarian' disturbances in the city with relish – between April and December 1935 suggests that a total of 38 criminal charges were brought in connection with sectarian incidents, with around two-thirds of those charged appearing to be active militant Protestants. Whilst this figure undoubtedly underestimates the level of religious tension and violence in the city, it does suggest that the extent of the disorder has been exaggerated in subsequent accounts. Militant Protestantism's effective street presence was, in any case, a brief phenomenon. In North Leith, during the 1936 election, PAS speakers were drowned out by opponents who 'kept up a continual barracking by the singing of Irish songs', an affront PAS was not strong enough to overcome.[23]

One reason for the exaggeration of the extent and effectiveness of PAS violence is the palpable shock experienced in a city relatively unused to sectarian controversy and where, until very recently, Catholic activities had been rarely publicly criticised, let alone physically challenged. Archbishop MacDonald complained that the fact that 'a riot ... did not actually take place' in Morningside was due only to police action 'deserving of the highest commendation' and to the 'commendable self-restraint' of Catholics. He further urged that steps be taken against 'incitement to violence'.[24] The scale of the remembered violence seems to have been rapidly magnified by the absence, in McDonald's view, of an adequately wide and sympathetic recognition of the Catholic experience.[25] These concerns were echoed by Gallagher: 'The fact that no major Edinburgh institution such as the Kirk, the police, or the press took a major stand against Cormack or consistently sought to deflect public opinion away from him ... causes apprehension even at a distance of fifty years.'[26]

In fact a number of institutions *were* resolutely consistent in their hostility to PAS, not least the press and the courts. Those convicted of sectarian offences received harsher treatment than that given for more serious offences without sectarian overtones, and there is some evidence of judicial leniency towards Catholics provoked into retaliation.[27] The police were praised by Archbishop MacDonald, and they undoubtedly handled the militants skilfully. The authorities, though, feared that prosecution would, far from chastening the militant Protestant leadership, afford them unprecedented publicity. In 1936 James Graham and a colleague were convicted of breach of the peace, the Sheriff declaring that the 'time had arrived when the authorities must take up a firm attitude and put down these disturbances'.[28] Charges were then unexpectedly preferred against three PAS leaders. The authorities seem to have been encouraged by the conviction of Graham, and while the prosecution was, technically speaking, a success it proved a publicity triumph for militant Protestantism. Cormack's trial and subsequent (brief) incarceration preceded the electoral peak of militant Protestantism in the city.

Initially, mainstream Protestantism insisted that militancy was not their problem, dismissing the movement as 'unchurched' and ignorant. By 1935, however, as the movement began to take off, Presbyterians were not slow in expressing disgust and dismay.[29] An outright condemnation not only of PAS but of 'Our attitude to the Church of Rome' was written by the Kirk's Principal Clerk, Rev. W. M. McGregor, and published as the lead article in *Life & Work*. McGregor warned: '[I]f Protestantism can be vindicated only in such ways, its day is nearly done,' and claimed that in the face of 'a rising tide of paganism both in faith and morals', '[i]t is not inconceivable that some day all who call Jesus Lord may be driven to stand together, acknowledging and assisting one another, in order to save the nation from the deluge.'[30] Here was a senior churchman condemning militant Protestantism *and* the Presbyterian anti-Irish campaign on the front page of the flagship publication of the Church of Scotland. The Kirk's Edinburgh presbytery noted that the PAS protests of June 1935 'had caused much heart-searching and deep concern to many of their people' and rejected as 'fundamentally unchristian': 'all methods of violence, all interference with personal freedom, and every word and action which expressed the spirit of hatred'. In 1936 the United Free Church's Edinburgh presbytery unanimously denounced PAS as 'unworthy of our religion and injurious to its good name'.[31]

In short, press, civic authorities and mainstream Presbyterians *did* oppose PAS, and the police seemed to have been very diligent in keeping its more physically minded elements in check. Far from causing 'apprehension', the actions of these bodies suggest a belief, perhaps a prescient one, that PAS was riding on an outburst of socio-economic anxiety and that, as one Kirk minister wrote to the press, 'mass hysteria, as experience shows, dies away as quickly as it arises'.[32]

Militant Protestantism reached its electoral zenith in 1936, winning the support of almost a third of Edinburgh's electorate. Who supported the militant Protestants, and why? The obvious answer is that they were supported by Protestants viewing the presence of Catholicism in their midst with apprehension and distaste. Yet such an answer begs two questions: why did anti-Catholicism become politically viable at *that* moment; and were militant Protestants most successful in religiously mixed wards? McLean, with regard to Glasgow, concludes that the SPL vote 'probably bore little relation to the proportion of Catholics [in the particular ward]. The enemy did not have to live next door to be hated or feared.'[33] Yet PAS took seats in precisely those areas where Catholics did have a fairly sizeable presence – in particular Leith, Canongate and Broughton. In part this was because Edinburgh's Catholics made up a considerably smaller proportion of the population and were less politically organised than their Glasgow brethren. Edinburgh's left was weak and there was no 'machine' to direct the Catholic vote. While militant Protestants were to avoid, or fail in, certain Glasgow wards because of a sizeable and organised Catholic political presence there were few such obstacles in Edinburgh.

By 1936 militant Protestants held nine seats across six Edinburgh wards. Detailed data are scarce, but some judgements can be made by ranking wards according to a measure of housing quality from the 1931 census: persons per 100 windowed rooms (PWR). Table 9.1 shows those wards where militant Protestants performed best in terms of the proportion of each ward's electorate who supported them. Using this measure (rather than the proportion of those who actually voted) most clearly illustrates underlying levels of support. The table also shows the number of times each ward was won by Labour candidates (excluding by-elections) between 1921 and 1938: Labour success is found only at the 'poorer' end of the PWR scale, suggesting that this measure is a useful, if crude, surrogate measure for class.[34] The table does not show Edinburgh's eight most affluent wards[35] (falling in a PWR range of 66 to 98) since Protestants rarely contested these wards, and when they did they polled very poorly indeed. Labour also failed miserably in these eight affluent wards achieving no electoral victories across the entire inter-war period.

Table 9.1 Protestant electoral record by ward

PWR ranking (out of 23 wards)		PWR	Labour wins	Highest % electorate voting Protestant
	MIXED WARDS			
9	West Leith	102	–	11
10	St Andrew's	108	–	13
11	Portobello	108	–	16
12	**Broughton**	109	–	24
	WORKING-CLASS WARDS			
13	Liberton	125	4	9
14	George Square	132	–	17
15	Calton	135	5	21
16	**South Leith**	144	–	29
17	**Gorgie**	152	14	25

PWR *ranking* (out of 23 wards)		PWR	Labour *wins*	Highest % electorate *voting Protestant*
18	Canongate	155	8	26
19	St Leonard's	160	15	27
20	St Giles'	162	8	15
21	Dalry	163	13	21
22	**Central Leith**	169	3	26
23	**North Leith**	183	9	26

Source: Census of Scotland, 1931; election returns, Scottish press (1921–38)

Militant Protestantism targeted the most working-class of the city's wards, with electoral success almost entirely limited to such districts. Incursions into mixed wards targeted working-class enclaves within them. Class geography never mapped neatly onto municipal boundaries, and PAS won Broughton in 1936 on the basis of their support in working-class Pilrig and Bonnington, both of which bordered North and Central Leith.

The militant Protestant vote was substantial in working-class wards, and in working-class enclaves within mixed wards, but largely non-existent outwith such areas. While this might seem unsurprising (Gallagher, for example, gives a good sense of PAS' proletarian character), the same was not true for the SPL in Glasgow, where support was strongest in affluent suburban wards.[36] It should also be stressed that the Protestant record was by no means consistent across working-class areas – Liberton and St Giles' wards resisted the PAS message, and North Leith developed into such a poor prospect that PAS had abandoned it by 1938. These three wards had relatively substantial Catholic populations, suggesting that PAS found it difficult to operate where its enemy was strong enough to vote tactically. Ironically, PAS engendered a self-fulfilling prophecy, with its fulminations about a (largely imaginary) Catholic 'bloc vote' bringing one into existence in parts of proletarian Edinburgh.

How did PAS and its allies attract this working-class vote? Broadly speaking, their approach can be divided into two phases – the development of popular support between c.1933 and 1936, and the failed consolidation of that support c.1936–39. This first phase was overwhelmingly characterised by 'the controversy' (i.e. traditional and often esoteric critiques of 'Popery') whilst the second was strongly characterised by 'secular' arguments and the relegation of anti-Catholic themes. Some degree of anti-Irish sentiment was present through the entire period, though very much in the background.

PAS and its allies followed a well-trodden path of anti-Catholic rhetoric in the 'Covenantal' tradition that Romanism was a pagan conspiracy.[37] Starting from the contention that 'Rome' was not simply un-Scriptural but *anti*-Scriptural, Catholicism was seen as much as a political conspiracy as a movement of faith. The danger of 'Rome' was that it actively conspired to enslave the temporal world, to crush freedom of thought and action. By the twentieth century, however, such views had retreated to the fringes of Protestant life and were seen by most mainstream clerics (as the tenor of the Presbyterian campaign suggests) as an embarrassing and best-forgotten anachronism. The 'controversy' remained alive on the evangelical fringes, in the gospel halls and evangelical missions, and had a redoubtable (if thoroughly eccentric) champion in Rev. Jacob Primmer, a missioner in the Church of Scotland. Primmer revelled in controversy, actively courting violent opposition (to 'prove' Catholic intolerance). In later life, till his death in 1914, Primmer held weekly meetings in Edinburgh, building up a small but intensely loyal following which was to form the core of later militant Protestantism.

The fare of militant Protestant meetings in the early 1930s was little different from that offered by Primmer and many before. In 1933, for example, James Graham's Edinburgh Protestant Society (EPS) held lectures on 'indulgences'; 'confessionals', '*Ne Temere*', and 'the Jesuits', whilst PAS offered a men-only expose on 'The priest, woman and confessional'. Although relations between these groups were hostile, both sang from the same lurid hymn sheet. Just weeks after PAS offered 'Startling truths about the popes! Facts, Pope Joan: What was "it"?' the EPS offered 'The truth about the she-pope'.[38] The rhetoric at this time focused upon the more salacious (and publicly appealing) aspects of 'the controversy', occasionally spiced up by specific reaction to local Catholic activities. The Catholic Evidence Guild (CEG) was active in Edinburgh and frequently the Mound witnessed simultaneous meetings of the CEG, PAS, EPS and myriad others each verbally (though rarely physically) attacking the other. Infighting on the Protestant fringe was endemic and bitter and brought to the fore a thorny problem for those immersing themselves in 'the controversy': in the struggle against Catholic*ism*, what approach was to be taken towards Catholic*s*?

In the abstract sense the answer was simple, if rarely practised: abhor the sin and love the sinner. But given that Catholicism as a system was viewed as a very real and immediate political conspiracy, Catholics were to be regarded as simultaneously the perpetrators *and* victims of 'Popery'. PAS argued that active opposition towards both the system and those sustaining it was necessary, and that the intolerance *of* Rome could only be countered by intolerance *towards* Rome: 'What is toleration? Why should wild beasts be caged? Because they are dangerous to life and limb. But it is intolerant to the beast and contrary to God's laws. The Papists, not because of their religion (which is certainly not Christian), but because of the fact that politics is the great factor through it, and in it, makes them a danger, and like wild beasts as far as our Protestantism is concerned. Therefore we must keep them in a ... position where they will be less dangerous.'[39]

In 1934 Cormack insisted that PAS could not co-operate with ex-Catholics, because they could not be trusted, and coined the slogan 'Once a papist, always a papist'. This broke the militant Protestant consensus (not always reflected in practice) that individual Catholics were redeemable, could be 'saved' by conversion. From its inception PAS was ambiguous on this point

– describing itself as '100 per cent Protestant' – but the slogan 'Once a papist' was specifically used against James Graham (an ex-Catholic) during a particularly tense moment of intra-militant conflict in 1934. By 1936 PAS was supporting Graham electorally, and Cormack never severed his long-standing connections to a number of ex-Catholic evangelists. Cormack addressed a mission hall, in 1931, on the question 'Should Protestants be bitter towards Roman Catholics?' His co-operation on the night with converted ex-Catholics provided the answer. The slogan, therefore, was a weapon against Graham and not a deeply-held principle. Its utility, though, was wider. When PAS urged that Catholic bodies be banned from public halls, Ratcliffe denounced them as 'intolerant pro-Romanists who would deprive Romanists of their rights'. For Ratcliffe, the touchstone of Protestantism was civil and political rights for all; the key character of Catholicism its denial of such rights. PAS' opposition to granting Catholics access to public halls could thus be said to 'savour of Popery'.[40] The cumbersome gymnastics of such 'logic' made 'Once a papist' attractive for its simplicity.

The 'controversy' alone cannot explain the rise of militant Protestantism in Edinburgh. After all, this militant critique of 'Rome' was hardly new; why did it appeal specifically at this time? The question is all the more telling when the SPL's Edinburgh Education Authority campaign of 1925 is considered. Then, militant Protestantism could muster only 2,666 votes throughout the entire city. The militant Protestant vote in 1935 totalled 18,109, almost doubled (to 35,002) in 1936, and even in 1937, when the movement was in clear decline, totalled 27,810. More telling was the situation in Leith: only 481 Leithers had voted for militant Protestants in 1925, compared with 8,015 in 1935 and 9,438 in 1936. If the anti-Popery message had not changed, the popular mood had. Militant Protestants in the 1930s were able to capitalise on very real and pressing fears within working-class communities that their economic and social conditions were not simply deteriorating, but collapsing. Slum clearance was tearing the heart from long-established communities and relocating (often very reluctant) tenants to the outer fringes of the city. The new estates were relatively far from places of work and leisure, far from the friends and family left behind, and ill served by affordable public transport. The great promise of Edinburgh's house-building schemes had collapsed in the mid-1930s, and while the ruling Moderates (closely associated with landlordism) pursued austerity the Labour Party was too weak, and too timid, to offer a real alternative.

In many clearance areas local opinion favoured rapid rebuilding and rehousing on the cleared sites themselves, opinion which only PAS was consistently to support in the council chamber. This was the key to electoral success, fitting 'the controversy' into specific and immediate secular concerns – in a sense, making 'Popery' a bread and butter issue. Protestant candidates did precisely that in the 1934 and 1935 elections, insisting (with considerable success) that Catholics were receiving preferential treatment at the hands of the corporation, monopolising the most secure of the unskilled posts in some municipal departments, and controlling recruitment in others. Redress from

Moderate policy would not come from the left (since the Labour Party was in thrall to a Catholic bloc vote) and thus the only way to protect and improve the lot of ordinary Protestants, it was argued, was through a specifically Protestant bloc vote. The first PAS council motion urged: 'That the religious denomination of all employees under this Corporation and of every future employee be obtained, and also the department to which they are allocated, in order that only 10 per cent of Corporation employment be given to Papists'.[41]

The attempted fusion of 'the controversy' with secular concerns became clear in 1935 when PAS adopted as its own policy a hodgepodge of public works proposals concocted by the independent Protestant George Horne. His 'Prosperous Times' policy argued that the corporation should raise a loan subscription of several millions to ride out the economic downturn and restart the housing programme. As a platform it was unsophisticated but its evident popularity amongst South Leith electors persuaded PAS to adopt it wholesale. This left PAS pushing a contradictory message – while their 'manifesto' proudly reminded voters that their sole plank was crushing the 'Papist Beast' their attached 'programme' offered a wide range of vague economic promises.[42]

PAS' appeal hinged on the fact that Edinburgh as a whole escaped the worst ravages of the depression and did not, therefore, qualify for Special Area Assistance. Deprived areas of the city felt doubly burdened – ignored not simply by the authorities in Westminster, but by Moderate austerity measures. Leith had particular grievances, remaining unhappy over its forced 1920 amalgamation with Edinburgh, and as a trading port was acutely sensitive to economic crisis. As one Leither complained: 'It is well known that Leith is one of the most distressed areas … but the port cannot be classified as such nor be given any special benefits because of her misfortune in being amalgamated with Edinburgh … Edinburgh and Leith are rather like Dives and Lazarus, Dives being utterly indifferent to the sores and pains of Lazarus at his gate. Dives does not want to be bothered or interrupted in his pleasures, and so he shuts his eyes to the misery so near by.'[43] In the mid-1930s Leith contained one-fifth of Edinburgh's population, a quarter of its total unemployed, over a third of those 'temporarily stopped', and 90 per cent of Edinburgh's unemployed who were 'normally in casual employment'.[44] Without political influence but with a strong and distinctive identity, Leith provided 27 per cent of the militant Protestant vote in 1936 as PAS harnessed resentment to the ruling Moderates and exasperation at the weakness of Labour. Although PAS' offices were in central Edinburgh, its social offices – running games nights; and mother and toddler, and pensioner groups – were in Leith's Corner Rooms. The remarkable range of militant Protestant activity in Leith suggests that anti-Catholicism was less immediately important than more secular, and time-specific, issues.

In the 1936 election secular and material issues were very much to the fore as Protestant candidates made Labour their key target, with the slogan 'Neglected Leith' used to good effect. So powerful was the effect of the Leith card that other parties tried, less convincingly, to use it. The proposal for corporation employment to be 90 per cent Protestant and attacks on the Catholic bloc vote remained, but PAS was now keen to move away from the view that it was a single-issue (i.e. anti-Catholic) party. Cormack insisted that PAS proposed: 'schemes and suggestions, which are both business-like and visionary, for the better working of the city of Edinburgh, and for the upholding and protection of our Protestant interests'.[45] The defiant words of 1934 and 1935 – the single plank of battling the 'Papist Beast' – were quietly forgotten in favour of 'business-like' economic populism. This contrasts directly with the strategies of other radical fringe groups in inter-war Britain who *began* with an economic platform but leavened it with the scapegoating of minorities (e.g. the increasing use of anti-Semitism by the British Union of Fascists and the Social Credit Party).

By November 1937 the 'controversy', whilst still evident in PAS propaganda, had receded even further into the background. Indeed the *Evening News* noted that PAS was increasingly more 'municipal' than 'sectarian'.[46] Of the eight points in the PAS election programme only two were explicitly sectarian; the Protestant employment proposal, and a policy towards the 'RC Irish' (a rare explicit reference by PAS to 'the Irish': 'We will take steps to prevent any further inroads of this community in our City, as they are a menace to our citizens').[47] In the subdued campaign of 1938, held under the cloud of Munich, PAS was especially anonymous. With their vote collapsing militant Protestantism began to drift back towards the political fringes. As it drifted, PAS returned to emphasising the 'controversy '– but its moment as a metaphor for working-class dissatisfaction had passed. Militant Protestantism had reaped the benefit of a moment of acute socio-economic anxiety amongst Edinburgh's working class. But it was only that, a moment. Once anxiety had passed the PAS vote simply evaporated. As the *Evening Dispatch* editorialised in 1938: 'It would appear as if the sectarian issue is losing ground. There will not be much regret about that.'[48]

It seems significant that Edinburgh's militant Protestants did not play the 'anti-Irish' card to any great extent. This is not to say that PAS was silent on the Irish for it was not – as its 1937 policy statement on the 'RC Irish' and occasional complaints of recently arrived 'Free Staters' acquiring municipal jobs indicates. However, the national character, real or perceived, of Catholics was never to the fore in PAS rhetoric. This returns us to the need to be cautious in relation to the 'Scottish equation'. If the equation worked in 1930s Edinburgh, if the terms Irish and Catholic were coterminous, we might reasonably expect to have found considerable slippage between the two terms in the rhetoric of militant Protestants. In fact we find relatively little, and the simplest explanation is that PAS attacked *Popery* because they were genuinely and sincerely opposed to *Catholicism*. Their enemy was first, foremost and supremely, Romanism as a global system and its local – 'Papist' – agents. If these Papists could be dismissed as 'Free Staters' with the implications of 'disloyalty' to British laws and values that might add, then so much the better. But these were added value, never crucial (nor indeed important) to the 'controversy'. PAS and its allies regarded themselves as the defenders of an essential Protestant tradition – leading back through the Covenanters to John Knox himself – that mainstream Presbyterians had abandoned. In other words, from our secularised twenty-first century viewpoint we should not underestimate ultra-conservative theology as a motivating political factor in 1930s Edinburgh.

There is much misunderstanding about the militant Protestant parties of the 1930s, not least because most accounts have focused upon their sensational and violent aspects rather than on the underlying basis of what was, essentially, a brief moment of electoral despair. What makes PAS so enigmatic is that the extent of its violence has been historically magnified and exaggerated. This exaggeration reflects the fact that Edinburgh, and in particular its Catholic minority, was simply stunned by the rise of PAS. In turn, the shock PAS delivered to the placid (indeed enervating) politics in Edinburgh illustrates precisely how marginal the 'controversy' had been over the first three decades of Scotland's twentieth century. Yet, intriguingly and disturbingly, much of Edinburgh's working class – frustrated at their lack of representation in a Moderate dominated and relatively prosperous city – turned to a party intent on crushing the 'Papist Beast'. PAS electrified and polarised Edinburgh's politics, inadvertently galvanising a hitherto ineffectual left and rapidly undermining much of the basis of its own appeal.

The PAS story might suggest the vibrancy and depth of anti-Catholic and anti-Irish politics in inter-war Scotland, and some authors have certainly interpreted it in this way. However, anti-Irishness was not a key theme in PAS rhetoric, and a broader view of its rise and fall demonstrates the long-standing marginality of religious particularism in Scottish politics. Unlike Northern Ireland there were no major secular issues dividing Scotland neatly across religious, ethnic or 'racial' cleavages. In Ulster, conservative Protestantism – and the anti-Catholic controversy it pursued – operated as a sacred canopy under which Protestants united in defence of their economic and political interests. In Scotland, two issues marked out a different historical trajectory. Firstly, mainstream Presbyterianism, notwithstanding its ugly and self-serving turn towards ethnocentrism in the 1920s, had largely abandoned the traditional critique of Catholicism. Ministers no longer immersed themselves in anachronistic and embarrassing pope-baiting activities. Secondly, Scotland's key socio-political cleavage was class, and here the Labour movement provided – where it was strong enough – a secular canopy within which workers of all religions and none found their economic interests represented. The 1930s saw not simply the peak, but also the dying kick, of militant Protestant populism. PAS (and the SPL) were strictly limited in time and location and left two distinct legacies. In the political realm they helped to revitalise and strengthen a Labour Party which, after the agonising split of 1931, seemed to have lost its way. In the cultural realm, they left a wealth of bitter memories.

10 The Orange Order in Scotland since 1860: A social analysis

Eric Kaufmann

The Orange Order is a fraternity founded in the north of Ireland in 1795 whose constitution commits its members to the defence of Protestantism and the British Crown, and has served as a major associational nexus for Protestant dominant ethnic groups in Scotland, Northern Ireland, north-western England and Canada. Its convivial and religious role has been matched by its political engagement. In the above locations, the order has supplied numerous local, provincial or national leaders and has attempted to influence the course of government policy in a unionist and Protestant direction.[1]

Two key questions run through the literature on Scottish Orangeism. First, whether the order was an Irish import or a native Scots-Protestant response to Irish-Catholic immigration. Second, was the 'Orange vote' a coherent political force, and the rise to prominence of several Orangemen as Scottish politicians significant? These are symbolically charged issues. Those who cleave to a Scottish nationalist perspective tend to downplay the role of Scots-Protestant antipathy toward the Irish, as well as the power of the Orange Order over Scottish politics. Scoto-Irish activists, will, by contrast, accentuate the power of native Scots' sectarianism and the role of Orangeism in Scottish politics. Where does the truth lie? On this, the academic authorities are divided. Elaine McFarland stresses the Irish-Protestant, working-class, immigrant basis of Scottish Orangeism. This suggests that Orangeism was an import that failed to capture the imagination of native Scots, who were more inclined toward socialism or 'liberal commonsense'.[2] In considering the inter-war period, Graham Walker reiterates McFarland's claim that the order was principally an Irish-Protestant ethnic association. Drawing on contemporary newspaper reports, he suggests that the order was 'maintained in the early decades of the twentieth [century] by immigrants and their Scottish-born descendants'.[3]

This did not, however, render the order politically impotent. Walker maintains that the political turbulence of the inter-war period led to a surge in Orange membership, a broader Scottish appeal and enhanced political activism. As evidence, he points to the sweeping success of Orange candidates in the 1919 Glasgow school board elections and notes the presence of a considerable number of Orange MPs in the twenties and thirties. Among these were Sir John Gilmour, Secretary of State for Scotland (1924–29) and Col A. D. McInnes Shaw.[4] A study of election results in this period, writes Walker, indicates that 'the Orange vote was a meaningful political factor' despite its inchoate and unpredictable nature.[5] Steve Bruce adds that the order helped deliver the Protestant working-class vote in west-central constituencies until the 1950s.[6] Ian Maclean, however, disagrees: even in the turbulent 1918–22 period, he contends that Orangemen were less likely to vote as a bloc than Catholics, and failed to affect Labour in any major electoral contest.[7] Others claim that the jury is still out as to the existence and efficacy of the Orange vote in the twentieth century.[8]

In terms of membership dynamics, Walker notes that Irish immigration slowed considerably between the wars, but he does not assert that this affected Orange membership. Rather, he suggests that events kept membership buoyant. This is an account that finds some resonance in the work of Bruce and McFarland, as well as other political historians of the order who emphasise the role of events.[9] Others point to the importance of class structure in reinforcing sectarian division, with the Orange Order in Northern Ireland viewed as a means for Protestant-dominated manufacturing interests to divide or control the working class.[10]

In terms of the more recent period, Steve Bruce suggests that slum clearance has been more of a factor than declining religiosity in the order's decline. Though not specifically addressing Orangeism, he also writes that the relatively low proportion of Catholics in Scotland, as compared to Ulster, has always limited the appeal of militant Protestant movements.[11] Some evidence for Bruce's contention is provided by the example of Liverpool, where Peter Day found that 60 per cent of Orange members he surveyed chose slum clearance as a reason for post-1945 membership decline – by far the largest factor cited by Orange respondents.[12]

This chapter builds upon the existing historical newspaper-based literature, but attempts to chart major trends with greater precision and makes a more concerted attempt to evaluate the relative strength of competing explanations for fluctuations in Orange strength. This necessarily relies on high-quality statistical data which has only been made possible by unprecedented access to the records of the Grand Orange Lodge of Scotland (GOLS). These provide a virtually complete run of annual membership data, across lodge and county, for the period 1860–2001.[13]

Membership Trends

Let us begin by considering the long-term trend in Scottish male Orange membership, expressed as a ratio per thousand males. For confidentiality reasons, actual membership figures cannot be displayed, but the general trend is clear.[14] Membership increases occurred in the periods 1863–77, 1902–9, 1919–26, 1941–53 and 1961–79. Notable declines took place during 1878–1900, 1913–18, 1927–41 and 1987-present. Spikes of over 20 per cent in membership took place during 1920, 1903, 1933, 1864 and 1865. Collapses of over 20 per cent occurred during 1885 and 1934 (see Figure 10.1).

In explaining patterns such as these, it is tempting to jump immediately to

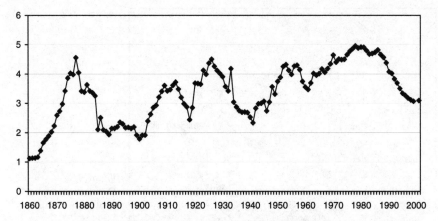

Figure 10.1 Orange membership, Scotland, per 1,000 males. Source: Grand Orange
Lodge of Scotland reports and return sheets; Census of Scotland

event-driven explanations. However, while certain historical junctures appear
to be relevant, we also need to be cognisant of the many events that seem to
have had a surprisingly limited effect (i.e. Great Depression, Home Rule Crises
of 1884–6 and 1916–22, Northern Ireland 'Troubles' of 1969–72). Appearances
can be deceiving, though, since events can counteract each other's influence and
mask underlying social trends. We therefore need to contextualise these patterns
against a background of both internal developments (i.e. dues increases) and
broader social, demographic and economic changes in order to assess the true
predictive power of these events. We will come to this later on.

Scottish Orangeism has been limited in strength, but has proven remarkably
durable. The tale of Orangeism in the latter half of the twentieth century
has been one of steady decline, but while Scottish Orange male membership
peaked as late as 1982, Ontario membership peaked in 1920 (a smaller peak
was attained in the late 1950s) and membership in both Northern Ireland and
Newfoundland peaked around 1960. These changes have been so profound
that today there are slightly more Orangemen in Scotland than in Canada!
Though the nature of these differences is beyond the scope of this essay, it
suggests that the Scottish context differs in important ways from those in other
Orange jurisdictions.

A further dimension to this study is geographic. Figures 10.2 and 10.3
map Scottish Orange Lodges in 2001, with points adjusted for size of
lodge membership. This is framed by pre-1973 Scottish county boundaries.
Notice the concentration of membership on the west coast of central
Scotland around Glasgow and North Lanarkshire, with spillover into adjacent
counties, notably West Lothian (the highest per capita concentration of
current membership), Renfrewshire and Ayrshire. This is partially explicable
by population distribution, given the primacy of Glasgow and the surrounding
Clydeside conurbation as the largest Scottish metropolitan area. Yet the

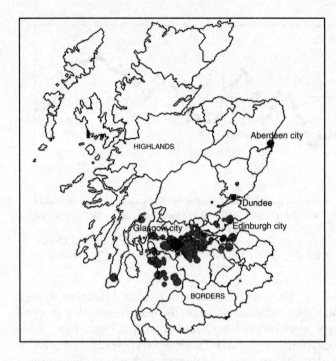

Figure 10.2 Distribution of Scottish Orange Lodges, 2001. Source: Grand Orange Lodge of Scotland 2001 Directory and return sheets. Digital boundaries courtesy of EDINA/UK Borders

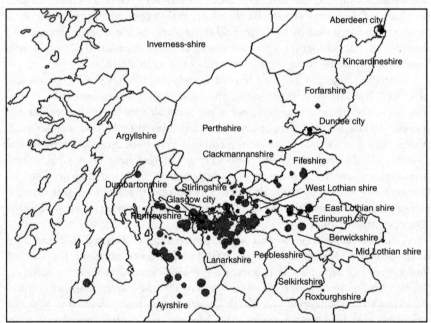

Figure 10.3 Distribution of Scottish Orange Lodges, by county, central Scotland, 2001. Source: Grand Orange Lodge of Scotland 2001 Directory and return sheets. Digital boundaries courtesy of EDINA/UK Borders

paucity of lodges in both the Highland and Borders regions and in populous Edinburgh, Dundee and Aberdeen is striking.

Orange Membership Density

It is very often forgotten that Orangeism was, and is, a worldwide fraternity, and could at one time be found throughout the British Empire. English-speaking Canada, not Ireland, has been the leading Orange jurisdiction, with Scotland, England, Australasia and the United States occupying a much smaller position within the organisation. One way of examining the impact of Orangeism in a particular location is membership density. Orange male membership density is calculated as the number of Orange male members per target population (adult male British Protestants). In these terms, the Scottish membership density has generally been little more than 1 per cent, and averaged barely 2 per cent in its Clydeside heartland during its membership peak. Even in its

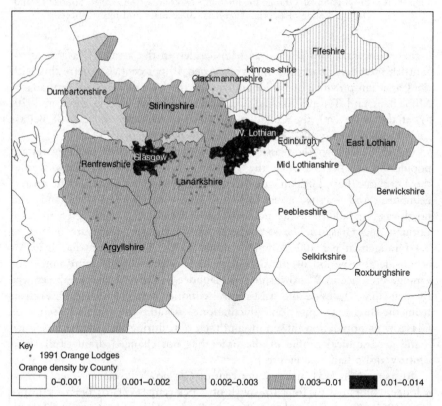

Figure 10.4 Orange Lodges and proportion of Orangemen in the adult male Protestant population, central Scotland, 1991. Source: Grand Orange Lodge of Scotland reports and return sheets; Census of Scotland; digital boundaries courtesy of EDINA/UK Borders

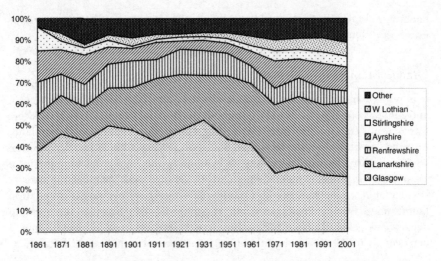

Figure 10.5 Proportion of Orange membership by county, 1861–2001. Source: Grand Orange Lodge of Scotland reports, directories and return sheets

highest concentrations (Govan and Rutherglen in the greater Glasgow area), Scottish membership density rarely exceeded 10 per cent. Compare this with the Canadian province of Newfoundland or the Irish counties of Fermanagh, Monaghan and Tyrone (all had a density of roughly one in three in 1920) or, at the lower end, the Canadian province of Ontario and city of Belfast (membership density of both was around 10 per cent in 1920).[15]

Figure 10.4 shows the density of Orangeism in the adult male Protestant population in 1991. Notice the strength of Orangeism in Glasgow and the Lothians (East Lothian's density is 0.0095) and its weakness in greater Edinburgh and – as we noted in Figure 10.2 – the Borders, Highlands and north-east. In addition, the numbers are astoundingly small: even in West Lothian and Glasgow, the strongholds of Orangeism, there are only 1 to 1.4 Orangemen per 100 Protestant adult males. This pattern has held for a considerable period of time. Though there was a slightly more numerous Orange presence in Wigtownshire and Dundee in the mid-nineteenth century, the principal Clydeside and west-central counties have dominated Orangeism from the outset. Despite some fluctuation – notably the rise and decline of Glasgow as population moved in, and then out, during the twentieth century – the geographical profile of the order has not changed dramatically in a century and a half (see Figure 10.5).

At its peak in 1951, under 2 per cent of Glasgow's Protestant men were in a lodge, compared to Toronto's peak of 7 per cent (1921) or Belfast's 16 per cent (1951). On the other hand, if we look at ward-level patterns in Glasgow based on 1931 and 1961 census data and attribute membership data based on lodge locations, we find that the greatest area of strength is in Govan district, where Orange density may have been as high as 16 per cent –18 per cent given the size of the district's Catholic population. This may be inflated due to commuting patterns, but in any case, density appears to be highest in the swath of south bank wards stretching from Govan in the west through present-day Ibrox (then Kinning Park and Fairfield) and Kingston. Orange density was also high in suburban Rutherglen (10 per cent–15 per cent) to the south-east, and in Cowcaddens (10 per cent –12 per cent) north of the centre. These areas thus were as Orange as much of Belfast.[16] There is little to suggest that these areas of Orange strength shifted after 1961, though members in the city lodges may have increasingly been commuting in from suburban estates. Gordon McCracken suggests that roughly half of Kelvingrove district's membership resides in Drumchapel, an estate developed north-west of the city after 1959. A similar tale can be told for other city districts.[17] Figure 10.6 shows Orange Lodges in the city by size in 1981, at the peak of the order's membership. The Clyde is the backbone of Orangeism in Glasgow. Notice the presence of the large Govan Lodge in Kingston ward and the lodge in

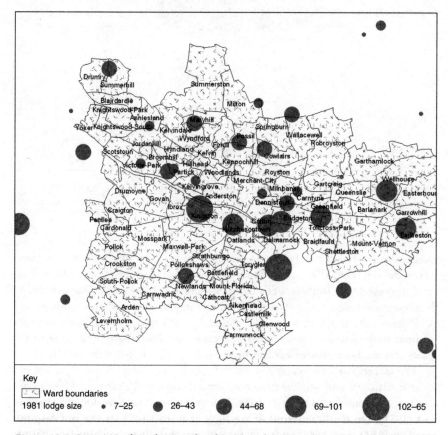

Figure 10.6 Orange Lodges, by membership size, showing Glasgow wards, 1981.
Source: Grand Orange Lodge of Scotland return sheets, 1981; digital boundaries courtesy of EDINA/UK Borders

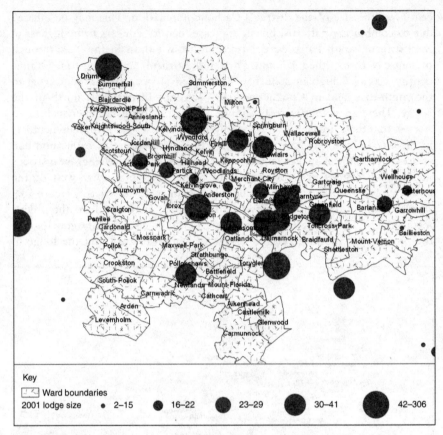

Figure 10.7 Orange Lodges, by membership size, showing Glasgow wards, 2001.
Source: Grand Orange Lodge of Scotland return sheets, 2001; digital
boundaries courtesy of EDINA/UK Borders

neighbouring Hutchesontown, despite significant Catholic presence in these
areas. By contrast, the greater Bridgeton-Calton-Dennistoun area in the East
End, though home to the order's headquarters and known as a 'Rangers area',
has fewer Catholics and thus a much lower Orange density than Govan. Figure
10.7 shows the city lodges in 2001. Little has changed, though there appears
to be membership loss in the outskirts (especially Baillieston-Wellhouse in the
east) and gains in greater Bridgeton as well as Maryhill-Possil-Cowlairs.

The Freemasons make for a useful contrast. Their ritual, symbolism,
degree structure and organisation are virtually identical to that of Orangeism.
Indeed, Orangeism explicitly drew upon Masonic models for inspiration.
Given a native Scots tradition of Masonry that goes back to the late fifteenth
century, it is unsurprising that this fraternity has done so well among Scottish
Protestants. In fact, Scotland's total of some 150,000 Masons gives this nation
the highest rate of Masonic membership in the world.[18] The Masons have

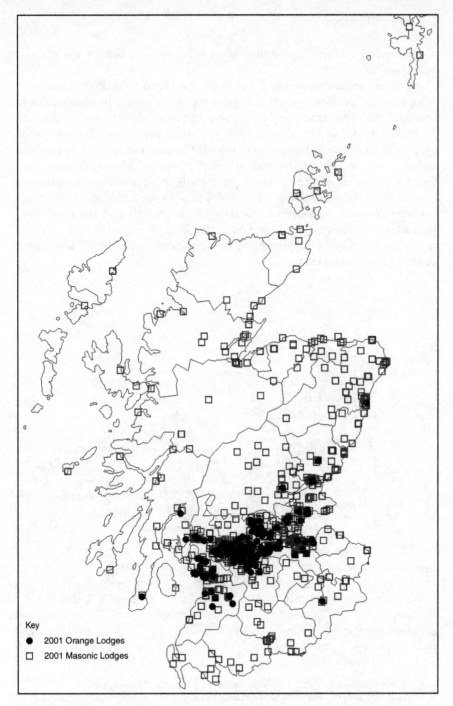

Figure 10.8 Orange Lodges and Masonic Lodges, Scotland, showing county
boundaries, 2001. Source: Grand Orange Lodge of Scotland return
sheets, 2001; *AFAM Grand Lodge of Scotland Yearbook, 2001*; digital
boundaries courtesy of EDINA/UK Borders

also served as one of the institutional vessels of both Scottish and popular Protestant identity.[19]

However, while Freemasonry has been associated with Protestantism in most English-speaking societies, its identity as an avowedly apolitical and non-religious organisation makes it a less convenient vehicle than Orangeism for Protestant or Loyalist identity. Here it is instructive to note the contrasting geography of Masonic lodges vis á vis their Orange counterparts in Scotland and in Glasgow (see Figures 10.8 and 10.9).[20] Notice Masonry's more even lodge distribution in the country – this maps much more neatly onto the broader Protestant population of Scotland as a whole: Clydeside is the major concentration, but lodges cover the Borders, Highlands and the north-east, with secondary concentrations in Edinburgh, Dundee and Aberdeen. Whereas nearly two-thirds of Orangemen live in Glasgow or Lanarkshire, less than a quarter of Scottish Masons do.

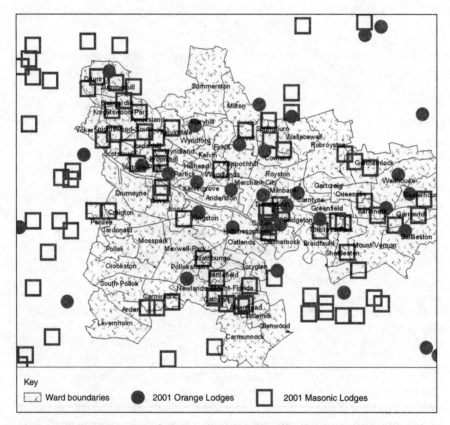

Figure 10.9 Orange Lodges and Masonic Lodges for Glasgow wards, 2001. Source: Grand Orange Lodge of Scotland return sheets, 2001; *AFAM Grand Lodge of Scotland Yearbook, 2001*; digital boundaries courtesy of EDINA/UK borders

Peering at trends in Glasgow in Figure 10.9, we find both Orange and Masonic Lodges absent from the largely Catholic south-western wards. Masonic Lodge halls, which far outnumber their Orange counterparts, are relatively absent from the deprived inner city zone from Kingston-Kelvingrove to the city centre. On the other hand, they are plentiful in the better-heeled west, and on the city's outskirts. This reflects a class division between these two fraternities, which we shall return to later on.

The Causes of Membership Change

Our next task is to explain membership dynamics in both their temporal and spatial dimensions. Orange membership has been computed from the annual reports of the Grand Lodge of Scotland 1860–1966, and annual returns for 1967 to 2001. Comparison data are drawn from decennial Scottish censuses, the annual reports of the Scottish Registrar-General and electoral data.[21] Geographic adjustments have been made in order to establish a continuous dataset for the 1961–1991 period, but 2001 data are not available.[22]

In order to figure out what is driving Orange membership, I compare against all available demographic, cultural and economic data from the 1861–1991 period. Variables are limited to those that span the entire 1861–1991 period as part of either the census or Registrar-General's series. The following variables were tested down for significance: *demographic* – population growth, population, sex ratio, population density, marriage rate, birth rate, infant mortality rate; *cultural* – religiosity (in terms of religious marriages as a percentage of total marriages), denomination (Church of Scotland, Roman Catholic, 'Nonconformist') and Irish born; and *economic* – proportions in agricultural sector, professions and manufacturing.

In addition, I try to isolate the impact of the Irish-Protestant ethnic factor to get at the question of whether Orangeism is brought by Irish Protestant immigrants, or is caused by the response of native Scots to Irish Catholics. Since the Irish-born population includes both Protestants and Catholics, we need to compare this figure with the proportion of Catholics. If the proportion of Irish-born is not significant, but the Catholic proportion of the population is, this suggests that we are observing a Scottish Protestant response to the presence of Irish Catholics. The use of fixed dates for the Irish-born variable (1851, 1901, 1921) is necessary due to the steady decline in the rate of Irish immigration after 1851.

Here I attempt to weigh the importance of the Irish-Protestant ethnic element by examining the ratio between the proportion Irish-born and the proportion Catholic at various dates (1901 was used for this model), a method used by Graham Walker.[23] If this ratio exceeds 1, for instance, there are likely to be more Irish-born who are not Catholic than if the number is much less than 1. When multiplied by the Irish-born population of 1901, this provides a term which measures the impact of the Irish-Protestant population in the absence of direct data. This interaction term can be expressed as follows: Irish

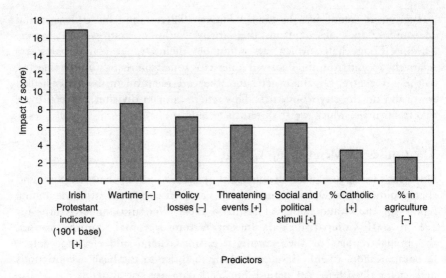

Figure 10.10 Predictors of Scottish Orange male density, 1860–1991. $N = 1,202$, $R2$
= 0.115, where N is the number of cases analysed and R^2 is a measure
of association where 0 is no correlation and 1 is perfect correlation.
Source: Eric Kaufmann, 'The Orange Order in Ontario, Newfoundland,
Scotland and Northern Ireland: a macro-social analysis', in David
A. Wilson (ed.), *The Orange Order in Canada* (Dublin, 2006).

Protestant Ethnic Group = (Irish-born % / Roman Catholic %) x Irish-born
%. This arrays cases between, on the one hand, counties like Argyllshire or
Aberdeenshire which possess larger native Scots Catholic populations but few
Irish descendants, and, on the other hand, counties with a large proportion of
Irish immigrants, but with relatively low Catholic populations. (Wigtownshire,
Ayrshire). Given our focus on the central belt, the former effect is not likely
greatly to influence our sample.

In statistical analyses which only include the main central belt counties, we
find that the strongest predictor of Orange density in a county over the period
1861–1991 is the Irish-Protestant percentage (z-score of 17 in Figure 10.10).
Next in importance are political events like the papal visit or Home Rule,
which are deemed to be political threats to Protestantism. The proportion
of Catholics is weaker than various events at explaining membership, but is
still significant.[24] This indicates that Elaine McFarland and Graham Walker
are correct in their appraisal that Irish-Protestant immigrants and their
descendants are the key to explaining Orange strength. The mere presence
of Irish Catholics, as in Dundee, is no guarantee of Orange strength, while
smaller numbers of Irish Catholics – as in Ayrshire or West Lothian – may
not directly correspond with lower Orange densities. Here we can see
parallels with Ontario, where Orangeism is much stronger in areas of historic
Irish-Protestant settlement, as well as Cumbria in northern England, where
virtually all Orangemen had Irish immigrant heritage. Newfoundland, where

Orange membership was the strongest of anywhere in the world, despite the absence of Irish-Protestant immigration, stands as a major exception to this pattern.

Another of the findings to emerge from this model is the importance of religio-ethnic variables as shown by the correlation between Orange membership density and the proportions of Irish-Protestant ethnicity and Catholic religion. The purely religious angle is not so vital: witness the insignificance of Protestant denomination (i.e. Church of Scotland v. Nonconformist) and religiosity in the analysis, thereby broadly confirming Bradley's survey evidence which shows that 27 per cent of Scots Orangemen belong to Churches other than the Church of Scotland while many are not regular churchgoers.[25] In contrast, socio-demographic and economic factors such as population density, infant mortality, illiteracy and proportion in manufacturing are insignificant, casting some doubt upon theories which link the spread of Orangeism to a 'labour aristocracy' in growing industries like shipping or textiles. Factors (rotated principal components) designed to simplify the full range of structural variables were also tested, with similar results.

The only (modestly) significant structural variable is the agricultural proportion of a county's population. This was found to be negatively associated with Orange participation at a z-score of around 3. In other words, more urban counties like Lanark and Renfrew are more Orange than rural ones like Stirlingshire. This contrasts with findings in Ontario, Northern Ireland and Newfoundland where rural populations were/are more close-knit and more Orange. This discrepancy is probably explained by the fact that Irish-Protestant immigrants came to Scotland to work in the industrial cities and towns while Orangeism remained a foreign import among the native Scots population, even in the agricultural areas of west-central Scotland.

What about the role of events? Many would leap to these in explaining membership trends over time. Generally speaking, major membership changes do not correspond very well to key historical events. Only in the case of the membership collapse of 1884–85 do we get some clue from printed sources. Elaine McFarland writes that some in the Govan area of south Glasgow complained of the impact of 'dull trade' on the membership during this period, though it must be asked why this recession could have such a decisive impact as compared with the Great Depression.[26] Another possible explanation is that the extension of voting rights to rural Scots (1884–85) obviated the need for participation in a political vehicle like the order. However, any explanation focused on the extension of voting rights to rural Scots must explain why the membership fall-off in a big city like Glasgow, where residents already could vote, was as severe as in rural areas and why the more significant 1918 franchise extension had no similar effect. Otherwise, there is no obvious reason for the Orange membership collapse of 1934 or the spikes of 1903, 1920, 1933, 1864 and 1865.

Individual events had surprisingly little explanatory power. Among the few important individual events affecting membership were the two Church of

Scotland-related crises (1868–69, 1962), the Boer War, the First World War and the first Home Rule crisis (1884–86). I then tested for broad categories of events. This involved amalgamating events that could be categorised as: (1) threats to Protestantism or the Union; (2) Protestant policy victories; (3) Protestant policy losses; (4) social or political stimuli; (5) wartime. Event variables were composed of the following events: (1) threatening events = Church of Ireland disestablishment controversy (1868–69), Scottish papal hierarchy restoration (1878), Church of Scotland disestablishment debate (1881–84), Irish Home Rule crises (1884–86; 1890–92; 1916–22), *Ne Temere* decree (1907–8), 1918 Education Act, Roman Catholic Relief Act (1926), visit to pope by Church of Scotland moderator (1962), Northern Ireland 'Troubles' (1969–72), Tullyvallen massacre at a Northern Ireland Orange hall (1975), first Roman Catholic chief constable (1977), first papal visit (1982), Anglo-Irish agreement (1986); (2) policy victories: first Glasgow Orange parade (1872), first two Home Rule crises' endpoints (1886, 1892), Catholic Bishop of Derry's visit halted at Edinburgh (1975); (3) policy losses: COI disestablishment (1869), restoration of papal hierarchy (1879), Irish independence (1922), Church of Scotland moderator visit – aftermath (1963), RC chief constable (1977), papal visit – aftermath (1983), Anglo-Irish agreement – aftermath (1987); (4) socio-political stimuli: union of competing Orange Order branches (1877), Boer War (1899–1901), Anti-Catholic mass activities of preacher George Wise (1903–6), Orange and Protestant political party (1923), height of John Cormack and Alexander Ratcliffe's Protestant parties in Edinburgh and Glasgow (1925–36), anti-Catholic riot in Edinburgh (1935); (5) wartime: Boer War (1899–1901), First World War (1914–18), Second World War (1939–45).

I also tested for the impact of economic recessions, dues increases and leadership changes – none of which proved significant. Of the five main groups of events, all but policy victories were significant in at least some of the models. The exigencies of war (notably a high Orange enlistment rate) and policy losses tend to lower Orange membership whereas political threats and stimuli from socio-political actors (like firebrand preacher George Wise or the Protestant political parties of John Cormack and Alexander Ratcliffe) tend to increase membership. By and large, all of these variables display effects that are weaker than that of Irish-Protestant ethnicity but stronger than that of the Catholic proportion of the population. One-year lags of the five event variables listed above proved insignificant. On this evidence, we can make the case that events occupy a middle causal ground between ethno-religious factors and structural factors in explaining Orange membership dynamics. There is one caveat to this: when we move from a county-level analysis to look at trends at ward level in Glasgow, we find that the proportion of Catholics in a ward becomes insignificant while structural forces seem more important. In particular, a high number of casual workers and high population density in a ward (both associated with poverty) seem to be associated with low Orange participation by Protestants while the proportion of skilled workers is linked to higher Orange participation. Saying this, the limitations of the Maclean and Gordon data suggest that we should treat such findings with some caution.

Social Makeup

Much of the analysis we have presented is based on county-level aggregate data which compare census data and membership. But individual-level records largely confirm our county-level findings (see Table 10.1). For instance, an analysis of all lodge masters and secretaries (256 in sample) from the Scottish Orange directory of 1881 against the nominal census of Scotland in that year paints a clearer picture: fully 72 per cent were Irish-born. The average age was 39, almost all were working-class (just 4.8 per cent were non-manual), with a slight majority in skilled as opposed to unskilled trades. Given the occupational background of most inhabitants of central Scotland at the time (which was not vastly dissimilar to this), the birthplace of Scottish Orangemen stands out far more dramatically than their occupational profile, which confirms our thesis regarding the relative importance of religio-ethnic over structural factors. It also confirms the ethnic Irishness of Scottish Orangeism which McFarland noticed in her Greenock data.

No ethnic data are freely available for years after 1881 (1891 and 1901 data are available for a fee), but we can still track occupational data through valuation rolls. Examining the valuation rolls of 1911 for Glasgow shows a much higher representation of petit-bourgeois occupations like shopkeeper and clerk than in Scotland as a whole in 1881. Of our sample of 99 masters and secretaries from the city 27 per cent were in this category in 1911. This has less to do with changes between 1881 and 1911 than it does with the geographical fact that Glasgow had a higher proportion of non-manual occupations than surrounding west-central belt towns. As with the 1881 Scottish lodge officers, the 1911 Glasgow Orangemen reflected the occupational structure of their city and this should dispel any notion that Orangeism was a unique product of class, as opposed to ethno-religious, relationships.

The class profile of Scottish Orangemen increasingly stood out after the 1950s because it was essentially the same as it was in 1881, while the country as a whole had shifted in a far more post-industrial and professional direction. We can see this in the limited professional and bourgeois representation within the Orangemen and women sampled in the twentieth century in Table 10.1 and Figure 10.11. If anything, the proportion of professionals, bourgeoisie and skilled workers to the unskilled (labelled in the table as the 'class ratio') was higher in the late nineteenth than in the late twentieth century. This reflects a 'class slippage' effect which was also noticeable in the Northern Irish organisation in the twentieth century.[27]

If we bring the tale forward to the present, class slippage becomes even more apparent – a pattern we also find in Northern Ireland.[28] Here we use postcode classification to get at a measure of status in Figure 10.12. Notice, for example, that the 527 Orange officebearers of 2001 are vastly under-

Table 10.1 Occupational class of Scottish rank-and-file Orange members

Date		Source	Total	Found	Class ratio	Prof	Bourgeois	Skill	Unskilled
1870–86	Greenock – largely lodge officebearers	Directories	93	53	1.5	5.7%	25%	30%	40%
1866–86	Paisley – largely lodge officebearers	Directories	n.a.	35	4.8	8.6%	51%	23%	17%
1881	Glasgow Loyal Orange Lodge No. 417 members	Census	17	8	1.7	0.0%	25%	38%	38%
1881	Orange Lodge officebearers (total)	Census	377	255	0.9	0.4%	4%	41%	50%
1881	Orange Lodge officebearers Glasgow	Census	106	79	2.1	0.0%	8%	61%	33%
1881	Orange Lodge officebearers Lanarkshire (outside Glasgow city)	Census	74	43	1.7	2.3%	9%	51%	37%
1881	Orange Lodge officebearers Renfrewshire	Census	54	33	1.8	0.0%	6%	58%	36%
1881	Orange Lodge officebearers Edinburgh and Dundee	Census	37	28	0.4	0.0%	0%	29%	71%
1881	Orange Lodge officebearers Ayrshire (inc. Wigtown district)	Census	81	48	0.0	0.0%	2%	2%	96%
1881	Orange Lodge officebearers Stirlingshire	Census	20	15	2.8	0.0%	13%	60%	27%
1892	Greenock – largely lodge officebearers	Directories	n.a.	38	0.9	0.0%	16%	29%	50%
1911	Glasgow – lodge officebearers	Val rolls	212	92	1.6	1.1%	27%	34%	38%
1921	Glasgow Primrose Ladies' Lodge members' husbands	Val rolls	201	83	1.1	0.0%	7%	46%	47%
1958–59	The Vigilant subscribers	Val rolls	66	6	1.0	0.0%	17%	33%	50%
1961	Glasgow Primrose Ladies' Lodge members' husbands	Val rolls	64	13	1.2	0.0%	8%	46%	46%
early 1990s	Members: Glasgow, Ayrshire, Lanarkshire, East of Scotland	Survey	111		1.3	6.0%	8%	42%	44%

Source: McFarland, *Protestants First*; Bradley, *Ethnic and Religious Identity*; 1881 Census of Scotland; City of Glasgow Valuation Rolls, 1911–1961; 1881 Grand Orange Lodge of Scotland (GOLS) *Reports of Proceedings*; *Vigilant* subscriber list 1958–59; LOL #417 roll book 1881 and Primrose Ladies' Lodge roll books 1921 and 1961.

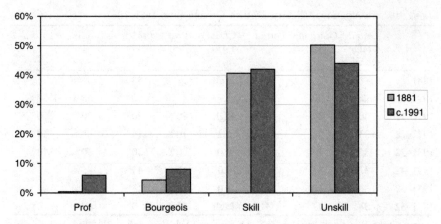

Figure 10.11 Class basis of Scottish Orangeism, 1881 and 1991. Source: Bradley,
Ethnic and Religious Identity; 1881 Census of Scotland; 1881 GOLS
Directory.

represented in the top MOSAIC postcode classifications (A and B) and
over-represented in public housing categories (E to H). The contrast with the
1,400-odd Freemason officebearers of the same year is particularly striking.
The post-industrial restructuring of Scotland's economy seems to have passed
the order by entirely.

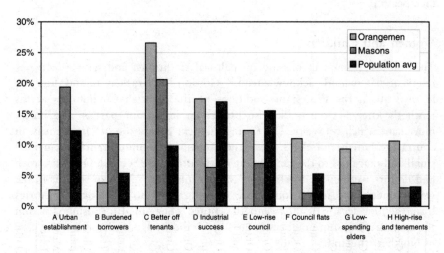

Figure 10.12 Proportion of Orangemen, Masons and Scottish population in main
MOSAIC categories, 2001. Source: GB MOSAIC 2002; 2001 GOLS
Directory.

Table 10.2 Occupational class of Scottish Orange elite, 1881–1961

	Grand Lodge total	Glasgow total	Found	Class ratio	Prof	Bourgeois	Skill	Unskill
1881			6	high	17%	33%	50%	
1901–2	n.a.	12	8	1.7	0%	0%	63%	38%
1911–12	30	11	10	high	10%	20%	70%	0%
1921–22	33	16	14	6.2	10%	14%	64%	14%
1931–32	35	15	10	9.0	0%	30%	60%	10%
1941–42	37	15	11	10.0	0%	45%	45%	9%
1951–52	36	12	8	1.0	0%	13%	38%	50%
1961–62	38	17	3	high	33%	0%	67%	0%

Source: GOLS Directories, 1881–1961; City of Glasgow Valuation Rolls, 1911–1962; 1881 Census of Scotland.

The elite of Scottish Orangeism differ only slightly from the rank-and-file of the lodges. Looking purely at Glasgow-based members of the Grand Lodge of Scotland in Table 10.2, we find a somewhat more elite social profile, albeit one which exhibits a static pattern in the period 1881–1961. Unfortunately the postcodes of Grand Lodge members cease to be listed for the recent period apart from those holding the top few positions. Of these, two appear to be from well-off postcodes (A, J) and two from poorer ones (D), but the sample size is too small to draw firm conclusions. However, if trends in the Grand Lodge of Ireland (GOLI) are anything to go by, it is likely that the Scottish Orange elite social profile differs little from that of the Scottish Orange mass membership.[29]

Women and Children

The role of women in passing on cultural traditions, and females' greater religiosity, is widely acknowledged.[30] Gordon McCracken relates how he learned about the Protestant traditions of the Scottish Covenanters at his mother's knee.[31] Women likewise played an important part in the junior movement which was critical to raising the next generation of Orangemen. In contrast to Northern Ireland, where the women's and junior branches remained small and marginal to the functioning of the order, the Scottish Orangewomen and juniors were in the forefront of the organisation.[32] We can see this in the way women's and junior lodges are incorporated into the lodge directories from the first decade of the twentieth century. They are also subsumed within the total membership numbers quoted by Grand Lodge, which is not the case in Northern Ireland.

The numerical ascent of these 'auxiliary' organisations after 1909 is striking. Figure 10.13 shows the relative membership of the three branches of Scottish Orangeism in the twentieth century at successive census dates.

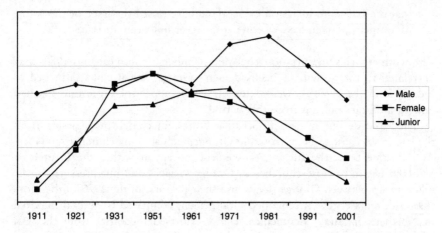

Figure 10.13 Scottish Orange membership, male, female, junior 1911–2002. Source: Grand Orange Lodge of Scotland reports and return sheets

Notice that the men's lodges are a near-minority within Orangeism by 1921. Between 1931 and 1951, the women's organisation actually supersedes that of the men and the juniors are not far behind. Only in the 1970s do adult men re-emerge as the majority within Scottish Orangeism. Even in Ontario, where the first women's lodges were formed in the late nineteenth century, women's lodges only enrolled about half the numbers that the men did. Thus Scotland appears to be distinct from other Orange jurisdictions in its twentieth-century gender profile.

War foreshadowed the decline of the men's organisation some 15 years later. In Scotland, a similar pattern seems to prevail, with junior strength cresting in the early 1970s, followed by a decline in the men's organisation in the 1980s. (see Figure 10.13). What is more difficult to explain is the slide in female membership from the 1950s. Canadian evidence from Ontario and Newfoundland shows that Orangemen's and women's associations declined in tandem, beginning in the late 1950s or early 1960s.[33] The decline in women's interest may have to do with changing gender roles or with alienation at falling Orange church membership since women tend to be far more pious than men.[34] Sister Helyne MacLean certainly hints that gender issues were prominent in the order in her bicentenary message to the membership:

> Women have always been regarded as an important part of the Institution in Scotland ... today they are being encouraged to take on a different role to that of the traditional 'tea makers' or 'fund raisers' ... Society is changing dramatically and it is inevitable that we will see changes within our Institution, for some, (women as well as men), change may be unwelcome and happen too fast while for others it may not happen fast enough. I wonder how often during the almost ninety years of its existence

that the Ladies Association of Scotland have raised the issue of the status of women ... or indeed whether it has ever not been an issue ...[35]

The Scottish men's organisation's buoyant membership into the mid-1980s may be related to the growth of licensed men's Orange social clubs (attached to lodges) after the 1960s as well as the masculine appeal of Protestant football and paramilitary culture from this period.[36]

The rapid decline in general Scottish Protestant church membership from the late 1950s came to be mirrored in Orangemen's slipping church attendance. At the same time, the surging ecumenical movement within the Church of Scotland began to close churches to Orange services and put pressure on the relationship between Orange flocks and their pastors. In the 1970s, little more than a dozen clergymen remained Orangemen, compared to several hundred in Northern Ireland.[37] Ecumenical clergy criticised the order from the left, while on the right, evangelical clergy like Jack Glass or David Cassels looked askance at Orange social clubs and their lack of piety.[38] In 2002, one Church of Scotland minister reflected the sentiment of many in the Kirk when he remarked that membership in the Church was incompatible with membership in the order.[39] Gordon McCracken adds that Orange membership can lead to Church of Scotland ecumenical elites blocking upward mobility for candidates within the Kirk.[40]

Seven clergymen are listed as Grand Chaplains in 1969–70, and this number remained steady until 1984. Importantly, just one of the seven Orange clerics in 1984 was present in 1970, suggesting that an important reservoir of new talent had risen to the level of Grand Chaplain. However, between 1984 and the present, no new blood has flowed into the Orange chaplaincy. Attrition culled the number of Grand Chaplains to just four by 1989. The resignation of Rev. Gordon McCracken in 1997 over the violence at Drumcree deprived the order of one of its leading intellectuals. By 2001, Rev. Ian Meredith, an English-based minister active in Orangeism in Paisley and Edinburgh, Rev. Ron Campbell, and possibly one or two other pastors from small independent churches comprised the sole remnant of an unbroken Orange clerical tradition dating from the 1830s.[41]

The consolidation of Glasgow Orange services within the walls of the Orange-friendly Glasgow Evangelical Church in Cathedral Square represents another facet of the contracting Orange connection to institutionalised religion.[42] 'Grand Secretary advised Grand Lodge of the great difficulties we were experiencing in obtaining a suitable venue for the Annual Divine Service, having written to several prospective locations without success,' bemoaned Grand Lodge in March 2000. Remarking upon the fact that just one district lodge from outside Glasgow had attended the annual Orange service in 1999 despite the hire of two separate facilities, the author opined that Glasgow Evangelical Church would suffice for the 2000 service.[43] Poor attendance at Orange services was matched by slackening religious surveillance of new members. Whereas an Orange initiate in the 1950s required a letter from his or her clergyman to join, this had become watered down to mere 'vouching' from a churchgoing fellow Orangeman by the 1970s.[44] Herein lies a possible explanation for the difference between Canada, where churchgoing remained strong into the 1960s and most Orangemen remain avid churchgoers, and Scotland, where the Kirk began to lose strength in the 1950s and secularisation within the ranks is high.[45] Secularisation may have reduced the appeal of Orangeism among women, a relatively religiously-motivated group.

Orange Policy and Links with Northern Ireland in the Recent Period

Developments in Scotland in the late 1950s show that the Scottish order was occasionally susceptible to a greater degree of militancy than its more cautious Ulster cousin. The Rev. Alan Hasson was integral to Scottish Orangeism's new radicalism. Hasson's genealogy was certainly unusual within Orangeism: his mother was Irish Catholic and his father Egyptian. Nonetheless, Hasson emerged as a charismatic minister who spearheaded opposition to ecumenism within the Church of Scotland in the 1950s and served as Grand Chaplain of the Scottish Orange Order. He visited Northern Ireland in 1959 and was instantly viewed as a troublemaker by the Grand Lodge of Ireland (GOLI). Likewise, Hasson's Orange-sponsored Scottish organ, *The Vigilant*, was the target of GOLI opprobrium.

This began when the Central Committee of the GOLI refuted *The Vigilant*'s outlandish claims that 'Senior Service' brand cigarettes subsidised the pope and pointed out that 'County Grand Lodges should not invite Rev. Hasson to speak at any demonstrations'. Grand Lodge need not have worried: *The Vigilant*'s 1958–59 subscriber list shows that no more than about 10 per cent of the 250-odd subscribers were from Northern Ireland.[46] It is noteworthy that Ulster condemnation provoked divisions within the clearly more militant Grand Lodge of Scotland. Though the Grand Lodge of Scotland agreed to apologise and pay compensation to the affected tobacco firm, Alan Hasson remained both editor of *The Vigilant* and an influential Orange chaplain; and became Grand Master of Scotland the following year.[47]

Hasson's activity and that of other ultras on *The Vigilant* led to a split between the paper and the Scottish Orange Committee assigned to oversee it, but the militant forces gained the upper hand, and it is evident that the small size of the Scottish order and its limited political responsibility allowed for a more radical ideology than was the case in Northern Ireland.[48] We see this a year later (1959) in the midst of the second Dungiven parade dispute in Co. Londonderry, when Hasson openly criticised Northern Ireland (Official Unionist and Orangeman) Minister of Home Affairs W. W. B. Topping at the platform at Finaghy during the Belfast Twelfth. When pressed to apologise for his heckling to both Belfast County organisers and Topping, Hasson responded with an aggressive phone message to the order's Belfast headquarters. Later, the Hasson-influenced Grand Lodge of Scotland's executive committee warned the Ulstermen to drop the charge against Hasson or face a serious inter-jurisdictional rift within Orange ranks. This was acceded to by the GOLI, and represented such a low point in relations between the two branches that one Ulsterman remarked that it would be unpleasant to go to Scotland in 1961 for the Triennial Council meetings.[49]

The exit of Hasson – who left in disgrace following an embezzling scandal – helped to heal the estrangement between the Irish and Scottish Grand Lodges. A period of quiescence followed, but old rifts were reawakened by the Northern Ireland Troubles of 1969–72. Gordon McCracken laments what he calls the 'Ulsterisation' of the order from this period, accompanied by a growing tendency for Scottish lodges and bands to go across by ferry to march in Northern Ireland. This was mirrored by the fading of distinctively Scottish Orange traditions: the pipe bands which once led Orange services dwindled while the Scottish and union flags which many districts once sported were replaced by the Red Hand of Ulster.[50]

The Scottish identity of most Scots Orangemen (50 per cent list it as their primary one) is nonetheless evident in surveys – albeit somewhat less prominent than among other Protestant Scots – and in the Scottish dancing which forms part of the order's youth programme. Yet it is the British identity of many Scots Orangemen that is most impressive: it comes across in the Union Jackery displayed in commemorative videos of Orange gatherings like the 1998 Scottish Orange Bicentenary Video or 'Brig'ton Pride' (about the celebrations which opened the new Orange headquarters in Bridgeton Cross, Glasgow, in September 1999), as well as in survey evidence which shows that Orangemen are far more likely to identify themselves as principally 'British' (14 per cent of those surveyed) than other groups of Protestant Glaswegians.[51]

This Britishness reinforces the concern for Northern Ireland issues, in marked contrast to Canada, where discussion about Ulster politics is virtually absent from reports of proceedings. Ulsterisation has been clearly evident in the content of Grand Lodge of Scotland reports to the membership since the early 1970s. From 1969, Ulster matters topped the list of concerns outlined in the annual reports, and in the regular Grand Master's addresses. Throughout the 1970s, concerns over Ulster's security and constitutional status were paramount. The early 1980s, when fears regarding the official status of the pope and the 1982 papal visit predominated, proved one of the few exceptions to the Ulsterisation rule. Even then, the hunger strike simmered just below the papal visit in the list of priorities. Thereafter, the Grand Lodge prioritised criticism of the Anglo-Irish agreement in the late 1980s, agitated on behalf of the 'UDR Four' in the early and mid-1990s and backed the protests at Drumcree in Portadown in the late 1990s. These concerns featured as the first agenda item in reports, with local education, parading and political matters rarely intruding into top spot. Addresses by leading Ulster Orangemen like Martin Smyth and James Molyneaux were afforded wide coverage.[52]

In 1972, following the collapse of the Protestant-dominated Northern Ireland parliament at Stormont, relations with the GOLI had improved to the point where the Grand Lodge of Scotland could act as a facilitator for intra-unionist talks between the 'established' wing of unionism (the order, Bill Craig's Vanguard and the Official Unionists) and the upstarts (Paisley's DUP and the paramilitaries) in pursuit of a united unionist front. Two Scottish Orange representatives acted as observers at the first United Ulster Unionist meetings. These were initially torpedoed by clashes between the established unionists (led by the order), who counselled against violence, and Ian Paisley over the inclusion of paramilitary representatives at the table.[53]

At this juncture, the Grand Lodge of Scotland tried to salvage the talks. Ulster Orangemen had been impressed by the vitality of Orangeism among young Scots and appreciated the generous donations from Scotland toward Orange social causes in Northern Ireland.[54] Scottish Orangemen were looking to play a more high profile role in Ulster, and the unity talks offered them an opportunity. Accordingly, the Scots envisaged inviting all shades of loyalist opinion over to Scotland for a conference. Failing to understand the depth of Orange-DUP schism, Scottish Grand Secretary John Adam insisted that 'there ARE points of unity which MUST be common to all [including the UVF, UDA or UPV paramilitaries] ... otherwise Ulster is fighting a losing battle.'[55]

Adam received a courteous reply from Belfast and a promise to consider the matter at the Grand Lodge of Ireland. This was not enough for Adam, who pointed out that 'the meeting, having represented only three bodies – no matter how influential – did not produce the effect of solidarity.' Once again, Adam offered his lodge's services to bring all parties together. After a month went by with no response from Northern Ireland, a follow-up letter was sent by the Scots.[56] At the GOLI Central Committee, the Scottish proposal was rebuffed, with some concerned about the influence of Paisley.[57] The eventual response to the Scots was cordial and thanked the Scottish order for its rallies and its hundreds of pounds' donation to the Orange distress fund, but stressed that the Ulster order 'unanimously agreed' that a unity conference 'would not be the answer to our many problems'. The letter concluded with an acknowledgement of Scottish-Ulster solidarity, which it was felt might extend to the military sphere: 'We know, that in certain ways, you will continue to prepare yourselves to support the Loyalists of Ulster should the present dangers increase.'[58] This solidarity could draw upon a history of Protestant mobilisation in Scotland for the Ulster Unionist cause. During the uncertain days of 1913–14, when Irish Home Rule – enforced by British troops in the north – seemed imminent, the seven Glasgow chapters of the paramilitary Ulster Volunteer Force organised as many as 2,000 men to defend Protestant Ulster.[59]

The Grand Lodge of Scotland (along with that of England) also became involved in Orange lobbying at Westminster for a return of Stormont and a hard line against terrorism.[60] This effort failed, but the Ulster Workers Council strike of 1974 brought the Sunningdale power-sharing agreement to its knees and was perceived as a major victory for Ulster unionism against the combined forces of Irish nationalism and British government complicity. At the GOLI, support from farmers and Scottish brethren for the strike was applauded.[61] Yet such goodwill seems to have been sorely tested by the more radical approach of the Scottish Grand Lodge. As in 1972, Scottish Orangemen seeking unionist unity failed to respect salient intra-unionist divisions between 'respectable' (Orange/UUP) and 'rebel' (DUP, paramilitary) unionists. In 1975, Martin Smyth and the Ulster Orangemen scolded the Grand Lodge of Scotland for meeting representatives of loyalist paramilitaries and making press statements. Their request to hold a joint meeting of the central committees of the Irish and Scottish associations was then rebuffed by Scottish Grand Master Thomas Orr.[62]

However, the Grand Lodge of Scotland under Orr's leadership remained highly tuned in to affairs in Ulster. In 1975, a 'campaign to assist Ulster' got under way, with plans for protest parades, petitions, lobbying, fundraising, visits to South Armagh and joint delegations with Ulster Orangemen to see the Prime Minister.[63] In a tersely worded telegram to Secretary of State for Northern Ireland Roy Mason, Orr castigated Mason's performance on security: 'The people of Scotland demand that you discard your smug and useless campaign of empty words. This latest outrage at Comber requires a policy of total extermination of the evil men and women of Ireland who glory in death and violence.'[64] Grand Secretary David Bryce took a more cerebral approach, but was no less insistent on tighter security for Northern Ireland.[65] In an interview following an announcement by the Scottish Grand Lodge that it had put its '80,000' (a heavily inflated figure) members on 'stand by alert', Bryce deflected questions of paramilitarism, claiming that he was referring only to humanitarian assistance to Northern Ireland victims of IRA violence.[66] Bryce was also keenly aware of Ulster unionism's image in mainland Britain, hence his letter to the Ulster Unionist Party 'expressing the abhorrence of the Members of the Order in Scotland at the racialist remarks of Mr. Enoch Powell, the Ulster Unionist M.P. for South Down ... [we] are deeply offended by Mr. Powell's comments on repatriation ... Mr. Powell is a luxury neither the Unionists, nor Ulster, can afford.'[67]

Throughout 1980–82, the Grand Lodge of Scotland co-ordinated its efforts with the Irish and English Grand Lodges to thwart the proposed papal visit and prevent the upgrading of the pope's diplomatic status. Lists of names of those to contact were provided by the GOLI to the Scottish brethren and a 'mammoth' London rally planned. The Scottish Grand Lodge helped to organise the printing of thousands of leaflets and over 100,000 stickers.[68] A protest rally was planned for Edinburgh, with the intention of halting the pope's progress. After a survey of the proposed papal route with local Edinburgh Orangemen, it was determined that:

> With sufficient strength in numbers a strong protest could be effective at the top of the Mound ...Approximately 700–800 of our people were present in that area and the whole of the Mound was there for the taking but unfortunately approximately 30 minutes prior to the arrival of the Pope's transport the Rev. Ian Paisley arrived and along with 20 of his supporters started singing which attracted the police and caused police

reinforcements to be brought to the area. Prior to the police reinforcements arriving there was every possibility that we would have been able to carry out the intention of blocking the Papal route by sitting across the road. Brother [Magnus] Bain [soon to be Grand Master] indicated that the protest had been effective but that more could have been achieved if a greater number of our members had been present.

In addition to castigating the apathy of the membership, Bain expressed 'amazement' that some members, including many from Central Committee, had opted to demonstrate in Glasgow on the same day, detracting from the Grand Lòdge strategy to focus on Edinburgh. That said, a subsequent report on the Glasgow events found that just 38 souls had attended the Mosspark Boulevard protest despite police permission for 150. The sister demonstration at George Square was also a fiasco, with Orange protesters and Ian Paisley harassed by drunken 'loyalist' elements while police moved in. All told, the day underscored the apathy of the Orange membership and its lack of mobilising capacity.[69]

The air was filled with recriminations after this disaster. Three Glasgow Orange districts called for the Grand Master's resignation. The large Govan district complained that Grand Lodge had failed to co-ordinate its protests with local trade unions. Reflecting Bryan's 'rough' Orangeism with its emphasis on action, these grassroots complaints also alleged that the Grand Lodge officers were too dignified in their protest. In response, Thomas Orr's Grand Lodge officers stood up for 'respectable' Orangeism: 'If the membership disagree[s] with the principal lodge office bearers ignoring the call for militant action that ha[s] come from certain quarters, calling for "walking through blood to protest on the Pope's visit" which the Trustees believed was a contradiction of Orange Christian principles then the principal office bearers [are] due a vote of no confidence.' Grand Lodge officers also excoriated the apathy of many within the organisation who had not supported the campaign.[70] Some observers see the papal visit failure as marking a turning point for Scottish Orangeism. Namely, that Scottish Orange membership achieved its post-1861 membership peak just after the papal visit of 1982 and went into steady decline from 1987.[71]

The order's activity also encompassed other realms, much like its Ulster counterpart. An education committee oversaw developments pertaining to the equitable funding of Catholic and non-denominational schools, as well as seeking to bolster the religious content of the latter. Ecumenism and relations with the main Churches (especially the Kirk) was another major sphere of activity and lobbying. Though few Orangemen were clerics, a wider number were active as church elders and could present their case this way as well as through letters which sought to bring forth motions in the General Assembly of the Church of Scotland. Though less active on this front than its Irish counterpart, the Scottish Grand Lodge also sought to promote sabbatarianism. Hence, at the request of the Grand Lodge of Ireland, the Scottish Grand Lodge pressed the Glasgow Rangers to desist from playing on a Sunday.[72] This was not acceded to, though the Rangers regularly granted the order permission to use Ibrox stadium for Orange services.[73]

Notwithstanding its half-hearted efforts at sabbatarianism, the Grand Lodge was alive to the reality of its members' habits. A motion for lodges to be allowed to meet in licensed premises (though not in pubs) was, accordingly, passed.[74] Not only this, but the Grand Lodge tiptoed around the issue of Orange social clubs: in March 1974, it agreed to permit dancing between the first and second parts of a cabaret show at an Orange social club on a Sunday. Resistance was token – 'it was emphasised by Grand Lodge, however, that there must be no organised dancing on Sunday, and it was emphatically decided furthermore that there must be no strip-tease show(s), nor any production of a crude or obscene nature'.[75] Commenting on the fact that a social club in Glasgow had been open on Sunday at the same time as a local junior Orange church parade was taking place, Grand Lodge made a recommendation that districts 'discuss' the possibility that Orange social clubs close on a Sunday 'if there is a church parade within a half mile radius of their premises'. Grand Lodge also urged that clubs move to a six-day opening, though no action appears to have been forthcoming on this issue.[76]

In Northern Ireland, the GOLI failed to win the battle against drink in lodge halls in the 1980s, but Sunday opening of social clubs in Scotland shows that Scottish Orangemen were far more 'secular' in their habits than their Irish brethren. Irish Grand Master Martin Smyth, who was embroiled in the conflict between 'wet' and 'dry' forces within Ulster Orangeism over hall licensing in the 1970s, threatened in one meeting that if the wets gained the upper hand, Ulster Orangeism would have cabaret and drinks on a Sunday as in Scotland.[77]

The issue of Scottish marching bands in Northern Ireland underscores the conflict between the 'rougher' brand of Orangeism in Scotland and the more traditional Orangeism of rural Ulster. In addition, the issue foregrounds the tension between Orangeism's desire to attract young members through spectacle and action, and its need to maintain respectability in the eyes of the Church, media and society.[78] The marching bands the order hires for parades and the spectators who line the streets to watch parades rarely display the decorum demanded by Orange ritual and laws. Together, the youthful bands and spectators often relegate the Orange marchers and platform speakers to the status of a sideshow. The order's attitude to these supporters is ambivalent, and views the spectators and bands as supporters but also as sources of trouble. In order to safeguard its image and pursue respectability, the order focused on enforcing band discipline. This was not merely a PR device: real action was taken against unruly bands and this topic is discussed regularly by the Grand Lodge.

The backdrop to this is the growth of 'blood and thunder' flute bands, as in Northern Ireland, from the early 1970s.[79] Prior to this, suspensions of bands were more often linked to non-payment of fees, and many bands were accordion bands rather than the simpler flute bands favoured by the new 'blood and thunder' or 'kick the pope' bands.[80] In the 1970s, individual bands were regularly suspended for poor behaviour.[81] Band contracts dating from the 1980s banned paramilitary insignia and provocative behaviour in Ireland. In Scotland, action was taken against unruly bands, and attempts made to regulate both their symbolism (i.e. paramilitary flags) and hymn tunes (i.e. sectarian songs).[82] For example, 'the County Grand Lodge of Glasgow gave notice of its intention to ban the Monkstown Flute and Ballynahinch Blue Star Flute Bands. Grand Lodge decided that the ban should apply throughout Scotland.'[83] By 1989, the problem had become so acute that the Grand Secretary's report warned: 'it was necessary to spend more time than normal on the matter of discipline to ensure the maintenance of our reformed principles and standards. Not least in the area of bands where three ... have been permanently banned. It was regrettable, but necessary to terminate the Scottish First Flute Band Association which was replaced by four band Liaison Committees.'[84]

The problem continued to flare during the 1990s.[85] Regular infringements led the topic to be seriously discussed at the 2002 meeting of Scottish, English and Ulster Orange leaders at Liverpool.[86] Discussions between the Scots and Irish over the conduct of bands also appears regularly in Irish reports in the early 1990s. Scottish bands are repeatedly singled out by the GOLI for their poor behaviour on parade, highlighting the often 'rougher' nature of Scottish unionist culture as compared with that of Ulster – especially rural Ulster.[87] Violent behaviour by Scottish bands on Stena Line ferries across the Irish Sea is another pressing concern. A particularly nasty incident concerned members of four Scottish bands returning from Northern Ireland after parading in the Belfast Twelfth. Stena Line wrote to Grand Orange Lodge of Ireland executive officer George Patton as follows: 'Members [of the band(s)] were involved in serious hooligan activity and loutish behaviour ... violent and intimidating behaviour ... included bottle throwing, fighting (with bottles), lewd and sectarian chants and even the manhandling of children travelling on board.'[88] In these cases, the Scottish and Irish Grand Lodges co-operated quickly with Stena Line and banned the bands from taking part in future Orange parades.[89]

Despite the hiccups of the Hasson period and the spats over Scottish interference in unionist unity intiatives in the early 1970s, the Scottish Grand Lodge has, like its Irish counterpart, served as a 'respectable' brake on the rougher attitudes of some members. In this, Dominic Bryan's 'rough vs. respectable' dichotomy between an often sectarian rank and file and a more image-conscious leadership is accurate.[90] However, the divide does not stem from the bourgeois composition of the Grand Lodge leadership, as Bryan maintains, since Scottish Orange leaders have sprung from humble backgrounds for decades. Rather it comes from the leadership's perception that it must seek to safeguard the organisation's wider respectability to the greatest extent possible – especially in the face of falling membership. As a Scottish-Irish-English inter-jurisdictional meeting agreed, the order must attempt to attract some businesspeople into its ranks.[91] Heightened co-operation is also evident on the parading issue, with Scots and Irish branches pooling their legal expertise on means of contesting parade bans. These bans became increasingly problematic for the Scottish order in the 1990s.[92] Indeed, the Scots refused to meet with Parades Commission representatives from Ulster in line with GOLI policy, despite the fact that the order in Ulster is deeply divided on this issue.[93]

One further area where the Irish and Scottish branches think alike is over the problem of paramilitarism. As in Ulster, Grand Lodge has taken a stand against paramilitaries and most – but not all – members disapprove of them. Already in 1974, complaints had been received from Glasgow lodges about UVF paramilitary circulars, and Grand Lodge commented on the 'negative attitude' of the UVF.[94] In a subsequent report, Grand Lodge read a letter from the Ulster Defence Association complaining that the Scottish Grand Lodge had not contributed assistance to the dependants of prisoners.[95] This was a deliberate Grand Lodge policy, since Grand Lodge claimed that monies for these funds were diverted to other UDA activities.[96] On 11 December 1976, the Grand Lodge passed a resolution 'rejecting any support for the activities within Scotland of the UDA or any other paramilitary body'. Interestingly, this was a mere year after the Grand Lodge of Scotland received a reprimand from the GOLI for seeking to bring representatives of loyalist paramilitaries together with mainstream Ulster unionists to further unionist unity.[97]

In 1988, the issue reared its head again when an Edinburgh member complained that his district master, James MacLean, failed to take action when two individuals dressed in UDA paramilitary uniforms made an appearance at an Edinburgh Orange district dance seeking donations. Other members complained that MacLean's activities as a spokesman for the 'Edinburgh Loyalist Coalition' led to the order being branded as 'sectarian'. MacLean had apparently voiced his opinion that he 'could not give any form of guarantee that there would be no violence should Republican parades be permitted' in his area. This led the Chief Constable to approve parade restrictions against MacLean's district, leading many members to express annoyance at MacLean's remarks. On a Grand Lodge ballot, MacLean was judged not guilty – perhaps because his defenders included high-ranking Orangewoman Helyne MacLean and several others. On the other hand, two lower-ranking members, Crawford and Cameron, who admitted taking up a collection for the UDA, were suspended from the order and six others from several lodges in district 5 were later expelled for UDA activities.[98]

Part of the explanation for Grand Lodge support for James MacLean may have been Grand Lodge's desire not to offend local sensibilities in district 5. Sometime in the following months, members of the wayward lodge from which the two suspended UDA men came shouted abuse at the Grand Master on an Orange platform.[99] Ten members of LOL 160, including its five office bearers, were later charged with not properly conducting the business of their lodge. It transpired that LOL 160 had simply ignored the overwhelming evidence against the two UDA brethren and failed to suspend them.[100] At the Grand Lodge hearing in December, just one of the ten accused turned up to answer charges. James MacLean was at the hearing and he strenuously defended LOL 160, warning Grand Lodge that action against the lodge could lead to court action. This was rebuffed by a legal opinion received from Donald Finlay QC. Despite this setback, MacLean maintained his resistance to action, but the 'rough' brand of Orangeism he represented clearly carried little weight among the gathered representatives of Scottish Orangeism: the vote to revoke the warrant of lodge 160 carried 116 to 5.[101]

This pattern of paramilitary 'outlaw' lodges has its Ulster counterpart in Belfast paramilitary lodges like LOL 633 'Old Boyne Heroes', known as the 'UVF Lodge'.[102] Yet, as in Northern Ireland, the 'rough' forces of sectarian Orangeism, with their pockets of strength in various locales, could not prevail at the higher levels of Orangeism. A similar dynamic holds for militant evangelical Protestantism, as when theological firebrands Ian Paisley and David Cassels were rejected by Grand Lodge as district speakers on Orange platforms in 1989–90.[103] Part of Grand Lodge's motivation has to do with the split between Orangeism, as a 'traditional' unionist organisation, and the street politics of 'rebel' unionism with its emphasis on action and its lack of deference to hierarchy and tradition.[104] The order is also aware of its plebeian make-up and the need to win public approval in order to have influence and retain the right to parade. Grand Lodge has had a running battle with the media in Scotland that has intensified in the 1990s. One of the major new advances within Grand Lodge at its new Olympia St headquarters is an extensive press file and an organised system of responding to allegations made in the print or electronic media.[105]

Politics

The nature of the political system in which the order operates is important in determining its policy influence. In Scotland, and in both Newfoundland and Ontario (as in Canada at the federal level), there is a Westminster system with pragmatic 'catchall' parties like the Liberal, Conservative or Labour/New Democratic Parties based on class ideology. The system makes it difficult for ethnic or religious parties to emerge and encourages parties to reach to the centre for votes beyond their ethno-religious base. Lines of class and region cross-cut the ethno-religious cleavage thereby making it much harder to mobilise voters along ethno-religious lines. Residential segregation is also much less pervasive, which undercuts ethnic appeals at ward and constituency level.

In Northern Ireland, by contrast, the political system has been based on the ethno-religious cleavage between Ulster Protestants and Catholic nationalists since partition. Competition between parties occurs within ethnic blocs and is aimed at 'outbidding' mainstream parties by appealing to the interests of one's own ethnic group only. This 'outbidding' dynamic has been noted in numerous other divided societies and arises because it is futile for parties to appeal across the communal divide since this strategy will gain few votes from the other ethnic group while losing many from a party's own group.[106] Unsurprisingly, the link between Orangeism and politics is strongest in Northern Ireland. During the Stormont period (1922–72) when the Unionist Party ruled the province, all prime ministers of Northern Ireland and all but three cabinet ministers were Orangemen.[107] In a year 2000 study, roughly half the Ulster Unionist Party's 900-member governing body (the Ulster Unionist Council) were shown to be Orangemen or women, and most UUP MPs and MLAs were as well.[108]

At the elite level, Orangeism has also wielded influence in other jurisdictions, but has never dominated to the same extent as in Northern Ireland. Canadian Orange strength goes some way to explaining why four Canadian and four Newfoundland prime ministers, many provincial premiers, federal MPs and numerous mayors (including over 30 in Toronto) were Orangemen while only a handful of Scottish Orangemen made the political grade.[109] In Scotland, lower Orange membership densities led to more limited electoral clout. Nonetheless, the Scottish order was very important in establishing a working-class Tory base in the 1880s through Working Men's Conservative Associations in the west of Scotland. In Glasgow, the order played an important part in municipal politics until the 1930s. Its influence was similar to that of the order in Liverpool, though it never dominated city politics to the same extent as in Toronto.[110] Nationally, in the 1880s and 1890s, James Bain, Archibald Campbell and William Whitelaw were the first Scottish Orange MPs. The surge in Orangeism and Protestant politics more generally in the 1920s and 1930s following the 1918 Education Act brought at least six new Orange MPs to Parliament. These included Sir John Gilmour, who served as Secretary of State for Scotland (1924–29), Col A. D. McInnes Shaw (also Grand Master), General Hunter Weston, Lt Col T. E. R. Moore, William Templeton and Sir John Baird.[111]

Overall, however, it is clear that the order in Scotland only furnished a fraction of the number of politicians it did in Canada and Northern Ireland. We may thus surmise that political influence seems to be linked to the numerical strength of Orange membership, with the caveat that cross-cutting cleavages tend to weaken Orange influence even if membership is very strong, as in the Canadian province of Newfoundland. In Scotland, as in Canada and Newfoundland, Orange MPs had little influence over the course of Tory/ unionist policy owing to the power of cross-cutting cleavages of class and the fact that sectarian issues had little resonance outside specific working-class locales in west-central Scotland. In the main, the Scottish unionists welcomed the Orange element as a way of mobilising a working-class vote, but kept the order at arm's length when it came to the party's policies and image.[112] The Scottish Orange MP Sir John Gilmour, for example, as Secretary of State for Scotland, rebuffed the Church of Scotland's appeal to regulate Irish immigration to Scotland which the Kirk feared was a 'menace' to the Scottish 'race'. Meanwhile, the Orange unionist councillor Sir Charles Cleland defended the 1918 Education Act against Protestant grassroots accusations of 'Rome on the Rates'.[113]

The turn of the Scottish Tory Party away from unionism alienated many Scottish Orangemen and west of Scotland working-class Protestants. This was symbolised by the dropping of the 'Unionist' label from the party's name in the 1960s and underscored by Thatcher's support for the Anglo-Irish agreement of 1985.[114] Having lost its direct political connections, the order concentrated on acting as a lobby for Protestant interests in education and on Northern Ireland issues. It first flirted with establishing a new Scottish Unionist Party in 1986, deciding later to focus on tactical voting against sitting Tory MPs. A hundred thousand leaflets on tactical voting were distributed and the order made the Scottish unionist position clear at a press conference prior to the election. The Grand Lodge of Scotland claimed that a large number of Tories lost their seats as a result of the Anglo-Irish agreement. 'Conservatives who had scoffed at the Orange vote had changed their tune. They now know it exists,' glowed Grand Lodge.[115] The GOLI accepted this version of events, claiming that the Scottish branch had 'persuaded electors to switch votes to punish Thatcher'.[116]

Despite such claims, in electoral terms, I could find no significant Orange effect on the Scottish national vote at either the county level (1861–1961) or in Glasgow at the ward level (1922–47) during eras of stronger Protestant politics. In both cases, Orange density is insignificant while class and the proportion of Catholics were highly significant electoral factors, suggesting that trade unions and Catholics were more highly mobilised (as Labour or Liberal supporters) than were Orangemen and women. In Glasgow, the Orange Order has had perhaps its greatest impact on municipal politics and attained an important degree of influence on the Tory Party between the wars.[117] However, using ward-level data across a limited range of census and electoral variables collected by Maclean and Gordon in a study of the Glasgow Labour movement during 1922–47, I found no significant relationship between Orange membership density and the vote for either Labour (we might expect a negative relationship) or even the militant Scottish Protestant League (SPL).[118] Several commentators have pointed to friction between Alexander Ratcliffe's SPL and the Orange Order, noting that the order distrusted the street politics of Ratcliffe while Ratcliffe criticised the Orange Order for its insufficient religiosity. This analysis supports such a claim.[119] Overall, given Orangeism's limited impact on the vote at both county and city levels, it seems that the puzzle of Orange political impotence needs to be qualified: Orangeism seems to have provided far more political figures than its electoral weight warranted.

Conclusion

In summary, we have shown that the order's strength within the Protestant majority in Scotland – even in the west-central belt – is and was much weaker than many believe. The order's growth was fuelled by Irish-Protestant immigrants and their descendants and is currently strongest in areas of historic

Irish-Protestant immigration. Broad categories of events like 'threats to the union' explain some of the fluctuation in membership trends over time, but – apart from the wars – no single historical event seems to have dramatically altered membership levels. Economic trends seem to bear an even weaker relationship to membership numbers. The decline in the religiosity of Scottish Protestants and the rise of Orange social clubs in the 1960s may account for the unusual pattern in which Ladies Orange membership began to fall some thirty years before the men's.

In ideological terms, the Scottish order is divided along similar lines to Ireland, with a 'respectable' Grand Lodge trying to enforce decorum against the 'rougher' sentiments of sections of the rank-and-file who desire militancy and action. Though unsuccessful in curbing alcohol use in lodge halls and on parade, the Grand Lodge of Scotland has kept a lid on paramilitarism and poor band behaviour. Having said this, comparisons with Ireland show that Scottish Orangeism has generally been rougher, more secular and occasionally more militant than its Ulster cousin. In political terms, the weakness of Orangeism within Protestant Scotland (as compared to Ulster) and the lower salience of ethno-religious as opposed to class issues there has resulted in a divided 'Orange vote' and little policy success. Given these realities, the fact that the order has provided so many political figures to Scottish politics is surprising – a testament to its efficacy in training men for elected office.

11 The End of Disadvantage? The descendants of Irish-Catholic immigrants in modern Scotland since 1945

T. M. Devine

The census of 2001 was the first in Scotland to include a specific question on the religious identity of respondents. According to the analysis of the data, 803,000 individuals declared their religious affiliation as Catholic or around 16 per cent of the total population of Scotland. Of course, by no means all of this number are of Irish origin. The descendants of the inhabitants of the traditional enclaves of Catholicism in Gaeldom and parts of the north-east, the Italians, Poles, Lithuanians and, not least, those Catholics among the extensive English immigrations of recent times, have all to be included in that description. But the vast majority of Scottish Catholics today are the children, grandchildren and great-grandchildren of the hundreds of thousands who left Ireland in the nineteenth and early twentieth centuries for work in Scotland. This is particularly true of the central Lowlands where over 80 per cent of Scottish Catholics live.

Therefore, in this chapter, because there is no alternative, data on Catholics in Scotland will be used as a general surrogate for the modern population of Irish-Catholic descent in the country. It is an old immigrant group. Large-scale movement of the Irish to Scotland peaked nearly a century ago in the years before the Great War. During the inter-war years it slowed to a trickle and, unlike the post-1950 Irish migrations to English cities, never really recovered in recent decades.[1] This also means that the crude correlation offered here between 'Catholic' and 'of Irish descent' cannot capture those who left the Church over the generations. From 1931 to 1951 an estimated 52,000 Catholics lost contact with the faith. 'Leakage' became even more acute between 1951 and 1976 when around 120,000 lapsed.[2] These numbers are certain to have increased further in the last few decades.

I

As Tom Gallagher has argued, it was possible for Scottish Catholics to feel a 'guarded optimism' about their future in the victorious aftermath of the Second World War.[3] The sectarian crises of the 1920s and 1930s petered out amid the struggle of a nation fighting for its very existence against an evil foe.

As in 1914–18, Irish Scots had acquitted themselves well during the war and their loyalty and contribution both on the home front and on the battlefield may have disarmed some critics who doubted their solidarity to the British cause. Similarly, those Scottish Catholics who served in the forces seem not to have experienced systematic discrimination on the grounds of either religion or ethnic origin.[4]

However, in the short term at least, tentative optimism was misplaced. It was true that the ferocity of the General Assembly of the Church of Scotland's attack on Catholics of Irish origin abated after the war. Indeed, the Church and Nation Committee of the General Assembly, which had itself produced the notorious report of 1923, on *The Menace of the Irish Race to our Scottish Nationality*, gave its support in 1952 to a policy which would 'oppose racial discrimination wherever it is found, at home or overseas; in particular to support and apply the principle of partnership in all relationships, official and personal, with other members of the multi-racial Commonwealth to which we belong'.[5] Knowledge of the horrors of the Holocaust had apparently helped to undermine the legitimacy of much of the racist discourse on which the anti-Irish campaign during the inter-war period was founded. Moreover, by the early 1950s, the Kirk itself had become a leading champion of the rights of native Africans in such colonial territories as Nyasaland against the threatened oppression by racist whites.[6] Yet, ironically, at home the old prejudices against Catholics in Scotland endured in the General Assembly's public pronouncements. Thus, in the same year as it condemned racial discrimination in such forthright terms, the Church and Nation Committee renewed its criticism of the Roman Catholic Church in language which, though more moderate, was redolent of the racist vocabulary of the past. Irish Catholics warranted condemnation for displacing 'the native Scots Protestant population from the industrial areas of the West'. They formed 'a compact community largely of alien origin with interests of its own' and their Church was 'coming to exercise an undue influence over public life'. The report concluded in terms which vividly recalled that of 1923: 'Above all, those who cherish the Protestant heritage of our country should realise it is being definitely menaced.'[7]

Some of the most vociferous critics of the Scoto-Irish in the 1930s, such as the nationalist, Andrew Dewar Gibb, also reopened old wounds in his *Scotland Resurgent* of 1950. For him the descendants of the immigrants remained 'a foreign element' in Scotland. Gibb, the Regius Professor of Scots Law at Glasgow University, then went on to claim that the Catholic Irish were 'responsible for most of the crime committed in Scotland, which otherwise would be the most law-abiding country in the world'. He asserted that 'Wherever knives and razors are used, wherever sneak thefts and mean pilfering are easy and safe, wheresoever dirty acts of sexual baseness are committed, there you will find the Irish in Scotland with all but a monopoly of the business.'[8] Dewar Gibb's printed polemics were paralleled in the world of sport by the tensions between the Scottish Football Association and Celtic FC, a club widely regarded as the sporting champions of the Irish Catholics and an anchor of identity for many in that community. In the early 1950s Celtic was threatened with expulsion from the Scottish League for refusing to end the tradition of flying the Irish tricolour in tribute to its Irish immigrant origins at its ground, in a campaign orchestrated by George Graham, SFA Secretary, a Freemason and leading member of the Orange Order. Despite the lengthy press coverage of the affair, no mention was made of the fact that Celtic's great rivals, Rangers FC, might also merit criticism for its traditional policy of opposing the employment of Catholics either as players or within the administration of the club.[9]

Perhaps, however, for most people of Irish-Catholic background these issues were more matters of irritation than of substance. The real concerns were likely to be the perceived discrimination in the labour market and the disadvantaged social and economic status of the community as a whole. The Church of Scotland had given powerful legitimacy and support in the 1930s to the idea that 'native' Scots should be given preference for jobs above those of 'alien' immigrant stock. In 1931, for instance, the General Assembly instructed its Church and Nation Committee to approach employers and advise them to confine their hiring of labour to 'those of the Scottish race'.[10] Moreover, in 1937, when the Kirk implicitly acknowledged that government support for its campaign to curb Irish immigration was unlikely to achieve success, one senior churchman, the Rev. John Maclagan, a parish minister from Glasgow, stated that the 'cure' for the Irish-Catholic problem now lay with the Scottish people rather than with the state. He advocated that all employers must give preference to Scottish labour while voters in council elections should try to ensure that no-one of Irish-Catholic origin could be employed in local government or public relief works. These remarks were warmly applauded by the ministers and elders of the General Assembly when Maclagan concluded his speech.[11]

While it is impossible to judge the impact of public statements such as these, the clarity of the message which was delivered was undeniable. The General Assembly of the Church of Scotland in the 1950s was possibly the most prestigious and respected forum in the land, regarded as the surrogate parliament of a stateless nation, with its proceedings reported annually at considerable length and in great detail in the Scottish press. It had resolved that those of Irish-Catholic stock, even if born in Scotland, were pariahs who did not deserve the same opportunities in the labour market as the majority who were of Scots blood and lineage. The message was clear: Scottish employers had a patriotic duty to discriminate in favour of those of the Scottish race.

How far this injunction was carried through in practice in the 1940s and 1950s cannot easily be determined. By its very nature discrimination takes place secretly and is difficult to prove. The Irish Scots came overwhelmingly from the poorer classes in Scottish society and in this period suffered from more serious educational disadvantages than the population as a whole. These factors alone would have presented powerful impediments in the labour market even if discrimination on religious or ethnic grounds had not been an important force.

Moreover, allegations of discrimination can often easily be dismissed as false perceptions, special pleading or easy excuses for personal failure.

Certainly, however, Catholics themselves believed that discrimination was a fact of life. The Catholic commentator, Patrick Reilly, talked about 'Himalayas of anecdotal evidence from almost every Catholic family as to alleged injustices suffered'.[12] In 1995, the present author edited a study of a Catholic parish in Hamilton, Lanarkshire, generally regarded as one which by that time had attracted significant numbers of professional and well-educated families. Of the sample of churchgoers taken in that year almost half believed that discrimination in favour of Protestants remained a social reality in Scotland and that it had had even deeper roots in previous decades. A number of shops, companies and establishments were specifically named as having had reputations locally as bastions of anti-Catholicism in the past. These included Lanarkshire Steel Works, the police service, the Clydesdale Bank and other banks, Colville's Steel Works, Anderson Boyce Engineering, Tunnocks Bakery and many others.[13] A broader and more systematic study, published in 2003, of employment discrimination in Glasgow by Patricia Walls and Rory Williams interestingly included the views of the majority Protestant community in the analysis. The interviews they recorded provided strong support from both denominations for the view that discrimination against Catholics in the work place was prevalent in the period before c.1970, though opinion was more mixed on the survival of such practices into the later twentieth century.[14]

While discrimination and its extent c.1950 remains an evidential and methodological minefield, there is less uncertainty about the social and economic status of Catholics of Irish descent in the middle decades of the twentieth century. Here a clear contrast can be drawn with Irish Americans in the same period. The American cousins of the Irish Scots achieved rough occupational and educational equality with the US population as a whole by the first decade of the twentieth century. From being the 'white negroes' at the time of the mass immigrations of the Famine period, the Irish and their descendants by the early 1900s considerably exceeded the 'new' European migrants, such as the Italians, Russians and Poles, in both social mobility and material success.[15] Their counterparts in Scotland, on the other hand, remained for the most part locked in disadvantage in terms of occupational profile, health and material standards and educational opportunity. Overwhelmingly Scottish Catholics were working class with only a relatively small sprinkling of professionals in teaching, law and medicine and an even tinier number of businessmen with most of them in the drinks trade, pawnbroking and groceries. Social disadvantage was omnipresent. Before 1965, 5 per cent of schools offering senior secondary education, and so preparation for university entry, were in the denominational sector although Catholics comprised over 19 per cent of the relevant age group. In one of the Irish-Catholic heartlands, the industrial county of Lanarkshire, there were only three Catholic senior secondaries in the 1950s.[16] Moreover, because of relative poverty among many families, there was often an unwillingness to support a child through five or six years of secondary education followed by another few years after that at university, when they could be gainfully employed leaving school at 15. Anecdotal evidence suggests that some families waited until older children were earning before helping a talented son (rarely a daughter) through higher education, a situation which was, of course, widespread throughout the Scottish working classes at the time, whatever their religious faith or background.

One consequence of this was the paucity of literary and academic achievement within the Catholic community of the 1950s. True, there were isolated examples of excellence, such as the foundation of the Scottish Catholic Historical Association in 1949, together with its admirable journal, the *Innes Review*; and the seminal books of the first historian of the Irish in Scotland, James Handley. But these accomplishments were few and far between. The effort to maintain a basic existence meant that creative pursuits were simply not an option for most people. As the late John McCaffrey has put it: 'Living in crowded tenements and trying to keep a good timekeeping record; the daily struggle, mainly by women, to establish a decent family life, was in itself an achievement, but it had been an energy-sapping process.'[17] A fascinating collection, *Across the Water* (2000), reproduces extracts from the works of 45 Scottish writers of Irish-Catholic origin but in only five cases were they originally published before 1950. As the editors point out: 'For the most part, Irish Scots were written about rather than writing themselves; and they were described in alarmed and unflattering terms as a set of social problems.'[18]

No scholar has yet explored the reasons for these dramatic contrasts in the life experience of the American Irish and the Irish Scots in the first half of the twentieth century and there is not the space here to present a detailed analysis. But a few brief suggestions may be in order. For a start, Irish immigrants to the USA possessed certain advantages. From the 1860s their country of settlement was the fastest growing economy in the world, and though this process of rapid transformation stalled briefly in the Great Depression it quickly recovered its dynamism in the 1940s and beyond. In contrast, Scotland's economic agony in the inter-war period was more enduring and, despite rearmament and post-war boom, the economy remained sluggish by American standards.[19] That contrast was the key reason why so many Scots continued to cross the Atlantic for a better life in the post-war years. Significantly, also, Irish immigration to Scotland never again recovered its pre-1914 levels. For them there were better pickings to be had elsewhere and the opportunities for upward mobility were more extensive and more varied in the USA.

In addition, the decline of American nativist opposition to the Irish (ironically much more ferocious in the 1850s than anything experienced by the Irish in Scotland) was likely to take place at a faster rate than the ebbing of Protestant hostility to Catholics in Scotland. Soon the nativists found other targets in mass black migration to the northern cities after the end of slavery and then successive waves of immigrants from central and eastern Europe who were more 'alien' in language and culture than the Irish had ever been.[20] In Scotland, on the other hand, the small numbers of Jewish, Lithuanian and

Italian migrants (no more than 30,000 in all before 1945) paled into insignif-icance alongside the massive Irish presence, especially in the west-central parts of the country.[21] It did not help that the population of the once proud Workshop of the British Empire suffered a major crisis of collective confidence in the economic crises of the 1920s and 1930s, which provided fertile soil for those who wished to confront and scapegoat the immigrants as a central cause of the nation's decline.

Finally, the vast scale of Irish immigration to the American cities in the nineteenth century proved a key advantage. In 1860 the Irish comprised no less than 40 per cent of the country's foreign-born population. By 1900 New York had become the largest Irish settlement in the world, exceeding the entire population of Dublin and Belfast combined. Scholars have described how the American Irish used this demographic muscle to good effect in New York, Boston, San Francisco and Chicago through machine politics, trade unions, the Catholic Church and the Democratic Party to promote ethnic solidarity and collective advancement.[22] In comparison, their Scottish cousins were in a much weaker position. The Labour Party, to which they had transferred their political loyalties in the early 1920s had limited electoral success until the historic and crushing victory in 1945. Catholics and ex-Catholics were able to assume positions of influence in some trade unions but there was little evidence that they were able or willing ruthlessly to promote the cause of their co-religionaries in the same way as Irish trade union leaders across the Atlantic. Irish Catholics remained a marginal and marginalised element in Scottish society, politics and culture in the first half of the twentieth century.

II

Yet, ironically, it was in the 1950s that the foundations were being laid for the transformation which was to come from that lowly position. First, the landslide Labour victory of 1945 led to a massive extension of state support for all irrespective of social class or ethnic origin. As one of the most underprivileged sections of Scottish society, Catholics were likely to gain more than most from 'the cradle to grave' security embodied in child allowances, universal retirement pensions, unemployment benefits and the National Health Service, with care free at the point of delivery for all.

Second, the same period saw a dramatic increase in state intervention in the economy through the nationalisation of coal (1947), railways and electricity (1948) and iron and steel (1949) while new work opportunities burgeoned in the expanding public service bureaucracies both at national and local level. At a stroke, entire new career possibilities opened up for Catholics keen to join the white-collar salariat in areas of employment which were perceived, rightly or wrongly, as being much freer from the kind of discriminatory practices that made upward mobility in the traditional industries and the older professions more challenging.[23]

Third, after the austerity of the immediate post-war era, the Scottish economy entered a period of sustained expansion for much of the 1950s. Unemployment, which in the 1930s had hit the most disadvantaged groups hardest in the old heartlands of heavy industry where the Irish had settled, fell to historically low levels. Between 1947 and 1957, numbers out of work in Scotland declined to between 2 and 3 per cent, despite a labour force increase of nearly 700,000 from 1945 to 1960. Jobs were now available for virtually everyone who wanted them. Indeed, the problem often became one of temporary labour shortage rather than surplus.[24] This new condition was bound to have an impact on discriminatory recruitment practices. The well-known trade unionist, Alex Ferry, later a president of the Amalgamated Engineering Union, recalled that in the early 1950s Catholics were markedly under-represented in the skilled trades in many shipyards and engineering shops because of the power of foremen with Orange and/or Masonic loyalties over hiring, firing and promotion. But he argued that the 1950s were a watershed in this respect since acute shortages of skilled labour forced a more liberal system of recruitment.[25] What accelerated this process was the unprecedented inward movement of both English and American firms in Scotland, employers who were entirely unfamiliar with old Scottish tribal prejudices. By the early 1970s, no less than 40 per cent of the Scottish workforce in manufacturing were employed by English-owned firms and many others such as the US giants Honeywell, IBM, Euclid, Goodyear and Caterpillar.[26]

Fourth, in the 1950s Scotland experienced a revolution in housing. The old city and town slums, where most of the descendants of the Irish Scots were concentrated, were broken up and house-building in green-field sites expanded at a staggering pace. In the two decades after 1945, 564,000 new dwellings were constructed in Scotland, over 80 per cent of them in the public sector. Not only were these decent homes with baths, indoor toilets and gardens but they were also available at subsidised rentals. Recent research on the huge rehousing programmes initiated by Glasgow Town Council suggests that Catholics were neither favoured nor penalised in the allocation processes, though, as one of the most underprivileged groups, they were likely to gain more than most from the destruction of the slums. Indeed, as Ian Paterson has perhaps over-optimistically argued, the revolution in housing may have 'contributed to the break-up of insular mentalities, softening of traditional tensions based on suspicions and mistrust and the stimulation of cross-community social interaction'.[27]

III

In the long-run, however, those foundations of greater social emancipation were but the prelude to the more radical changes which set in from the 1960s and accelerated at an even faster pace from the late 1980s. At the heart of this process of transformation were three key influences which will be considered in turn: the educational factor, the post-1980 emergence of a new economic system in Scotland, and the significance of secularisation and ecumenism.

Educational expansion both in secondary schooling and in the university sector formed the ladder of opportunity out of the manual working classes for many Scottish Catholics from the 1960s. In particular, the introduction of comprehensive education in 1964 and the end of selection at 11-plus in state schools were of critical importance. The Bishop of Motherwell, Joseph Devine, argued that in his view they were 'more beneficial to the Catholic community than anything since the Catholic Emancipation Act of 1829 and the repeal of the penal laws'.[28] In his diocese of Motherwell, for instance, covering Lanarkshire and parts of Greater Glasgow, the number of Catholic secondary schools offering courses through to the level of university entrance more than quadrupled from three in 1964 to thirteen by the late 1970s. It also helped that, as recent educational research has shown, the secondary denomi- national sector has had a particularly good record in providing academic qualifications for pupils from poorer backgrounds.[29] The introduction of more generous grants for all students in higher education was equally influential. Bursaries from local authorities for university students were already available but the new legislation of 1962 offered grants to all who gained a place in higher education and were designed to cover all costs. At the same time the expansion in university places advised by the Robbins Committee in 1963 began in earnest. By 1970 the figure of 52,000 students in the new universities and extended ancient institutions was a doubling of numbers in a decade and more than a tripling since the 1930s. Bishop Devine, then chaplain to the Catholic community at Glasgow University in 1974, saw the dramatic impact of these changes. In 1967 there were around 700 Catholic undergraduates at Glasgow. Five years later that number had nearly tripled to 2000. A survey at the time revealed that nine out of ten were the first of their families to have experience of tertiary education.[30]

However, the ladder of opportunity was not simply constructed on the basis of academic infrastructure and state support. The general economic context was also crucial. Rising living standards from the 1950s meant that many more Catholic families could afford to send not only their sons but also increasingly their daughters to university. The contraceptive revolution made possible by the availability of the Pill also helped to enhance material position from the 1960s by enabling the reduction of family size. The warnings of the papacy and the bishops about moral failure often fell on deaf ears. The continuing expansion of employment in the public services also ensured that the new graduates who remained in Scotland were able to obtain employment. Certainly, anecdotal evidence suggests that the overwhelming majority of this Catholic graduate cadre found work in primary and secondary school teaching, local government and related public services, a pattern which partly helps to explain their continuing loyalty to the Labour Party despite newly acquired middle-class status.

From the 1980s, the unprecedented transformation of Scotland's traditional economic structure was to have further major effects on Catholic occupational and class structures. The end of the heavy industrial economy in that decade and the large-scale unemployment which it caused (male employment in

Scotland fell by 234,000 between 1979 and 1994) hit the Catholics of Scotland hard because so many of them were still employed as manual workers. But the long-term consequences were more positive. With deindustrialisation the old citadels of perceived discrimination in heavy engineering and shipbuilding crumbled. By 2001 all manufacturing accounted for less than a fifth of Scottish GDP; and the service sector, comprising almost 70 per cent of GDP became the commanding force in the nation's economy. The public sector alone in 2006 had a total spend of £44 billion per annum which represented about 55 per cent of GDP.[31] Scotland, during these years, reinvented itself as a post-modern economy in which the new motors of growth, in addition to the public services, became finance, insurance, oil and gas, tourism, light engineering and science-based industry. It is an economic system where to a great extent merit, certification and credentials are king, both in obtaining posts in the first place and then achieving later promotion. The old traditions of nepotism, clientage, discrimination and patronage might not have entirely gone but they now lost much of their potency.[32] In 2004, for instance, only eight out of 8,000 employment tribunal cases were brought in Scotland under the UK Employment Equality (Religion or Belief Act) of 2003; and a mere four of these had any sectarian connection.[33]

Before exploring the magnitude of that change in more detail a third key change in the national social context deserves consideration. Hostility from the Church of Scotland to Roman Catholics of Irish origin, still alive and overt in the 1950s as seen above, soon became a thing of the past as ecumenism fostered closer and mutually respectful relations. In 1975 a senior Roman Catholic clergyman, Archbishop Thomas Winning, addressed the General Assembly for the first time while, in 1982, the Moderator met with Pope John Paul II during his highly successful visit to Scotland under the statue of John Knox in New College, Edinburgh. Four years later the General Assembly formally withdrew those clauses in the Westminster Confession of 1647 which had described the Moderator's distinguished guest as the anti-Christ. Finally, in May 2002 the wheel came virtually full circle when the Assembly publicly repented for its notorious role in the anti-Irish Catholic campaigns of the 1920s and 1930s, a decision described by one commentator as 'a defining moment in the cultural history of Scotland'.[34]

Even the bloody sectarian conflict in Ulster, which erupted in the late 1960s and continued for many years afterwards, failed to impede the movement to better inter-communal relations in Scotland. Given the strong historical connections between these two parts of the United Kingdom, this may at first be surprising. As one commentator noted, 'the west of Scotland was the part of mainland Britain closest to Northern Ireland not just geographically but emotionally and also in terms of the ethnic composition of its inhabitants and their religious ties.'[35] Some observers had also seen Glasgow as a city marked by the same sectarian sickness as Belfast, while still recognising that the problem was much more deep-rooted in the north of Ireland.[36]

Of course, Scotland did not remain immune from the terrible trauma across the North Channel.[37] There is evidence that the Orange Order in Scotland drew fresh impetus and increased membership from the Troubles, while the slogans, PIRA, UDA and UFA, became common graffiti on bus shelters and factory walls.[38] There were Scottish paramilitaries, especially on the Loyalist side. But the Scottish police were an effective constraint on their activities. Over 100 people were convicted of arms and explosives offences in the 1970s and 1980s but serious incidents were rare. In one such, when bombs were planted in two Catholic bars in Glasgow, only minor injuries resulted. A seasoned member of the city's CID dismissed the UDA contemptuously as 'the Union of Dumb Amateurs'.[39] Sectarian divisions were neither as rigid nor as bitter as those of Ulster. Scottish society, whether Protestant or Catholic in sympathy, was appalled by the ferocity of the violence in Ireland and absolutely determined that it could not be allowed to cross the 60 miles of sea which separated the two countries. The more mindless the carnage, the more resolute and unbending this attitude became.[40] Crucially, the Provisional IRA did not take its campaign of terror to Liverpool or Glasgow. These two cities with historically large Irish immigrant populations were spared the atrocities visited upon London, Birmingham and Manchester. It is impossible to speculate what might have happened if that dispensation had not been in place.

However, by the end of the century, Irish-Scottish relations in general had improved appreciably. Scottish nationalists were impressed by the performance of the Irish 'Tiger Economy' and saw in it a possible model for an independent Scotland. Devolution after 1999 was also significant and Dublin established a high-profile consulate general in Edinburgh to develop closer relations with the new Scottish Executive and Parliament. Young Scots of all religious backgrounds in the 1990s found Irish culture 'cool', whether that meant traditional music, themed bars or stag parties in Dublin.[41] Perhaps of even more enduring value was the lively development of Irish-Scottish academic studies with the formation of the Irish-Scottish Academic Initiative in 1995, a consortium involving some of the leading universities of the two countries, followed by the establishment of the first advanced centre of research in the field at Aberdeen University in 1998. Two years later a similar development in Irish-Scottish Studies was launched at Trinity College, Dublin.[42] This was all a far cry from the racist disparagement of Irish culture in the 1920s, when the great poet, Hugh MacDiarmid, was almost a lone voice when he called the so-called 'Irish invasion of Scotland' as 'destined to be the best thing that happened to it [Scotland] for over 200 years at least'.[43]

For the first time, too, in the late 1990s Scotland's hidden sectarian demons were liberated and became matters of intense public disputation and debate. They were ushered into the open in a sensational lecture, given in the full blaze of publicity, by the Catholic composer, James MacMillan, at the Edinburgh International Festival, Scotland's most prestigious cultural event, in the summer of 1999. Entitled 'Scotland's Shame', MacMillan's address bitterly denounced Scotland as a place of 'sleep-walking bigotry' where the professions, academe, politics and the media were riddled with 'a visceral anti-Catholicism'.[44] For some weeks afterwards the nation's broadsheets were crammed with letters passionately arguing for or against this remarkable polemic. Pandora's Box had truly been opened in spectacular fashion. A subject which, like a bad odour, was usually never mentioned, and especially not in polite company (though everyone was fully aware of its existence), now became of obsessive interest to the nation's chattering classes. Since then the subject of 'sectarianism', rarely defined and often misunderstood, has not been far away from the political and media agenda. It became an issue of concern to the infant Scottish Parliament, elected for the first time in 1999, and eventually attracted the attention of the First Minister, Jack McConnell, who dubbed sectarianism 'Scotland's Secret Shame' (with obvious reference to the title of the MacMillan lecture). He proceeded to frame an anti-sectarian policy which, inter alia, produced a new offence of religiously aggravated criminality.

However, from the perspective of the history of Irish Catholics in Scotland, even more interesting was the fact that a speech like MacMillan's had been delivered at all. Flawed, exaggerated and unconvincing in parts it might have been, but the lecture's importance lay in the fact that it was a decisive and dramatic break with past Catholic behaviour. The response of the community to suspicion, hostility and a dominant Presbyterian hegemony had long been to maintain a low profile and respond to injustice with stoic silence. MacMillan's lecture challenged that tradition head-on. Indeed, he himself admitted that 'there are older Catholics who would be appalled at me raising the issue. That generation has survived through the avoidance of conflict, not putting their heads above the parapet.' It was hardly a surprise when some of his most bitter critics came from the ranks of his fellow Catholics – MacMillan had not simply rocked the boat, he had nearly capsized the vessel and no good would come of it! Was the real significance of the MacMillan intervention, then, that it was a symbol of a new, more confident Catholicism in Scotland; a sign that disadvantage was more of the past than of the present? The final part of this chapter will consider this and related questions.

IV

Some scholars favour the concept of the 'ghetto' when considering the experience of the Catholic community in Scotland at the beginning of our period. Steve Bruce first used the term in an *Innes Review* article and it subsequently appeared in a collection edited by Raymond Boyle and Peter Lynch entitled, *Out of the Ghetto. The Catholic Community in Modern Scotland* (published in 1998). In the same volume, David McCrone and Michael Rosie wrote that hostility to Catholicism coupled with the Catholic Church's fear of its flock being 'contaminated' by a broadly Protestant culture, 'led to a ghettoisation of the Catholic community ... the walls of the ghetto were fortified with suspicion and mistrust on both sides'.[45] The concept implies the introversion of a mainly closed community, homogeneous in faith and class and retaining few linkages with the mainstream society.

As such the description does have some partial force. Catholics of Irish descent c.1950 were overwhelmingly working class, usually married a person of the same faith and, in political terms, were overwhelmingly loyal to the Labour Party. The denominational educational system was a key marker of their identity. A collective sense was further fostered by high levels of Mass attendance and the mobilisation of the laity in a host of voluntary organisations which included the St Vincent de Paul Society to provide succour to the poor; the Catholic Young Men's Society, whose role was to fortify spiritual life; the Rosary Association; Children of Mary; Legion of Mary; Confraternity of the Sacred Heart; and many others. But to portray the community as 'ghettoised' goes too far. Introspection there might have been, but the so-called 'walls' between host and immigrant societies were remarkably porous, not least through the 'lapsing' of many of Catholic birth from the faith when they reached adulthood. Protestants and Catholics worked together and were also active in the same trade unions. Both shared in the popular recreations of dancing, the cinema and football. No Catholic or Irish political party was founded in Scotland to advance ethnic interests. Instead, adherence to the Labour Party led the descendants of the Irish into the mainstream of Scottish and UK politics. The short-lived anti-Partition campaign in Lanarkshire between 1948 and 1950 was the last popular movement with a particular focus on Ireland; nowadays republican clubs attract only a tiny minority of Catholics. Scottish Catholics had also shared equally with the rest of the Scottish nation in the bloody sacrifices of the First and Second World Wars. Even the portrayal of the community as segregated in housing is largely a myth. Some areas of Glasgow and other parts of the west of Scotland did become identified as 'Orange' and 'Green' but few districts were homogeneous in this respect. 'Catholic' enclaves in Glasgow, such as the Gorbals and Garngad, were partly mixed in much the same way as the so-called 'Protestant' strongholds of Bridgeton and Govan. The local branches of the Independent Labour Party were never divided along ethnic or religious lines simply because of the absence of rigid patterns of residential segregation. What did exist, however, was a coherent community, socially disadvantaged and broadly uniform in class terms. It is this which started to pass into history from the 1970s as a consequence of the factors for change outlined in the early sections of this chapter.

Three particular manifestations of this transformation can be identified. First, Catholics, like large numbers of other Scots, have experienced substantial social mobility from the manual working class into professional and middle-class status. Table 11.1 below is informative in this respect.

In 2001 Catholics were still more likely than Protestants to work in lower-status jobs. But the tabulation illustrates that this pattern has been changing fast over the last two decades. Older Catholics, aged 55+, are behind their Protestant counterparts, but among those between 18 and 34 the gap has closed dramatically. A further analysis of the 2001 Scottish census and the Scottish Household Survey of the same year confirm the historic disadvantage

Table 11.1 Religion of upbringing by class and age, Scotland, 2001 (%)

Age group	Percentage of each group in a non-manual occupation				
	Roman Catholic	Church of Scotland	No religion	Other religion	All
18–34	58	63	45	65	58
35–54	47	58	45	62	55
55+	26	49	33	63	48

Source: Scottish Social Attitudes Survey 2001, as reported in Steve Bruce et al. (eds), *Sectarianism in Scotland* (Edinburgh, 2004), p. 78

of older Catholics who have higher than average levels of long-term sickness and disability, but also suggest that Catholics are no longer under-represented among Scotland's managers, senior officials and professionals.[46]

That process of achieving occupational and social parity may well still be ongoing. Table 11.2 describes the proportion of free school meal provision (one index of relative deprivation) in denominational and non-denominational secondary schools in Lanarkshire. The data suggest little substantive difference between the two sectors, with the proportion in Catholic schools slightly more favourable than in non-denominational schools. Furthermore, Tables 11.3 and 11.4, which outline the academic performance of secondaries in the more deprived areas of Glasgow, suggest that one of the motors of Catholic mobility, namely the capacity of the faith schools to outperform others in preparing children from underprivileged social backgrounds for university entrance, is still proving very effective. Indeed, the data in these two tabulations suggest a yawning gap in performance despite similar levels of pupil deprivation as judged by the free school meal index.

Table 11.2 Free school meals: Average percentage of all pupils, South and North Lanarkshire, 2006

South Lanarkshire	Denominational schools	16.6%
	Non-denominational schools	17.4%
North Lanarkshire	Denominational schools	16.1%
	Non-denominational schools	18%
South and North Lanarkshire combined average:		
	Denominational	16.35%
	Non-denominational	17.7%

Source: www.scottishschoolsonline.gov.uk

Second, this social transformation has been a key foundation for a much higher profile and more influence by Catholics in Scottish life. A new confidence now radiates from the leadership of the Catholic Church and the low-profile policy has been well and truly jettisoned. The late Cardinal

Table 11.3 Performance of Glasgow Catholic and denominational schools, 2006 (confined to those with 30% of pupils and above eligible for free school meals)

Catholic	Non-denominational	% S4 pupils gaining 3+ Higher grades A-C in S5	% school leavers gaining university entrance	% pupils eligible for free school meals
All Saints		5	16	40.5
	Castlemilk	5	9	49.1
	Drumchapel	3	6	56.7
	Eastbank	2	15	32
	Govan	n/a	n/a	44.2
John Paul Academy		11	21	36.1
	Lochend	n/a	n/a	47.5
	Smithycroft	6	11	40.9
	Springburn	0	n/a	43.1
St Andrews		5	20	34.8
St Margaret Mary's		n/a	12	50.2
St Mungo's		5	15	36
St Paul's		7	13	44
St Roch's		5	n/a	53.6
St Thomas Acquinas		16	26	30
	Whitehill	6	n/a	41.8

Notes: n/a not available
Source: www.scottishschoolsonline.gov.uk

Table 11.4 Average performance of Glasgow Catholic and non-denominational schools, 2006 (confined to those with 30% of pupils and above eligible for free school meals)

Percentage of S4 pupils gaining 3+ Higher grades A-C in S5	
Catholic:	7.37
Non-denominational:	2.75
Glasgow Council averages (state schools): 12	
Percentage of school leavers gaining university entrance	
Catholic:	15.37
Non-denominational:	5.12
Glasgow Council averages (state schools): 22	
Percentage of pupils eligible for free school meals	
Catholic:	40.65
Non-denominational:	44.41
Glasgow Council averages (state schools): 31.8	

Note: n/a in both types of school counted as zero
Source: www.scottishschoolsonline.gov.uk

Winning – dubbed Scotland's most influential clergyman by the media – and his successor, Cardinal Keith Patrick O'Brien, together with other members of the hierarchy, comment robustly and often controversially on the great moral issues of the day. People of Irish-Catholic stock, though not necessarily practising Catholics themselves, have established national and international reputations in their field – Billy Connolly, James MacMillan, William McIlvanney, Tom McGrath, John Byrne, Sean Connery, John Reid and Helen Liddell – to name but a few of the best-known names. Scottish Catholics also produced in the 1990s around three-quarters of MPs in the west of Scotland, two Secretaries of State for Scotland, eleven successive Lord Provosts of Glasgow and at least two of the current members of the judiciary. Some critics have even started to voice concern about the newly 'privileged position' of Roman Catholics, while one academic commentator in 2000 could describe the 'perceptions of Protestants' about 'the relative coherence and purposefulness of the Catholic community, and the decline symbolically and materially of Presbyterianism in Scotland'.[47]

Third, the fuller integration of Catholics into Scottish society proceeded apace. By 2000 attendances at Sunday Mass had plummeted to around 30 to 40 per cent of the faithful, although these figures concealed considerable disparities between the continuation of relatively high levels in middle-class parishes alongside an astonishing collapse of numbers in those serving poorer communities. That pattern was in itself telling proof of the erosion of old ethnic and religious solidarities. Several of the old Church organisations also went into terminal decline as state welfare, television and alternative popular pursuits made their rationale or attraction redundant.[48] Both the Church of

Scotland and the Catholic Church were therefore on similar trajectories of declining membership, though the haemorrhages of the former had started to occur from an earlier date. Levels of 'mixed marriages' also reached unprecedented levels. One study in 2004 found that almost all married Catholics aged 65–74 (94 per cent) had a Catholic spouse. For those aged 25–34, on the other hand, more than half the Catholics were married to non-Catholics.[49]

The old political loyalties also showed signs of fraying at the edges though, as this is written, the traditional Catholic support for Labour is still only slowly eroding. One half of middle-class Catholics voted Labour in the 2001 general election while two-thirds of church-going Catholics in general did so. But Catholic suspicions of Scottish nationalism and fears of a Kirk and Presbyterian-dominated devolved Scotland seem to have disappeared, especially among those in the younger and middle-aged groups. Social scientists point out that levels of Scottish identity among Catholics are now comparable with the national level and, strikingly, support for devolution and even independence is even higher among them than Protestants.[50]

It would be a mistake to paint too rosy a picture. Health and social disadvantage among older Catholics, an inheritance from the more impoverished times of the past, remains. Deep pools of concentrated deprivation still exist in parts of Glasgow, Lanarkshire and Ayrshire in areas of the country which were traditional places of settlement of the Catholic Irish in earlier generations. Living in them are the victims of the self-same economic transformation which has provided opportunity for their more fortunate and better qualified fellow Catholics.[51] Also, 25 per cent of the prison population in Scotland are baptised Catholics, a much higher proportion than one might expect from their numbers in the population as a whole.[52] In addition, while labour market discrimination may have largely gone, attitudinal sectarianism endures in some parts of the country. Many Catholics, rightly or wrongly, view the continuing public controversy over the existence of the denominational school sector as evidence of lingering bigotry and question why Catholic schools flourish easily in other countries without fuss or comment.[53] The director of the Catholic Media Office in December 2006 pointed to a 'staggeringly intolerant attitude … symptomatic of a simplistic belief that educating children in a faith-based environment is wrong and will inevitably lead to conflict and strife in society'.[54] As if to confirm the depth of differing opinion on this vexed issue, one letter writer to The Scotsman in the same month proclaimed that the 'Catholic school system is the greatest example of institutional racism' in the land and demanded that for the good of the nation it should be abolished forthwith.[55] The hierarchy of the Catholic Church increasingly sees the publicity given to such sentiments as proof of an underlying intolerance of pluralism perpetuated by the survival of ancient animosities and more recently buttressed by the new forces of secular humanism. Indeed, when it was reported in 2006 that sectarian crimes were more likely to be committed against Catholics under cases resulting from the Criminal Justice (Scotland) Act of 2003, Cardinal O'Brien, the leader of the community, publicly complained that the root of the problem was not 'sectarianism' but 'blatant anti-Catholicism'.[56] These negative aspects may counsel against exaggerating the extent of the transformation of the position of Catholics in modern Scottish society. Yet, in the long-run perspective of history, the evidence confirms that a transformation there has undoubtedly been. It may, however, take somewhat longer for the sense of victimhood to disappear among some of the many descendants of the immigrants from Ireland who now comprise such an important part of the modern Scottish nation.

Notes

1 Irish Catholics in the West of Scotland in the Nineteenth Century: Despised by Scottish workers and controlled by the Church?

1 For a fuller discussion of historians' views on the Irish in Scotland see Martin J. Mitchell, *The Irish in the West of Scotland, 1797–1848: Trade Unions, Strikes and Political Movements* (Edinburgh, 1998), pp. 5–11. Since its publication, other works have appeared which support such views of the immigrants. See, for example, David McCrone and Michael Rosie, 'Left and liberal: Catholics in modern Scotland', in Raymond Boyle and Peter Lynch (eds), *Out of the Ghetto? The Catholic Community in Modern Scotland* (Edinburgh, 1998), pp. 66–7; Donald M. MacRaild, *Irish Migrants in Modern Britain, 1750–1822* (Basingstoke, 1999), p. 167; W. W. Knox, *Industrial Nation: Work, Culture and Society in Scotland, 1800-Present* (Edinburgh, 1999), pp. 102–3, 142–3, 173–4; Anon, 'Scots on the Move 1850–1914', in Edward Cowan and Richard J. Finlay (eds), *Scotland since 1688: Struggle for a Nation* (London, 2000), pp. 88–9; R. A. Houston and W. W. J. Knox, 'Introduction: Scots and their histories', in R. A. Houston and W. W. J. Knox (eds), *The New Penguin History of Scotland: from the Earliest Times to the Present Day* (London, 2001), p. xxii; Joseph M. Bradley (ed.), *Celtic Minded: Essays on Religion, Politics, Society, Identity ... and Football* (Glendarvel, 2004), pp. 21, 31; I. G. C. Hutchison, 'Workshop of the Empire: the nineteenth century', in Jenny Wormald (ed.), *Scotland: A History* (Oxford, 2005), pp. 221–3.

2 Tom Gallagher, *Glasgow, the Uneasy Peace: Religious Tension in Modern Scotland* (Manchester, 1987), p. 16.

3 Gallagher, *Uneasy Peace*, chapter 1.

4 Gallagher, *Uneasy Peace*, p. 32.

5 Michael Fry, *Patronage and Principle: a Political History of Modern Scotland* (pbk edn, Aberdeen, 1991), p. 106.

6 Anon, 'Scots on the Move', p. 88.

7 Callum G. Brown, *Religion and Society in Scotland since 1707* (Edinburgh, 1997), p. 120.

8 Brown, *Religion and Society*, p. 32.

9 W. M. Walker, 'Irish immigrants in Scotland: their priests, politics and parochial life', *Historical Journal* 15 (4) (1972), p. 657.

10 Tom Gallagher, 'The Catholic Irish in Scotland: in search of identity', in T. M. Devine (ed.), *Irish Immigrants and Scottish Society in the Nineteenth and Twentieth Centuries* (Edinburgh, 1991), p. 21. See also, Gallagher, *Uneasy Peace*, pp. 47–8.

11 Christopher Harvie and Graham Walker, 'Community and culture', in W. Hamish Fraser and R. J. Morris (eds), *People and Society in Scotland Volume II, 1830–1914* (Edinburgh, 1990), p. 342.

12 Graham Walker, *Intimate Strangers: Political and Cultural Interaction between Scotland and Ulster in Modern Times* (Edinburgh, 1995), p. 8.
13 Walker, 'Irish immigrants', pp. 663–4.
14 Walker, 'Irish immigrants', p. 663.
15 Knox, *Industrial Nation*, pp. 173–4. See also pp. 102–3, 142.
16 See, for example, James Handley, *The Irish in Scotland, 1798–1845* (2nd edn, Cork, 1945), chapters 5, 6 and 8; Handley, *The Irish in Modern Scotland* (Cork, 1947), chapters 4 and 8; Bernard Aspinwall, 'Popery in Scotland: image and reality, 1820–1920', *Records of the Scottish Church History Society* 22 (1986), pp. 236–57; Colin Kidd 'Race, Empire and the limits of nineteenth-century Scottish nationhood', *Historical Journal* 46 (4) (2003), pp. 873–92.
17 In 1841, 93,258, or almost 75 per cent, of the 126,321 people of Irish birth in Scotland lived in the west of the country (the counties of Lanarkshire, Renfrewshire, Ayrshire and Dunbartonshire). In 1861 the proportion was 144,148 out of 204,083 (70.6 per cent), and in 1911 140,370 out of 174,715 (80.3 per cent). Figures extracted from Handley, *Irish in Modern Scotland*, pp. 44, 247–8.
18 Mitchell, *Irish in the West of Scotland*, chapter 1; Alan B. Campbell, *The Lanarkshire Miners: a Social History of their Trade Unions, 1778–1874* (Edinburgh, 1979), chapter 7.
19 See Handley, *Irish in Scotland*, chapter 4 and *Irish in Modern Scotland*, chapter 5.
20 Campbell, *Lanarkshire Miners*, pp. 81, 102, 181.
21 Campbell, *Lanarkshire Miners*, pp. 194–201.
22 Campbell, *Lanarkshire Miners*, pp. 194–5; Mitchell, *Irish in the West of Scotland*, pp. 38–40.
23 Alan B. Campbell, *The Scottish Miners, 1874–1939, Volume One: Industry, Work and Community* (Aldershot, 2000), p.–342; A. M. McDonagh, 'Irish immigration and labour movements in Coatbridge and Airdrie' (BA Dissertation, Department of History, University of Strathclyde, n.d.), pp. 38–45.
24 See, for example, Glasgow Archdiocesan Archive (GAA) General Correspondence, GC/6/1/11, James MacIntosh to Charles Eyre, 20 May 1874; *Glasgow Observer*, 9, 16 and 30 March, 13 and 20 April 1912.
25 For an examination of the role of the Irish in the labour movement in the first half of the nineteenth century see Mitchell, *Irish in the West of Scotland*, chapter 1.
26 Parliamentary Papers, 1836 (40), XXXIV, *Report on the State of the Irish Poor in Great Britain*, p. 109.
27 For the Irish in the weavers' unions see Mitchell, *Irish in the West of Scotland*, pp. 40–5.
28 Mitchell, *Irish in the West of Scotland*, pp. 20–33.
29 National Archives of Scotland, Lord Advocate's Papers, AD14/37/453, Declaration of Henry Cowan, 15 November 1837.
30 Mitchell, *Irish in the West of Scotland*, pp. 29–33.
31 W. Hamish Fraser, 'Trades councils in the labour movement in nineteenth-century Scotland', in Ian MacDougall (ed.), *Essays in Scottish Labour History* (Edinburgh, 1978), p. 7; P. W. Morris, 'The Irish in Glasgow and the labour movement, 1891–1922' (BLitt Thesis, Oxford, 1989), pp. 58, 60.
32 William Kenefick, *'Rebellious and Contrary': The Glasgow Dockers, 1853–1932* (East Linton, 2000), chapter 5; Morris, 'Irish in Glasgow', p. 59.
33 Kiernan and Murphy were leading Irish nationalists in the west of Scotland at this time. Morris, 'Irish in Glasgow', pp. 57–62.
34 McDonagh, 'Irish immigration', pp. 47–8.
35 For repeal see Mitchell, *Irish in the West of Scotland*, chapters 7–8; for Home Rule, see Handley, *Irish in Modern Scotland*, chapter 9.
36 Mitchell, *Irish in the West of Scotland*, chapter 3.
37 Mitchell, *Irish in the West of Scotland*, chapter 5.

38 The Six Points of the Charter were: universal male suffrage, annual parliaments, the secret ballot, equal electoral districts, payment of MPs and abolition of the property qualifications for MPs. Mitchell, *Irish in the West of Scotland*, chapters 6–7. See also Martin J. Mitchell, 'The Catholic Irish and Chartism in the west of Scotland', in Terry Brotherstone, Anna Clark and Kevin Whelan (eds), *These Fissured Isles: Ireland, Scotland and British History, 1798–1848* (Edinburgh, 2005), pp. 178–94.

39 Ian Wood, 'Irish immigrants and Scottish radicalism, 1880–1906', in I. MacDougall (ed.), *Essays in Scottish Labour History* (Edinburgh,1978), pp. 65–89; James J. Smyth, *Labour in Glasgow, 1896–1936: Socialism, Suffrage, Sectarianism* (East Linton, 2000), chapter 4. See also Catriona M. M. MacDonald, *The Radical Thread in Political Change in Scotland, Paisley Politics, 1885–1924* (East Linton, 2000), pp. 99–105.

40 For the Irish and temperance in the 1830s and 1840s see Martin J. Mitchell, 'The Catholic Irish in the west of Scotland: "A Separate and Despised Community?"' in T. M. Devine and J. F. McMillan (eds), *Celebrating Columba: Irish-Scottish Connections 597–1997* (Edinburgh, 1999), pp. 60–2; Handley, *Irish in Scotland*, pp. 244–8.

41 Campbell, *Lanarkshire Miners*, pp. 316–19. His discussion of some of these events is on pp. 182–94. See also Handley, *Irish in Modern Scotland*, chapter 4. For sectarian clashes in Lanarkshire in the 1880s and 1890s see Campbell, *Scottish Miners*, pp. 332–40.

42 Callum G. Brown, *The People in the Pews: Religion and Society in Scotland since 1780* (Scottish Economic and Social History Society, 1993), p. 36.

43 Campbell, *Lanarkshire Miners*, pp. 180–1; Handley, *Irish in Scotland*, pp. 110–12; Mitchell, *Irish in the West of Scotland*, pp. 33–40.

44 For the Airdrie riot see Handley, *Irish in Scotland*, pp. 289–90 and Campbell, *Lanarkshire Miners*, pp. 182–3. For events in Greenock and Gourock see Handley, *Irish in Modern Scotland*, pp. 95–6, and Frances M. Dunlop, *St Mary's Greenock: the Story of a Community* (Greenock, 2001), pp. 52–7.

45 GAA, Western District Papers, WD5 Condon Memoirs, Hamiltonia (1850–59), pp. 85, 132, 262.

46 For example, see *Glasgow Chronicle*, 22 June 1829, 27 August 1841.

47 John McCaffrey, 'Roman Catholics in Scotland in the nineteenth and twentieth centuries', *Records of the Scottish Church History Society* 21 (1983), pp. 290–1. See also his 'Irish immigration' in Michael Lynch (ed.), *The Oxford Companion to Scottish History* (Oxford, 2001), p. 332. For anti-Irish activity in England and Wales see Alan O'Day, 'Varieties of anti-Irish behaviour in Britain, 1846–1922', in Panikos Panayi (ed.), *Racial Violence in Britain 1840–1950* (Leicester, 1993) and MacRaild, *Irish Migrants*, chapter 6.

48 Elaine McFarland, *Protestants First: Orangeism in Nineteenth-Century Scotland* (Edinburgh, 1990).

49 For Ratcliffe see Gallagher, *Uneasy Peace*, pp. 150–7.

50 For events in the early 1850s see Handley, *Irish in Modern Scotland*, pp. 93–113; John Wolffe, *The Protestant Crusade in Great Britain, 1829–1860* (Oxford, 1991), chapters 5, 7 and 8. More research is needed on the riots in Greenock and Gourock. The fact that the mob was stirred into action by a Protestant preacher on 12 July suggests that there was an Orange – and therefore a Protestant Irish – element to the proceedings.

51 Quoted in Knox, *Industrial Nation*, p. 103. For Crawfurd see William Knox (ed.), *Scottish Labour Leaders 1918–39: a Biographical Dictionary* (Edinburgh, 1984), pp. 81–6.

52 J. Devon, 'The Calton fifty years ago', *Transactions of the Old Glasgow Club* 6 (1930–31), p. 31, quoted in I. G. C. Hutchison, 'Politics and society in mid-Victorian Glasgow' (PhD, University of Edinburgh, 1975), pp. 484, 486.

53 T. C. Smout, *A Century of the Scottish People 1830–1950* (pbk edn, London, 1987), pp. 247–8.

54 For a detailed examination of Scottish-Irish relations in the first half of the nineteenth century see Mitchell, 'Catholic Irish in the west of Scotland', pp. 50–83.

55 Members of the middle class disliked the Catholic Irish for a number of reasons, such as the immigrants' race, nationality and religion, and because the Irish were seen as a burden on the poor rates, and the cause of most of the social problems that afflicted urban life, such as crime, poverty, drunkenness and disease. See works cited in n. 16.

56 *Report on the State of the Irish Poor*, p. 112. See also pp. 116–17.

57 *Report on the State of the Irish Poor*, p. 118.

58 *Report on the State of the Irish Poor*, p. 110.

59 Quoted in Handley, *Irish in Modern Scotland*, p. 240.

60 Bernard Aspinwall, 'The ties that bind and loose: the Catholic community in Galloway, 1800–1998', *Records of the Scottish Church History Society* 29 (1999), pp. 96–7.

61 GAA, GC3/3/2, Paul McLaughlin to Charles Eyre, 20 June 1871.

62 GAA, GC10/40/1, Louis J. C. MacIntyre to Charles Eyre, 29 July 1878.

63 GAA, GC10/1/1, James McIntosh to Charles Eyre, 2 March 1878.

64 Aspinwall, 'Ties that bind and loose', p. 98.

65 Aspinwall, 'Ties that bind and loose', p. 99. According to Aspinwall 'Even after 1878 the numbers of mixed marriages and infants baptized from mixed-faith marriages [in certain parishes in the west of Scotland] ran from one in six to four out of five …' Bernard Aspinwall, 'Faith of our fathers living still … the time warp or woof! woof!', in T. M. Devine (ed.), *Scotland's Shame?: Bigotry and Sectarianism in Modern Scotland* (Edinburgh, 2000), p. 113.

66 See, for example, Gallagher, *Uneasy Peace*, p. 49 and T. M. Devine, *The Scottish Nation, 1700–2000* (London, 1999), p. 493.

67 For the growth and development of the Catholic community in the nineteenth century see the following works by Bernard Aspinwall: 'The formation of the Catholic community in the west of Scotland', *Innes Review* 33 (1982), pp. 44–57; 'Children of the dead end: the formation of the archdiocese of Glasgow, 1815–1914', *Innes Review* 43 (1992), pp. 119–44; 'A long journey: the Irish in Scotland', in Patrick O'Sullivan (ed.), *The Irish World Wide Volume Five: Religion and Identity* (Leicester, 1996), pp. 146–82. See also Mary McHugh, 'The development of the Catholic community in the western province (Roman Catholic Dioceses of Glasgow, Motherwell and Paisley) 1878–1962' (PhD Thesis, University of Strathclyde, 1990).

68 McHugh, 'Development of the Catholic community', p. 65.

69 For the Glasgow Catholic Association and its activities see Mitchell, *Irish in the West of Scotland*, chapter 4.

70 For Scottish attitudes to emancipation see Ian Muirhead, 'Catholic emancipation: Scottish reaction in 1829', *Innes Review* 24 (1973), pp. 26–42; Mitchell, 'Catholic Irish in the west of Scotland', pp. 63–6.

71 Scottish Catholic Archives, Blairs Letters, BL/5/180/1, Andrew Scott to William Reid, 7 February 1825.

72 The Catholic Emancipation Act allowed Catholics to sit in Parliament and hold public office (except Lord Lieutenant of Ireland, and Lord Chancellor).

73 Mitchell, *Irish in the West of Scotland*, pp. 152–7.

74 Mitchell, *Irish in the West of Scotland*, chapter 5.

75 Mitchell, *Irish in the West of Scotland*, chapters 7 and 8.

76 For Irish clergy in the region during this period see Martin J. Mitchell, ' "In general they do not answer well": Irish priests in the western lowlands of Scotland, 1838–50', in Oonagh Walsh (ed.), *Ireland Abroad: Politics and Professions in the Nineteenth Century* (Dublin, 2003), pp. 147–59.

77 Mitchell, 'Irish priests in the western lowlands', pp. 150–1.
78 Handley, *Irish in Modern Scotland*, chapter 3; Vincent Alan McClelland, 'The Irish clergy and Archbishop Manning's apostolic visitation of the western district of Scotland, 1867', *Catholic Historical Review* 53 (April and July 1967), pp. 1–27, 229–50; James Walsh, 'Archbishop Manning's visitation of the western district of Scotland in 1867', *Innes Review* 18 (1967), pp. 3–18; David McRoberts, 'The restoration of the Scottish Catholic hierarchy in 1878', *Innes Review* 29 (1978), pp. 3–29; McCaffrey, 'Roman Catholics in Scotland', pp. 278–88'; Bernard Aspinwall, 'Scots and Irish clergy ministering to immigrants, 1830–78', *Innes Review* 47 (1996), pp. 45–68.
79 For Eyre's period in charge see Bernard Aspinwall, 'Anyone for Glasgow? The strange nomination of the Rt Rev. Charles Eyre in 1868', *Recusant History* 23 (4) (1997), pp. 596–8.
80 McHugh, 'Development of the Catholic community', chapter 2; Gallagher, *Uneasy Peace*, pp. 46–7, 53–8; Aspinwall, 'Formation of the Catholic community'; Aspinwall., 'Children of the dead end'; Aspinwall 'A long journey'.
81 Gallagher, 'The Catholic Irish', pp. 21–2; Walker, 'Irish immigrants'; Michael Lynch, *Scotland: a New History* (London, 1991), pp. 404–5.
82 Hutchison, 'Politics and society', pp. 480–1; Sheridan Gilley, 'Catholics and socialists in Scotland, 1900–30', in Roger Swift and Sheridan Gilley (eds), *The Irish in Britain, 1815–1939* (London, 1989), p. 215. Eyre intervened during the 1900 general election campaign by sending a circular to all his parishes informing them that the Church advocated rate support for its schools in Scotland, and the creation of a Catholic university in Ireland. Those Catholics who had the vote were asked to establish what the views of parliamentary candidates were on these issues. Wood, 'Irish immigrants and Scottish radicalism', p. 82.
83 Gallagher, *Uneasy Peace*, p. 64; McHugh, 'Development of the Catholic community', p. 82.
84 GAA, LB2/7, James McLachlan to Father Hughes, 17 February 1886; GAA, GC18/5/2, J. Hughes to John McLachlan, 18 February 1886; GAA, MY82/21, John Ritchie to Rev. J. Taylor, 14 February 1902.
85 GAA, GC27/1/3, John Dougan to J. A. Maguire, 17 December 1885.
86 Bernard Aspinwall, 'The making of the modern diocese of Galloway', in Raymond McCluskey (ed.), *The See of Ninian: a History of the Medieval Diocese of Whithorn and the Diocese of Galloway in Modern Times* (Ayr, 1997), pp. 130–2.
87 For the involvement of some Irish priests in Irish nationalist politics see Bernard Canning, *Irish-Born Secular Priests in Scotland, 1829–1979* (Inverness, 1979), p. 147; Raymond McCluskey, *St Joseph's Kilmarnock, 1847–1997: a Portrait of a Parish Community* (Kilmarnock, 1997), p. 92; Martin J. Mitchell, 'The Catholic community in Hamilton, c.1800–1914', in T. M. Devine (ed.), *St Mary's Hamilton: a Social History, 1846–1996* (Edinburgh, 1995), pp. 53–4; Wood, 'Irish immigrants and Scottish radicalism', p. 78; Gallagher, *Uneasy Peace*, p. 64.
88 Condon and Danaher were among the first canons of the Glasgow Cathedral chapter when it was established in January 1884. Canning, *Irish-born Secular Priests*, pp. 48–54, 71–4.
89 Wood, 'Irish immigrants and Scottish radicalism', p. 74.
90 *Glasgow Observer*, 26 December 1885, quoted in Wood, 'Irish immigrants and Scottish radicalism', p. 75.
91 McHugh, 'Development of the Catholic community', p. 82; E. W. McFarland, *John Ferguson, 1836–1906: Irish Issues in Scottish Politics* (East Linton, 2003).
92 Handley, *Irish in Modern Scotland*, pp. 270–1; Hutchison, 'Politics and society', p. 481.
93 McCaffrey, 'Roman Catholics in Scotland', p. 290.
94 Quoted in Handley, *Irish in Modern Scotland*, pp. 118–19.

95 Handley, *Irish in Modern Scotland*, pp. 118–19; Robert Duncan, *Steelopolis: the Making of Motherwell, c.1750–1939* (Motherwell, 1991), p. 151.

96 Aspinwall, 'Making of the modern diocese', p. 133 and see also pp. 133–5 for Murphy's subsequent activities; Hutchison, 'Politics and society', pp. 482–3, 500. For further divisions within a Catholic community over local politics, see Geraldine Vaughan's chapter in this volume.

97 The Fenian movement emerged in America at the same time as in Ireland. Jonathan Bardon, 'Ribbonmen' and Oliver P. Rafferty, 'Fenian movement', in Brian Lalor (ed.), *The Encyclopaedia of Ireland* (Dublin, 2003), pp. 382–3, 929; Oliver P. Rafferty, *Catholicism in Ulster, 1603–1983: an Interpretative History* (Dublin, 1994), pp. 162–5; GAA, GC128, H. Morgan to Charles Eyre, 20 January 1873.

98 GAA, GC128, J. Shaw to 'My Lord', 3 November 1874; GAA, GC128, James McIntosh to 'My Dear Lord', 4 March 1875; GAA, LB2/3, A. MacFarlane to Rev. Dr Glancy, 16 August 1878. Eyre's predecessors in charge of the Church in the west of Scotland also had to deal with Fenianism and Ribbonism. See Handley, *Irish in Scotland*, pp. 161, 310; Handley, *Irish in Modern Scotland*, pp. 59, 262–9; Mitchell, *Irish in the West of Scotland*, p. 119; Elaine W. McFarland, 'A reality and yet impalpable: the Fenian panic in mid-Victorian Scotland', *Scottish Historical Review* 77 (1998), pp. 199–223.

99 GAA, RI3/6/2, 'Report of the Commission on Secret Societies 1882'.

100 GAA, RI3/1, Episcopal circular on 'St Patrick's Hibernian Society and St Patrick's Fraternal Society' (originally published 1883, reprinted 1888, 1894). The St Patrick's Fraternal Society – ostensibly a benefit society – had been viewed with suspicion in the archdiocese of Glasgow for some time. See the correspondence in GAA, RI3/21, St Patrick's Fraternal Society, 1874–5, undated; GAA, GC128, H. Morgan to Charles Eyre 20 January 1873; GAA, GC128, Samuel H. B. Rowson to Charles Eyre, 11 December 1874.

101 Handley, *Irish in Modern Scotland*, p. 283; McHugh, 'Development of the Catholic community', pp. 82–3.

102 GAA, GC29, George William Ritchie to John Maguire, 26 June 1897.

103 GAA, GC128, Patrick Graham to Charles Eyre, 18 December 1898.

104 Cardinal Rampolla to Archbishop Smith, 15 December 1909, quoted in McHugh, 'Development of the Catholic community', p. 83. See also Handley, *Irish in Modern Scotland*, pp. 292–3.

105 GAA, GC128, printed circular, 'Instructions regarding condemned societies from the archbishops and bishops of Scotland, printed by their order on July 31st, 1899'.

106 GAA, RI5/15/1, Charles Eyre, printed circular, 18 October 1888.

107 For an account of the League of the Cross in the Glasgow archdiocese see McHugh, 'Development of the Catholic community', pp. 66–70.

108 GAA, RI5/13/1 Charles Eyre, 'To the faithful of the archdiocese', printed circular, 13 May 1889.

109 *Catholic Directory for Scotland*, 1892, pp. 212–13.

110 GAA, RI5/15/2, Charles Eyre, Printed Circular, 13 March 1892.

111 McHugh, 'Development of the Catholic community', pp. 66–70; Mitchell, 'Catholic community in Hamilton', pp. 37–41; Gallagher, *Uneasy Peace*, p. 56.

112 Brown, *Religion and Society*, p. 119; Gallagher, *Uneasy Peace*, p. 56; Aspinwall, 'Children of the dead end', p. 136; Aspinwall., 'Anyone for Glasgow', p. 597.

113 GAA, GC22/45/1, Patrick Gaule to John Maguire, 10 March 1890.

114 *Glasgow Observer*, 31 October 1891.

115 *Glasgow Observer*, 2 April 1892.

116 GAA, GC31a/56 John Nyhan to 'My Lord', 24 May 1899.

117 McHugh, 'Development of the Catholic community', p. 68. The temperance cause was strongest in Glasgow and its immediate suburbs, whereas the coal, iron and steel districts of Lanarkshire were, overall, the worst performing areas. The membership

in the 1901 report breaks down as follows: Glasgow District – 22,688; Lanarkshire – 4,612; Renfrewshire and Ayrshire – 4,807; Dumbartonshire – 1,200.

118 See, for example, the works cited in n. 67.

119 T. M. Devine, 'Industrialisation', in T. M. Devine, C. H. Lee and G. C. Peden (eds), *The Transformation of Scotland: the Economy since 1700* (Edinburgh, 2005), pp. 34–70.

120 Handley, *Irish in Scotland*, p. 142.

121 For attitudes to the Catholic community in the inter-war period see Handley, *Irish in Modern Scotland*, chapter 10; Steve Bruce, *No Pope of Rome: Militant Protestantism in Modern Scotland* (Edinburgh, 1985), chapters 2 and 3; Tom Gallagher, 'Protestant extremism in urban Scotland 1930–39: its growth and contraction', *Scottish Historical Review* 64 (1985), pp. 143–67; Gallagher, *Uneasy Peace*, chapter 4; Gallagher, *Edinburgh Divided: John Cormack and No Popery in the 1930s* (Edinburgh, 1987); Stewart J. Brown, ' "Outside the Covenant": the Scottish Presbyterian Churches and Irish immigration, 1922–1938', *Innes Review* 42 (1991), pp. 19–45; Richard J. Finlay, 'Nationalism, race, religion and the Irish Question in inter-war Scotland, *Innes Review*, 42 (1991), pp. 46–67; Finlay, 'National identity in crisis: politicians, intellectuals and the "End of Scotland", 1920–1939, *History* 79 (1994), pp. 242–59; Smyth, *Labour in Glasgow*, chapter 6; Steve Bruce, Tony Glendinning, Ian Paterson and Michael Rosie, *Sectarianism in Scotland* (Edinburgh, 2004), chapter 2; Michael Rosie, *The Sectarian Myth in Scotland: of Bitter Memory and Bigotry* (Basingstoke, 2004), chapters 5–8. See also Michael Rosie's chapter in this volume.

122 For the famine Irish immigrants, and Scottish attitudes towards them, see Handley, *Irish in Modern Scotland*, chapter 2; Frank Neal, *Black '47: Britain and the Famine Irish* (Basingstoke, 1998), chapter 6; John F. McCaffrey, 'Reactions in Scotland to the Irish famine' in Stewart J. Brown and George Newlands (eds), *Scottish Christianity in the Modern World* (Edinburgh, 2000), pp. 155–76; and Tom Devine's chapter 2 in this volume.

123 Handley, *Irish in Modern Scotland*, chapter 3.

2 The Great Irish Famine and Scottish History

1 There is now a substantial modern historiography on the Irish Famine. See, *inter alia*, P. M. A. Bourke, 'The visitation of God' in Jacqueline Hill and Cormac Ó Gráda (eds) *'The Visitation of God?': the Potato and the Great Irish Famine* (Dublin, 1993); M. E. Daly, *The Famine in Ireland* (Dundalk, 1986); James S. Donnelly, Jr, *The Great Irish Potato Famine* (Sutton, 2001); Peter Gray, *The Irish Famine* (London, 1995); L. Kennedy, P. S. Ell, E. M. Crawford and L. S. Clarkson, *Mapping the Great Irish Famine* (Dublin, 1999); Christine Kinealy, *This Great Calamity: the Irish Famine, 1845–52* (Dublin, 1994); Cormac Ó Gráda, *Black '47 and Beyond* (Princeton, NJ, 1999); C. Póirtéir (ed.), *The Great Irish Famine* (Cork and Dublin, 1995).

2 Kerby Miller, *Emigrants and Exiles: Ireland and the Irish Exodus to North America* (Oxford, 1985), p. 291.

3 John F. McCaffrey, 'Reactions in Scotland to the Irish Famine', in S. J. Brown and G. Newlands (eds), *Scottish Christianity in the Modern World* (Edinburgh, 2000), p. 157.

4 James Handley, *The Irish in Modern Scotland* (Cork, 1947), pp. 20–46.

5 Frank Neal, *Black '47. Britain and the Famine Irish* (Basingstoke, 1998).

6 McCaffrey, 'Reactions in Scotland to the Irish Famine', pp. 155–76.

7 *Glasgow Herald*, 11 June 1847.

8 *Blackwood's Edinburgh Magazine* 70 (August 1851), p. 129. This was a much exaggerated figure and it did not take into account those large numbers who were temporary migrants.

9 *Glasgow Chronicle*, 6 January 1847.

10 Scottish Catholic Archives, Edinburgh (SCA), Blairs Letters, BL6/545/1, John Murdoch to Donald Carmichael, 4 January 1847.
11 SCA Presholme Letters, PL3/347/3, John Murdoch to James Kyle, 15 June 1847.
12 McCaffrey, 'Reactions in Scotland to the Irish Famine', pp. 157, 164–7.
13 Quoted in Ó Gráda, *Black '47*, p. 109.
14 SCA, Oban Letters, OL2/76/11, John Murdoch to Alexander Smith, 18 October 1848.
15 L. M. Cullen, *An Economic History of Ireland since 1660* (London, 1972), p. 132.
16 Donnelly, *Great Irish Potato Famine*, pp. 169–86.
17 S. H. Cousens, 'The regional pattern of emigration during the Great Irish Famine, 1846–51', *Transactions of the Institute of British Geographers* 28 (1966), p. 123.
18 Liam Kennedy and Philip Ollerenshaw (eds), *An Economic History of Ulster, 1820–1940* (Manchester, 1985), pp. 62–71.
19 Cousens, 'Regional Pattern of Emigration', pp. 123, 125.
20 R. H. Campbell, 'Irish paupers in Wigtownshire after 1845', *Scottish Archives* 2 (1996), pp. 61–2.
21 *Glasgow Herald*, 29 January 1847.
22 Neal, *Black '47*, p. 165.
23 SCA, Blairs Letters, BL6/545/15, John Murdoch to James Kyle, 21 May 1847.
24 SCA, Blairs Letters, BL6/545/15, John Murdoch to James Kyle, 21 May 1847.
25 Neal, *Black '47*, pp. 123–56.
26 *Scotch Reformers Gazette*, 26 February 1848.
27 T. M. Devine, *The Great Highland Famine. Hunger, Emigration and the Scottish Highlands in the Nineteenth Century* (Edinburgh, 1988).
28 *The Witness*, 21 and 25 November, 1846.
29 National Archives of Scotland (NAS), HD6/2, Treasury Correspondence, Mr Campbell to Sir John McNeill, 2 March 1847.
30 NAS, HD6/2, Treasury Correspondence, Major Halliday to Sir E. P. Coffin, 4 March 1847.
31 Devine, *Great Highland Famine*, pp. 147–70.
32 *Glasgow Herald*, 22 March 1847.
33 *Scotch Reformers Gazette*, 26 February 1848.
34 Glasgow City Archives (GCA), Glasgow Parochial Board Minutes, 30 November 1847.
35 *Blackwood's Edinburgh Magazine* (March 1851), p. 369.
36 Devine, *Great Highland Famine*.
37 C. W. J. Withers, *Urban Highlanders, 1700–1900* (East Linton, 1998), pp. 84–132.
38 *The Scotsman*, 24 November 1850.
39 *The Witness*, 19 July 1851.
40 Market reports for these years in *The Scotsman* and *Glasgow Herald*.
41 Neal, *Black '47*, p. 281.
42 *Glasgow Herald*, 15 February 1847.
43 Handley, *Irish in Modern Scotland*, p. 31.
44 SCA, Blairs Letters, BL5/545/4, John Murdoch to John Kyle, 2 February 1847; *Glasgow Chronicle*, 29 January 1847.
45 *Glasgow Saturday Post*, 12 June 1847; James Paterson, 'Statistics of the Barony Fever Hospital of Glasgow in 1847–48', *Edinburgh Medical and Surgical Journal* 70 (1848), pp. 357–66.
46 GCA, Glasgow Parochial Board Minutes, 29 July 1847.
47 Neal, *Black '47*, pp. 253, 258, 279.
48 *Glasgow Herald*, 1 April 1850.
49 Quoted in Handley, *Irish in Modern Scotland*, p. 25, n. 8.
50 P. Mackenzie, *Old Reminiscences of Glasgow and the West of Scotland*, vol. 3 (Glasgow, 1858), pp. 507–12.

51 William Sloan, 'Religious affiliation and the immigrant experience: Catholic Irish and Protestant Highlanders in Glasgow, 1830–1850'. in T. M. Devine (ed.), *Irish Immigrants and Scottish Society in the Nineteenth and Twentieth Centuries* (Edinburgh, 1991), pp. 69–70.

52 Sloan, 'Religious affiliation', p. 70.

53 William Sloan, 'Employment opportunities and migrant group assimilation: the Highlanders and Irish in Glasgow', in A. J. G. Cummings and T. M. Devine (eds), *Industry, Business and Society in Scotland since 1700* (Edinburgh, 1994), pp. 207–8.

54 SCA, Blairs Letters, BL5/545/4, John Murdoch to James Kyle, 2 February 1847; Glasgow Archdiocesan Archives, Western District Papers, WD5, Condon Diaries, p. 483.

55 *Scotch Reformers Gazette*, 19 February 1848.

56 F. Neal, *Sectarian Violence. The Liverpool Experience 1819–1914* (Manchester, 1988), pp. 80–175.

57 Handley, *Irish in Modern Scotland*, pp. 93ff.

58 Quoted in Handley, *Irish in Modern Scotland*, p. 100.

59 Colin Kidd, 'Race, empire and the limits of nineteenth-century Scottish nationhood', *The Historical Journal* 46 (4) (2003), pp. 873–92.

60 John Steill, *Scotland for the Scotch and Reasons for Irish Repeal* (Glasgow, 1848?).

61 McCaffrey, 'Reactions in Scotland to the Irish Famine', p. 175.

3 Catholic Devotion in Victorian Scotland

1 Charles D. Plater, 'Popular retreats since 1912', *Month*, 135 (1920) pp. 248–56, 248. He visited Glasgow earlier and met the Red Clydesiders.

2 *Scottish Catholic Directory*, 1848. Also Rev. George Porter SJ, 'The wants of Catholicism in Scotland', *Glasgow Free Press*, 12 September 1863 – union in one nation, diligence, temperance improved housing and real homes.

3 Emmet Larkin,'The devotional revolution in Ireland', *American Historical Review* 77 (1972), pp. 625–52, especially p. 649. He quotes Irish Dominican Rev. Thomas Burke, a regular visitor to Scotland and USA, p. 119. J. Derek Holmes, *More Roman than Rome* (London, 1978) and his *The Triumph of the Holy See: a Short History of the Papacy in the Nineteenth Century* (London, 1978); Mary Heimann, *Catholic Devotion in Victorian England* (Oxford, 1995), p. 170.

4 Bernard Aspinwall, '*Rerum Novarum* and the Church in the transatlantic world', in R. Boutry (ed.), *Rerum Novarum: Ecriture, Contenu et Reception* (Rome, 1997), pp. 465–95; and Kevin Collins, *Catholic Churchmen and the Celtic Revival in Ireland, 1848–1916* (Dublin, 2002), pp. 140–60.

5 Their dire poverty appalled the Cambridge convert Scot – Scots College Archives Rome (SCAR) 16/137, Rev J. A. Stothert to Rev. Dr A. Grant, 19 June 1850. The clerical clash of Irish temperance and the 'Hielan' dram may have fuelled some of the 1860s divisions.

6 These concerns bedevilled the Edinburgh trustee controversy in the 1820s as much as in the USA. Bishop John MacDonald, Aberdeen opposed restoring the hierarchy on financial grounds, Scritti e Riferiti Scozzese, Archives of Propaganda, Rome (APR), letter to Propaganda, 21 April 1880, vol. 8, fols 224–5. Ibid., Archbishop C. Eyre to Bishop J. Rigg, Dunkeld, 30 April 1880, fol. 225. said none realised the scale of debt at the restoration. There were several ecclesiastical and civil court cases over misuse of the Mitchell Fund and priests' pensions. The Rev. John Carmont, *Regarding the Past Administration and Present Condition of the Mitchell Fund*, APR, vol. 8, fols 14–19 and further correspondence. See also J. F. McCaffery, 'The stewardship of resources: financial strategies of Roman Catholics in the Glasgow district, 1800–70', *Studies in Church History* 24 (1987), pp. 359–70.

7 SCAR, 16/58, Bishop A. Carruthers to Rev A. Grant, 24 January 1845, re 16 acres purchased at Greenhills.

8 Heimann, *Catholic Devotion*; David W. Miller, 'Mass attendance in Ireland in 1834', in S. J. Brown and D. W. Miller (eds), *Piety and Power, 1760–1960: Essays In Honour of Emmet Larkin* (Notre Dame, 2000), pp. 158–79; T. G. McGrath, 'The tridentine evolution of modern Irish Catholicism, 1563–1962: a re-examination of the "devotional revolution" thesis', *Recusant History* 20 (1991), pp. 512–23; Ann Taves, *The Household of Faith: Roman Catholic Devotions in Mid-Nineteenth Century America* (Notre Dame, 1986): Colleen McDannell, *The Christian Home in Victorian America, 1840–1900* (Bloomington, 1986); Jay P. Dolan, *Catholic Revivalism: the American Experience, 1830–1900* (Notre Dame, 1978); Holmes, *More Roman than Rome*; Emmet Larkin, 'The devotional revolution in Ireland 1850–1875', *American Historical Review* 77 (1975), pp. 1,244–76.

9 Cf. Charlotte Eaton, *Rome in the Nineteenth Century*, 3 vols (Edinburgh, 1820), vol. 3, p. 125: 'Every pulpit resounds with the stentorian voice of some friar, denouncing, with all the vehemence of Italian energy and gesticulation, the horrors of hell, and demonstrating that his congregation are in the fair way to tumble into that fiery abyss. A preacher has not the smallest chance of popularity here who does not frighten his auditor out of their senses.' Also vol. 3, p. 151 for a sobbing congregation.

10 APR vol. 4, fol. 384, Bishop A. Scott, 10 Oct 1832, and APR, vol. 4, fol. 322, Rev. J. Gordon to Propaganda, c.1830. Rev. J. Strain, later Archbishop of Edinburgh, introduced many confraternities, medals and rosaries in his scattered Dalbeattie area, SCAR, 16/85B, letter to Rev. A. Grant, 2 February 1846; SCAR 16/103, Bishop A. Smith, 9 August 1849,

11 SCAR, 16/140, Rev. J. A. Stothert to Rev A. Grant, 18 February 1851.

12 Jesuit, Redemptorist, Vincentian and Passionist missions. SCAR, 16 /222, J. Murdoch to Rev. A. Grant, 1 June 1865. Italian-speaking Rosminians also came.

13 APR, vol. 7 fols 953–4, Rev. A. Taylor, 4 February 1875 on Rev. Edmund Vaughan's mission. On Greenock in 1890 see John Sharp, *Reapers of the Harvest: the Redemptorists in Great Britain and Ireland, 1843–1898* (Dublin, 1989), p. 228.

14 Bernard Aspinwall, 'The formation of the Catholic community in the west of Scotland: some preliminary outlines', *Innes Review* 33 (1982), pp. 44–57.

15 *Parliamentary Papers*, 1854. *The Religious Census of Scotland*, 1851. Rev. Francis McKerrell reported 1,200 Catholics in and around Linlithgow, 9 December 1851.

16 Earlier a politically active Irish priest, Rev. William Byrne (or O'Beirne) in Rothesay served Inverary – 60 miles, Lochgilphead – 40 miles and Largs – 22 miles, travelling by land and sea every fourth Sunday: APR, vol. 4, fols 425–7, Rev. W. Byrne, 1 February 1833. Rev. Michael Condon at Campbeltown also served a vast area.

17 SCAR, 16 /128, Rev. J. McLachlan to Rev. A. Grant, 26 June 1850.

18 The figure would suggest less than 10 per cent Sunday Mass observance.

19 Italian Rev. Joseph Bruschini served four years then died of typhus, 1865; APR, vol. 6, fol. 772, Bishop J. Murdoch, 26 January 1865.

20 For example the census for 1901 shows some 27 French nuns in Dumfries.

21 Bernard Aspinwall, 'The formation of British identity within Scottish Catholicism, 1830–1914' in R. Pope (ed.), *Religion and National Identity: Wales and Scotland, c.1700–2000* (Cardiff, 2001), especially pp. 285–6. In 1887 Jesuits heard 100,000 confessions. Confessional boxes appeared for the first time in Scotland. Advertising of devotional books and objects massively increased from mid-century, in *Scottish Catholic Directory*.

22 D. McRoberts (ed.), *Modern Scottish Catholicism, 1878–1978* (Glasgow, 1979), p. 233; and David Miller, 'Irish Catholicism and the Great Famine'. *Journal of Social History* 9 (1975) pp. 81–98 is persuasive in terms of the impact on Scotland.

23 Figures from *Scottish Catholic Directory, 1850–1920*. Aberdeen did not make returns

until after 1885. In 1828, 50 priests cared for 28,000 faithful or one to every 560. In 1881, 273 priests ministered to an estimated 321,000, or one to 1,176: APR, vol. 8 fols 745–7, Report, 23 June 1885,

24 In 1847 Rev. John Carmont, intent on studying for a DD with the renowned Rev. Professor Passaglia had to return to the 'fevered' Irish immediately on ordination. He hankered to go back later: APR, vol. 8, fols 44–5, Rev. J. Carmont to Propaganda, 8 February 1879; and Bishop Hay (with added material by John Carmont), *History of the Scottish Clerical Quota Fund to which is added 'Observation on Quota Fund'* (Girvan, 1878). It was published by Rev. J. O'Shaughnessy who saw the restoration as a means of controlling Scottish bishops. Carmont later took his pension case to Rome, backed by Bute, and defeated the bishops. He did not receive a penny. He later published a severe indictment of the bishops, *An Episode in the Management of the Mitchell Fund* (Blairgowrie, 1901). Ultramontanism had odd supporters and even more odd consequences.

25 That mood is captured in Gary Wills, *Bare Ruined Choirs: Doubt, Prophecy and Radical Religion* (Garden City, 1972); as did portable medals, rosaries and hymns which lingered in the memory.

26 MC4/9, Scottish Catholic Archives (SCA), Edinburgh, Rev. I. Spencer to Agnes Trail, 27 Oct 1832, A talented convert artist, Trail entered the Ursulines in France, and became superior of St Margaret's Convent in Edinburgh, the first Scottish foundation since the Reformation. Spencer, a close friend of Monteith died on his estate after his mission at Greenock. His prayer crusade for the conversion of England had counter-revolutionary overtones for the Irish, while his confident optimism chimed in with Irish rather than 'Hielan' pastoral attitudes in Scotland.

27 SCAR, 16/85E, Rev. P. McLachlan to Rev. A. Grant, 24 November 1847.

28 *Dumfries Times*, 22 August 1837. Aristocratic Catholic Whig Philip Howard (1801–83), MP for Carlisle, 1830–47 and 1848–52, attended. See Thomas Muir, 'Ad majorem dei gloriam: Catholic Church music at Everingham and Stonyhurst, 1839–1914'. www.bpmonline.org.uk/bpm5-admajorem.html for William Constable Maxwell's desire to enrich the liturgy. Gillis attended the lavishly orchestrated opening of Everingham chapel in 1839.

29 Established July 1838and included in its members della Torre. See inside covers of pamphlets issued 1838–44. The Scottish Catholic Truth Society only began fifty years later.

30 Its 350 members walked through 80,000 on Edinburgh streets: SCAR 16/45, Rev. J. Gillis to Rev. A. Grant, 1 January 1845,

31 Raymond Jonas, *France and the Cult of the Sacred Heart: an Epic Tale of Modern Times* (Berkeley, 2000).

32 APR, vol. 5, fols 557–8, Bishop John Murdoch, 13 March 1845.

33 SCAR, 17/30, Rev. Alexander Munro to Rev. A. Grant, 27 April 1867. Munro himself was a Presbyterian convert from Aberdeen.

34 APR, vol. 4 fol. 6, Vicars-Apostolic Report, 25 September 1801, reports 400 going; Rev. Paul McPherson, 24 December 1804 ibid f22; V-apostolic, 15 August 1804; APR, vol. 4, fols 102–3, Rev. N. MacDonald, 27 February 1819; APR, vol. 4, fol. 150, 5 November 1824; APR, vol. 5, fols 510–11, Rev. C. McPherson, Barra, 30 Oct 1851, notes 400 leaving; APR, vol. 5, fol. 520, Rev. C. MacDonald, 8 November 1851.

35 APR, vol. 6, Rev. Eugene Small, 29 July 1855.

36 APR, vol. 4, fol. 357, Rev. Eneas MacDonald, 1 February 1832. Even in late nineteenth-century Glasgow, one in four children died before reaching five years of age.

37 APR, vol. 5, fols 63–7, Report, 1835. Fifty years later, Argyll and the Isles, heavily depleted by clearances, depended on Catholic landlords: Howard of Glossop, Lord Lovat, Bute and the laird of Glenfinnan: APR, vol. 8, fols 772–81 Bishop's Report, 24 September 1885.

38 *Census 1851. Religious Worship*, pp. 44–5. In 1838, England and Wales had 429

chapels; in 1853, 855 priests and 88 religious houses – 73 for women – and 616 chapels: *Scottish Catholic Directory* 1838, 1850, 1855.

39 *Scottish Catholic Directory*, 1880, 1920 – quality of buildings and staff salaries lagged far behind state schools.

40 There are editions of 1846, 1849, 1851, 1854, 1857, 1875 and 1896 in the National Library of Scotland. Many more can be found in the Library of Congress catalogue.

41 *Scottish Catholic Directory*, 1850, pp. 65–6. By 1855 almost 1,200 were in regular schools, *Scottish Catholic Directory*, 1855, pp. 64–70; and Dundee had 600 in day and 1,600 in Sunday schools.

42 *Scottish Catholic Directory*, 1855, pp. 82–9.

43 Bernard Aspinwall, 'Catholic teachers for Scotland: the Liverpool connection', *Innes Review* 45 (1994), pp. 47–70.

44 *Scottish Catholic Directory*, 1870. Thanks mainly to nuns and lay school teachers.

45 *Scottish Catholic Directory*, 1838 and 1910.

46 After 1868 Eyre introduced Quarant'Ore to the west. Letter to the author from Rev. Mgr John McIntyre, former Rector Scots College, Rome and Professor at Blairs College, 28 April 2003. His nineteenth-century migrant Donegal family regarded Benediction as 'new fangled.' Edinburgh Cathedral has a monstrance presented by the exiled Bourbons. The Duchess of Angouleme zealously encouraged the later Bishop Gillis.

47 *Scottish Catholic Directory*, 1855, 1910 and 1914.

48 *Scottish Catholic Directory*, 1850, 1860, 1910, 1914.

49 Kilwinning, *Scottish Catholic Directory*, 1873–8 and 1905, p. 139. In that he reinforced the smears of *The Scottish Protestant*, 29 June 1851.

50 *Scottish Catholic Directory*, 1838–1914. The Jesuit-inspired Apostleship of Prayer grew from one in 1866 to 138 branches in 1914.

51 Annual Returns, Irvine, 1866–72; Rev P. J. O'Gorman to Archbishop C. Eyre, 11 January 1869; Annual Returns, Newton Stewart, 1856–1869, Glasgow Archdiocesan Archive (GAA).

52 APR, vol. 6, fols 238–42, Rev. E. Small to Propaganda, 31 December 1856.

53 *Scottish Catholic Directory*, 1838 and 1855. By 1853 Glasgow had 4,000 in Sunday and 3,300 in day schools. In Edinburgh, seven nuns and three novices ran a Sunday school for 1,000 girls.

54 SCAR, 16/ 96, 'I am sorry to say that the missioners taken as a whole are far from being of a first rate description. The Irish priests I find to be almost one and all of them unfit priests to take charge of missions,' Bishop J. Murdoch, 6 December 1846. Also SCAR, 16/49, 16/50, 16/57, Bishop J. Murdoch to Rev. A. Grant, 12 March 1845; and 'I do not like political priests', 3 November 1848, Bishop A. Scott, 2 January, 16 May, 3 December 1845, 7 November 1852.

55 E.g. SCAR 16/51, Bishop A. Scott, 3 December 1845; and SCAR, 17/ 31, Rev. A. Munro to Rev. A. Grant, 28 May 1867.

56 SCAR, 16/119, 120, 121, 151, 154, Bishop Smith to Rev. A. Grant, 12 April, 8 May, 13 June 1850; 2 February, 18 July 1852. The cost was estimated to be in the region of £400,000! Rosemary Hill, *God's Architect. Pugin and the Building of Romantic Britain* (2007), p. 420 shows their great enthusiasm for such schemes.

57 SCAR, 16/ 49 and 50, 'There is too much Irish nationality in Irish Catholicism' and 'Ireland will never be quiet while O'Connell lives', Bishop A. Scott to Rev. A. Grant, 16 May, 2 June 1845.

58 SCAR 17/31, Rev. Alexander Munro to Rev. Dr A. Grant, 28 May 1867.

59 SCAR 16/21, Bishop J. Murdoch to Rev. Dr A. Grant, 8 August 1864.

60 SCAR 17/26 and 17/78, Rev. Coll MacDonald, 20 May 1867 and Rev. H. Gall to Rev. A. Grant, 3 November 1868.

61 Cullen Papers, Dublin Archdiocesan Archives, Bishop J. Lynch to Archbishop Cullen,

2 January, 24 February, 24 September, 15 October, 12 December, 1868. His doctor father trained at Edinburgh University.

62 Aspinwall, 'British identity', p. 284.

63 Aspinwall, 'British identity' p. 283. Jesuits began the modern cult of Rev. John Ogilvie SJ about 1874, to stress the *Scottish* nature of *Roman* Catholicism.

64 GAA, DD 2/6, p. 2, MS Rev. Thomas Keane's copy of minutes and receipts and expenditures, St John's, Barrhead, 1858–71.

65 GAA, DD 2/6, MS Keane 1863, p. 27. Bute also gave the new Scottish bejewelled mitres and crosiers.

66 GAA, DD 2/6, MS Keane 1866, pp. 38–9, for a drunken gravedigger with convert family and a stonemason.

67 See, for example, APR, vol. 7 fol. 1,292, 3rd Marquess of Bute, letter 10 January 1877 criticising 'the obstinacy of Eyre and the vanity of Strain' on the eve of the restoration of the hierarchy. Also APR, vol. 9, fols 738–9, n.d., c.1892 re his proposals for an orphanage, choir and cathedral; and APR, vol. 9, fols 787–8, 19 April 1891. He also published *A Book of Prayers for the Use of Catholics Unable to Hear Mass on Sundays* (London, 1896) and tried to build a seminary at the University of St Andrews. APR, vol. 9, fols 693–4, Lord Ralph Kerr wanted to fund a Benedictine foundation in Jedburgh, n.d., and 15 June 1891.

68 M. Constable Maxwell, *Religious Intolerance: or a Statement of Fact with Reference to the Appointment of a Matron to the Creighton Royal Institution, Dumfries* (Edinburgh, 1859); *Tablet*, 23 April 1859; Rayomnd McCluskey (ed.), *The See of Ninian. A History of Whithorn and the Diocese of Galloway in Modern Times* (Glasgow, 1997), pp. 93–4, 106. The Christian Brothers arrived at New Abbey in 1916, *New Abbey and History of Thomas Bagnall and New Abbey Centre* at www.thomasbagnallcentre.org/history.htm

69 *Scottish Catholic Directory*, 1880.

70 *Scottish Catholic Directory*, 1881, 1888.

71 *Tablet*, 8 November 1879; 15 April 1882; 5 May 1917; SCAR, 17/170, letter, c.15 April 1871.

72 APR, vol. 7, fol. 1,213, Bute gave £125,000; the Duke of Norfolk, £50,000; and a sister of Lord Lovat, £25,000. Fort Augustus Founding, n.d., 1876.

73 A graduate of Glasgow and Cambridge, Monteith tried unsuccessfully to settle Rev. Ignatius Spencer and the Passionists, the Redemptorists and other male and female religious to his estate. Bernard Aspinwall, 'Robert Monteith and the origins of modern Catholic social thought', *Downside Review* 97 (1979), pp. 46–68.

74 *Tablet*, 28 February 1880. The Maxwells, Bishop Gillis and the Jesuits played a prominent role in developing congregational singing. See Thomas Muir, '*Ad majorem dei gloriam*' and Aspinwall, 'British identity', pp. 268–306. Evringham was Marmaduke Maxwell, Lord Herries' Yorkshire estate.

75 Quoted in E. D. Steele, *Irish Land and British Politics: Tenant Right and Nationality, 1865–1870* (Oxford, 1974), p. 43.

76 APR, vol. 9, fols 787–8 'the daily singing of vespers and compline drew people to the Church and was a known fact and feature of the two which among the most frequented resorts of tourists in Great Britain,' Bute, 19 April 1891. At Cumnock the choirmaster kept him informed. Unsatisfactory clergy were likely to be moved on. Bute was equally concerned about daily office and Vespers at Oban, APR, vol. 9, fol. 610, extract of Bute letter, 21 November 1890.

77 *Scottish Catholic Directory*, 1855, 1860, 1870, 1900, 1910 and 1914.

78 APR, vol. 9, fol. 212, Irvine parish returns, GAA and *Irvine Herald*, 2 August 1879.

79 Evidence varies on this point. See Kirby Papers, Irish College Archives, Rome, *Second Report of the Commissioners of Religious Instruction*, 1837, pp. 16, 92, 94; *7th Report*, April 1838, pp. 454–5; *8th Report*, 1838, pp. 218–19, 316–17; Rev. 'Raineron' (?) to Mgr W. Kirby, 20 Oct 1850; APR, vol. 6, fols 280–1 and fols 343–4,

Rev. C. Conroy, 28 May 1858; APR, vol. 6, fols 280–1, Rev. R. Innes, Edinburgh, 17 December 1859; APR, vol. 8, fol. 807, Bishop J. McLachlan, Report, 1879–85.

80 Bernard Aspinwall, 'A Glasgow pastoral plan, 1855–1860: social and spiritual renewal', *Innes Review* 35 (1984), pp. 33–6; and *Glasgow Post Office Directory*, 1886, p. 32; 1890, p. 28 and 1895, p. xxxi which list seven, six and four parish savings banks with hours of operation usually and significantly, on a Saturday evening between 5 p.m. and 8 p.m. and less often on Mondays 7p.m.–8p.m.

81 SCAR 16 /104, Bishop A. Smith, 18 October 1849; SCAR, 16/152, 'I fear we are not yet prepared for the good sisters however much their services may be required in Babylon', Bishop J. Murdoch to Rev. A. Grant, 16 December 1852; APR, vol. 6, fol. 208, Monteith and Maxwell of Terregles gave £1,150 to the Good Shepherd convent, Glasgow, 24 March 1856. 32 different orders arrived by 1920.

82 E.g. Monteith unsuccessfully offered a 19-acre site to the Jesuits and episcopal opposition blocked his Passionist scheme: SCAR, 16/135, Bishop J. Murdoch to Rev. A. Grant, 15 October 1851; SCAR 16/254, Bishop A. Smith, 2 February 1852.

83 Bernard Aspinwall, 'The transatlantic Catholic conservatism of Colm Brogan', *Innes Review* 53 (2002), pp. 201–25; and 'Varieties of modern Scottish Catholic conservatism', in Sheridan Gilley (ed.), *Victorian Churches and Churchmen. Essays Presented to Vincent Alan McClelland* (Woodbridge, 2005), pp. 110–38.

84 George Hay, *Devout Christian Instructed in the Faith of Christ* (Glasgow, 1831); and *Works* (5 vols edited by Bishop J. Strain, Edinburgh, 1872). *The Garden of the Soul* was reprinted in Edinburgh, 1874 and Glasgow, 1875.

85 Monteith's popular 'Arise from the dreams of time' was still in the 1966 *St Andrew's Hymnal*.

86 APR, vol. 6, fols 753–5, Rev. E. Small, 31 December 1864.

87 E.g. APR, vol. 7, fols 721–2, Rev. Michael Fox, Mossend, 26 December 1891.

88 J. Magnier, 'After a mission', *Irish Ecclesiastical Record* 16 (1895), pp. 894–904.

89 GAA, DD 2/6, MS Keane, pp. 5–8. Also APR, vol. 7, fols 933–4, Rev. M. Brady, Edinburgh, 18 August 1874 on his St Patrick's Institution providing alternative 'to wandering idly through the streets'.

90 GAA, DD 2/6, MS Keane, pp. 10 and 17. Gas and running water came even later.

91 John Wolffe, *The Protestant Crusade in Great Britain, 1829–1860* (Oxford, 1991).

92 GAA, DD 2/6, MS Keane, 1868, p. 41, Robert Monteith declined to underwrite it.

93 GAA, DD 2/6, MS Keane, June 1868 on Rev. Dr Scully.

94 GAA, DD 2/6, MS Keane, p. 39, 1866, Rev. Kavanagh, Vincentian and Rev. Robert Whitty, SJ.

95 GAA, DD 2/6, MS Keane, p. 58, 1869, and see my 'Scots and Irish clergy ministering to immigrants, 1830–1878', *Innes Review* 47 (1996), pp. 45–68; and my 'Anyone for Glasgow? The strange nomination of Rt Rev. Charles Eyre in 1868', *Recusant History* 23 (1997), pp. 589–601.

96 *Scottish Catholic Directory*, 1914. A similar case can be made for the other dioceses.

97 Aspinwall, 'British identity', pp. 268–306.

98 Aspinwall, 'British identity', p. 293.

99 E.g. interspersed at APR, vol. 8, fols 447–53, John C. Maxwell-Scott, 31 July 1883, Joseph Maxwell-Scott, 3 August 1883; and fols 456–57, R. S. Kerr, Marquess of Lothian to Propaganda, 27 August 1883, wanting to retain the excellent Jesuits against the archbishop.

100 Belaney initially brought them to Glasgow, Hope-Scott and aristocratic converts brought them to Oban and the Borders. See Francis Edwards, *The Jesuits in England* (Tunbridge Wells, 1985), pp. 278–83.

101 Aspinwall, 'British identity', especially p. 276.

102 Rev. Archibald Campbell SJ, who founded the Glasgow Caledonian Society to safeguard Gael faith and temperance and to protect women, travelled extensively

in that campaign: Aspinwall, 'British identity', p. 293. His zeal was sharpened by the clearances of Col MacDonald, Tory MP,. brother of the Archbishop of Edinburgh.

103 Heimann, *Catholic Devotion*, p. 172. Since this chapter was written, the recent researches of Alasdair Roberts 'William McIntosh in the west Highlands: changing the practice of religion', *Innes Review* 54 (2003), pp. 111–41, Michael Turnbull's forthcoming history of the archdiocese of Edinburgh, Gracewing Press, and my recent book on St Mary's, Saltcoats may have added to our knowledge but they do not significantly affect my interpretation here.

104 E.g. Patrick Macgill, *Children of the Dead End* (London, 1914), p. 289.

4 Irish Migrants in the Scottish Episcopal Church in the Nineteenth Century

1 Marion Lochhhead, *Episcopal Scotland in the Nineteenth Century* (London, 1966), p. 223.

2 Irene Maver, 'The Scottish Episcopal Church: a new history by Gavin White', reviewed in *Scottish Historical Review* 207 (April, 2000), pp. 124–5.

3 Callum G. Brown, *Religion and Society in Scotland since 1707* (Edinburgh, 1997), p. 36.

4 *Scottish Guardian*, February 1872.

5 Rowan Strong, *Episcopalianism in Nineteenth-Century Scotland* (Oxford, 2002), p. 27.

6 Historians in the late nineteenth and first half of the twentieth century included James S. Gordon, William Perry, George Grub, Marion Lochhead, Gordon Donaldson and Frederick Goldie. It has only been more recent historians such as Gavin White and particularly Rowan Strong who have noted the presence of the Irish in any significant number.

7 Alan Acheson, *A History of the Church of Ireland 1691–1996* (Dublin, 1997), pp. 139, 184.

8 Irene Maver, 'The Scottish Episcopal Church', p. 125.

9 Elaine McFarland, *Protestants First: Orangeism in Nineteenth-Century Scotland* (Edinburgh, 1990), p. 133.

10 Brown, *Religion and Society*, p. 15.

11 The Scottish Episcopal United Diocese of Glasgow and Galloway was reconstituted in 1837 and covers the counties of Dunbartonshire, Lanarkshire, Renfrewshire, Ayrshire, Wigtownshire, Kirkcudbrightshire and Dumfriesshire.

12 T. M. Devine in T. M. Devine (ed.), *Irish Immigrants and Scottish Society in the Nineteenth and Twentieth Centuries* (Edinburgh, 1990), p. vi.

13 James E. Handley, *The Irish in Scotland* (Glasgow, 1964).

14 William Sloan, 'Religious affiliation and the immigration experience', in Devine (ed.), *Irish Immigrants*, p. 68.

15 D. H. Akenson, *Small Differences: Irish Catholics and Irish Protestants 1815–1922* (Dublin, 1988), p. 3.

16 Tom Gallagher, 'The Catholic Irish in Scotland', in Devine (ed.), *Irish Immigrants*, p. 20.

17 Graham Walker, 'The Protestant Irish in Scotland', in Devine (ed.), *Irish Immigrants*, p. 49.

18 McFarland, *Protestants First*, p. 104.

19 Handley, *Irish in Scotland*, pp. 42–51.

20 Walker, 'The Protestant Irish', p. 49.

21 Walker, 'The Protestant Irish', p. 52.

22 Walker, 'The Protestant Irish', p. 49.

23 Acheson, *The Church of Ireland*, p. 19. These figures relate to the whole of Ireland. In Ulster, Presbyterians outnumbered Anglicans.

24 James D. Reid, *History of the Presbyterian Church in Ireland*, 3 vols (London, 1853), vol. 3, p. 579.

25 Cecil J. Houston and William Smith, *Irish Emigration and Canadian Settlement* (Toronto, 1990), p. 8.

26 Donald M. Macraild, *Irish Migrants in Modern Britain 1750–192* (Basingstoke, 1999), p. 103.

27 David Hempton and Myrtle Hill, *Evangelical Protestantism in Ulster Society 1740–1890* (London, 1992), p. 18.

28 Desmond Bowen, *The Protestant Crusade in Ireland* (Montreal, 1978), p. 32.

29 Bowen, *Protestant Crusade*, p. 32.

30 Dundee City Archives CP/DE/6/1, *General Register of Inmates of Dundee Poor House, 1861*.

31 Handley, *Irish in Scotland*, p. 356.

32 Joseph M. Bradley, *Ethnic and Religious Identity in Modern Scotland* (Aldershot, 1995), p. 83.

33 Bowen, *Protestant Crusade*, p. 31.

34 A. C. Anderson, *The Story of the Presbyterian Church in Ireland* (Belfast, 1965), p. 77.

35 Finlay Holmes, *Our Irish Presbyterian Heritage* (Belfast, 1985), p. 90.

36 David Bryce, *Our Blood is on their Hands: the Girvan Riots, 1831* (Hamilton, 2001), p. 5.

37 John D. Brewer and Gareth I. Higgins, *Anti-Catholicism in Northern Ireland 1600–1998* (Basingstoke, 1998), p. 66.

38 Diocese of Glasgow and Galloway Archives (DGGA), TD 1382/173/11, R. J. S. Speir to Bishop Wilson, Christmas 1878.

39 DGGA, TD 1382/173/10, Rev. W. E. Bradshaw to Bishop Wilson, 20 December 1878.

40 *Scottish Guardian*, 31 March 1882.

41 Desmond Bowen, *The History and Shaping of Irish Protestantism* (New York, 1995), p. 252.

42 DGGA, TD 1382/803, Edith Hill, mss. 'St John's Mission, Irvine' (1889–1902).

43 *Minutes of the Grand Orange Lodge of Scotland*, June 1881, p. 10. A note appended to the resolution added that features of ritualistic furniture and ornaments of churches included: 'The Twelve Apostles in the chancel, the Virgin Mary and Gabriel, two lighted candles, the figure of our saviour on the cross, a chancel screen with large cross on top of it, and at Easter and other occasions, processions with crossbearers'.

44 John P. Lawson, *The History of the Scottish Episcopal Church* (Edinburgh, 1843), pp. 63–9.

45 *Scottish Guardian*, 10 October, 1901.

46 *Scottish Chronicle*, 15 February, 1907.

47 James Cleland, *Enumeration of the Inhabitants of the City of Glasgow and County of Lanark, 1831* (Glasgow, 1831), p. 30.

48 *Minutes of the Vestry of St Andrew's Church*, 31 August 1815.

49 Barbara Thatcher, 'The Episcopal Church in Helensburgh in the mid-nineteenth century', in John Butt and J. T. Ward (eds), *Scottish Themes* (Edinburgh, 1976), pp. 107, 111.

50 *Scottish Ecclesiastical Journal*, 20 January 1859.

51 William Perry, *Anthony Mitchell: Bishop of Aberdeen and Orkney* (London, 1920), p. 91. The church became a 'byword in the neighbourhood' by the lack of any baptismal discipline on the part of Dr Gordon. He would baptise any child 'for half a crown' and so around 1,000 were baptised every year.

52 *Scottish Chronicle*, 5 November 1915.

53 Walker, 'The Protestant Irish', p. 49.

54 Parliamentary Papers, *Appendix to the Second Report of the Commissioners of Religious Instruction, Scotland, 1836–1839*, pp. 314–15.
55 David Aitchison, *A Vindication of the Ambassadors of Christ – Addressed to the Protestant Episcopalians Scattered throughout the Eastern Districts of Glasgow* (Glasgow, 1839), p. 17.
56 David Aitchison, *A Pastoral Letter Addressed to his Flock* (Glasgow, 1837), p. 8.
57 Sheena Macleod, *St Mary's Episcopal Church, Glasgow 1871–1908* (Glasgow, 1994), p. 11.
58 DGGA, TD 1382/147/2, W. M. Biggar to Rev. W. E. Bradshaw, 28 October 1878.
59 DGGA, TD 1382/173/10, Rev. W. E. Bradshaw to Bishop Wilson, 20 December 1878.
60 DGGA, TD 1382/173/11, R. T. N. Speir to Bishop Wilson, Christmas 1878.
61 DGGA, TD 1382/147/11, Rev. Charles H. Brooke to Bishop Wilson, 18 August 1879.
62 DGGA, TD 1382/147/12, Rev. Charles H. Brooke to Bishop Wilson, 18 August 1879.
63 *Scottish Chronicle*, 21 January 1910.
64 *St Rollox and Springburn Express*, 22 December 1892.
65 Handley, *The Irish in Scotland*, p. 47, quoting McMaster's evidence to the *Parliamentary Report on the Irish Poor in Great Britain, 1835.*
66 Peter McMaster, 'The parish of Girvan', *New Statistical Account of Scotland* (Edinburgh, 1845), p. 397.
67 Bryce, *The Girvan Riots*, p. 5.
68 Martin J. Mitchell, *The Irish in the West of Scotland 1797–1848: Trade Unions, Strikes and Political Movements* (Edinburgh, 1998), p. 147.
69 McMaster, *New Statistical Account*, p. 404.
70 DGGA, TD 1382/146, petition to Bishop Russell to form an Episcopal Church in Girvan, 2 March 1846.
71 *Church News: Scotland*, September 1870.
72 John Strawhorn and William Boyd (eds), *The Third Statistical Account of Scotland: Ayrshire* (Edinburgh, 1951), p. 818.
73 *Stephen's Ecclesiastical Journal*, August 1833, quoting Wade's sermon at the opening of Trinity Chapel, 19 May 1833.
74 William Wade, *Ten Sermons Preached at Trinity Episcopal Church* (Paisley, 1830), p. 154.
75 Wade, *Ten Sermons*, p. 137.
76 Mary McCarthy, *A Social Geography of Paisley* (Paisley, 1969), p. 109.
77 DGGA, TD 1382/154/9, Rev. Thomas Fullarton to Bishop Wilson, 7 May 1885.
78 *Report of the Protestant and Orange Soiree held in Paisley 5 November 1856* (Paisley, 1856), p. 9.
79 *North British Daily Mail*, 14 July 1868.
80 *Paisley Papers, 1871*, 'Obituary of the Rev. James Stewart'.
81 *Church News: Scotland*, March 1871.
82 *Paisley and Renfrewshire Gazette*, 8 November 1873.
83 *Minute Book of 'King William' Loyal Orange Lodge No. 102*, Paisley, 26 June 1882.
84 D. D. A. Lockhart, *Holy Trinity Church, Paisley: Centenary of the Church Building* (Paisley, 1933), p. 20.
85 DGGA, TD 1382/154/9, Rev. Thomas Fullerton to Bishop Wilson, 7 May 1885.
86 This group affiliated with an English schismatic group known as the Reformed Episcopal Church, founded in 1877, which later amalgamated with the Free Church of England.
87 *Scottish Chronicle*, 30 January 1914.
88 Sean Damer, *Glasgow: Going for a Song* (London, 1990), p. 57.
89 *Scottish Chronicle*, 26 February 1909.

90 Brown, *Religion and Society*, pp. 32–3.
91 *Scottish Churchman*, September 1926.
92 *Scottish Churchman*, September 1926.
93 *Scottish Chronicle*, 10 October 1910.
94 *Scottish Chronicle*, 26 April 1912.
95 *Scottish Chronicle*, 12 March 1909.
96 Walter J. Trower (Bishop of Glasgow and Galloway), *Letter to the Rev. A. J. D. D'Orsey, Incumbent of St John's Episcopal Church, Glasgow on Certain Recent Changes in the Ritual of his Church* (Glasgow, 1851), p. 4.
97 Strong, *Episcopalianism*, p. 236.
98 Strong, *Episcopalianism*, p. 236.
99 *Scottish Chronicle*, 4 April 1912.
100 Steve Bruce et al., *Sectarianism in Scotland* (Edinburgh, 2004), pp. 41–2.
101 DGGA, TD 1382/285, Rev. Frank Bins to Bishop John How, 22 January 1940.
102 These would have included families like the Sykes family of Springburn. Seth Sykes, baptised at St James-the-Less Church in 1892 left the Episcopal Church after an 'evangelical conversion' and became superintendent of the railway mission in Springburn and a national figure of the working-class 'mission hall' movement.
103 *Scottish Chronicle*, 26 February 1909.

5 Sectarianism, Segregation and Politics on Clydeside in the Later Nineteenth Century

1 James Purdie, 'Reminiscences of the municipal and political life of Old Govan', *Old Govan Club Transactions* 4 (1) (1917–18), p. 16 (Mitchell Library, Glasgow).
2 Steven Fielding, *Class and Ethnicity: Irish Catholics in England 1880–1939* (Buckingham, 1993) p. 11.
3 D. Fitzpatrick, '"A curious middle place": the Irish in Britain 1871–1921', in R. Swift and S. Gilley (eds), *The Irish in Britain 1815–1939* (London, 1989) pp. 11–59.
4 A. C. Hepburn, *A Past Apart: Studies in the History of Catholic Belfast 1850–1950* (Belfast, Ulster Historical Foundation, 1996) pp. 50–4; Catherine Hirst, *Religion, Politics and Violence in Nineteenth-Century Belfast: the Pond and Sandy Row* (Dublin, 2002).
5 Fitzpatrick, 'A curious middle place'.
6 J. Foster, M. Houston, and C. Madigan, 'Distinguishing Catholics and Protestants among Irish immigrants to Clydeside: a new approach to immigration and ethnicity in Victorian Britain', *Irish Studies Review* 10 (2) (2002), pp. 171–92.
7 Fitzpatrick, 'A curious middle place', gives this estimate based on the Barlinnie prison register. Our own sample replicated this.
8 R. J. Morris, 'Inequality, social structure and the market in Belfast and Glasgow 1820–1914', in S. Connolly, R. Houston and R. Morris (eds), *Conflict, Identity and Economic Development* (London, 1995) pp. 189–203 provides a very similar argument. We are grateful to Professor Morris for comments on an earlier version of this paper.
9 R. D. Lobban, 'The Irish community in Greenock in the nineteenth century', *Irish Geography* 6 (1971), pp. 270–81.
10 A. Slaven,'Shipbuilding in 19th-century Scotland', in Simon Vile (ed.), *Shipbuilding in the United Kingdom in the Nineteenth Century* (*Research in Maritime History* 4 (St John's Newfoundland, 1993), pp. 153–76.
11 Robert Steele, who ran the biggest shipbuilding firm in Greenock, told the Royal Commission on Labour in 1867 that the proportion of labourers in iron shipbuilding on the Clyde was 'about half' but in wood 'very trifling indeed': Question 17363, *Ninth Report RC Trade Unions, Parliamentary Papers 1867–68* (3980 – v) 39.
12 Patrick Donnelly, *Govan on the Clyde* (Glasgow City Libraries, 1994)

13 Robert Steele of Greenock claimed in 1867 that the Clyde rate was 'fully 30 per cent below the Thames': Question 17426, *Ninth Report RC Trade Unions*.

14 Angela Tuckett, *The Blacksmiths' History* (London, 1974) p. 60.

15 J. E. Mortimer, *History of the Boilermakers' Society, 1836–1906*, vol. 1 (London, 1973) p. 65.

16 Tuckett, *Blacksmiths' History*, p. 62.

17 Cited by S. Damer, 'Property relations in Victorian Glasgow', *Discussion Papers in Social Research* 15, Glasgow University (1976).

18 It appears that the main impetus for the formation of the burgh came from pre-existing property owners and tradesmen who had been seeking to defend property rights, commons and rights of way against the shipyard developments over the previous two decades: James Houston JP, 'Civic life in old Govan', *Old Govan Club Transactions* 1 (1914–15), p. 21.

19 T. C. Brotchie, *A History of Govan* (Glasgow, 1905).

20 Andrew McMahon, *A History of Kinning Park and District, Glasgow* (Queens Nursing Institute of Scotland, 2003) pp. 179–88 (quays), pp. 195–210 (firms) and pp. 167–8 (churches).

21 P. J. Dollan, *Jubilee History of the Kinning Park Cooperative Society Limited* (Glasgow, 1913).

22 *1881 Census of Scotland*, vol. 2, pp. 715 and 770.

23 *1881 Census of Scotland*, vol. 2, pp. 365–7 (c. 3657 1883).

24 The sample is drawn from streets identified on the *Post Office Directory* map of 1890 and includes the four wards of Govan together with a section of Kinning Park, which is socially integrated with Govan though outside the burgh boundary. This area of Kinning Park is bounded to the south by the Glasgow and Paisley Joint Railway and to the east by the Harbour branch of the Caledonian Railway.

25 Confidence intervals (95 per cent) for this difference are 0.03 to 0.26. Thus we cannot exclude the possibility that the true difference is as low as 0.03.

26 S. Pollard and P. Robertson, *The British Shipbuilding Industry 1870–1914* (Boston, MA 1979), p. 157.

27 Hepburn, *A Past Apart*, pp. 50–4.

28 Hirst, *Religion, Politics and Violence*, pp. 156–80; C. Kinealy and G. MacAtasney, *The Hidden Famine: Hunger, Poverty and Sectarianism in Belfast* (London, 2000) pp. 189–92.

29 If Ward 3 (Ibrox) is dropped, Protestants are under-represented in Ward 1, over-represented in Wards 3 and 4 and roughly as expected in Kinning Park.

30 Paul Doherty and Michael Poole, *Ethnic Residential Segregation in Belfast* (Belfast, 1995) pp. 20–2.

31 Hepburn, *A Past Apart*, pp. 50–54.

32 F. Boal, C. Murray and M. Poole, 'Belfast; the urban encapsulation of a national conflict', in S. Clarke and J. Obler (eds), *Urban Ethnic Conflict* (Chapel Hill, NC, 1976) p. 77–131.

33 R. D. Lobban, 'The Irish community in Greenock in the nineteenth century', *Irish Geography* 6 (1972), pp. 270–81.

34 Hepburn, 'Irish Catholics in Belfast and Glasgow in the early twentieth century' in *A Past Apart*, pp. 203–17.

35 Foster, Houston and Madigan, 'Distinguishing Catholics and Protestants', pp. 182–4.

36 Clydeside Shipbuilders Association (CSA) Minute Books (Mitchell Library Archive, Glasgow TD 241).

37 Robert Steele in evidence, Questions 17254–7 and 17267, *Ninth Report RC Trade Unions*.

38 Shipbuilders on the Clyde (CSA) Minutes, 3 and 6 July 1866, 27 June 1871 and 28 July 1871 (TD 241/1/1: Strathclyde Regional Archives).

39 *Glasgow Sentinel*, 1 September 1866; CSA Minutes, 11 March 1868, 7 June 1871 and 5 July 1872.
40 Glasgow Shipwrights Society Minute Book 1872–76: Minutes of Strike Committee 12–19 April 1877 (TD 389/59: Strathclyde Regional Archives).
41 Glasgow Shipwrights Society Minute Book, 15 September 1875.
42 *Glasgow Sentinel*, 26 October 1876.
43 *Glasgow Sentinel*, 16 September 1865 reports that after a four-week strike by shipwrights and blacksmiths in Dumbarton 'most had found work elsewhere' and there were only 133 on the strike roll; for 2 September 1871 the *Sentinel* reports a meeting of striking Govan shipwrights discussing the removal of members to Leith. The Clyde Shipbuilders discussed the same practice from their own perspective at their meeting of 18 May 1866.
44 Evidence by J. C. Proudfoot representing Glasgow trades, Question 2886, *SC on Masters and Operatives Parliamentary Papers 1856*, 343 (13) most of the 700 workers locked out in January 1855 had moved away; Robert Steele refers to the same episode in answer to question Question 17284, *Ninth Report RC Trade Unions*.
45 *Glasgow Sentinel*, 19 May and 2 June 1866; CSA Minutes, 2 April and 30 April, 18 May and 18 June 1866.
46 Glasgow Shipwrights Society Minute Book, 3 March 1875: printing and distribution of bills 'across country'; vigilant reports 12 April 1877; *Glasgow Sentinel*, 19 June 1875, report from shipwrights to Glasgow Trades Council on Vigilance Committee intercepting three men outside Napiers yard who were discovered to be detective officers; *Glasgow Sentinel*, 10 July 1877 reports plain clothes police now stationed all down Govan Road.
47 *Glasgow Sentinel*, 17 July 1875 and 18 August 1875.
48 John Paterson Smith answering Questions 17470 and 17471, *Ninth Report RC Trade Unions*.
49 *Glasgow Sentinel*, 7 April 1866.
50 CSA Minutes, 18 May 1866 and *Glasgow Sentinel*, 16 June 1866.
51 *Glasgow Sentinel*, 7 April 1866.
52 *Glasgow Sentinel*, 21 October 1876 reporting issue being raised in Glasgow Trades Council; 4 November issue reports a meeting by shipwrights in Govan to raise collections.
53 The only instance is the action by the stevedore employers in 1888 against the Harbour Mineral Labourers. The response by Glasgow Trades Council is to 'condemn in the most unqualified terms the malicious action of the said stevedores in endeavouring to import into the present struggle a spirit of sectarianism': Minutes of Glasgow Trades Council, 19 September 1888, Glasgow Mitchell Library.
54 Minutes of Glasgow Trades Council, 30 April and 13 May 1858.
55 *Glasgow Sentinel*, 3 and 10 March 1866; *Glasgow Sentinel*,13 January 1866 (Midlothian farm servants), 3 February (Tranent), 10 February (Kennoway and Selkirk) and 24 February (Dalkeith) are some of the early entries.
56 *Glasgow Sentinel*, 29 January 1870 (railway carters), 17 May (horse keepers), 16 September (Caledonian Railway).
57 *Glasgow Sentinel*, 12 January 1870, 17 May 1870, 16 September 1870.
58 CSA Minutes, 23 February 1880, 31 January 1882, 29 May 1882, 30 August 1882, 11 September 1882, 21 November and 1 December 1883.
59 J. Foster, 'William Pearce: annual lecture at Govan Old', *Annual Report Society of Friends of Govan Old* (December 1997), pp. 19–32 provides considerably more detail.
60 *Govan Press*, 16 July 1885.
61 *Govan Press*, 28 November 1885.
62 *Govan Press*, 5 December 1885.
63 *Govan Press*, 26 June 1886, 3 and 10 July 1886.

64 *Glasgow Herald*, 13 and 16 July 1874.
65 *Glasgow Herald*, 14 August 1875, p. 4. The issue of 16 August 1875 reports that Govan was quiet over the weekend.
66 *Forward*, 8 November 1913.

6 Shaping the Scottish Past: Irish migrants and local politics in the Monklands in the second half of the nineteenth century

1 P. McGill, *Children of the Dead End* (London, 1914), p. 268.
2 *Airdrie and Coatbridge Advertiser*, 5 January 1907.
3 T. M. Devine, *The Scottish Nation* (London, 2000), p. 217.
4 *Glasgow Free Press*, 21 August 1858.
5 In 1861, the Irish-born represented 18.45 per cent of the Airdrie population and 14 per cent in 1871; in 1851 an estimate made for Coatbridge showed a total of 21.44 per cent; in 1869 the Catholic population represented 35 per cent of the total Coatbridge population; in 1901 the Irish-born amounted to 15 per cent of the burgh population (see various census reports).
6 Coatbridge Town Council was established in 1885, when the town was elevated to burgh status.
7 The town and parish councils were elected by the parliamentary electors residing within the area, together with women and peers who would be disqualified but for their rank or sex. The school boards were elected by all persons of lawful age entered in the valuation roll as an owner or occupant of lands of £4 annual value or upwards.
8 W. M. Walker, 'Irish immigrants in Scotland: their priests, politics and parochial life', *The Historical Journal* 15 (4) (1972), pp. 649–67.
9 *Airdrie and Coatbridge Advertiser*, 3 November 1860: during a public meeting of ratepayers and electors in Airdrie concerning the forthcoming municipal elections, John Devlin, a Catholic Irishman complained of the high rates in Airdrie (he established a comparison between these and the notoriously high rates of the burgh of Hamilton).
10 With the passing of the Education (Scotland) Act in 1872, which transferred burgh and parish schools to local elected school boards under the supervision of the Scotch Education Department, the administration of the schooling system was shifted to an elected secular authority supported by local rates. As ratepayers, Catholics supported the public rate-aided schooling system, although they refused to send their children to the public schools and maintained separate Catholic schools.
11 *Airdrie and Coatbridge Advertiser*, 14 April 1900.
12 *Glasgow Observer*, 7 April 1888.
13 *Airdrie and Coatbridge Advertiser*, 5 April 1902: two prominent Irish Catholic local gentlemen, ex-Bailie McKillop and Daniel Carlin (parish councillor) acted as croupiers for the Airdrie and district Licensed Trade Defence Association.
14 The list is thus composed: John Benson, Daniel Carlin, John Lavell, James McAuley, Alexander McKillop, Arthur Malone, George Mulvey, John Mulvey, Charles O'Neill.
15 Even though the magistrate of the licensing court was not to be engaged in the spirit trade.
16 *Airdrie and Coatbridge Advertiser*, 7 April 1894.
17 Glasgow City Archives (GCA), COI 5/1/8/7: *Minute Book of Old Monkland School Board (1893–95)*, p. 198.
18 *Airdrie and Coatbridge Advertiser*, 12 September 1900.
19 See for example, a report on the meeting of first ward electors in 1905, where Patrick Agnew challenged Councillor Louden, the retiring member seeking re-election, on his position on the Unemployment Bill. *Airdrie and Coatbridge Advertiser*, 21 October 1905.

20 *The Coatbridge Express*, 19 October 1901: at an annual meeting of the third ward electors of Coatbridge, Charles O'Neill expressed his satisfaction at the buying of the water works, and advocated pursuit of the purchase of gas works.

21 Here follows a list of Roman Catholic Irishmen who served on parochial boards, parish councils, school boards and town councils: Henry Bannen (member of Old Monkland Parish Council, bailie for Coatbridge from 1885 to 1898); Daniel Carlin (member of New Monkland Parochial Board from the mid-1850s up to his death in 1907, court house commissioner); James Flannigan (native of County Cavan, member of Old Monkland Parish Council from 1900); John Lavell (Coatbridge town councillor then elected bailie in 1885); Arthur Malone (member of Old Monkland Parochial Board in 1884, member of Old Monkland School Board from 1890); Alexander McKillop (member of New Monkland Parochial Board, first Roman Catholic councillor in Airdrie, 1887–98; JP in 1898); Hugh O'Hear (member of Old Monkland Parochial Board in the late 1860s, Coatbridge town councillor from 1885 and school board member from 1891); John Mulvey, spirit merchant (member of New Monkland Parochial Board 1878–87); George Mulvey (member of Airdrie School Board in 1905).

22 *Airdrie and Coatbridge Advertiser*, 10 September 1881.

23 *Glasgow Examiner*, 22 August 1903 and 23 December 1905.

24 *Airdrie and Coatbridge Advertiser*, 5 November 1898.

25 *Glasgow Examiner*, 3 January 1903.

26 *Airdrie and Coatbridge Advertiser*, 4 October 1862.

27 *Airdrie and Coatbridge Advertiser*, 29 April 1882.

28 *Airdrie and Coatbridge Advertiser*, 4 May 1889.

29 *Airdrie and Coatbridge Advertiser*, 26 October 1872.

30 In 1901, there were 5,607 Irish-born in Coatbridge (see *Eleventh Decennial Census of the Population of Scotland, taken 31st March 1901 with Report*, vol. 2, p. 382) which is 15 per cent of the population; and in 1896 the *Glasgow Examiner* claimed that Coatbridge had 11,000 Catholics (2 May); *Glasgow Examiner*, 3 January 1903.

31 *Airdrie and Coatbridge Advertiser*, 21 November 1868.

32 J. McCaffrey, 'The Irish vote in Glasgow in the later nineteenth century: a preliminary survey', *Innes Review* 21 (1970), pp. 30–6.

33 North Lanarkshire Archives (NLA), UA 1/13/05: 'List of persons entitled to vote in the parliamentary and municipal elections in Airdrie, year 1894–95'.

34 *Airdrie and Coatbridge Advertiser*, 4 April 1900.

35 Glasgow Archdiocese Archives (GAA), GC 29/95: letter from Dr O'Neill, Coatbridge, 15 December 1897. See also *Glasgow Observer*, 12 November 1892, where John Lavell states to have been elected as town councillor for the fourth time with the votes of both Catholics and 300 Protestants.

36 *Glasgow Observer*, 7 January 1888.

37 *Glasgow Observer*, 13 April 1889.

38 See, for example, the 1885 meeting held in St Margaret's schoolroom, Airdrie, chaired by Fr James McIntosh on the subject of school board elections: *Airdrie and Coatbridge Advertiser*, 14 March 1885.

39 *Airdrie and Coatbridge Advertiser*, 29 October 1859.

40 *Airdrie and Coatbridge Advertiser*, 29 October 1859.

41 *Airdrie and Coatbridge Advertiser*, 1 October 1892: at the Coatbridge Voters Registration Court, Charles O'Neill, acting on the behalf of Irish nationalists, succeeded in 12 of the 13 claims he defended.

42 *Glasgow Observer*, 18 April 1891. See also GAA, GC 29/95: during the 1897 Coatbridge municipal election, out of 138 Roman Catholic fourth ward electors living in Whifflet parish, only two failed to record their votes.

43 In comparison, for Irish Protestant local political participation and campaigning, little evidence is available: nevertheless, a press report in 1890 stated that at a meeting

of the Coatbridge District Loyal Orange Lodge (No. 22), a resolution was adopted – 'a committee be appointed to draw up a scheme or organisation to give expression to our views in any contest, whether Municipal or Parliamentary': see *Airdrie and Coatbridge Advertiser*, 15 November 1890. In 1895, the same lodge decided to run two candidates in the Old Monkland parish elections, one of whom, John Stewart Bell, was a 25-year-old Irish-born coal miner: *Coatbridge Express*, 6 February 1895.

44 *Airdrie and Coatbridge Advertiser*, 7 April 1900. The four Roman Catholic candidates finished in third, fifth, seventh and ninth positions (respectively, Father Hughes with 4,672 votes; Hugh O'Hear with 4,334 votes; Charles O'Neill with 4,245 votes and Father Kirke with 4,080 votes).

45 Walker, 'Irish immigrants', p. 657.

46 J. E. Handley, *The Irish in Scotland* (Glasgow, 1964), pp. 298–320.

47 *Glasgow Observer*, 3 March 1888.

48 *Airdrie and Coatbridge Advertiser*, 15 February 1873.

49 *Airdrie and Coatbridge Advertiser*, 15 March 1873: at the meeting of ratepayers, Father McIntosh declined to be nominated, by stating that: 'It had been said that the ministers should not go upon the Board: and he made up his mind to decline doing so (hear, and some slight hisses).'

50 See *Catholic Directory*, 1848, p. 116: Michael O'Keeffe, born in County Limerick in 1818, ordained in 1845, was appointed to the Coatbridge Mission in 1848. He remained there until his death in 1893.

51 GCA, COI 5/1/8/1: *Minute Book of Old Monkland School Board (1873–79)*, pp. 4–5: of the ten members to be returned, only one Catholic layman was elected (James McAuley, in third position with 2,661 votes); Father O'Keeffe (defeated) came in 19th position with only nine votes.

52 GCA, COI 5/1/8/2: *Minute Book of Old Monkland School Board (1880–84)*, p. 108 (31 October 1881).

53 For Old Monkland School Board: Father Thomas O'Reilly (a native of County Meath, appointed to Coatbridge in 1879) was elected in 1882; Father Daniel Thomas Browne (assistant priest in Coatbridge from 1884) sat on the board from 1885 to 1891; and Father John Hughes was elected (appointed to Langloan in 1892) in 1900. On the New Monkland School Board, Father John Nyhan (appointed to Longriggend in 1890) sat as representative of Catholic ratepayers from 1900 to 1903, when he was replaced by Father Muller.

54 *Glasgow Observer*, 18 April 1891.

55 Walker, 'Irish immigrants in Scotland', p. 659: 'Nevertheless, Catholic Social Organisation was inimical to free expression and suspicious of spontaneity.' He compares the role of priests with that of Communist Party secretaries in the USSR, vis-a-vis parochial organisation.

56 See for example a 'Meeting of Roman Catholics' described in the *Airdrie and Coatbridge Advertiser* 30 October 1869, chaired by Father MacIntosh in the St Margaret Schoolroom in Airdrie. For the coming municipal elections, the priest recommended 'Mr Deedes [a Conservative] as a fit and proper person to represent them', but his motion 'fell to the ground'.

57 *Coatbridge Express*, 15 August 1900.

58 *Coatbridge Express*, 15 August 1900.

59 GAA, GC 29/95, Charles O'Neill to Archbishop Eyre, 12 December 1897.

60 GAA, GC 29/95, Charles O'Neill to Archbishop Eyre, 12 December 1897.

61 GAA, GC 29/95, Charles O'Neill to Archbishop Eyre, 12 December 1897.

62 GAA, GC 29/14, Canon McCay to Archbishop Eyre, 6 December 1897.

63 GAA, GC 29/95, Charles O'Neill to Archbishop Eyre, 12 December 1897.

64 GAA, GC 29/95, Charles O'Neill to Archbishop Eyre, 12 December 1897.

65 GAA, GC 29/95, Charles O'Neill to Archbishop Eyre, 12 December 1897.

66 GAA, GC/ 26/14/24, John McCay to Archbishop Eyre, March 1894.
67 A few remarks may be made concerning the attitude of Irish Protestant ministers in the Monklands. For example, the Irish minister of the Coatbridge Episcopal Church appointed in 1895, Rev. William Winter, often expressed his views on municipal affairs. He was an active Orangeman too, and manifested his opinions on local boards. In 1900, he headed a delegation sent to the Old Monkland School Board, objecting to a Roman Catholic being nominated in place of a dead Catholic member. The deputation brought to the board a memorial signed by 1,150 electors, but it failed in its request, as Arthur Malone, a familiar figure of Irish Catholic politics was elected in place of the late Father Hughes. On this state of affairs, the infamous Rev. Jacob Primmer, in a conventicle held in Coatbridge in 1901, addressing Irish Protestants, stated that it was scandalous that 'in Coatbridge there should be four Papists looking after the education of their Protestant children', and despised what he described as the Catholic way of canvassing (and obtaining votes from Protestants): 'Catholics went, say to a grocer, and told him that if he did not vote for the Catholic candidate the Catholics wouldn't buy his sugar': *Airdrie and Coatbridge Advertiser*, 10 July 1901.
68 J. McCaffrey, 'Politics and the Catholic community since 1878', *Innes Review* 29 (1978), p. 144.
69 GAA, GC/11/1/1, James McIntosh to Archbishop Eyre, 24 April 1879.
70 *Coatbridge Express*, 10 July 1901.
71 The Irish-born poor were a numerous category: in 1863, out of 290 boarded paupers, 96 were born in Ireland (33 per cent or a third of the total inmate population); in 1872, out of the total number of poor relieved in the Old Monkland (1977), 430 were Irish-born (21 per cent); in 1874, of the 208 applicants for the Old Monkland Poorhouse, 91 were natives of Erin (45 per cent): see *Airdrie and Coatbridge Advertiser*, 8 August 1863, 1 June 1872 and 14 March 1874.
72 GCA, CO1/50/12: *New Monkland Parochial Board Poorhouse (Committee) Minute Book (1863–78)*.
73 *Coatbridge Express*, 13 April 1892.
74 *Glasgow Observer*, 16 April 1892.
75 GCA, CO1/50/12, *New Monkland Parochial Board Poorhouse (Committee) Minute Book (1863–78)*: during a meeting (19 October 1865), the governor of the poor-house read a minute passed by the Board of Supervision, stating that the poor-house committee 'is not legally bound to supply the Roman Catholic Inmates with Roman Catholic prayer-books'.
76 GCA, CO1/50/1: *New Monkland Parochial Board Minute Book (1878–81)*, p. 415: at a meeting (29 April 1880) John Mulvey, the superintendent of St Margaret RC cemetery made a request that the board should pay the same fees for the interment of paupers in the Catholic cemetery as they paid for burial in the New Monkland (Protestant) cemetery.
77 GCA, CO1/50/1: *New Monkland Parochial Board Minute Book (1878–81)*, pp. 33–4: meeting of 2 April 1878.
78 *Airdrie and Coatbridge Advertiser*, 22 April 1882.
79 *Airdrie and Coatbridge Advertiser*, 1 November 1873.
80 *Airdrie and Coatbridge Advertiser*, 30 March 1878; GCA, CO1/5/1/8/1, *Minute Book of Old Monkland School Board (1873–79)*.
81 *Airdrie and Coatbridge Advertiser*, 30 March 1878.
82 See, for example, *Coatbridge Express*, 1 June 1904: Arthur Malone proposed an amendment opposing the increase of headmasters' salaries, supported by Charles O'Neill and Hugh O'Hear, at the meeting of the Old Monkland School Board (31 May 1903).
83 *Airdrie and Coatbridge Advertiser*, 21 May 1903.
84 *Airdrie and Coatbridge Advertiser*, 22 April 1882.

85 *Airdrie and Coatbridge Advertiser*, 21 April 1906.
86 *Glasgow Examiner*, 3 January 1903. The Irish Catholics who became JPs in the Monklands before the First World War were: Alexander McKillop (1898); Thomas Lavell, Hugh O'Hear and Dr Charles O'Neill (1910).
87 *Airdrie and Coatbridge Advertiser*, 28 January 1893.
88 See, for example, the annual supper of the Coatbridge Burns Club, where Bailie Lavell and Councillor O'Neill were present: *Airdrie and Coatbridge Advertiser*, 29 January 1898.
89 See, for instance, the Irish Catholic local politicians' reaction towards the coronation celebrations: in 1902, at the Old Monkland School Board monthly meeting (March), where none of the Irish members made any proposals in connection with coronation day, Father Kirke 'jocularly remarked that he was not a loyalist': *Coatbridge Express*, 26 March 1902.
90 Although one should always carefully consider obituaries, as Honoré de Balzac reminds us in his novel *Bureaucracy* (Chapter 5: 'The machine in motion') – where a character, Du Bruel, is asked to write an obituary on a politician: ' "Du Bruel, we must get ten or a dozen lines about the worthy late director into the papers; his Excellency will glance them over, – he reads the papers. Do you know the particulars of old La Billardiere's life?" Du Bruel made a sign in the negative. "No?" continued des Lupeaulx. "Well then; he was mixed up in the affairs of La Vendee, and he was one of the confidants of the late King. Like Monsieur le Comte de Fontaine he always refused to hold communication with the First Consul. He was a bit of a 'chouan'; born in Brittany of a parliamentary family, and ennobled by Louis XVIII. How old was he? never mind about that; just say his loyalty was untarnished, his religion enlightened,– the poor old fellow hated churches and never set foot in one, but you had better make him out a 'pious vassal'. Bring in, gracefully, that he sang the song of Simeon at the accession of Charles X … But be very careful what you say; weigh your words, so that the other newspapers can't laugh at us; and bring me the article when you've written it."
91 GCA, CO1/5/1/8/2: *Minute Book of Old Monkland School Board (1880–84)*, p. 98.
92 *Coatbridge Express*, 2 January 1907.
93 *Airdrie and Coatbridge Advertiser*, 21 December 1907.
94 Walker, 'Irish immigrants in Scotland', pp. 121–2.
95 *Glasgow Observer*, 21 November 1891.
96 *Airdrie and Coatbridge Advertiser*, 29 October 1859, 12 and 19 November 1859.
97 *Airdrie and Coatbridge Advertiser*, 3 November 1860.
98 *Airdrie and Coatbridge Advertiser*, 4 October 1862.
99 NLA, UA/1/11/2/3: *Airdrie Poll Register detailing Elections of Councillors (1861–67)*. The Irishmen identified were: James McAuley; Daniel Carlin; Michael McKillop, pawnbroker (father of Alexander McKillop); John Lavell, pawnbroker; Charles M'Geechan, grocer; Francis M'Kearney, spirit dealer.
100 *Airdrie and Coatbridge Advertiser*, 4 October 1862.
101 *Airdrie and Coatbridge Advertiser*, 4 October 1862: 'the political parties are so equally balanced with us.'
102 *Airdrie and Coatbridge Advertiser*, 25 October 1862.
103 NLA, UA/1/11/2/3: Airdrie municipal election, 5 November 1861. James McAuley, Michael McKillop, Charles M'Geechan and Daniel Carlin voted for: J. Colquourn, Peter Thompson, James Black and James Know. John Lavell polled for D. Mitchell and John Dalziel (Conservatives), Peter Thompson (Liberal) and James Black, the 'Publicans' candidate'.
104 *Glasgow Free Press*, 22 October 1862.
105 *Glasgow Free Press*, 29 November 1862.
106 *Glasgow Free Press*, 6 December 1862.
107 NLA, UA/1/11/2/3: Airdrie municipal election, 7 November 1865. John Lavell, Daniel

Carlin, James McAuley and Charles M'Geechan voted for J. Forrester, J. Watson (Liberals) and Robert Hamilton and George Gentles (Conservatives).

108 GAA, GC 29/95, Charles O'Neill to Archbishop Eyre, 12 December 1897.
109 *Glasgow Examiner*, 4 November 1893.
110 *Glasgow Observer*, 6 July 1895.
111 *Airdrie and Coatbridge Advertiser*, 15 April 1899.
112 *Airdrie and Coatbridge Advertiser*, 21 November 1868.
113 *Airdrie and Coatbridge Advertiser*, 8 December 1860.
114 *Airdrie and Coatbridge Advertiser*, 5 February 1870.
115 *Coatbridge Express*, 6 November 1901.
116 Joseph Primmer (1842–1914) toured Scotland every summer from 1890 to 1903, defending the reformed faith and attacking the Roman Catholic Church. See T. Gallagher, *Glasgow the Uneasy Peace. Religious Tension in Modern Scotland* (Manchester, 1987), pp. 35–6.
117 *Coatbridge Express*, 10 July 1901.
118 *Airdrie and Coatbridge Advertiser*, 6 March 1875.
119 *Coatbridge Express*, 29 January 1896.
120 *Airdrie and Coatbridge Advertiser*, 14 April 1900.
121 *Airdrie and Coatbridge Advertiser*, 14 April 1900.
122 Yet this was not the case in all Scottish towns: in Greenock, for instance, reactions concerning Irish participation in local politics were much more violent.
123 GCA, CO1/50/1: *New Monkland Parochial Board Minute Book (1878–81)*, pp. 663–4.
124 *Airdrie and Coatbridge Advertiser*, 22 September 1900.
125 *Airdrie and Coatbridge Advertiser*, 21 December 1907.
126 *Airdrie and Coatbridge Advertiser*, 28 November 1868: 'An election ballad'.
127 *Glasgow Observer*, 30 March 1895.
128 See T. M. Devine's lecture, 'Racism and anti-Catholicism in Scotland from the Irish Famine to World War Two', in the Gonzaga Lectures, St Aloysius' College, *In Search of an Identity – Catholicism in Scotland since the Reformation*, 25 March 2003.
129 *Airdrie and Coatbridge Advertiser*, 21 December 1907.
130 J. Lavelle, *Looking Back* (Airdrie, 1934), p. ii.
131 Martin Mitchell suggests this in his study of the Hamilton Irish community: see M. J. Mitchell, 'The Catholic community in Hamilton, c.1800–1914', in T. M. Devine (ed.), *St Mary's Hamilton, a Social History 1846–1996* (Edinburgh, 1995), pp. 31–70.
132 *Coatbridge Leader*, 11 September 1909.
133 'What makes Scotland Scotland is fast disappearing': Walter Scott quoted by T. M. Devine in *The Scottish Nation*, p. 286.
134 J. McCaffrey, *Scotland in the Nineteenth Century* (London, 1998), p. 66.
135 McCaffrey, 'Politics and the Catholic community since 1878', p. 140.

7 A Winnowing Spirit: Sinn Féin in Scotland, 1905–38

1 Colm Brogan, *The Glasgow Story* (London, 1952), p. 190.
2 My preference in this essay has been for Gaelic titles as these are most readily used in the contemporary sources, hence Conradh na Gaeilge rather than the Gaelic League, Cumann Lúthchleas Gael instead of the Gaelic Athletic Association, *craobhacha* instead of 'branches', and *cumann* and its plural *cumainn* to designate Sinn Féin branches.
3 Brogan, *Glasgow Story*, p. 190; *Glasgow Observer*, 13 May 1911; National Archives of Ireland (NAI), Crime Branch Special (CBS), S Files, 18588/S, report dated 13 February 1899 from Sergeant Maguire, Royal Irish Constabulary (RIC), Glasgow to Inspector-General, Dublin Castle.

4 E. W. McFarland, *Ireland and Scotland in the Age of Revolution* (Edinburgh, 1994); Martin J. Mitchell, *The Irish in the West of Scotland 1797–1848* (Edinburgh, 1998), pp. 231–56.

5 Máirtín Ó Catháin, 'The Fenian movement in Scotland, 1858–1916' (PhD thesis, University of Ulster, 2001), p. 100, p. 185 and p. 345. This last figure of 1,700 includes Irish National Brotherhood (INB) men (the IRB's main rival), as well as the latter organisation.

6 Ó Catháin, 'The Fenian movement', Chapter 4; Máirtín Ó Catháin, 'Michael Davitt and Scotland', *Saothar* 25 (2000), pp. 19–26.

7 Ó Catháin, 'The Fenian movement', p. 195, p. 252 and p. 358; Robert Mitchell Henry, *The Evolution of Sinn Féin* (Dublin, 1920), p. 47.

8 *United Irishman*, 6 October 1900; John Hutchinson, *The Dynamics of Cultural Nationalism* (London, 1987), pp. 68–9; Owen McGee, *The IRB: the Irish Republican Brotherhood from the Land League to Sinn Féin* (Dublin, 2005), pp. 288–9.

9 Hutchinson, pp. 172–7; Tom Garvin, *Nationalist Revolutionaries in Ireland, 1858–1928* (Oxford, 1987), pp. 94–5; Brian Maye, *Arthur Griffith* (Dublin, 1977), pp. 84–7; McGee, *The IRB*, p. 300.

10 *United Irishman*, 15 December 1900, 6 July 1901 and 1 November 1902; In 1901 the Emmet anniversary was marked only by Partick Home Rulers and the main Manchester Martyrs celebration of 1902 was organised by the Home Government Branch (see *Glasgow Observer*, 9 March 1901 and *Glasgow Examiner*, 29 November 1902). The former leader of Scotland's Parnellites rather than the Fenians brought to light the case of destitute ex-dynamitard prisoner Henry McCann in 1902 (see *United Irishman*, 25 January 1902).

11 Seán Ó Fiannaí, *Conradh na Gaeilge (Gaelic League) in Scotland* (Glaschú, 1995), p. 35, p. 1 and p. 14; Pádraig Ó Baoighill, 'Conradh na Gaeilge in Albain – *na blianta tosaigh*', *Feasta* 44 (3) (Márta 1996); and Bernard J. Canning, *Pádraig H. Pearse and Scotland* (Glasgow, 1979), p. 5; *Glasgow Examiner*, 14 June 1902.

12 *United Irishman*, 22 and 29 November, and 13 December 1902. Belfast, Cork, Limerick, Tullamore, Castlebar, Edenderry, Carron, Dun Laoghaire, Rathmines, Glenmornan, Terenure, Dublin City, Liverpool, London and Newry all had Cumann na nGaedheal branches before Glasgow (see *United Irishman*, 1 November 1902), and for Fenians in the Belfast, Derry, Liverpool, Manchester and London Cumann na nGaedheal, see *United Irishman*, 20 and 27 October, 1 December 1900, and 23 May and 7 November 1903); Mark Ryan, *Fenian Memories* (Dublin, 1945), p. 200ff.

13 *Glasgow Star and Examiner*, 11 April 1903. There was actually a mention of the Irish National Club in November when it appears to have changed into a branch of Cumann na nGaedheal under the presidency of Patrick McCauley, leader of the AOH and the IRB in Port Glasgow (see *United Irishman*, 5 December 1903).

14 Maye, *Arthur Griffith*, p. 69; NAI, CBS, S Files, 29621/S, report dated 18 May 1904 from Sergeant Harrington, RIC, Glasgow to Inspector-General, Dublin Castle.

15 *United Irishman*, 10 October 1903; *Glasgow Observer*, 17 October 1903.

16 *United Irishman*, 24 October, 7, 14 and 28 November 1903, and 3 September 1904; *Glasgow Observer*, 28 January 1905.

17 Michael Thomas Foy, 'The Ancient Order of Hibernians: an Irish political-religious pressure group, 1884–1975' (MA thesis, Queen's University Belfast, 1976), pp. 24–30. Even a passing scan of the newspapers from 1904 over 1905, 1906 and 1907 show a remarkable rise in violent sectarian band riots and ethnic clashes in places such as Springburn, Kilsyth, Rutherglen, Partick, Motherwell, Cambusnethan, Hamilton, Blantyre, Saltcoats and Kilwinning. While these do not explain the rise of the AOH – most of these events did not involve them – they indicate a climate of tension and hostility between the internal and external contexts which made the continued existence and growth of groups such as the AOH somewhat inevitable (see *Glasgow*

Observer, 3 December 1904, 25 March, 1 April [founding of the Glasgow and District Flute Band Association – an Irish nationalist band alliance led by a Registered AOH and Sinn Féin leader in Govan], 22 and 29 April, 24 June, 8 July 1905, 3 February, 26 May, 2 and 3 June, 28 July 1906, and 6 April, 1 June and 31 August 1907); Hugh P. Hagan, 'Ancient Order of Hibernians in Scotland, 1880–1914' (unclassified dissertation, Ruskin College Oxford, 1987), pp. 37–9; *Glasgow Star and Examiner*, 23 February 1906; *Glasgow Observer*, 21 July 1906; *Glasgow Observer*, 17 March 1906 for Rossa's visit, and 16 June 1906 for MacManus visit.

18 *Glasgow Observer*, 12 December 1908 (for dramatics and industrial committee); *Peasant*, 2 May 1908 (for various Sinn Féin activities); *Glasgow Observer*, 3 April 1909 (for MS journal); *Glasgow Observer*, 21 March 1908 (for Irish in the schools); *Peasant*, 10 August 1907 (for Catholic Boys Brigade in St Mungo's); *Glasgow Observer*, 25 April 1908 (for Sinn Féin support towards Irish Co-operative Society); and see letters of Patrick McCauley on this in *Glasgow Observer*, 15 February and 7 March 1908.

19 *Glasgow Observer*, 20 April 1907, 7 November and 11 July 1908, 10 April 1909, 28 May and 19 November 1910.

20 *Glasgow Observer*, 29 August 1908.

21 *Peasant*, 6 July 1907.

22 *Glasgow Observer*, 23 November 1907; *Sinn Féin*, 30 November 1907; *Peasant*, 23 November 1907; National Library of Ireland (NLI), Patrick McCormick MS 15,337, p. 2.

23 *Peasant*, 16 November 1907; *Glasgow Observer*, 23 November 1907; (for James O'Neill see *United Irishman*, 13 October 1900 and for Gillespie, *Glasgow Examiner*, 31 July 1897). Sorcha O'Neill (or Ní Néill), was an Irish dancing teacher (see *Glasgow Observer*, 5 December 1908).

24 *Glasgow Observer*, 17 and 31 October 1908 and 15 January and 5 February 1910; *An Phoblacht*, 17 December, 1932, for Sarah O'Kane's obituary.

25 Pádraic Colum, *Arthur Griffith* (Dublin, 1959), pp. 92–3.

26 John F. McCaffrey, *Scotland in the Nineteenth Century* (Hampshire, 1998), pp. 113–16. For a range of anti-Catholic outbursts in places such as Hamilton, Kelso, Ayr and Motherwell, see *Glasgow Observer*, 17 April 15 and 22 May, 12 June and 21 August 1909.

27 *Glasgow Observer*, 6 and 13 March 1909 for MacDiarmada; 4 December 1909 for Daly; 14 August 1909 for last Coiste Ceanntair Albain meeting and proposed branches in Dumbarton, Falkirk and Coatbridge; 27 March, 24 April and 15 May 1909 for the Irish Club; 2 October 1909 for O'Meagher Condon/O'Callaghan visit; Hagan, 'Ancient Order of Hibernians in Scotland', pp. 57–8; Foy, 'The Ancient Order of Hibernians', pp. 88–9; A. C. Hepburn, 'The Ancient Order of Hibernians in Irish politics, 1905–14', *Cithara* 4 (1971), p. 7.

28 *Glasgow Observer*, 2 October 1909, 31 August 1912.

29 *Glasgow Observer*, 15 and 29 March 1913. Perhaps a return visit by Major John McBride the previous December to give the Manchester Martyrs oration for a second year running stretched already thin financial resources, and Craobh Éire Óg decided to withhold applications for speakers in 1913.

30 *Glasgow Observer*, 17 May, 21 June and 6 September 1913.

31 *Glasgow Observer*, 10 and 17 January 1914.

32 *Glasgow Observer*, 2 May, 28 February, 4 and 18 April 1914; figures are based on numbers given at inauguration of companies (from *Glasgow Observer*, 25 April, 16, 23 and 30 May, 6, 13, 20 and 27 June, 4, 11 and 18 July and 29 August 1914); Iain D. Patterson, 'The activities of Irish republican physical force organisations in Scotland, 1919–21', *Scottish Historical Review* 72 (1) 193 (April 1993), p. 67 and p. 47fn. Police records quoting a total of 3,000 Volunteers are probably quite accurate despite Patterson's misgivings; Military Archives (MA), Bureau of Military History

1913–21 (BMH), witness statements WS/627, statement of Séamus Reader, member of Glasgow IRB, 1914, later OC Scottish Brigade, Irish Republican Army, 1920, p. 5.

33 Leon Ó Broin, *Revolutionary Underground* (Dublin, 1976), p. 153 and p. 155; *Irish Volunteer*, 24 October and 14 November 1914; this figure is confirmed by one of the most senior IRB figures in Scotland at the time, Dan Branniff (see MA, BMH, witness statements WS/222, statement of Daniel Branniff, member of Dungannon Clubs, Newcastle-on-Tyne and Belfast, 1907, co-opted member of Supreme Council, IRB 1912–14, p. 2).

34 NLI, Frank Gallagher MS 21,265, p. 60 and appendices, various letters to the *Sunday Press* re Séamas Robinson and the Glasgow Fianna, undated (March, 1954?); *An tÓglach*, St Patrick's Day, 1962, Easter 1963, summer 1964 and Easter 1965; *Irish Volunteer*, 30 October 1915; *An Phoblacht*, 29 January 1926; *Irish Press*, 18 October 1949; James E. Handley, *The Irish in Modern Scotland* (Cork, 1947), p. 298; and letter (undated) from Frank McGowan, late quartermaster, IRA, Glasgow, in possession of author.

35 Pádraig Ó Baoighill, *Óglach na Rosann: Niall Pluincéad Ó Baoighill* (Baile Átha Cliath, 1994), pp. 149–76; Owen Dudley Edwards, 'The Catholic press in Scotland since the restoration of the hierarchy', in David McRoberts (ed.), *Modern Scottish Catholicism 1878–1978* (Glasgow, 1979), pp. 169–73.

36 *An Phoblacht*, 29 January 1926; Dorothy McArdle, *The Irish Republic* (London, 1937), p. 348; Ó Baoighill, *Óglach na Rosann*, p. 165; MA, BMH, witness statements WS/863, statement of H. Warren Hutchinson (father of the poet, Pearse Hutchinson who was born in Glasgow in 1927), member of Sinn Féin, Glasgow, 1913–? and member of the IRA, Glasgow, 1916–22, p. 12.

37 National Archives of Scotland (NAS), Irish Disturbances files, HH055/00062, 63, 65, 66 all contain references to the 'Sinn Féin Volunteers' and 'Sinn Féin raids'; and Stephen Coyle, 'The smashing of the van', unpublished article and research notes, donated to author by kind permission of Stephen Coyle, Glasgow.

38 Seán O'Farrell, 'Irish republicanism in Scotland, 1916–1923' (BA dissertation, Politics/ Sociology, Department of Social Sciences, University College Galway, undated), pp. 16–18; Eunan O'Halpin, *Defending Ireland: the Irish State and its Enemies since 1922* (Oxford, 1999), pp. 20–1; Peter Hart, 'Operations abroad': The IRA in Britain, 1919–23', *English Historical Review* (February 2000), pp. 94–102; *An Phoblacht*, 29 January 1926. Cumann Poblacht na hÉireann nAlbain took the place of Sinn Féin as the main anti-treaty voice in Scotland after the party Poblacht na hÉireann was founded by de Valera and supporters in March 1922, though it faded from view and was replaced once more by Sinn Féin after 1924.

39 Bernard Aspinwall, 'A long journey: the Irish in Scotland', in Patrick O'Sullivan (ed.), *The Irish World Wide: History, Heritage, Identity Vol. V: Religion and Identity* (Leicester, 1996), pp. 146–52; Harold J. Abramson, 'On the sociology of ethnicity and social change: a model of rootedness and rootlessness', in *Economic and Social Review* 8 (1) (October 1976), pp. 43–59; C. Desmond Greaves, *The Life and Times of James Connolly* (London, 1972), pp. 368–9; James D. Young, 'John Maclean, socialism and the Easter Rising', *Saothar* 16 (1991), pp. 30–2; Robert Stewart, *Breaking the Fetters* (London, 1967), pp. 152–3.

40 Aspinwall, 'A long journey', p. 169; Tom Gallagher, 'The Catholic Irish in Scotland: in search of identity', in T. M. Devine (ed.), *Irish Immigrants and Scottish Society* (Edinburgh, 1991), pp. 29–31; T. M. Devine, *The Scottish Nation 1700–2000* (London, 1999), pp. 497–8.

41 Michael Lynch, *Scotland: a New History* (London, 1992), pp. 430–1; Brenda Collins, 'The Irish in Britain, 1780–1921', in B. J. Graham and L. J. Proudfoot (eds), *An Historical Geography of Ireland* (London, 1993), p. 393.

42 Hart, 'Operations abroad', p. 73; Aspinwall, 'A long journey', p. 169; O'Farrell, 'Irish republicanism in Scotland', p. 12. NAS records released in 1994 confirmed the

police had information in 1920 suggesting 30,000 active republicans, see *Scotsman*, 25 August 1994. This number would mean that around 14 per cent of the Irish-born population in Scotland was in or supporting the IRA. The release of the Bureau of Military History witness statements by the Military Archives in Dublin's Cathal Brugha Barracks sheds some new light on these disputed figures. It is known that the Scottish Brigade of the IRA's second battalion, for example, covering much of mid-Lanarkshire, was composed of some nine companies in 1919–20, comprising around 300 men (though the battalion area intriguingly had around 600 IRB men); and before the Third Battalion was formed covering the Lothians, the Falkirk Company alone had 100 men. Even relatively small towns such as Denny and Alloa had IRA companies to rival places such as Motherwell which had 70 IRA men (see MA, BMH, witness statements WS/828, statement of James Byrne, quarter-master, Second Battalion, Scottish Brigade IRA 1919-, p. 2; WS/777, statement of Patrick Mills, lieutenant, Motherwell Company, Scottish Brigade, IRA 1918-, pp. 2–3; WS/696, statement of Henry O'Hagan, adjutant Third [Edinburgh] Battalion, Scottish Brigade IRA, 1920-, pp. 4–5).

43 Brian Hanley, *The IRA, 1926–1936* (Dublin, 2002), p. 12, table 2; University College Dublin Archives (UCDA), Moss Twomey Papers, P69/174 (54), letter dated 8 May 1925 from Pete Hughes to Frances Carty. The 1925 feud related to difficulties between the IRA's 'H' company (Cambuslang, Wellshot, Carmyle and Rutherglen), and the Glasgow Officer Commanding over their stewarding of rowdy Glasgow concerts and dances; *An Phoblacht*, 18 September, 16 October, 20 November, 4 and 11 December 1925 and 29 January, 5 March, 16 April and 29 October 1926; *Glasgow Observer*, 11 December 1926.

44 *An Phoblacht*, 15 August 1927, 14 April, 7 July, 11 August, 24 November and 1 December 1928, and 23 July 1929.

45 O'Keeffe, who was a Sinn Féin organiser, later returned to Dublin to found and become president of the Irish National League of the Blind trade union, but returned to Glasgow many times over the years; see Pat Lyons, *A Place in the Sun: a Brief History of the National League of the Blind in Ireland* (Dublin, 1999).

46 *An Phoblacht*, 14 December 1929 and 29 January 1926; Hanley, *The IRA*, p. 97 and p. 110; Hugh MacDonald, 'Amlaibh MacAindreas: another Scots fighter for Ireland', undated, unreferenced article donated by Stephen Coyle. The Irish Citizen Army had a grouping in Glasgow from 1916; see Patterson, 'The activities', p. 49 and p. 56; Brian Hanley, 'The Irish Citizen Army after 1916', *Saothar* 28 (2003), p. 47, Note 68. I am deeply indebted again to Stephen Coyle for his detailed knowledge of the period and of Scottish solidarity links to Irish republicanism in particular.

47 *An Phoblacht*, 28 December 1929; UCDA, Moss Twomey Papers, p69/172, IRA transfer requests to Scottish units.

48 Taped interview with Frank McGowan, late quartermaster, IRA, Glasgow, 8 January 1997, conducted by author; Uinseann MacEoin, *The IRA in the Twilight Years: 1923–1948* (Dublin, 1997), pp. 879–81.

8 'Our Country's Heroes': Irish Catholics in Scotland and the Great War

1 J. C., 'Day Dreams', *Glasgow Observer*, July 1916.

2 K. Jeffery, *Ireland and the Great War* (Cambridge, 2000); A. Gregory and S. Paseta, *Ireland and the Great War: 'A War to Unite Us All'?* (Manchester, 2002); N. C. Johnson, *Ireland, the Great War and the Geography of Remembrance* (Cambridge, 2003); D. Hall, *World War I and Nationalist Politics in County Louth, 1914–20* (Dublin, 2005).

3 P. J. Casey, 'Irish casualties in the First World War', *Irish Sword* 20 (1997), pp. 193–206. Casualties identified number 330 in the HLI, 230 in the Cameronians. (These include Catholics and Protestants of Irish birth). For examples of regimental and

battalion histories see: L. B. Oates, *The 17th HLI: Record of War Service* (Glasgow, 1920); H. C. Wylly, *A Short History of the Cameronians (Scottish Rifles) 1689–1924* (Aldershot, 1924); T. Chalmers, *An Epic of Glasgow. History of the 15th Battalion HLI* (Glasgow, 1934); and *A Saga of Scotland. The History of the 16 th Battalion HLI* (Glasgow, n.d.).

4 *Glasgow Observer*, 26 July 1919.

5 *Glasgow Observer*, 23 July 1921.

6 *Glasgow Observer*, 28 August 1916, 13 January 1917.

7 Some caution is necessary as the UILGB figures – apparently compiled from local branch and parish returns – were used for explicitly political purposes, but they are useful in that they include first- and second-generation Irish Catholics, while excluding Irish-born Protestants. Unfortunately, it is impossible to express Irish recruitment figures as a reliable percentage of adult males of military age, as the 1911 census includes those of Irish birth, without specifying religious denomination. There may also be a measure of conflation with reservists and regular soldiers already in the ranks. For a summary of Scottish weekly recruiting totals see D. Young, 'Voluntary recruitment in Scotland 1914–16' (PhD Thesis, University of Glasgow, 2001), p. 430.

8 *Parliamentary Debates: House of Lords Vol. XVIII, 1914 (Nov. 11-May 19)*, p. 383.

9 G. L. Mosse, *Fallen Soldiers. Reshaping the Memory of the World Wars* (Oxford, 1999), pp. 53–69.

10 For a fuller treatment of volunteering among Irish Catholics in Scotland, see E. W. McFarland, 'How the Irish paid their debt: Irish Catholics in Scotland and voluntary enlistment, August 1914-July 1915', *Scottish Historical Review* 82 (2) 214 (2003), pp. 261–84.

11 Young, 'Voluntary recruitment', p. 380.

12 *Census Report, 1911*, vol. 3, pp. 24–5.

13 *Census Report, 1911*, vol. 3, pp. 24–5. See P. E. Dewey, 'Military recruiting and the British labour force during the First World War', *The Historical Journal* 27 (1984), p. 1.

14 *Glasgow Observer*, 4 November 1916.

15 *Glasgow Observer*, 13 February, 2 October 1915.

16 P. Simkins, *Kitchener's Army: the Raising of the New Armies 1914–16* (Manchester, 1988); J. M. Osborne, *The Voluntary Recruitment Movement in Britain 1914–16* (Garland, NY, 1982).

17 McFarland, 'How the Irish paid their debt', pp. 268–9.

18 See John Ferguson, *Three Centuries of Irish History. From the Reign of Mary the Catholic to that of Victoria the Protestant. An Unbroken Record of Confiscation and Persecution, Mixed with Massacre, and Terminating in Extermination by Unjust and Ruinous Taxation* (Glasgow, c.1897), pp. 125–6.

19 The 1911 census indicated 174,715 people of Irish birth in Scotland, representing 3.7 per cent of the total population compared with 6.2 per cent 40 years before: *Census Report, 1911*, vol. 2, p. 503.

20 *Glasgow Star*, 10 July 1914.

21 *Glasgow Observer*, 8 August 1914.

22 *Glasgow Observer*, 15 August 1914.

23 *Glasgow Observer*, 13 December 1914.

24 Thornton eventually won the DSO: *Glasgow Observer*, 13 January 1917. For the demand for chaplain postings see Glasgow Archdiocesan Archives (GAA), General Correspondence, GC46/4–5, J. Richie to S. Thornton, 8 and 15 August 1914. By October 1916, 17 from this diocese alone had volunteered. A shortage of Catholic chaplains persisted, however, possibly reflecting the scant ratio of priests to parishioners in Scotland: B. Flynn to J. Richie, 13 October 1916. See also *Glasgow Observer*, 24 July 1915.

25 *Freeman's Journal*, 4 August 1914.
26 *Glasgow Observer*, 8 August 1914.
27 T. P. Dooley, ' Politics, bands and marketing: army recruitment in Waterford City, 1914–15', *Irish Sword* 18, pp. 205–19. Redmond also rejected pleas to prevent the call-up of reservists serving in the Irish Volunteers until Home Rule was granted.
28 See *Glasgow Herald*, 9 September 1914.
29 *Freeman's Journal*, 21 September 1914.
30 *Glasgow Observer*, 26 September 1914.
31 *Glasgow Observer*, 19 September 1914.
32 See, for example, *Glasgow Observer*, 3 October 1914; *Glasgow Star*, 14 October 1914.
33 *Forward*, 8 August 1914.
34 *Glasgow Observer*, 4 September 1914.
35 *Irish Volunteer*, 10 and 24 October 1914.
36 *Glasgow Star*, 16 October 1914.
37 *Glasgow Star*, 2 January, 8 May 1915.
38 *Dundee Advertiser*, 15 February 1915. For comparative figures for Irish recruitment in England see *House of Lords Vol. XVIII*, p. 383. The London total was suggested at 5,000, with 15,000 in the north of England.
39 *Glasgow Observer*, 15 and 29 May 1915.
40 *Glasgow Observer*, 22 August 1914.
41 *Glasgow Observer*, 7 August 1915.
42 GAA, GC 46/30–3.
43 *Glasgow Observer*, 9 January, 13 February 1915.
44 *Glasgow Observer*, 8 May 1915.
45 *Glasgow Star*, 8 April 1916.
46 *Glasgow Star*, 13 February 1915.
47 Basil Williams, *Raising and Training the New Armies* (London, 1918), p. 6; R. Douglas, 'Voluntary enlistment in the First World War and the work of the Parliamentary Recruiting Committee', *Journal of Modern History* 42 (1970), pp. 565–85.
48 *Glasgow Observer*, 24 October 1914; 20 March 1915; 8 and 22 May 1915. St John's Portobello, for example, had five killed at Gallipoli and many wounded out of a total serving of 140.
49 *Glasgow Observer*, 9 and 16 October 1915.
50 K. Grieves, *The Politics of Manpower, 1914–1918* (Manchester, 1988), p. 21.
51 J. M. Osborne, *The Voluntary Recruitment Movement in Britain 1914–16* (Garland, NY, 1982), p. 92.
52 T. P. Dooley, *Irishmen or English Soldiers?* (Liverpool, 1995), pp. 163–4.
53 *Glasgow Observer*, 10 July, 14 and 28 August 1915; *The Scotsman*, 21 August 1915.
54 P. Callan, 'Ambivalence towards the Saxon shilling: the attitudes of the Catholic Church in Ireland towards enlistment during the First World War', *Archivum Hibernicum* 41 (1986), pp. 99–111.
55 *Glasgow Observer*, 10 July 1915.
56 *Glasgow Observer*, 24 July 1915.
57 NLI, Redmond Papers, R. Brade to J. Redmond, 21 Feb. 1915. The situation appeared serious enough to warrant the War Office suggestion of a joint approach from Redmond and Carson.
58 *General Reports on the British Army, Parliamentary Papers 1921*, 20, *p. 113*.
59 Jeffery, Ireland and the Great War, pp. 6–7; P. Callan, 'Recruiting for the British army in Ireland during the First World War', *Irish Sword* 27 (1987), pp. 42–56.
60 R. Douglas, *Steelopolis: the Making of Motherwell 1790–1939* (Motherwell, 1991), p. 150.
61 See, for example, *Motherwell Times*, 3 March 1916.

62 *Peace Souvenir. Motherwell's Part in the Fight for Freedom* (Motherwell, n.d.).

63 *Motherwell Times*, 12 November 1914, 4 June 1915.

64 *Motherwell Times*, 28 May, 11 June 1915.

65 *Motherwell Times*, 30 June 1916.

66 *Motherwell Times*, 26 June 1915. Note parallels with the anti-German riots in Scotland of May 1915: C. M. M. Macdonald, 'May 1915: race, riot and representations of war', in C. M. M. Macdonald and E. W. McFarland, *Scotland and the Great War* (East Linton, 1999), pp. 145–72.

67 *Glasgow Star*, 7 July 1915.

68 *Motherwell Times*, 14 August 1915.

69 *Glasgow Observer*, 4 August 1917: in the midst of the city's by-election, George Baxter, the chair of the Dundee Conservatives astutely paid tribute to Dundee Irishmen at the front.

70 *Glasgow Herald*, 17 August 1915; *Evening Citizen*, 18 August 1915.

71 *Glasgow Herald*, 20 August 1915.

72 *Glasgow Observer*, 2 July 1915.

73 *Glasgow Observer*, 28 August 1915.

74 See *Glasgow Observer*, 9 October 1915 for 'Knoxism made in Germany', and 26 June for the weekly activities of 'Loyal Orange Lodge "Kaiser Wilhelm"'.

75 D. Gwynn, *The Life of John Redmond* (London, 1932), pp. 402–9. See also N. Perry, 'Nationality in the Irish infantry regiments in the First World War', *War and Society* 12 (1) (1994), pp. 76–7.

76 *Glasgow Observer*, 26 December 1914; 9 January, 15 May 1915. One contemporary later estimated that 5,000 of Scotland's 35,000 serving Irish Catholics were in Irish regiments: *Motherwell Times*, 30 June 1916.

77 *Glasgow Star*, 29 January 1916.

78 NLI, Redmond Papers, MS 15259, memos: 'Recruiting in Ireland'. See also, MS 15261, Rev. M. Brogan to John Redmond, 15 November 1915. For a general discussion see T. Denman, *Ireland's Unknown Soldiers. The 16th (Irish) Division in the Great War* (Dublin, 1992), pp. 40–2.

79 N. Perry, 'Nationality in the Irish infantry regiments in the First World War', *War and Society* 12 (1994), pp. 69–78; C. A. Cooper Walker, *The Book of the 7th Service Battalion Royal Enniskillen Fusiliers* (Dublin, 1920).

80 *Glasgow Observer*, 7 August, 11 September 1915. The RIF established their own office in Glasgow.

81 In August 1917 a quarter of the Glasgow Irish Foresters' 200 casualties were reported to have been from those in Irish regiments: *Glasgow Observer*, 18 August 1917. Following conscription, those who were called up could elect to join an Irish regiment if they could claim Irish parentage or descent. Arrangements for battalion transfers were also put in place: Denman, *Unknown Soldiers*, p. 141. Some were disappointed: Pat Moran who had registered under the Derby Scheme requested to join the Connaught Rangers, but was told when reporting for service in 1916 that the unit was full. He was instead directed to the 7th Argylls – 'his face tripping him because he felt that as an Irishman he should never have been put in a foreign regiment'. Mary-Jane Moran (1890–1975), oral testimony, recorded September 1975.

82 *Glasgow Observer*, 22 May, 1915; 5 July 1915 for anniversary Mass at Catterick Camp for soldiers killed at Gallipoli.

83 *Glasgow Observer*, 5 February, 26 August, 25 November 1916; *Derry Journal*, 24 March 1916.

84 J. V. McCabe, *A History of St Aloysius College 1859–1999* (Glasgow, 2000), p. 103.

85 *Glasgow Observer*, 5 August 1916.

86 *Glasgow Observer*, 23 December 1916.

87 The number of Catholic Irish soldiers winning gallantry awards rose steadily during the war. See for example: *Glasgow Observer*, 29 January 1916, and 14 April for William Young VC.
88 *Glasgow Observer*, 1 and 22 April, 25 May 1916.
89 *Glasgow Observer*, 1 January 1916.
90 *Glasgow Observer*, 3 March 1917.
91 GAA, GC48/45.
92 *Glasgow Observer*, 11 March 1916.
93 *Glasgow Star*, 30 October 1915.
94 J. L. Macleod, '"Greater love hath no man than this": Scotland's conflicting religious responses to death in the Great War', *Scottish Historical Review* 81 (1) 211 (2002), pp. 70–96.
95 *Glasgow Observer*, 14 November 1914, 13 November 1915.
96 *Glasgow Observer*, 15 April 1916: 'Our Lady of the Trenches' by Denis A. McCarthy.
97 D. Fitzpatrick, *Politics and Irish Life, 1913–1921* (Dublin, 1977), pp. 107–15.
98 *Glasgow Observer*, 12 June 1916.
99 *Glasgow Observer*, 22 January 1916.
100 *Glasgow Observer*, 29 April, 6 May 1916.
101 NLI, Redmond MS 15235/5, J. Cruden to J. Redmond, 19 Jul. 1916 and 24 May 1916.
102 *Glasgow Observer*, 6 May 1916.
103 *Glasgow Herald*, 26 April 1916; *Evening Citizen*, 27 April 1916; *Daily Record*, 26 April 1916.
104 *Motherwell Times*, 5 December 1915: only two out of 100 'unstarred' men came forward.
105 *Motherwell Times*, 9 June 1916.
106 *Glasgow Observer*, 19 August 1916; *Motherwell Times*, 11 August 1916; *Derry Journal*, 16 August 1916.
107 *Glasgow Observer*, 13 May, 10 June 1916.
108 Irish Military Archives, Bureau of Military History, Daniel Kelly statement, doc. 1004; Joseph Booker Statement, doc. 776; Patrick Mills (Motherwell) statement, doc. 777.
109 For relations with Labour, see article by George Barnes, *Glasgow Observer*, 8 January 1916.
110 *Glasgow Observer*, 1 September 1917.
111 *Glasgow Observer*, 25 August, 13 July 1917.
112 *Glasgow Observer*, 26 Jan. 1917.
113 Grieves, *Politics of Manpower*, p. 9.
114 Such cases were pursued with remarkable energy: see National Archives of Ireland, CSORP 15, 202, CO 2 (Hamilton) District to Inspector General RIC, 7 Aug. 1916, enclosing list of suspected absentees (approximately 240), and asking that they be apprehended.
115 *Glasgow Observer*, 1 September 1917.
116 *Glasgow Observer*, 4 August 1917.
117 *Glasgow Observer*, 3 November 1917.
118 *Derry Journal*, 3 August 1917.
119 *Glasgow Observer*, 8 December 1917.
120 *Glasgow Observer*, 4 August 1917.
121 See *Glasgow Observer*, 16 March 1918.
122 *Glasgow Observer*, 23 March 1918.
123 *Glasgow Observer*, 13 April, 11 May 1918.
124 *Glasgow Observer*, 4, 18, 25 May, 1 June 1918.
125 *Glasgow Observer*, 28 September 1918. The AOH did, however, approve the action of its Irish brethren in opposing conscription.

126 *Evening Times*, 9 July 1918. See A. Gregory, '"You might as well recruit Germans": British public opinion and the decision to conscript the Irish in 1918', in Gregory and Paseta, *Ireland and the Great War*, pp. 123–32.

127 *Glasgow Observer*, 11 May 1918.

128 *Forward*, 13 April 1918.

129 *Glasgow Observer*, 3, 13 and 27 April 1918.

130 *Glasgow Observer*, 24 February 1917.

131 *Glasgow Observer*, 13 April, 4 May 1918.

132 D. Fitzpatrick, *The Two Irelands, 1912–1939* (Oxford, 1999), p. 29.

133 *Freeman's Journal*, 20 August 1918.

134 *Glasgow Observer*, 24 August 1918.

135 *Glasgow Observer*, 24 August 1918. See also 3 August, 2 November.

136 *Glasgow Observer*, 31 August 1918.

137 *Glasgow Observer*, 19 October 1918.

138 *Glasgow Star*, 17 November 1918.

139 One of the last soldiers to be profiled in 'Our Country's Heroes' was Sgt John Moran of Dundee who died of pneumonia in 1919. He had served with the Leinsters at Mons and spent over four years in captivity: *Glasgow Observer*, 14 April 1919.

140 J. O'Connor, 'Some examples of Irishmen enlisted in the Australian Imperial Force, 1914', *Irish Sword* 21 (1998), pp. 88–9.

9 Protestant Action and the Edinburgh Irish

1 On the Kirk campaign, see Stewart J. Brown, '"Outside the Covenant": the Scottish Presbyterian Churches and Irish immigration, 1922–1938', *Innes Review* 42 (1) (1991), pp. 19–45; Michael Rosie, *The Sectarian Myth in Scotland: of Bitter Memory and Bigotry* (Basingstoke, 2004), pp. 100–6.

2 James E. Handley, *The Irish in Modern Scotland* (Cork, 1947), p. 305; Joseph M. Bradley, 'Religious cleavage and aspects of Catholic identity in modern Scotland', *Scottish Church History Society* 25 (3) (1995), pp. 442–68 – see p. 464.

3 Bernard Aspinwall, 'Faith of our fathers living still … the time warp or Woof! Woof!', in Tom Devine (ed.), *Scotland's Shame? Bigotry and Sectarianism in Modern Scotland* (Edinburgh, 2000), p. 106.

4 *The Times*, 31 May 1927; *The Scotsman*, 29 May 1928.

5 (Edinburgh) *Evening News*, 29 September 1920; *Glasgow Herald*, 29 September 1920.

6 Iain McLean, *The Legend of Red Clydeside* (Edinburgh 1983), p. 280.

7 *Evening News*, 12 October 1934.

8 Steve Bruce's contribution includes *No Pope of Rome: Militant Protestantism in Modern Scotland* (Edinburgh 1985) and 'Militants and the margins: British political Protestantism', *Sociological Review* 34 (4) (1986), pp. 797–811. Tom Gallagher's includes 'Protestant extremism in urban Scotland, 1930–1939: its growth and contraction', *Scottish Historical Review* 64 (2) (1985), pp. 143–67; *Glasgow, the Uneasy Peace: Religious Tension in Modern Scotland, 1819–1914* (Manchester, 1987); and, *Edinburgh Divided: John Cormack and No Popery in the 1930s* (Edinburgh 1987).

9 Gallagher, *Edinburgh Divided*, p. 158.

10 See, for example: Gallagher, *Edinburgh Divided*, p. 35; Graham Walker, *Intimate Strangers: Political and Cultural Interaction between Scotland and Ulster in Modern Times* (Edinburgh, 1995), p. 75; William Knox, *Industrial Nation: Work, Culture and Society in Scotland, 1800-Present* (Edinburgh, 1999), p. 201.

11 *Evening News*, 1 February, 14 and 23 May, 5 and 6 June 1934.

12 *Evening News*, 24 and 25 April 1935.

13 On the left's acceptance of 'ruffianism' from their own supporters see *New Statesman & Nation*, 9 November 1935.
14 *Evening News*, 18 April 1935; *The Scotsman*, 27 April 1935.
15 Tom Devine, *The Herald*, 18 July 1998.
16 *The Scotsman*, 29 April 1935; *Evening News*, 29 April 1935.
17 Gallagher, *Edinburgh Divided*, p. 49.
18 *The Scotsman*. 25 May 1935; *Evening News*. 26 June 1935.
19 See Scottish Catholic Archives (SCA) documents DE162/51.
20 Letter from Abbot Alban Boultwood OSB, to Michael Turnbull, June 1999. I am very grateful to both for permission to cite their correspondence.
21 *Evening News*, 26 May 1935; *The Scotsman*, 27 June 1935.
22 *Evening News*, 1 and 3 August 1935; Bruce, *No Pope of Rome*, p. 73. On Klan anti-Catholicism, see Kenneth T. Jackson, *The Ku Klux Klan in the City, 1915–1930* (Chicago, 1967).
23 *Evening News*, 15 October 1936.
24 SCA DE 162/49/4, letter from Archbishop MacDonald to Sir Godfrey Collins, 16 July 1935.
25 See *The Times*, 6 and 14 August 1935; *The Spectator* 9 and 16 August 1935
26 Gallagher, *Edinburgh Divided*, p. 187.
27 See, for example, court reports in *Evening News*, 1 August and 6 November 1935.
28 *Evening News*, 30 January and 22 February 1936; (Edinburgh) *Evening Dispatch*, 10 March 1936.
29 See, for example, *The Scotsman*, 27 June 1935; *Evening News*, 18 July 1935.
30 *Life & Work*, September 1935.
31 *Evening News*, 2 October 1935; *Evening Dispatch*, 5 March 1936.
32 Letters to the editor, *Evening News*, 26 April 1935.
33 McLean, *Legend of Red Clydeside*, p. 225.
34 On the utility of this measure at ward level see William Miller, 'Politics in the Scottish city, 1832–1982', in George Gordon (ed.), *Perspectives of the Scottish City* (Aberdeen, 1985).
35 The most affluent wards were: Morningside, Haymarket, Newington, Corstorphine and Cramond, Merchiston, St Bernard's, Colinton, St Stephen's.
36 See Rosie, *Sectarian Myth*, pp. 130–5.
37 On forms of anti-Catholicism, see John Brewer with Gareth Higgins, *Anti-Catholicism in Northern Ireland, 1600–1998: the Mote and the Beam* (Basingstoke, 1998).
38 See the classified notices in *Evening News* on successive Saturdays between 14 October 1933 and 28 April 1934.
39 Letters to the editor, *Evening News*, 20 April 1935.
40 See the classified notices in *Evening News*, 1 September 1934, 2 May 1931, 2 and 8 April 1935.
41 *Evening News*, 5 April 1935.
42 SCA GD11/45, see collection of PAS literature.
43 Letters to the editor, *Evening News*, 14 February 1935.
44 *Evening News*, 7 November 1933 and 8 September 1936.
45 *Evening News*, 2 November 1936.
46 *Evening News*, 29 October 1937.
47 SCA GD11/45, see collection of PAS literature.
48 *Evening Dispatch* 2 November 1938

10 The Orange Order in Scotland since 1860: A social analysis

1 Hereward Senior, *Orangeism, the Canadian Phase* (McGraw-Hill Ryerson, 1972); Cecil Houston and William J. Smyth, *The Sash Canada Wore: a Historical Geography*

of the Orange Order in Canada (Toronto, 1980); P. J. Waller, *Democracy and Sectarianism: a Political and Social History of Liverpool 1868–1939* (Liverpool, 1981); Frank Neal, *Sectarian Violence; the Liverpool Experience, 1819–1914: an Aspect of Anglo-Irish history* (Manchester, 1987); Dominic Bryan, *Orange Parades: the Politics of Ritual, Tradition and Control* (Pluto, 2000); Eric Kaufmann, *The Orange Order: a Contemporary Northern Irish History* (Oxford, 2007).

2 Elaine McFarland, *Protestants First: Orangeism in Nineteenth-Century Scotland* (Edinburgh, 1990).

3 Graham Walker, 'The Orange Order in Scotland between the wars', *International Review of Social History* 37 (2) (1992), p. 178.

4 Tom Gallagher, *Glasgow; the Uneasy Peace: Religious Tension in Modern Scotland* (Manchester, 1987), pp. 144–5.

5 Walker, 'The Orange Order in Scotland between the wars', pp. 187–9.

6 Steve Bruce, *No Pope of Rome: Anti-Catholicism in Modern Scotland* (Edinburgh, 1985).

7 Iain Maclean, *The Legend of Red Clydeside* (Edinburgh, 1983), pp. 200–1.

8 Graham Walker and Tom Gallagher, 'Protestantism and Scottish politics', in Graham Walker and Tom Gallagher (eds), *Sermons and Battle Hymns: Protestant Popular Culture in Modern Scotland* (Edinburgh, 1990), pp. 91–2.

9 William Marshall, *The Billy Boys: a Concise History of Orangeism in Scotland* (Edinburgh, 1996), p. 105; Gallagher, *The Uneasy Peace*, pp. 293–5; Gordon McCracken, *Bygone Days of Yore: the Story of Orangeism in Glasgow* (County Grand Orange Lodge of Glasgow, 1990), p. 35.

10 Bryan, *Orange Parades*, p. 20.

11 Bruce, *No Pope of Rome*, pp. 167, 246; Steve Bruce, *Comparative Protestant Politics* (Oxford, 1998), p. 111.

12 Peter Day, 'The Orange Order and the July 12th parade in Liverpool since 1945' (PhD Dissertation, University of Liverpool, 2006), p. 32.

13 1908 is the only missing year and has been linearly interpolated from adjacent years. We would like to record our debt to Rev. Gordon McCracken, an ex-Orangeman and former Deputy Grand Master of the Orange Order, who painstakingly collected and scanned in reports of proceedings from all over Scotland for the period 1860–1966, compiling these onto CD. His assistance and advice have been invaluable, as has that of former Grand Secretary Jack Ramsay and current Grand Secretary Donald Hatcliffe.

14 Those wishing to gain access to this data should contact the author. Data will be released through the UK Data Archive subject to the approval of the Grand Orange Lodge of Scotland and Rev. McCracken.

15 Calculated from County (N. Ireland) and Provincial (Canada) Grand Orange Lodge reports of proceedings and return sheets, and respective historical censuses.

16 Assumes target population at half electorate. Iain Maclean and J. C. Gordon, 'Labour elites and electorates in Glasgow, 1922–1974' (UKDA ref. SN1007, 1976).

17 Interview with Rev. Gordon A. McCracken, former Deputy Grand Master, and former Grand Secretary David Bryce, Olympia House, Glasgow, 28 August 2002.

18 Brian Bessel, 'MLC – Masonic Leadership Centre webpage, international Masonic statistics', http://www.bessel.org/intstats.htm (14 November 2006).

19 Gerry P. T. Finn, 'In the grip?: A psychological and historical exploration of the social significance of freemasonry in Scotland', in Walker and Gallagher, *Sermons and Battle Hymns*, pp. 160–92.

20 Memberships at lodge level are not available for the Masonic Order, hence the lack of size differentials on the map.

21 I have drawn upon Michael Hechter's UK County dataset for the 1851–1966 period. See Michael Hechter, *UK County Data 1851–1966* (UKDA ref. 430, 1976). This

comprehensive dataset encompasses variables from the census, registrar-general's reports and elections of 1885, 1892, 1900, 1910, 1924, 1931, 1951 and 1966. Election data have been matched to their closest census year. A second source of electronic data is Maclean and Gordon, 'Labour elites', which provides census and electoral data for Glasgow in the mid-twentieth century. These data have been augmented by text sources where necessary.

22 Thanks to the important geographic areal interpolation work of Danny Dorling, David Martin and Richard Mitchell on the Linking Censuses Together project, we are able to establish a set of county-level data for the 1971–91 period which is continuous with Hechter's 1851–1961 county data. See Danny Dorling, David Martin and Richard Mitchell, *Linking Censuses Together Project* (2001) http://www.mimas. ac.uk/lct/. 2001 data, though now available using the post-1973 geography, have not been similarly covered by the LCT program and thus cannot be used in our county-level study.

23 Graham Walker, 'The Protestant Irish in Scotland', in T. M. Devine (ed.), *Irish Immigrants and Scottish Society in the Nineteenth and Twentieth Centuries* (Edinburgh, 1991), pp. 44–66.

24 Z-score is a measure of statistical significance (derived from comparing the coefficient of a variable with its standard error). TSCS refers to time-series cross sectional pooling, R sq (R squared) is a measure of how well the independent variables predict the dependent variable (in this case Orange density).

25 Joseph M. Bradley, *Ethnic and Religious Identity in Modern Scotland: Culture, Politics and Football* (Avebury, 1995).

26 McFarland, *Protestants First*.

27 Kaufmann, *Orange Order*.

28 Kaufmann, *Orange Order*.

29 Kaufmann, *Orange Order*.

30 B. Hayes, 'Gender differences in religious mobility in Britain', *British Journal of Sociology*, 47 (4), pp. 643–56.

31 Interview with Rev. Gordon A. McCracken, former Deputy Grand Master, and former Grand Secretary David Bryce, Olympia House, Glasgow, 28 August 2002.

32 There were roughly 5,500 juniors in Northern Ireland in 1954, down to 3,900 by 1970. See Grand Orange Lodge of Ireland (GOLI) junior returns. In 1997, just 1 per cent of Ulster Orangemen claimed to have passed through a junior programme. See Loyal Orange Institution Commission (GOLI, 1997) The Loyal Orangewomen of Ireland are said to number 7,000 or 8,000 members. (Interview with George Patton, former Grand Secretary of Ireland, Sept. 2000)

33 Kaufmann, 'The Orange Order in Ontario'.

34 Hayes, 'Gender differences'.

35 Sister Helyne MacLean, 'Scottish Orange women', in Grand Orange Lodge of Scotland Bicentenary Booklet (GOLS, 1998).

36 Interview with Rev. Gordon A. McCracken and David Bryce, August 2002; interview with Jim McLean, Deputy Grand Secretary, Grand Orange Lodge of Scotland, 27 August, 2002; McFarland, *Protestants First*, p. 215.

37 Interview with Rev. Gordon A. McCracken and David Bryce, August 2002; Duncan Morrow, Derek Birrell, John Greer and Terry O'Keefe, *The Churches and Inter-Community Relationships* (Centre for the Study of Conflicts, 1991).

38 McFarland, *Protestants First*, p. 215.

39 GOLI *Reports of Proceedings*, Sept. 2002, p. 30.

40 Interview with Rev. Gordon A. McCracken and David Bryce, August 2002.

41 GOLS *Reports of Proceedings*, 1969–2002.

42 Interview with Rev. Gordon A. McCracken and David Bryce, August 2002; correspondence with Gordon McCracken, August 2006.

43 GOLS *Reports of Proceedings*, 4 March 2000, p. 10.

44 Interview with Rev. Gordon A. McCracken and David Bryce, August 2002.
45 For more on the decline of the Church of Scotland, see Callum G. Brown, *Religion and Society in Scotland since 1707* (Edinburgh, 1997).
46 Central Committee of the GOLI Minutes, 27 March 1957; *Vigilant* subscriber list 1958–59.
47 McFarland, *Protestants First*, p. 215.
48 Gordon A. McCracken, 'Scottish Orangeism in the twentieth century', paper presented at conference on 'Orangeism and Protestant politics', University of Ulster at Jordanstown, Belfast; GOLS *Reports of Proceedings*, June 1957, June and December 1958.
49 Central Committee of the GOLI Minutes, 29 July, 16 October and 3 December 1959, 30 December 1960.
50 Interview with Rev. Gordon A. McCracken and David Bryce, August 2002.
51 Bradley, *Ethnic and Religious Identity*, p. 94; bicentenary video 1998.
52 GOLS *Reports of Proceedings* 1969–2001.
53 Minutes of Unionist Unity Conference, 23 August 1972.
54 Central Committee of the GOLI Minutes, 10 September and 8 December 1971.
55 Letter from Scottish Grand Secretary John Adam to Irish Grand Secretary Williams, 11 September 1972.
56 Letters from John Adam to Walter Williams, 13 September and 20 October 1972.
57 Central Committee of the GOLI Minutes, 27 October 1972.
58 Letter from Walter Williams to John Adam, 10 November 1972.
59 Marshall, *Billy Boys*, p. 99.
60 Central Committee of the GOLI Minutes, 27 October 1972.
61 Central Committee of the GOLI Minutes 10 June 1974.
62 Central Committee of the GOLI Minutes, 5 December 1975.
63 GOLS *Reports of Proceedings*, 6 September 1975, pp. 23–4.
64 GOLS press release, 18 February 1978.
65 Letter from David Bryce to Harold Wilson, 2 December 1975; letter from A. R. Williams, Northern Ireland Office (NIO) to David Bryce, 22 December 1975.
66 BBC TV transcript, 6 January 1978.
67 Letter from David Bryce to Norman Hutton, UUP Secretary, 6 October 1976.
68 GOLS *Reports of Proceedings*, 6 March 1982, pp. 5–7.
69 GOLS *Reports of Proceedings*, 12 June 1982, pp. 16–17.
70 GOLS *Reports of Proceedings*, 4 September 1982, pp. 24–5.
71 McCracken, 'Scottish Orangeism in the twentieth century'.
72 GOLI *Reports of Proceedings*, June 1984, pp. 16–17.
73 GOLS *Reports of Proceedings*, 3 March 1990.
74 GOLS *Reports of Proceedings*, 2 March 1985, p. 7.
75 GOLS *Reports of Proceedings*, March 1974, p. 15.
76 GOLS *Reports of Proceedings* 07/09/91:12.
77 Central Committee of the GOLI Minutes, 13 December 1978.
78 McFarland, *Protestants First*, pp. 215–19.
79 Bryan, *Orange Parades*.
80 GOLS *Reports of Proceedings*, 8 June 1967.
81 GOLS *Reports of Proceedings*, March 1974, p. 13; 22 June 1974.
82 GOLS *Reports of Proceedings*, 4 September 1982; 5 September 1987.
83 GOLS *Reports of Proceedings*, 11 June 1988, p. 15.
84 GOLS *Reports of Proceedings*, 21 January 1989, p. 1.
85 GOLS *Reports of Proceedings*, 1990, p. 8.
86 GOLI *Reports of Proceedings*, June 2002, p. 29.
87 GOLI *Reports of Proceedings*, June 1992, pp. 17–18; December 1992, p. 17; December 1993, p. 16; June 1998, p. 17.
88 Letter from Stena Line to Grand Secretary of GOLI, George Patton, 3 March 2001.

89 GOLI *Reports of Proceedings*, September 2001, p. 4; September 2002, p. 3.

90 Bryan, *Orange Parades*.

91 GOLI *Reports of Proceedings*, June 2002, p. 29.

92 GOLS *Reports of Proceedings*, June 1995, p. 6.

93 GOLI *Reports of Proceedings*, June 2002, p. 29; Kaufmann, *Orange Order*.

94 GOLS *Reports of Proceedings*, 7 December 1974, p. 30.

95 GOLS *Reports of Proceedings*, 1 March 1975, p. 16.

96 GOLS *Reports of Proceedings*, 2 September 1989, p. 20.

97 GOLS *Reports of Proceedings*, 21 January 1989, p. 5; Central Committee of the GOLI Minutes, 5 December 1975.

98 GOLS *Reports of Proceedings* 25/02/89: 5–6, 03/03/90: 2.

99 LOL.#160; GOLS *Reports of Proceedings*, 1 September 1990, p. 12.

100 GOLS *Reports of Proceedings*, 8 December 1990, p. 17.

101 GOLS *Reports of Proceedings*, 8 December 1990, p. 17.

102 Brian Kennaway, *The Orange Order: a Tradition Betrayed* (Methuen, 2006).

103 GOLS *Reports of Proceedings*, 2 September 1989, p. 20; 3 March 1990, p. 3.

104 Kaufmann, *Orange Order*.

105 GOLS *Reports of Proceedings* 1990, p. 13, 1991, p. 2, 1998, p. 28.

106 Donald L. Horowitz, *Ethnic Groups in Conflict* (California, 1985), Chap. 8.

107 J. F. Harbinson, *The Ulster Unionist Party 1882–1973* (Blackstaff Press, 1973).

108 Jonathan Tonge and Jocelyn A. J. Evans, 'Party members and the Good Friday Agreement in Northern Ireland', *Irish Political Studies* 17 (2), pp. 59–73.

109 I am indebted to Alex Rough of the County Grand Lodge of Toronto for his personal directory of prominent Orangemen, compiled painstakingly over many decades.

110 Houston and Smyth, *The Sash Canada Wore*; Neal, *Sectarian Violence*; Kaufmann, 'The Orange Order in Ontario'; Peter Day, "The Orange Order".

111 Gallagher, *The Uneasy Peace*, pp. 144–5; McFarland, *Protestants First*, pp. 192–3; McCracken, *Bygone Days of Yore: the Story of Orangeism in Scotland*.

112 Walker, 'The Orange Order in Scotland between the wars', p. 187.

113 Steve Bruce, 'Comparing Scotland and Northern Ireland', in T. M. Devine (ed.), *Scotland's Shame?: Bigotry and Sectarianism in Modern Scotland* (Edinburgh, 2000), p. 139,

114 Interview with Rev. Gordon A. McCracken and David Bryce, August 2002; Marshall, *Billy Boys*.

115 GOLS *Reports of Proceedings*, 13 June 1987.

116 GOLI *Reports of Proceedings*, December 1987, p. 20.

117 Gallagher, *The Uneasy Peace*, pp. 144–5; Walker, 'The Orange Order in Scotland between the wars'.

118 Maclean and Gordon, 'Labour elites'.

119 Gallagher, *The Uneasy Peace*; Marshall, *Billy Boys*; interview with Rev. Gordon A. McCracken and David Bryce, August 2002.

11 The End of Disadvantage? The descendants of Irish-Catholic immigrants in modern Scotland since 1945

1 John F. McCaffrey, 'Roman Catholics in Scotland in the 19th and 20th century', *Records of the Scottish Church History Society*, vol. 21 (1981–83), pp. 275–300.

2 John Cooney, *Scotland and the Papacy* (Edinburgh, 1982), p. 95.

3 Tom Gallagher, *The Uneasy Peace* (Manchester, 1987), p. 227.

4 Gallagher, *The Uneasy Peace*, p. 227.

5 Cited in Elinor Kelly, 'Challenging sectarianism in Scotland: the prism of racism', *Scottish Affairs* 42 (2003), pp. 35–56.

6 M. Fry, *The Scottish Empire* (Edinburgh, 2001), pp. 412–24.

7   Cited in Kelly, 'Challenging sectarianism', pp. 35–56.
8   A. D. Gibb, *Scotland Resurgent* (Stirling, 1950), p. 83.
9   Bill Murray, *The Old Firm* (Edinburgh, 1984), p. 63.
10 *Reports on the Schemes of the General Assembly of the Church of Scotland, 1931*, pp. 571–4.
11 *Proceedings and Debates of the General Assembly of the Church of Scotland, 1937*, pp. 382–5.
12 Patrick Reilly, 'Kicking with the left foot: being Catholic in Scotland', in T. M. Devine (ed.), *Scotland's Shame? Bigotry and Sectarianism in Modern Scotland* (Edinburgh, 2000), p. 31.
13 T. M. Devine (ed.), *St Mary's Hamilton: a Social History 1846–1996* (Edinburgh, 1995), pp. 91–3.
14 Patricia Walls and Rory Williams, 'Sectarianism at work: accounts of employment discrimination against Irish Catholics in Scotland', *Ethnic and Racial Studies* 26 (4) (July, 2003), pp. 632–62.
15 Kevin Kenny, *The American Irish* (Harlow, 2000), p. 181; Patrick J. Blessing, 'Irish emigration to the United States, 1800–1920: an overview', in P. J. Drudy (ed.), *The Irish in America: Emigration, Assimilation, Impact* (Cambridge, 1985), pp. 13–18.
16 J. Devine, 'A Lanarkshire perspective on bigotry in Scottish society', in Devine (ed.), *Scotland's Shame?*, pp. 102–3; S. Bruce et al., *Sectarianism in Scotland* (Edinburgh, 2004), p. 71.
17 John F. McCaffrey, 'Irish immigration', in Michael Lynch (ed.), *The Oxford Companion to Scottish History* (Oxford, 2001), p. 333.
18 J. McGonigle, D. O'Rourke and H. Whyte (eds), *Across the Water. Irishness in Modern Scottish Writing* (Glendarvel, 2000), p. 14.
19 T. M. Devine, *The Scottish Nation, 1700–2007* (London, 2006), pp. 555–65.
20 Kerby A. Miller, 'Assimilation and alienation: Irish emigrants: responses to industrial America', in Drudy (ed.), *Irish in America*, pp. 91–3.
21 Devine, *The Scottish Nation, 1700–2007*, pp. 507–22.
22 The very extensive writing on this phenomenon is synthesised in Kenny, *Irish America*, pp. 181–279.
23 Walls and Williams, 'Sectarianism at work', p. 653; Lindsay Paterson, 'The social class of Catholics in Scotland', *Journal of the Royal Statistical Society* A (2000) 163 (3), pp. 363–79.
24 P. L. Payne, *Growth and Contraction: Scottish Industry c.1860–1990* (Glasgow, 1992).
25 Interview with Ferry reported in Gallagher, *The Uneasy Peace*, pp. 252–3.
26 J. Scott and J. Hughes, *The Anatomy of Scottish Capital* (London, 1980), p. 200.
27 Iain Paterson, 'Sectarianism and municipal housing allocation in Glasgow', *Scottish Affairs* 39 (spring, 2002), pp. 47–53.
28 Devine, 'A Lanarkshire perspective', p. 102.
29 Lindsay Paterson, 'Salvation through education? The changing social status of Scottish Catholics', in Devine (ed.), *Scotland's Shame?*, pp. 145–57.
30 Devine, 'A Lanarkshire perspective', p. 103.
31 *Scotland on Sunday*, 9 October 2005.
32 Lindsay Paterson, Frank Bechhofer and David McCrone, *Living in Scotland: Social and Economic Change since 1980* (Edinburgh, 2004), pp. 42–58.
33 *The Scotsman*, 17 February 2005.
34 Kelly, 'Challenging sectarianism in Scotland', pp. 32–56.
35 Gallagher, *The Uneasy Peace*, p. 291.
36 Gallagher, *The Uneasy Peace*, p. 291.
37 Gallagher, *The Uneasy Peace*, p. 292.
38 Eric Kaufmann, 'The dynamics of Orangeism in Scotland', *Social Science History* 30 (2), 2006, pp. 263–92.

39 Steve Bruce, *No Pope of Rome! Militant Protestantism in Modern Scotland* (Edinburgh, 1984), p. 184.

40 Gallagher, *The Uneasy Peace*, pp. 290–8.

41 For all these developments, see the special issues on Irish-Scottish relations of *The Scotsman* and *The Irish Times*, 30 November 1999.

42 For the academic rapprochement, see T. M. Devine, 'Making the Caledonian connection: the development of Irish and Scottish Studies', The O'Malley Lecture, New York University, 2001, *Radharc: A Journal of Irish Studies* 3 (2002), pp. 3–13.

43 C. M. Grieve, *Contemporary Scottish Studies* (London, 1926), p. 10.

44 The lecture is printed in Devine (ed.), *Scotland's Shame?*, pp. 13–24.

45 David McCrone and Michael Rosie, 'Left and liberal: Catholics in modern Scotland', in R. Boyle and P. Lynch (eds), *Out of the Ghetto? The Catholic Community in Modern Scotland* (Edinburgh, 1998), p. 68.

46 Paterson, Bechhofer and McCrone, *Living in Scotland*, pp. 56–7, 90, 101.

47 Graham Walker, 'Sectarian tensions in Scotland: social and cultural dynamics and the politics of perception', in Devine (ed.), *Scotland's Shame?*, p. 131.

48 B. Aspinwall, 'Roman Catholic community', in M. Lynch (ed.), *The Oxford Companion to Scottish History* (Oxford, 2001), pp. 529–30.

49 Bruce et al., *Sectarianism in Scotland*, p. 97.

50 Michael Rosie and David McCrone, 'The past is history: Catholics in modern Scotland', in Devine (ed.), *Scotland's Shame?*, pp. 199–218.

51 Devine, *Scottish Nation*, pp. 563–5.

52 *The Scotsman*, 28 November 2006.

53 See regular correspondence in the letters pages of the *Scottish Catholic Observer*, the newspaper of the Catholic community in Scotland.

54 *The Sunday Times*, 24 December 2006.

55 *The Scotsman*, 16 December 2006.

56 *The Scotsman*, 28 November 2006.

Index